Lecture Notes in Computer Science   9663

Commenced Publication in 1973
Founding and Former Series Editors:
Gerhard Goos, Juris Hartmanis, and Jan van Leeuwen

Xinyi Huang · Yang Xiang
Kuan-Ching Li (Eds.)

Green, Pervasive, and Cloud Computing

11th International Conference, GPC 2016
Xi'an, China, May 6–8, 2016
Proceedings

 Springer

Editors
Xinyi Huang
Fujian Normal University
Fuzhou
China

Yang Xiang
Deakin University
Burwood
Australia

Kuan-Ching Li
Providence University
Taichung
Taiwan

and

Hubei University of Education
Wuhan, Hubei
China

ISSN 0302-9743   ISSN 1611-3349 (electronic)
Lecture Notes in Computer Science
ISBN 978-3-319-39076-5   ISBN 978-3-319-39077-2 (eBook)
DOI 10.1007/978-3-319-39077-2

Library of Congress Control Number: 2016939059

LNCS Sublibrary: SL1 – Theoretical Computer Science and General Issues

Printed on acid-free paper

This Springer imprint is published by Springer Nature
The registered company is Springer International Publishing AG Switzerland

Preface

On behalf of the Organizing Committee, it is our pleasure to welcome you to the proceedings of the 11th International Conference on Green, Pervasive and Cloud Computing (GPC 2016), held in Xi'an, China, during May 6–8, 2016. The conference was organized by Xidian University, China, and sponsored by Suzhou Super Cluster Information Technologies Inc.

GPC aims at bringing together international researchers and practitioners from both academia and industry who are working in the areas of green computing, pervasive computing, and cloud computing. GPC 2016 was the next event in a series of highly successful events focusing on pervasive and environmentally sustainable computing. In the last 10 years, the GPC conference has been successfully held and organized all over the world: Taichung, Taiwan (2006), Paris, France (2007), Kunming, China (2008), Geneva, Switzerland (2009), Hualien, Taiwan (2010), Oulu, Finland (2011), Hong Kong (2012), Seoul, Korea (2013),Wuhan, China (2014), and Plantation Island, Fiji (2015).

This year the value, breadth, and depth of the GPC conference continued to strengthen and grow in importance for both the academic and industrial communities. The strength was evidenced this year by having a number of high-quality submissions resulting in a highly selective program. GPC 2016 received 94 submissions on various aspects including green computing, cloud computing, virtualization, data and storage, and network security. All submissions received at least three reviews via a high-quality review process involving 43 Program Committee members and a number of additional reviewers. The review and discussion were held electronically using EasyChair. On the basis of the review results, 20 papers were selected for presentation at the conference, giving an acceptance rate lower than 22 %. In addition, the conference also featured four invited talks given by Hui Li, Keqiu Li, Kenli Li, and Qingguo Zhou.

We sincerely thank all the chairs, Steering Committee members, and Program Committee members. Without their hard work, the success of GPC 2016 would not have been possible.

Last but certainly not least our thanks go to all authors who submitted papers and to all the attendees. We hope you enjoy the conference proceedings!

May 2016

Xinyi Huang
Yang Xiang
Kuan-Ching Li

Organization

General Chairs

Elisa Bertino   Purdue University, USA
Muhammad Khurram   King Saud University, Kingdom of Saudi Arabia
    Khan
Jianfeng Ma   Xidian University, China

Technical Program Chairs

Xinyi Huang   Fujian Normal University, China
Yang Xiang   Deakin University, Australia

Organizing Chairs

Xiaofeng Chen   Xidian University, China
Hui Li   Xidian University, China

Publicity Chair

Yu Wang   Deakin University, Australia

Steering Committee

Hai Jin   Huazhong University of Science and Technology, China (Chair)
Nabil Abdennadher   University of Applied Sciences, Switzerland
Christophe Cerin   University of Paris XIII, France
Sajal K. Das   Missouri University of Science and Technology, USA
Jean-Luc Gaudiot   University of California - Irvine, USA
Kuan-Ching Li   Providence University, Taiwan, China
Cho-Li Wang   The University of Hong Kong, SAR China
Chao-Tung Yang   Tunghai University, Taiwan, China
Laurence T. Yang   St. Francis Xavier University, Canada

Program Committee

Saadat M. Alhashmi	University of Sharjah, Sharjah, UAE
Luciana Arantes	Université Pierre et Marie Curie-Paris 6, France
Shehzad Ashraf Chaudhry	International Islamic University, Pakistan
Zeyar Aung	Masdar Institute of Science and Technology, UAE
Ioan Marius Bilasco	Université Lille 1, France
Aniello Castiglione	University of Salerno, Italy
Christophe Cerin	University of Paris XIII, France
Yuanfang Chen	Institute Mines-Telecom, France
Xiaowen Chu	Hong Kong Baptist University, Hong Kong, SAR China
Raphaël Couturier	University of Bourgogne Franche Comte, France
Noel Crespi	Telecom SudParis, France
Talbi El-Ghazali	University of Lille, France
Dan Grigoras	University College Cork, Ireland
Shamim Hossain	IBM Australia
Ching-Hsien Hsu	Chung Hua University, Taiwan
Kuo-Chan Huang	National Taichung University of Education, Taiwan
Hai Jiang	Arkansas State University, USA
Yong-Kee Jun	Gyeongsang National University, Korea
Chen Liu	Clarkson University, USA
Damon Shing-Min Liu	National Chung Cheng University, Taiwan
Victor Malyshkin	Russian Academy of Sciences, Russia
Tomas Margalef	Universitat Autonoma de Barcelona, Spain
Mario Donato Marino	Leeds Beckett University, UK
Rodrigo Mello	University of Sao Paulo, Brazil
Tommi Mikkonen	Tampere University of Technology, Finland
Alfredo Navarra	Università degli Studi di Perugia, Italy
Xiao Nong	State Key Laboratory of High Performance Computing, National University of Defense Technology, China
Francesco Palmieri	University of Salerno, Italy
Jun-Jie Peng	Shanghai University, China
Ron Perrott	Oxford University, UK
Dana Petcu	West University of Timisoara, Romania
Florin Pop	University Politehnica of Bucharest, Romania
Wasim Raad	King Fahd University of Petroleum and Minerals, Saudi Arabia
Kewei Sha	University of Houston, Clear Lake, USA
Pradip Srimani	Clemson University, USA
Kazunori Takashio	Keio University, Japan
Jie Tang	South China University of Technology, China
Niwat Thepvilojanapong	Mie University, Japan
Chien-Min Wang	Academia Sinica, Taiwan

Ding Wang	Peking University, China
Yu Wang	Deakin University, Australia
Yulei Wu	University of Exeter, UK
Chen Yu	Huazhong University of Science and Technology, China
Yanmin Zhu	Shanghai Jiao Tong University, China

Contents

Network Security

Green Computing

An Efficient Dynamic Programming Algorithm for STR-IC-STR-EC-LCS Problem

Daxin Zhu[1], Yingjie Wu[2], and Xiaodong Wang[3($\boxtimes$)]

[1] Quanzhou Normal University, Quanzhou 362000, China
[2] Fuzhou University, Fuzhou 350002, China
[3] Fujian University of Technology, Fuzhou 350108, China
wangxd135@139.com

Abstract. In this paper, we consider a generalized longest common sub-sequence problem, in which a constraining sequence of length s must be included as a substring and the other constraining sequence of length t must be excluded as a substring of two main sequences and the length of the result must be maximal. For the two input sequences X and Y of lengths n and m, and the given two constraining sequences of length s and t, we present an $O(nmst)$ time dynamic programming algorithm for solving the new generalized longest common subsequence problem. The time complexity can be reduced further to cubic time in a more detailed analysis. The correctness of the new algorithm is proved.

1 Introduction

The longest common subsequence (LCS) problem is a well-known measurement for computing the similarity of two strings. It can be widely applied in diverse areas, such as file comparison, pattern matching and computational biology [3,4,8,9].

Given two sequences X and Y, the longest common subsequence (LCS) problem is to find a subsequence of X and Y whose length is the longest among all common subsequences of the two given sequences.

For some biological applications some constraints must be applied to the LCS problem. These kinds of variants of the LCS problem are called the constrained LCS (CLCS) problem. Recently, Chen and Chao [1,5,6,10] proposed the more generalized forms of the CLCS problem, the generalized constrained longest common subsequence (GC-LCS) problem. For the two input sequences X and Y of lengths n and m,respectively, and a constraint string P of length r, the GC-LCS problem is a set of four problems which are to find the LCS of X and Y including/excluding P as a subsequence/substring, respectively.

In this paper, we consider a more general constrained longest common subsequence problem called STR-IC-STR-EC-LCS, in which a constraining sequence of length s must be included as a substring and the other constraining sequence of length t must be excluded as a substring of two main sequences and the length of the result must be maximal. We will present the first efficient dynamic programming algorithm for solving this problem.

X. Huang et al. (Eds.): GPC 2016, LNCS 9663, pp. 3–17, 2016.
DOI: 10.1007/978-3-319-39077-2_1

The organization of the paper is as follows.

In the following 4 sections, we describe our presented dynamic programming algorithm for the STR-IC-STR-EC-LCS problem.

In Sect. 2 the preliminary knowledge for presenting our algorithm for the STR-IC-STR-EC-LCS problem is discussed. In Sect. 3 we give a new dynamic programming solution for the STR-IC-STR-EC-LCS problem with time complexity $O(nmst)$, where n and m are the lengths of the two given input strings, and s and t the lengths of the two constraining sequences. In Sect. 4, the time complexity is further improved to $O(nms)$. Some concluding remarks are located in Sect. 5.

2   Characterization of the Generalized LCS Problem

A sequence is a string of characters over an alphabet $\sum$. A subsequence of a sequence X is obtained by deleting zero or more characters from X (not necessarily contiguous). A substring of a sequence X is a subsequence of successive characters within X.

For a given sequence $X = x_1 x_2 \cdots x_n$ of length n, the ith character of X is denoted as $x_i \in \sum$ for any $i = 1, \cdots, n$. A substring of X from position i to j can be denoted as $X[i : j] = x_i x_{i+1} \cdots x_j$. If $i \neq 1$ or $j \neq n$, then the substring $X[i : j] = x_i x_{i+1} \cdots x_j$ is called a proper substring of X. A substring $X[i : j] = x_i x_{i+1} \cdots x_j$ is called a prefix or a suffix of X if $i = 1$ or $j = n$, respectively.

An appearance of sequence $X = x_1 x_2 \cdots x_n$ in sequence $Y = y_1 y_2 \cdots y_m$, for any X and Y, starting at position j is a sequence of strictly increasing indexes $i_1, i_2, \cdots, i_n$ such that $i_1 = j$, and $X = y_{i_1}, y_{i_2}, \cdots, y_{i_n}$. A compact appearance of X in Y starting at position j is the appearance of the smallest last index i_n. A match for sequences X and Y is a pair (i, j) such that $x_i = y_j$. The total number of matches for X and Y is denoted by δ. It is obvious that $\delta \leq nm$.

In the description of our new algorithm, a function σ will be mentioned frequently. For any string S and a fixed constraint string P, the length of the longest suffix of S that is also a prefix of P is denoted by function $\sigma(S)$.

The symbol $\oplus$ is also used to denote the string concatenation.

For example, if $P = aaba$ and $S = aabaaab$, then substring aab is the longest suffix of S that is also a prefix of P, and therefore $\sigma(S) = 3$.

It is readily seen that $S \oplus P = aabaaabaaba$.

For the two input sequences $X = x_1 x_2 \cdots x_n$ and $Y = y_1 y_2 \cdots y_m$ of lengths n and m, respectively, and two constrained sequences $P = p_1 p_2 \cdots p_s$ and $Q = q_1 q_2 \cdots q_t$ of lengths s and t, the STR-IC-STR-EC-LCS problem is to find a constrained LCS of X and Y including P as a substring and excluding Q as a substring.

Definiton 1. *Let $Z(i, j, k, r)$ denote the set of all LCSs of $X[1 : i]$ and $Y[1 : j]$ such that for each $z \in Z(i, j, k, r)$, z includes $P[1 : k]$ as a substring, and excludes Q as a substring and $\sigma(z) = r$, where $1 \leq i \leq n, 1 \leq j \leq m, 0 \leq k \leq s$, and $0 \leq r < t$. The length of an LCS in $Z(i, j, k, r)$ is denoted as $f(i, j, k, r)$.*

Definiton 2. *Let $U(i, j, k, r)$ denote the set of all LCSs of $X[1 : i]$ and $Y[1 : j]$ such that for each $u \in U(i, j, k, r)$, u includes $P[1 : k]$ as a suffix, and excludes Q as a substring and $\sigma(z) = r$, where $1 \leq i \leq n, 1 \leq j \leq m, 0 \leq k \leq s$, and $0 \leq r < t$. The length of an LCS in $U(i, j, k, r)$ is denoted as $g(i, j, k, r)$.*

Definiton 3. *Let $V(i, j, r)$ denote the set of all LCSs of $X[1 : i]$ and $Y[1 : j]$ such that for each $v \in V(i, j, r)$, v excludes Q as a substring and $\sigma(v) = r$, where $1 \leq i \leq n, 1 \leq j \leq m, 0 \leq r < t$. The length of an LCS in $V(i, j, r)$ is denoted as $h(i, j, r)$.*

According to the definitions above, for the given two input sequences $X = x_1 x_2 \cdots x_n$ and $Y = y_1 y_2 \cdots y_m$, and the two constrained sequences $P = p_1 p_2 \cdots p_s$ and $Q = q_1 q_2 \cdots q_t$, if the STR-IC-STR-EC-LCS problem has a solution z, then there must be an index $d, 0 \leq d < t$, such that $z \in Z(n, m, s, d)$, and

$$f(n, m, s, d) = \max_{0 \leq r < t} \{f(n, m, s, r)\} \tag{1}$$

Similarly, if the STR-IC-STR-EC-LCS problem has a solution z, and z includes P as a suffix, then there must be an index $e, 0 \leq e < t$, such that $z \in U(n, m, s, e)$, and

$$g(n, m, s, e) = \max_{0 \leq r < t} \{g(n, m, s, r)\} \tag{2}$$

In this case we have,

$$\max_{0 \leq r < t} \{f(n, m, s, r)\} = \max_{0 \leq r < t} \{g(n, m, s, r)\} \tag{3}$$

The following theorem characterizes the structure of an optimal solution based on optimal solutions to subproblems, for computing the LCSs in $U(i, j, k, r)$, for any $1 \leq i \leq n, 1 \leq j \leq m, 0 \leq k \leq s$, and $0 \leq r < t$. The length of an LCS in $U(i, j, k, r)$ is denoted as $g(i, j, k, r)$.

For each character $x \in \sum$ and any $1 \leq i \leq n, 1 \leq j \leq m, 0 \leq k \leq s$, $0 \leq r < t$, let

$$\alpha(i, j, k, r) = \max_{0 \leq d < t} \{g(i - 1, j - 1, k, d) | \sigma(Q[1 : d] \oplus x_i) = r\}$$

The index of $d, 0 \leq d < t$, achieving the maximum is denoted as $\beta(i, j, k, r)$, i.e.,

$$\alpha(i, j, k, r) = g(i - 1, j - 1, k, \beta(i, j, k, r)).$$

Theorem 1. *If $Z[1 : l] = z_1, z_2, \cdots, z_l \in U(i, j, k, r)$, then the following formula holds:*

For any $1 \leq i \leq n, 1 \leq j \leq m, 0 \leq k \leq s$, and $0 \leq r < t$, $g(i, j, k, r)$ can be computed by the following recursive formula (4).

$$g(i, j, k, r) =$$

$$\begin{cases} \max\{g(i-1,j,k,r), g(i,j-1,k,r)\} & \text{if } x_i \neq y_j \\ \max\{g(i-1,j-1,k,r), 1+\alpha(i,j,k,r)\} & \text{if } k = 0 \wedge x_i = y_j \\ \max\{g(i-1,j-1,k,r), 1+\alpha(i,j,k-1,r)\} & \text{if } k > 0 \wedge x_i = y_j = p_k \\ g(i-1,j-1,k,r) & \text{if } k > 0 \wedge x_i = y_j \wedge x_i \neq p_k \end{cases}$$

(4)

The boundary conditions of this recursive formula are
$g(i, 0, 0, r) = g(0, j, 0, r) = 0$ for any $0 \leq i \leq n, 0 \leq j \leq m$, and $0 \leq r \leq t$ and
$g(i, 0, k, r) = g(0, j, k, r) = -\infty$ for any $0 \leq i \leq n, 0 \leq j \leq m, 1 \leq k \leq s$, and
$0 \leq r \leq t$.

Proof. 1. In the case of $x_i \neq y_j$, there are two subcases to be distinguished.

(1.1) If $z_l \neq x_i$, then $Z[1 : l]$ must be a common subsequence of $X[1 : i-1]$ and $Y[1 : j]$ including $P[1 : k]$ as a suffix, and excludes Q as a substring and $\sigma(z) = r$. It is obvious that $Z[1 : l]$ is also an LCS of $X[1 : i-1]$ and $Y[1 : j]$ including $P[1 : k]$ as a suffix, and excludes Q as a substring and $\sigma(z) = r$, i.e., $Z[1 : l] \in U(i-1, j, k, r)$.

(1.2) If $z_l \neq y_j$, then $Z[1 : l]$ must be a common subsequence of $X[1 : i]$ and $Y[1 : j-1]$ including $P[1 : k]$ as a suffix, and excludes Q as a substring and $\sigma(z) = r$. It is obvious that $Z[1 : l]$ is also an LCS of $X[1 : i]$ and $Y[1 : j-1]$ including $P[1 : k]$ as a suffix, and excludes Q as a substring and $\sigma(z) = r$, i.e., $Z[1 : l] \in U(i, j-1, k, r)$.

Therefore, in the case of $x_i \neq y_j$, we have, $g(i, j, k, r) = \max\{g(i-1, j, k, r), g(i, j-1, k, r)\}$.

2. In the case of $k = 0$ and $x_i = y_j$, we have no constraints on P, due to $k = 0$. There are also two subcases to be distinguished.

(2.1) If $x_i = y_j \neq z_l$, then $Z[1 : l]$ must be a common subsequence of $X[1 : i-1]$ and $Y[1 : j-1]$ excluding Q as a substring and $\sigma(z) = r$. It is obvious that $Z[1 : l]$ is also an LCS of $X[1 : i-1]$ and $Y[1 : j-1]$ excluding Q as a substring and $\sigma(z) = r$, i.e., $Z[1 : l] \in U(i-1, j-1, 0, r)$.

(2.2) If $x_i = y_j = z_l$, then $Z[1 : l-1]$ must be a common subsequence of $X[1 : i-1]$ and $Y[1 : j-1]$ excluding Q as a substring and $\sigma(z) = d$ for some $0 \leq d < t$ and $\sigma(Q[1 : d] \oplus x_i) = r$. Therefore,

$$l - 1 \leq \alpha(i, j, 0, r)$$

(5)

On the other hand, for any $z' \in U(i-1, j-1, 0, d)$ and $\sigma(Q[1 : d] \oplus x_i) = r$, $z' \oplus x_i$ is a common subsequence of $X[1 : i]$ and $Y[1 : j]$ excluding Q as a substring and $\sigma(z' \oplus x_i) = r$ and thus

$$l \geq 1 + \alpha(i, j, 0, r)$$

(6)

Combining (5) and (6) we have $l = 1 + \alpha(i, j, 0, r)$.

Therefore, in the case $k = 0$ and $x_i = y_j$, we have $g(i, j, k, r) = \max\{g(i-1, j-1, 0, r), 1 + \alpha(i, j, 0, r)\}$.

3. In the case of $k > 0$, $x_i = y_j$ and $x_i \neq p_k$, if $x_i = y_j = z_l$, then $z_l \neq p_k$, and thus $P[1 : k]$ is not a suffix of $Z[1 : l]$. Therefore, we have $x_i = y_j \neq z_l$, and $Z[1 : l]$ must be a common subsequence of $X[1 : i - 1]$ and $Y[1 : j - 1]$ including $P[1 : k]$ as a suffix, and excluding Q as a substring and $\sigma(z) = r$, i.e., $Z[1 : l] \in U(i-1, j-1, k, r)$. Therefore, in this case we have, $g(i, j, k, r) = g(i - 1, j - 1, k, r)$.

4. In the case of $k > 0$ and $x_i = y_j = p_k$, There are also two subcases to be distinguished.

   (4.1) If $x_i = y_j \neq z_l$, then $Z[1 : l]$ must be a common subsequence of $X[1 : i - 1]$ and $Y[1 : j - 1]$ including $P[1 : k]$ as a suffix, and excluding Q as a substring and $\sigma(z) = r$. It is obvious that $Z[1 : l]$ is also an LCS of $X[1 : i - 1]$ and $Y[1 : j - 1]$ including $P[1 : k]$ as a suffix, and excluding Q as a substring and $\sigma(z) = r$, i.e., $Z[1 : l] \in U(i - 1, j - 1, k, r)$, and thus $g(i, j, k, r) = g(i - 1, j - 1, k, r)$ in this subcase.

   (4.2) If $x_i = y_j = z_l$, then $Z[1 : l - 1]$ must be a common subsequence of $X[1 : i - 1]$ and $Y[1 : j - 1]$ including $P[1 : k - 1]$ as a suffix, and excluding Q as a substring and $\sigma(z) = d$ for some $0 \leq d < t$ and $\sigma(Q[1 : d] \oplus x_i) = r$. Therefore,

$$l - 1 \leq \alpha(i, j, k - 1, r) \tag{7}$$

   On the other hand, for any $z' \in U(i - 1, j - 1, k - 1, d)$ and $\sigma(Q[1 : d] \oplus x_i) = r$, $z' \oplus x_i$ is a common subsequence of $X[1 : i]$ and $Y[1 : j]$ including $P[1 : k]$ as a suffix, and excluding Q as a substring and $\sigma(z' \oplus x_i) = r$ and thus

$$l \geq 1 + \alpha(i, j, k - 1, r) \tag{8}$$

   Combining (7) and (8) we have $l = 1 + \alpha(i, j, k - 1, r)$.
   Therefore, in the case of $k > 0$ and $x_i = y_j = p_k$, we have $g(i, j, k, r) = \max\{g(i - 1, j - 1, k, r), 1 + \alpha(i, j, k - 1, r)\}$.

The proof is completed.   □

3   A Simple Dynamic Programming Algorithm

Based on the recursive formula (4), our algorithm for computing $g(i, j, k, r)$ is a standard dynamic programming algorithm which can be implemented as the following Algorithm 1.

To implement our new algorithm efficiently, the most important thing is to compte $\sigma(Q[1 : k] \oplus x_i)$ for each $0 \leq k < t$ and $x_i, 1 \leq i \leq n$ efficiently.

It is obvious that $\sigma(Q[1 : k] \oplus x_i) = k + 1$ for the case of $x_i = q_{k+1}$. It will be more complex to compute $\sigma(Q[1 : k] \oplus x_i)$ for the case of $x_i \neq q_{k+1}$. In this case the length of matched prefix of Q has to be shortened to the largest $r < k$ such that $q_{k-r+1} \cdots q_k = q_1 \cdots q_r$ and $x_i = q_{r+1}$. Therefore, in this case, $\sigma(Q[1 : k] \oplus x_i) = r + 1$.

Algorithm 1. Suffix

Input: Strings $X = x_1 \cdots x_n$, $Y = y_1 \cdots y_m$ of lengths n and m, respectively, and two constrained sequences $P = p_1 p_2 \cdots p_s$ and $Q = q_1 q_2 \cdots q_t$ of lengths s and t
Output: $g(i, j, k, r)$, the length of z, an LCS of $X[1 : i]$ and $Y[1 : j]$ including $P[1 : k]$ as a suffix, and excluding Q as a substring and $\sigma(z) = r$, $1 \le i \le n, 1 \le j \le m, 0 \le k \le s$, and $0 \le r < t$.

1: **for all** i, j, k, r, $0 \le i \le n, 0 \le j \le m, 0 \le k \le s$ and $0 \le r \le t$ **do**
2:   $g(i, 0, k, r), g(0, j, k, r) \leftarrow -\infty, g(i, 0, 0, 0), g(0, j, 0, 0) \leftarrow 0$ {boundary condition}
3: **end for**
4: **for all** i, j, k, r, $1 \le i \le n, 1 \le j \le m, 0 \le k \le s$ and $0 \le r \le t$ **do**
5:   **if** $x_i \ne y_j$ **then**
6:     $g(i, j, k, r) \leftarrow \max\{g(i - 1, j, k, r), g(i, j - 1, k, r)\}$
7:   **else if** $k = 0$ **then**
8:     $g(i, j, k, r) \leftarrow \max\{g(i - 1, j - 1, k, r), 1 + \alpha(i, j, k, r)\}$
9:   **else if** $x_i = p_k$ **then**
10:     $g(i, j, k, r) \leftarrow \max\{g(i - 1, j - 1, k, r), 1 + \alpha(i, j, k - 1, r)\}$
11:   **else**
12:     $g(i, j, k, r) \leftarrow g(i - 1, j - 1, k, r)$
13:   **end if**
14: **end for**

Algorithm 2. Prefix Function

Input: String $Q = q_1 \cdots q_t$
Output: The prefix function kmp of Q

1: $kmp(0) \leftarrow -1$
2: **for** $i = 2$ to t **do**
3:   $k \leftarrow 0$
4:   **while** $k \ge 0$ and $q_{k+1} \ne q_i$ **do**
5:     $k \leftarrow kmp(k)$
6:   **end while**
7:   $k \leftarrow k + 1$
8:   $kmp(i) \leftarrow k$
9: **end for**

This computation is very similar to the computation of the prefix function in KMP algorithm for solving the string matching problem [2,3,7].

For the constraint string $Q = q_1 \cdots q_t$ of lengths t, its prefix function kmp can be pre-computed in $O(t)$ time as follows.

With this pre-computed prefix function kmp, the function $\sigma(Q[1 : k] \oplus ch)$ for each character $ch \in \sum$ and $1 \le k \le t$ can be described as follows.

If we pre-compute a table λ of the function $\sigma(Q[1 : k] \oplus ch)$ for each character $ch \in \sum$ and $1 \le k \le t$, then we can speed up the computation of $\alpha(i, j, k, r)$ and $\beta(i, j, k, r)$).

The time cost of above preprocessing algorithm is obviously $O(t|\Sigma|)$. By using this pre-computed table λ, the value of function $\sigma(Q[1 : k] \oplus ch)$ for each character $ch \in \sum$ and $1 \le k < t$ can be computed readily in $O(1)$ time.

Algorithm 3. $\sigma(k, ch)$

Input: String $Q = q_1 \cdots q_t$, integer k and character ch
Output: $\sigma(Q[1:k] \oplus ch)$
1: **while** $k \geq 0$ **and** $q_{k+1} \neq ch$ **do**
2:     $k \leftarrow kmp(k)$
3: **end while**
4: **return** $k + 1$

Algorithm 4. $\lambda(1:r, ch \in \Sigma)$

Input: String $Q = q_1 \cdots q_t$, alphabet Σ
Output: A table λ
1: **for all** $a \in \Sigma$ **and** $a \neq q_1$ **do**
2:     $\lambda(0, a) \leftarrow 0$
3: **end for**
4: $\lambda(0, q_1) \leftarrow 1$
5: **for** $r = 1$ **to** $t - 1$ **do**
6:     **for all** $a \in \Sigma$ **do**
7:       **if** $a = q_{r+1}$ **then**
8:         $\lambda(r, a) \leftarrow r + 1$
9:       **else**
10:        $\lambda(r, a) \leftarrow \lambda(kmp(r), a)$
11:       **end if**
12:     **end for**
13: **end for**

It is obvious that with these preprocessing, the algorithm requires $O(nmst)$ time and space. For each value of $g(i, j, k, r)$ computed by algorithm *Suffix*, the corresponding LCS z of $X[1:i]$ and $Y[1:j]$ including $P[1:k]$ as a suffix, and excluding Q as a substring and $\sigma(z) = r$, can be constructed by backtracking through the computation paths from (i, j, k, r) to $(0, 0, 0, 0)$. The following algorithm $back(i, j, k, r)$ is the backtracking algorithm to obtain the LCS, not only its length. The time complexity of the algorithm $back(i, j, k, r)$ is obviously $O(n + m)$.

It is readily seen that the key problem is to find the LCSs in $Z(n, m, s, r)$, $0 \leq r < t$, according to formula (1). The algorithm above can only be applied in the case when the given problem has a solution including P as a suffix according to the formulas (2) and formula (3).

If we extend the string $P = p_1 p_2 \cdots p_s$ to a generalize string $P = p_1 p_2 \cdots p_s p_{s+1}$ and let $p_{s+1} = *$ be a wildcard character, which can match zero or any number of characters, then we can build the following result.

Theorem 2. *For the given two input sequences $X = x_1 x_2 \cdots x_n$ and $Y = y_1 y_2 \cdots y_m$ of lengths n and m, and the two constrained sequences $P = p_1 p_2 \cdots p_s$ and $Q = q_1 q_2 \cdots q_t$ of lengths s and t, if we extend the string $P[1:s] = p_1 p_2 \cdots p_s$ to a generalize string $P[1:s+1] = p_1 p_2 \cdots p_s p_{s+1}$ and let $p_{s+1} = *$ be a*

Algorithm 5. $back(i, j, k, r)$

Input: Integers i, j, k, r
Output: The LCS z of $X[1 : i]$ and $Y[1 : j]$ including $P[1 : k]$ as a suffix, and excluding Q as a substring and $\sigma(z) = r$

```
 1: if i < 1 or j < 1 then
 2:    return
 3: end if
 4: if xᵢ = yⱼ then
 5:    if k = 0 then
 6:       if g(i, j, k, r) = g(i − 1, j − 1, k, r) then
 7:          back(i − 1, j − 1, k, r)
 8:       else
 9:          back(i − 1, j − 1, k, β(i, j, k, r))
10:          print xᵢ
11:       end if
12:    else if xᵢ = pₖ then
13:       if g(i, j, k, r) = g(i − 1, j − 1, k, r) then
14:          back(i − 1, j − 1, k, r)
15:       else
16:          back(i − 1, j − 1, k − 1, β(i, j, k − 1, r))
17:          print xᵢ
18:       end if
19:    else
20:       back(i − 1, j − 1, k, r)
21:    end if
22: else if g(i, j, k, r) = g(i − 1, j − 1, k, r) then
23:    back(i − 1, j − 1, k, r)
24: else
25:    back(i − 1, j − 1, k, r)
26: end if
```

---

wildcard character, which can match zero or any number of characters, then $Z(n, m, s, r) = U(n, m, s + 1, r)$ for all $0 \leq r < t$.

Proof. For each $Z[1 : l] = z_1, z_2, \cdots, z_l \in Z(n, m, s, r)$, $Z[1 : l]$ includes $P[1 : s]$ as a substring, and excludes Q as a substring and $\sigma(z) = r$. Let $P = (z_{l'-s+1}, \cdots, z_{l'}), s \leq l' \leq l$, then $(z_{l'+1}, \cdots, z_l)$ is a substring of z with length $l - l'$. By the definition of $p_{s+1} = *$, p_{s+1} can match the substring $(z_{l'+1}, \cdots, z_l)$, and thus $P[1 : s + 1]$ is also a suffix of $Z[1 : l]$. It is obvious that in this case $Z[1 : l]$ is also an LCS including $P[1 : s+1]$ as a suffix, and excluding Q as a substring and $\sigma(Z[1 : l]) = r$. We then have $Z[1 : l] \in U(n, m, s + 1, r)$. Therefore,

$$Z(n, m, s, r) \subseteq U(n, m, s + 1, r) \tag{9}$$

On the other hand, for each $Z[1 : l] = z_1, z_2, \cdots, z_l \in U(n, m, s+1, r)$, let $P = (z_{l'-s+1}, \cdots, z_{l'}), s \leq l' \leq l$, and p_{s+1} match the substring $(z_{l'+1}, \cdots, z_l), s \leq l' \leq l$, then $Z[1 : l]$ includes $P[1 : s]$ as a substring, and excludes Q as a substring and $\sigma(z) = r$.

It is obvious that in this case $Z[1 : l]$ is also an LCS including $P[1 : s]$ as a substring, and excluding Q as a substring and $\sigma(Z[1 : l]) = r$. We then have $Z[1 : l] \in Z(n, m, s, r)$. Therefore,

$$U(n, m, s + 1, r) \subseteq Z(n, m, s, r) \tag{10}$$

Combining (9) and (10) we have proved $Z(n, m, s, r) = U(n, m, s + 1, r)$ for all $0 \le r < t$.

The proof is completed.   □

For this generalized constrained string $P[1 : s + 1]$, the formula (4) in Theorem 1 must be changed to

$g(i, j, k, r) =$

$$\begin{cases} \max\{g(i - 1, j, k, r), g(i, j - 1, k, r)\} & \text{if } x_i \ne y_j \\ \max\{g(i - 1, j - 1, k, r), 1 + \alpha(i, j, k, r)\} & \text{if } k = 0 \wedge x_i = y_j \\ \gamma(i, j, k, r) & \text{if } k > s \wedge x_i = y_j \\ \max\{g(i - 1, j - 1, k, r), 1 + \alpha(i, j, k - 1, r)\} & \text{if } k > 0 \wedge x_i = y_j = p_k \\ g(i - 1, j - 1, k, r) & \text{if } k > 0 \wedge x_i = y_j \wedge x_i \ne p_k \end{cases} \tag{11}$$

where,

$\gamma(i, j, k, r) = \max\{g(i - 1, j - 1, k, r), g(i, j, k - 1, r), 1 + \alpha(i, j, k - 1, r), 1 + \alpha(i, j, k, r)\}$.

In this formula, the item $g(i - 1, j - 1, k, r)$ corresponds to the case $x_i = y_j \ne z_l$; the item $g(i, j, k - 1, r)$ corresponds to the case $x_i = y_j$ and p_{s+1} matches none of characters; the item $1 + \alpha(i, j, k - 1, r)$ corresponds to the case $x_i = y_j = z_l$ and p_{s+1} matches one character z_l; the item $1 + \alpha(i, j, k, r)$ corresponds to the case $x_i = y_j = z_l$ and p_{s+1} matches a substring $z_{l'+1}, \cdots, z_l, l - l' > 1$.

The dynamic programming algorithm based on this formula can then be described as follows.

It is obvious that the extended algorithm requires $O(nmst)$ time and space. By using this dynamic programming algorithm, we can find $f(n, m, s, r)$, the length of the LCSs in $Z(n, m, s, r)$ according to Theorem 2 as $g(n, m, s + 1, r)$, and finally our solution is $\max_{0 \le r < t}\{f(n, m, s, r)\} = \max_{0 \le r < t}\{g(n, m, s + 1, r)\}$.

The backtrack algorithm for the algorithm *Suffix* can be changed accordingly to find the LCS, not only its length.

4   Improvements of the Algorithm

Deorowicz [3] proposed the first quadratic-time algorithm for the STR-IC-LCS problem. A similar idea can be used to improve the time complexity of our dynamic programming algorithm for solving the STR-IC-STR-EC-LCS problem. The improved algorithm is also based on dynamic programming with some preprocessing. To show its correctness it is necessary to prove some more structural properties of the problem.

Algorithm 6. DP

Input: Strings $X = x_1 \cdots x_n$, $Y = y_1 \cdots y_m$ of lengths n and m, respectively, and two constrained sequences $P = p_1 p_2 \cdots p_s p_{s+1}$ and $Q = q_1 q_2 \cdots q_t$ of lengths $s + 1$ and t, where $p_{s+1} = *$ is a wildcard character, which can match zero or any number of characters.

Output: $g(i, j, k, r)$, the length of z, an LCS of $X[1 : i]$ and $Y[1 : j]$ including $P[1 : k]$ as a suffix, and excluding Q as a substring and $\sigma(z) = r$, $1 \leq i \leq n, 1 \leq j \leq m, 0 \leq k \leq s + 1$, and $0 \leq r \leq t$.

1: **for all** i, j, r, $0 \leq i \leq n, 0 \leq j \leq m$, and $0 \leq r \leq t$ **do**
2:    $g(i, j, s + 1, r) \leftarrow -\infty$
3: **end for**
4: **for all** i, j, k, r, $0 \leq i \leq n, 0 \leq j \leq m, 0 \leq k \leq s + 1$ and $0 \leq r \leq t$ **do**
5:    $g(i, 0, k, r), g(0, j, k, r) \leftarrow -\infty, g(i, 0, 0, 0), g(0, j, 0, 0) \leftarrow 0$ {boundary condition}
6: **end for**
7: **for all** i, j, k, r, $1 \leq i \leq n, 1 \leq j \leq m, 0 \leq k \leq s$ and $0 \leq r \leq t$ **do**
8:    **if** $x_i \neq y_j$ **then**
9:        $g(i, j, k, r) \leftarrow \max\{g(i - 1, j, k, r), g(i, j - 1, k, r)\}$
10:   **else if** $k = 0$ **then**
11:       $g(i, j, k, r) \leftarrow \max\{g(i - 1, j - 1, k, r), 1 + \alpha(i, j, k, r)\}$
12:   **else if** $k > s$ **then**
13:       $g(i, j, k, r) \leftarrow \max\{g(i - 1, j - 1, k, r), g(i, j, k - 1, r), 1 + \alpha(i, j, k - 1, r), 1 + \alpha(i, j, k, r)\}$
14:   **else if** $x_i = p_k$ **then**
15:       $g(i, j, k, r) \leftarrow \max\{g(i - 1, j - 1, k, r), 1 + \alpha(i, j, k - 1, r)\}$
16:   **else**
17:       $g(i, j, k, r) \leftarrow g(i - 1, j - 1, k, r)$
18:   **end if**
19: **end for**

Let $Z[1 : l] = z_1, z_2, \cdots, z_l$ be a constrained LCS of X and Y including P as a substring and excluding Q as a substring. Let also $I = (i_1, j_1), (i_2, j_2), \cdots, (i_l, j_l)$ be a sequence of indices of X and Y such that $Z[1 : l] = x_{i_1}, x_{i_2}, \cdots, x_{i_l}$ and $Z[1 : l] = y_{j_1}, y_{j_2}, \cdots, y_{j_l}$. From the problem statement, there must exist an index $d \in [1, l - t + 1]$ such that $P = x_{i_d}, x_{i_{d+1}}, \cdots, x_{i_{d+t-1}}$ and $P = y_{j_d}, y_{j_{d+1}}, \cdots, y_{j_{d+t-1}}$.

Theorem 3. *Let $i'_d = i_d$ and for all $e \in [1, s - 1]$, i'_{d+e} be the smallest possible, but larger than i'_{d+e-1}, index of X such that $x_{i_{d+e}} = x_{i'_{d+e}}$. The sequence of indices*

$$I' = (i_1, j_1), (i_2, j_2), \cdots, (i_{d-1}, j_{d-1}), (i'_d, j_d), (i'_{d+1}, j_{d+1}), \cdots,$$
$$(i'_{d+t-1}, j_{d+t-1}), (i_{d+t}, j_{d+t}), \cdots, (i_l, j_l)$$

defines the same constrained LCS as $Z[1 : l]$.

Proof. From the definition of indices i'_{d+e}, it is obvious that they form an increasing sequence, since $i'_d = i_d$, and $i'_{d+t-1} \leq i_{d+t-1}$. The sequence $i'_d, \cdots, i'_{d+t-1}$ is of course a compact appearance of P in X starting at i_d. Therefore, both components of I' pairs form increasing sequences and for any (i'_u, j_u), $x_{i'_u} = y_{j_u}$. Therefore, I' defines the same constrained LCS as $Z[1 : l]$. The proof is completed.   □

The same property is also true for the jth components of the sequence I. Therefore, we can conclude that when finding a constrained LCS of the given STR-IC-STR-EC-LCS problem, instead of checking any common subsequences of X and Y it suffices to check only such common subsequences that contain compact appearances of P both in X and Y. The number of different compact appearances of P in X and Y will be denoted by δ_x and δ_y, respectively. It is obvious that $\delta_x \delta_y \leq \delta$, since a pair (i, j) defines a compact appearance of P in X starting at ith position and compact appearance of P in Y starting at jth position only for some matches.

Base on Theorem 3, we can reduce the time complexity of our dynamic programming from $O(nmst)$ to $O(nmt)$. The improved algorithm is composed of three main stages. In the first stage, both sequences X and Y are preprocessed to determine two corresponding arrays lx and ly. For each occurrence i of the first character p_1 of P in X, the index j of the last character p_s of a compact appearance of P in X is recorded as $lx_i = j$. A similar preprocessing is applied to the sequence Y.

Algorithm 7. Prep

Input: X, Y

Output: For each $1 \leq i \leq n$, the minimal index $r = lx_i$ such that $X[i : r]$ includes P as a subsequence

For each $1 \leq j \leq m$, the minimal index $r = ly_j$ such that $Y[j : r]$ includes P as a subsequence

1: **for** $i = 1$ to n **do**
2:     **if** $x_i = p_1$ **then**
3:         $lx_i \leftarrow left(X, n, i)$
4:     **else**
5:         $lx_i \leftarrow 0$
6:     **end if**
7: **end for**
8: **for** $j = 1$ to m **do**
9:     **if** $y_j = p_1$ **then**
10:         $ly_j \leftarrow left(Y, m, j)$
11:     **else**
12:         $ly_j \leftarrow 0$
13:     **end if**
14: **end for**

In the algorithm Prep, function $left$ is used to find the index lx_i of the last character p_s of a compact appearance of P.

In the second stage of the improved algorithm, the DP matrices $h(i, j, k)$ for the STR-EC-LCS problem, defined by Definition 3, is computed. The formula (4) can be modified somewhat to solve this problem, since it is a special case of $k = 0$ in the formula (4).

Algorithm 8. $left(X, n, i)$

Input: Integers n, i and $X[1 : n]$
Output: The minimal index r such that $X[i : r]$ includes P as a subsequence

1: $a \leftarrow i + 1, b \leftarrow 2$
2: **while** $a \leq n$ **and** $b \leq s$ **do**
3:    **if** $x_a = p_b$ **then**
4:       $b \leftarrow b + 1$
5:    **else**
6:       $a \leftarrow a + 1$
7:    **end if**
8: **end while**
9: **if** $b > s$ **then**
10:    **return** $a - 1$
11: **else**
12:    **return** 0
13: **end if**

Algorithm 9. STR-EC-LCS

Input: Strings $X = x_1 \cdots x_n$, $Y = y_1 \cdots y_m$ of lengths n and m, respectively, and a constrained sequence $Q = q_1 q_2 \cdots q_t$ of length t
Output: $h(i, j, r)$, the length of an LCS z of $X[1 : i]$ and $Y[1 : j]$ excluding Q as a substring and $\sigma(z) = r$, for all $1 \leq i \leq n, 1 \leq j \leq m, 0 \leq r < t$.

1: **for** $i = 1$ to n **do**
2:    **for** $j = 1$ to m **do**
3:       **for** $r = 0$ to $t - 1$ **do**
4:          **if** $x_i \neq y_j$ **then**
5:             $h(i, j, r) \leftarrow \max\{h(i - 1, j, r), h(i, j - 1, r)\}$
6:          **else**
7:             $h(i, j, r) \leftarrow \max\{h(i - 1, j - 1, r), 1 + \alpha(i, j, 0, r)\}$
8:          **end if**
9:       **end for**
10:    **end for**
11: **end for**

$$h(i, j, r) = \begin{cases} \max\{h(i - 1, j, r), h(i, j - 1, r)\} & \text{if } x_i \neq y_j \\ \max\{h(i - 1, j - 1, r), 1 + \alpha(i, j, 0, r)\} & \text{if } x_i = y_j \end{cases} \quad (12)$$

Based on the recursive formula (12), the algorithm for computing $h(i, j, r)$ can be implemented as the following Algorithm 6.

In the last stage, two preprocessed arrays lx and ly are used to determine the final results. To this end for each match (i, j) for X and Y the ends (lx_i, ly_i) of compact appearances of P starting at position i in X and j in Y are read. The length of an STR-IC-STR-EC-LCS, $g(n, m, s + 1, r)$ defined by Definition 2, containing these appearances of P is determined as a sum of three parts. The first part is, for some indices i, j, r', $h(i - 1, j - 1, r')$, the length of u, the constrained LCS which is a prefix of X and Y ending at positions $i - 1$ and $j - 1$, excluding Q

as a substring and $\sigma(u) = r'$. The second part is s, the length of the constrained string P. The third part is $h(lx_i+1, ly_j+1, r+1)$, the length of v, the constrained LCS which is a suffix of X and Y starting at positions $lx_i + 1$ and $ly_j + 1$, such that $z = u \bigoplus P \bigoplus v$ excludes Q as a substring and $\sigma(z) = r$.

We will show how to compute the third part for all $0 \leq r < t$.

Algorithm 10. $modify$

Input: The DP matrices $h(i, j, r)$ computed in stage 2
Output: The modified DP matrices $h(i, j, r)$

1: **for** $i = 1$ to n **do**
2:    **for** $j = 1$ to m **do**
3:      **if** $lx_i > 0$ and $ly_j > 0$ **then**
4:        **for** $r = 0$ to $t - 1$ **do**
5:          **if** $\zeta(r) < t$ **then**
6:            $h(lx_i, ly_j, \zeta(r)) \leftarrow \max\{h(lx_i, ly_j, r), h(i - 1, j - 1, r) + s\}$
7:          **end if**
8:        **end for**
9:      **end if**
10:    **end for**
11: **end for**
12: **for** $r = 0$ to $t - 1$ **do**
13:    **for** $i = 1$ to n **do**
14:      **for** $j = 1$ to m **do**
15:        **if** $h(i, j, r) < \max\{h(i - 1, j, r), h(i, j - 1, r)\}$ **then**
16:          $h(i, j, r) \leftarrow \max\{h(i - 1, j, r), h(i, j - 1, r)\}$
17:        **end if**
18:        **if** $h(i, j, r) < 0$ **then**
19:          $h(i, j, r) \leftarrow -\infty$
20:        **end if**
21:      **end for**
22:    **end for**
23: **end for**

For each $0 \leq r < t$, let

$$\zeta(r) = \sigma(Q[1 : r] \bigoplus P[1 : s]) \tag{13}$$

For each LCS z of $X[1 : i]$ and $Y[1 : j]$ excluding Q as a substring and $\sigma(z) = r$, computed in stage 2, if the ends (lx_i, ly_i) of compact appearances of P starting at position i in X and j in Y are valid, then $z' = z \bigoplus P$ is an LCS including P as a suffix, and excluding Q as a substring and $\sigma(z') = \zeta(r)$, where $1 \leq i \leq n, 1 \leq j \leq m, 0 \leq r < t$. Therefore, we can modify the DP matrix $h(i, j, r)$ computed in stage 2 in these ends (lx_i, ly_i) to $h(lx_i, ly_i, \zeta(r)) = h(i - 1, j - 1, r) + s$.

With these modified values as boundary values, a dynamic programming algorithm for the STR-EC-LCS problem can then be applied to find the third part of the value $h(n, m, r) = g(n, m, s + 1, r)$.

Algorithm 11. $\zeta(1:r)$

Input: Strings $P = p_1 \cdots p_s$ and $Q = q_1 \cdots q_t$
Output: A table ζ
  1: **for** $r = 1$ to $t - 1$ **do**
  2:     $\zeta(r) \leftarrow r$
  3: **end for**
  4: **for** $i = 1$ to s **do**
  5:     **for** $j = 1$ to $t - 1$ **do**
  6:         **if** $\zeta(j) < t$ **then**
  7:             $\zeta(j) \leftarrow \lambda(\zeta(j), p_i)$
  8:         **end if**
  9:     **end for**
10: **end for**

The following algorithm $modify$ will modify the DP matrix $h(i, j, r)$ computed in stage 2 to our purpose.

Then a dynamic programming algorithm for the STR-EC-LCS problem is applied to this modified DP matrix. Finally, we have $f(n, m, s, r) = g(n, m, s + 1, r) = h(n, m, r)$, and thus the length of the LCSs of X and Y including P as a substring and excluding Q as a substring is $\max\limits_{0 \leq r < t} \{h(n, m, r)\}$.

In our improved algorithms, the two dynamic programming algorithms for the STR-EC-LCS problem require both $O(nmt)$ time and space. In the algorithm $modify$, the values of $\zeta(r)$ for all $0 \leq r <$ can be pre-computed as follows.

The time complexity of this algorithm is obviously $O(st)$. With this pre-computed table, the value of $\zeta(r)$ for each $0 \leq r <$ can then be computed readily in $O(1)$ time. Therefore, the time complexity of the algorithm $modify$ is also $O(nmt)$.

According to the matrix $h(i, j, r)$, backtracking can be used to obtain the optimal subsequence, not only its length.

Finally we can conclude that our improved algorithm for solving the STR-IC-STR-EC-LCS problem requires $O(nmt)$ time and to $O(nmt)$ space in the worst case.

5   Concluding Remarks

We have suggested a new dynamic programming solution for the new generalized constrained longest common subsequence problem STR-IC-STR-EC-LCS. The first dynamic programming algorithm requires $O(nmst)$ in the worst case, where n, m, s, t are the lengths of the four input sequences respectively. The time complexity can be reduced further to cubic time in a more thorough analysis. Numerous other generalized constrained longest common subsequence (GC-LCS) problems have similar structures. It is not clear that whether the same technique of this paper can be applied to these problems to achieve efficient algorithms. We will investigate these problems further.

References

1. Chen, Y.C., Chao, K.M.: On the generalized constrained longest common subsequence problems. J. Comb. Optim. **21**(3), 383–392 (2011)
2. Crochemore, M., Hancart, C., Lecroq, T.: Algorithms on Strings. Cambridge University Press, Cambridge (2007)
3. Deorowicz, S.: Quadratic-time algorithm for a string constrained LCS problem. Inf. Process. Lett. **112**(11), 423–426 (2012)
4. Deorowicz, S., Obstoj, J.: Constrained longest common subsequence computing algorithms in practice. Comput. Inform. **29**(3), 427–445 (2010)
5. Gotthilf, Z., Hermelin, D., Lewenstein, M.: Constrained LCS: hardness and approximation. In: Ferragina, P., Landau, G.M. (eds.) CPM 2008. LNCS, vol. 5029, pp. 255–262. Springer, Heidelberg (2008)
6. Gotthilf, Z., Hermelin, D., Landau, G.M., Lewenstein, M.: Restricted LCS. In: Chavez, E., Lonardi, S. (eds.) SPIRE 2010. LNCS, vol. 6393, pp. 250–257. Springer, Heidelberg (2010)
7. Gusfield, D.: Algorithms on Strings, Trees, and Sequences: Computer Science and Computational Biology. Cambridge University Press, Cambridge (1997)
8. Peng, Y.H., Yang, C.B., Huang, K.S., Tseng, K.T.: An algorithm and applications to sequence alignment with weighted constraints. Int. J. Found. Comput. Sci. **21**(1), 51–59 (2010)
9. Tang, C.Y., Lu, C.L.: Constrained multiple sequence alignment tool development and its application to RNase family alignment. J. Bioinform. Comput. Biol. **1**, 267–287 (2003)
10. Tseng, C.T., Yang, C.B., Ann, H.Y.: Efficient algorithms for the longest common subsequence problem with sequential substring constraints. J. Complex. **29**, 44–52 (2013)

A Polynomial Time Algorithm for a Generalized Longest Common Subsequence Problem

Xiaodong Wang[2], Yingjie Wu[3], and Daxin Zhu[1]([✉])

[1] Quanzhou Normal University, Quanzhou 362000, China
dex@qztc.edu.cn
[2] Fujian University of Technology, Fuzhou 350108, China
[3] Fuzhou University, Fuzhou 350002, China

Abstract. In this paper, we consider a generalized longest common subsequence problem with multiple substring exclusive constraints. For the two input sequences X and Y of lengths n and m, and a set of d constraints $P = \{P_1, \cdots, P_d\}$ of total length r, the problem is to find a common subsequence Z of X and Y excluding each of constraint string in P as a substring and the length of Z is maximized. A very simple dynamic programming algorithm to this problem is presented in this paper. The correctness of the new algorithm is demonstrated. The time and space complexities of the new algorithm are both $O(nmr)$.

1 Introduction

The longest common subsequence (LCS) problem is a classic computer science problem, and has applications in bioinformatics. It is also widely applied in diverse areas, such as file comparison, pattern matching and computational biology [3,4,8,9]. Given two sequences X and Y, the longest common subsequence problem is to find a subsequence of X and Y whose length is the longest among all common subsequences of the two given sequences. It differs from the problems of finding common substrings: unlike substrings, subsequences are not required to occupy consecutive positions within the original sequences. The most referred algorithm, proposed by Wagner and Fischer [29], solves the LCS problem by using a dynamic programming algorithm in quadratic time. Other advanced algorithms were proposed in the past decades [2–4,16,17,19,21]. If the number of input sequences is not fixed, the problem to find the LCS of multiple sequences has been proved to be NP-hard [23]. Some approximate and heuristic algorithms were proposed for these problems [6,25].

For some biological applications some constraints must be applied to the LCS problem. These kinds of variants of the LCS problem are called the constrained LCS (CLCS) problem. One of the recent variants of the LCS problem, the constrained longest common subsequence (CLCS) which was first addressed by Tsai [27], has received much attention. It generalizes the LCS measure by introducing of a third sequence, which allows to extort that the obtained CLCS has some special properties [26]. For two given input sequences X and Y of lengths m and

X. Huang et al. (Eds.): GPC 2016, LNCS 9663, pp. 18–29, 2016.
DOI: 10.1007/978-3-319-39077-2_2

n, respectively, and a constrained sequence P of length r, the CLCS problem is to find the common subsequences Z of X and Y such that P is a subsequence of Z and the length of Z is the maximum. The most referred algorithms were proposed independently [5,8], which solve the CLCS problem in $O(mnr)$ time and space by using dynamic programming algorithms. Some improved algorithms have also been proposed [11,18]. The LCS and CLCS problems on the indeterminate strings were discussed in [20]. Moreover, the problem was extended to the one with weighted constraints, a more generalized problem [24].

Recently, a new variant of the CLCS problem, the restricted LCS problem, was proposed [14], which excludes the given constraint as a subsequence of the answer. The restricted LCS problem becomes NP-hard when the number of constraints is not fixed. Some more generalized forms of the CLCS problem, the generalized constrained longest common subsequence (GC-LCS) problems, were addressed independently by Chen and Chao [7]. For the two input sequences X and Y of lengths n and m, respectively, and a constraint string P of length r, the GC-LCS problem is a set of four problems which are to find the LCS of X and Y including/excluding P as a subsequence/substring, respectively. The four generalized constrained LCS [7] can be summarized in Table 1.

Table 1. The GC-LCS problems

Problem	Input	Output
SEQ-IC-LCS	X, Y, and P	The longest common subsequence of X and Y including P as a subsequence
STR-IC-LCS	X, Y, and P	The longest common subsequence of X and Y including P as a substring
SEQ-EC-LCS	X, Y, and P	The longest common subsequence of X and Y excluding P as a subsequence
STR-EC-LCS	X, Y, and P	The longest common subsequence of X and Y excluding P as a substring

For the four problems in Table 1, $O(mnr)$ time algorithms were proposed [7]. For all four variants in Table 1, $O(r(m+n)+(m+n)\log(m+n))$ time algorithms were proposed by using the finite automata [12]. Recently, a quadratic algorithm to the STR-IC-LCS problem was proposed [10], and the time complexity of [12] was pointed out not correct.

The four GC-LCS problems can be generalized further to the cases of multiple constraints. In these generalized cases, the single constrained pattern P will be generalized to a set of d constraints $P = \{P_1, \cdots, P_d\}$ of total length r, as shown in Table 2.

The problem M-SEQ-IC-LCS has been proved to be NP-hard in [13]. The problem M-SEQ-EC-LCS has also been proved to be NP-hard in [14,28]. In addition, the problems M-STR-IC-LCS and M-STR-EC-LCS were also declared

Table 2. The Multiple-GC-LCS problems

Problem	Input	Output
M-SEQ-IC-LCS	X, Y, and a set of constraints $P = \{P_1, \cdots, P_d\}$	LCS of X and Y including each of constraint $P_i \in P$ as a subsequence
M-STR-IC-LCS	X, Y, and a set of constraints $P = \{P_1, \cdots, P_d\}$	LCS of X and Y including each of constraint $P_i \in P$ as a substring
M-SEQ-EC-LCS	X, Y, and a set of constraints $P = \{P_1, \cdots, P_d\}$	LCS of X and Y excluding each of constraint $P_i \in P$ as a subsequence
M-STR-EC-LCS	X, Y, and a set of constraints $P = \{P_1, \cdots, P_d\}$	LCS of X and Y excluding each of constraint $P_i \in P$ as a substring

to be NP-hard in [7], but without a proof. The exponential-time algorithms for solving these two problems were also presented in [7].

We will discuss the problem M-STR-EC-LCS in this paper. The failure functions in the Knuth-Morris-Pratt algorithm [22] for solving the string matching problem have been proved very helpful for solving the STR-EC-LCS problem. It has been found by Aho and Corasick [1] that the failure functions can be generalized to the case of keyword tree to speedup the exact string matching of multiple patterns. This idea can be very supportive in our dynamic programming algorithm. This is the principle idea of our new algorithm.

The organization of the paper is as follows.

In the following 3 sections, we describe our presented dynamic programming algorithm for the M-STR-EC-LCS problem.

In Sect. 2 the preliminary knowledge for presenting our algorithm for the M-STR-EC-LCS problem is discussed. In Sect. 3 we give a new dynamic programming solution for the M-STR-EC-LCS problem with time complexity $O(nmr)$, where n and m are the lengths of the two given input strings, and r is the total length of d constraint strings. In Sect. 4, we consider the issues to implement the algorithm efficiently.

2   Preliminaries

A sequence is a string of characters over an alphabet $\sum$. A subsequence of a sequence X is obtained by deleting zero or more characters from X (not necessarily contiguous). A substring of a sequence X is a subsequence of successive characters within X.

For a given sequence $X = x_1 x_2 \cdots x_n$ of length n, the ith character of X is denoted as $x_i \in \sum$ for any $i = 1, \cdots, n$. A substring of X from position i to j can be denoted as $X[i : j] = x_i x_{i+1} \cdots x_j$. If $i \neq 1$ or $j \neq n$, then the substring $X[i:j] = x_i x_{i+1} \cdots x_j$ is called a proper substring of X. A substring $X[i:j] = x_i x_{i+1} \cdots x_j$ is called a prefix or a suffix of X if $i = 1$ or $j = n$, respectively.

For the two input sequences $X = x_1 x_2 \cdots x_n$ and $Y = y_1 y_2 \cdots y_m$ of lengths n and m, respectively, and a set of d constraints $P = \{P_1, \cdots, P_d\}$ of total length r, the problem M-STR-EC-LCS is to find an LCS of X and Y excluding each of constraint $P_i \in P$ as a substring.

Keyword tree (Aho-Corasick Automaton) [1,9,15] is a main data structure in our dynamic programming algorithm to process the constraint set P of the M-STR-EC-LCS problem.

Definiton 1. *The keyword tree for set P is a rooted directed tree T satisfying 3 conditions: 1. each edge is labeled with exactly one character; 2. any two edges out of the same node have distinct labels; and 3. every string P_i in P maps to some node v of T such that the characters on the path from the root of T to v exactly spell out P_i, and every leaf of T is mapped to some string in P.*

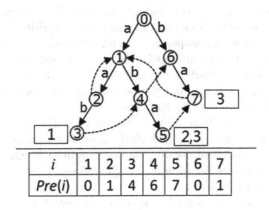

i	1	2	3	4	5	6	7
$Pre(i)$	0	1	4	6	7	0	1

Fig. 1. Keyword trees

In order to identify the nodes of T, we assign numbers $0, 1, \cdots, t-1$ to all t nodes of T in their preorder numbering. Then, each node will be assigned an integer $i, 0 \le i < t$, as shown in Fig. 1. For each node numbered i of a keyword tree T, the concatenation of characters on the path from the root to the node i spells out a string denoted as $L(i)$. The string $L(i)$ is also called the label of the node i in the keyword tree T. For example, Fig. 1 shows the keyword tree T for the constraint set $P = \{aab, aba, ba\}$, where $P_1 = aab, P_2 = aba, P_3 = ba$, and $d = 3, r = 8$. Clearly, every node in the keyword tree corresponds to a prefix of one of the strings in set P, and every prefix of a string P_i in P maps to a distinct node in the keyword tree T. The keyword tree for set P of total length r of all strings can be easily constructed in $O(r)$ time for a constant alphabet size.

The keyword tree can be extended into an automaton, Aho-Corasick automaton, which is composed of three functions, a goto function, an output function and a failure function. The goto function is presented as the solid edges of the keyword tree and the output function indicates when the matches occur and which strings are output. For each node i, its output function is denoted as O_i, a set of indices which indicate when the node i is reached then for each index $j \in O_i$, the string P_j is matched. For example, the output sets of nodes 3, 5 and 7 are $O_3 = \{1\}, O_5 = \{2, 3\}$ and $O_7 = \{3\}$, which means that the outputs of node 3, 5 and 7 are $\{P_1 = aab\}, \{P_2 = aba, P_3 = ba\}$ and $\{P_3 = ba\}$, respectively.

The failure function indicates which node to go if there is no character to be further matched. It is a generalization of the failure functions in the Knuth-Morris-Pratt algorithm for solving the string matching problem. It is represented by the dashed edges in Fig. 1.

For any node i of T, define $lp(i)$ to be the length of the longest proper suffix of string $L(i)$ that is a prefix of some string in T. It can be verified readily that for each node i of T, if A is an $lp(i)$-length suffix of string $L(i)$, then there must be a unique node $pre(i)$ in T such that $L(pre(i)) = A$. If $lp(i) = 0$ then $pre(i) = 0$ is the root of T.

The ordered pair $(i, pre(i))$ is called a failure link. The failure link is a direct generalization of the failure functions in the KMP algorithm. For example, in Fig. 1, failure links are shown as pointers from every node i to node $pre(i)$ where $lp(i) > 0$. The other failure links point to the root and are not shown. The failure links of T define actually a failure function pre for the constraint set P. As stated in [1,9], for a constant alphabet size, in the worst case, the failure function pre can be computed in $O(r)$ time.

The failure list of a given node is the ordered list of the nodes which locate on the path to the root via dashed edges. For example, for the nodes $i = 1, 2, 3, 4, 5, 6, 7$, the corresponding values of failure function are $pre(i) = 0, 1, 4, 6, 7, 0, 1$. The failure list of node 5 is $\{7 \rightarrow 1 \rightarrow 0\}$, and the failure list of node 6 is $\{0\}$, as shown in Fig. 1.

The failure function pre is used to speedup the search for all occurrences in a text Z of strings from P. For each node i of T, and a character $c \in \sum$, if no edges out of the node i is labeled c, then the failure link of node i direct the search to the node $pre(i)$. It is equivalent to add the edge $(i, pre(i))$ labeled c to the node i. This set matching method generalized the next function in KMP algorithm to the Aho-Corasick-next function as follows.

Definiton 2. *Given a keyword tree T and its failure function, for each node i of T and each character $c \in \sum$, Aho-Corasick-next function $\delta(i, c)$ denotes the destination of the first node in i's failure list which has an edge labeled c. If there exists no such node in the failure list, the function returns the root.*

Table 3 shows the Aho-Corasick-next function δ corresponding to the example in Fig. 1.

We take node 4 as an example. It can be seen from Fig. 1 that $\delta(4, a) = 5$ and $\delta(4, b) = 0$. It is easy to understand that each element of Aho-Corasick-next function can be computed in constant time.

Table 3. Aho-Corasick-next function

δ	0	1	2	3	4	5	6	7
a	1	2	1	4	5	1	7	1
b	6	4	3	0	0	1	0	1

The symbol $\oplus$ is also used to denote the string concatenation. For example, if $S_1 = aaa$ and $S_2 = bbb$, then it is readily seen that $S_1 \oplus S_2 = aaabbb$.

3   Our Main Result: A Dynamic Programming Algorithm

Let T be a keyword tree for the given constraint set P, and $Z[1 : l] = z_1, z_2, \cdots, z_l$ be any common subsequence of X and Y. If we search the set matching of Z from the root of T in the direction of the Aho-Corasick-next function δ of T, then the search will stop in a node i of T. All such common subsequence of X and Y can be classified into a group k, $0 \le k < t$. These t groups can be used to distinguish the different states in our dynamic programming algorithm. For each integer k, $0 \le k < t$, the state k represents the set of common subsequence of X and Y in group k.

Definiton 3. *Let $Z(i, j, k)$ denote the set of all LCSs of $X[1 : i]$ and $Y[1 : j]$ with state k, where $1 \le i \le n, 1 \le j \le m$, and $0 \le k < t$. The length of an LCS in $Z(i, j, k)$ is denoted as $f(i, j, k)$.*

If we can compute $f(i, j, k)$ for any $1 \le i \le n, 1 \le j \le m$, and $0 \le k < t$ efficiently, then the length of an LCS of X and Y excluding P must be $\max\limits_{0 \le k < t} \{f(n, m, k) | O_k = \emptyset\}$.

By using the keyword tree data structure described in the last section, we can give a recursive formula for computing $f(i, j, k)$ by the following theorem.

Theorem 1. *For the two input sequences $X = x_1 x_2 \cdots x_n$ and $Y = y_1 y_2 \cdots y_m$ of lengths n and m, respectively, and a set of d constraints $P = \{P_1, \cdots, P_d\}$ of total length r, let $Z(i, j, k)$ and $f(i, j, k)$ be defined as in Definition 3. Suppose a keyword tree T for the constraint set P has been built, and the t nodes of T are numbered in their preorder numbering. Then, for any $1 \le i \le n, 1 \le j \le m$, and $0 \le k < t$, $f(i, j, k)$ can be computed by the following recursive formula.*

$$f(i,j,k) = \begin{cases} \max\{f(i-1,j,k), f(i,j-1,k)\} & \text{if } x_i \ne y_j, \\ \max\left\{f(i-1,j-1,k), 1 + \max\limits_{\bar{k} \in S(k, x_i)} \{f(i-1,j-1,\bar{k})\}\right\} & \text{if } x_i = y_j. \end{cases} \quad (1)$$

where,

$$S(k, x_i) = \{\bar{k} | 0 \le \bar{k} < t, \delta(\bar{k}, x_i) = k\} \quad (2)$$

The boundary conditions of this recursive formula are $f(i, 0, 0) = f(0, j, 0) = 0$ for any $0 \le i \le n, 0 \le j \le m$.

Proof. For any $0 \leq i \leq n, 0 \leq j \leq m$, and $0 \leq k < t$, suppose $f(i,j,k) = l$ and $z = z_1 \cdots z_l \in Z(i,j,k)$.

First of all, we notice that for each pair $(i',j'), 1 \leq i' \leq n, 1 \leq j' \leq m$, such that $i' \leq i$ and $j' \leq j$, we have $f(i',j',k) \leq f(i,j,k)$, since a common subsequence z of $X[1:i']$ and $Y[1:j']$ with state k is also a common subsequence of $X[1:i]$ and $Y[1:j]$ with state k.

(1) In the case of $x_i \neq y_j$, we have $x_i \neq z_l$ or $y_j \neq z_l$.

   (1.1) If $x_i \neq z_l$, then $z = z_1 \cdots z_l$ is a common subsequence of $X[1:i-1]$ and $Y[1:j]$ with state k, and so $f(i-1,j,k) \geq l$. On the other hand, $f(i-1,j,k) \leq f(i,j,k) = l$. Therefore, in this case we have $f(i,j,k) = f(i-1,j,k)$.

   (1.2) If $y_j \neq z_l$, then we can prove similarly that in this case, $f(i,j,k) = f(i,j-1,k)$.

   Combining the two subcases we conclude that in the case of $x_i \neq y_j$, we have

$$f(i,j,k) = \max\left\{f(i-1,j,k), f(i,j-1,k)\right\}.$$

(2) In the case of $x_i = y_j$, there are also two cases to be distinguished.

   (2.1) If $x_i = y_j \neq z_l$, then $z = z_1 \cdots z_l$ is also a common subsequence of $X[1:i-1]$ and $Y[1:j-1]$ with state k, and so $f(i-1,j-1,k) \geq l$. On the other hand, $f(i-1,j-1,k) \leq f(i,j,k) = l$. Therefore, in this case we have $f(i,j,k) = f(i-1,j-1,k)$.

   (2.2) If $x_i = y_j = z_l$, then $f(i,j,k) = l > 0$ and $z = z_1 \cdots z_l$ is an LCS of $X[1:i]$ and $Y[1:j]$ with state k.

Let the state of $(z_1, \cdots, z_{l-1})$ be $\bar{k}$, then we have $\bar{k} \in S(k, x_i)$, since $z_l = x_i$. It follows that $z_1 \cdots z_{l-1}$ is a common subsequence of $X[1:i-1]$ and $Y[1:j-1]$ with state $\bar{k}$. Therefore, we have

$$f(i-1,j-1,\bar{k}) \geq l-1$$

Furthermore, we have

$$\max_{\bar{k} \in S(k,x_i)} \left\{f(i-1,j-1,\bar{k})\right\} \geq l-1$$

In other words,

$$f(i,j,k) \leq 1 + \max_{\bar{k} \in S(k,x_i)} \left\{f(i-1,j-1,\bar{k})\right\} \tag{3}$$

On the other hand, for any $\bar{k} \in S(k, x_i)$, and $v = v_1 \cdots v_h \in Z(i-1,j-1,\bar{k})$, $v \oplus x_i$ is a common subsequence of $X[1:i]$ and $Y[1:j]$ with state k. Therefore, $f(i,j,k) = l \geq 1 + h = 1 + f(i-1,j-1,\bar{k})$, and so we conclude that,

$$f(i,j,k) \geq 1 + \max_{\bar{k} \in S(k,x_i)} \left\{f(i-1,j-1,\bar{k})\right\} \tag{4}$$

Combining (3) and (4) we have, in this case,

$$f(i, j, k) = 1 + \max_{\bar{k} \in S(k, x_i)} \left\{ f(i - 1, j - 1, \bar{k}) \right\} \tag{5}$$

Combining the two subcases in the case of $x_i = y_j$, we conclude that the recursive formula (1) is correct for the case $x_i = y_j$.

The proof is complete.   ∎

4   The Implementation of the Algorithm

According to Theorem 1, our algorithm for computing $f(i, j, k)$ is a standard 3-dimensional dynamic programming algorithm. By the recursive formula (1), the dynamic programming algorithm for computing $f(i, j, k)$ can be implemented as the following Algorithm 1.

Algorithm 1. M-STR-EC-LCS

Input: Strings $X = x_1 \cdots x_n$, $Y = y_1 \cdots y_m$ of lengths n and m, respectively, and a set of d constraints $P = \{P_1, \cdots, P_d\}$ of total length r

Output: The length of an LCS of X and Y excluding P

1: Build a keyword tree T for P
2: **for all** i, j, $0 \le i \le n, 0 \le j \le m$ **do**
3:     $f(i, 0, 0) \leftarrow 0, f(0, j, 0) \leftarrow 0$ {boundary condition}
4: **end for**
5: $S \leftarrow \{0\}$ {current set of states}
6: **for** $i = 1$ to n **do**
7:     **for** $j = 1$ to m **do**
8:         **for each** $k \in S$ **do**
9:             **if** $x_i \ne y_j$ **then**
10:                 $f(i, j, k) \leftarrow \max\{f(i - 1, j, k), f(i, j - 1, k)\}$
11:             **else**
12:                 $\bar{k} \leftarrow \delta(k, x_i)$
13:                 **if** $|O_{\bar{k}}| = 0$ **then**
14:                     $f(i, j, \bar{k}) \leftarrow \max\{f(i - 1, j - 1, \bar{k}), 1 + f(i - 1, j - 1, k)\}$
15:                     $S \leftarrow S \bigcup \{\bar{k}\}$
16:                 **end if**
17:             **end if**
18:         **end for**
19:     **end for**
20: **end for**
21: **return** $\max_{0 \le k < t} \{f(n, m, k)\}$

In Algorithm 1, T is the keyword tree for set P. The root of the keyword tree is numbered 0, and the other nodes are numbered $1, 2, \cdots, t - 1$ in their preorder numbering. $\delta(\alpha, c)$ is the Aho-Corasick-next function defined in

Definition 2, which can be computed in $O(1)$ time. O_k is the output set of node k in T. The variable S is used to record the current states created. When a node is visited first time, a new state may be created. Therefore, in Algorithm 1, the current state set S is extended gradually while the for loop processed. In the worst case, the set S will have a size of r, the total lengths of the constrained strings. The body of the triple for loops can be computed in $O(1)$ time in the worst case. Therefor, the total time of Algorithm 1 is $O(nmr)$. The space used by Algorithm 1 is also $O(nmr)$.

The number of constraints is an influent factor in the time and space complexities of our new algorithm. If a string P_i in the constraint set P is a proper substring of another string P_j in P, then an LCS of X and Y excluding P_i must also exclude P_j. For this reason, the constraint string P_j can be removed from constraint set P without changing the solution of the problem. Without loss of generality, we can put forward the following two assumptions on the constraint set P.

Assumption 1. *There are not any duplicated strings in the constraint set P.*

Assumption 2. *No string in the constraint set P is a proper substring of any other string in P.*

If Assumption 1 is violated, then there must be some duplicated strings in the constraint set P. In this case, we can first sort the strings in the constraint set P, then duplicated strings can be removed from P easily and then Assumption 1 on the constraint set P is satisfied. It is clear that removed strings will not change the solution of the problem.

For Assumption 2, we first notice that a string A in the constraint set P is a proper substring of string B in P, if and only if in the keyword tree T of P, there is a directed path of failure links from a node v on the path from the root to the leaf node corresponding to string B to the leaf node corresponding to string A [1,9]. For instance, in Fig. 1, there is a directed path of failure links from node 5 to node 7 and thus we know the string ba corresponding to node 7 is a proper substring of string aba corresponding to node 5.

With this fact, if Assumption 2 is violated, we can remove all proper super strings from the constraint set P as follows. We first build a keyword tree T for the constraint set P, then mark all the leaf nodes pointed by a failure link in T by using a depth first traversal of T. All the strings corresponding to the marked leaf node can then be removed from P. Assumption 2 is now satisfied on the new constraint set and the keyword tree T for the new constraint set is then rebuilt. It is not difficult to do this preprocessing in $O(r)$ time. It is clear that the removed proper substrings will not change the solution of the problem.

If we want to compute the longest common subsequence of X and Y excluding P, but not just its length, we can also present a simple recursive backtracking algorithm for this purpose as the following Algorithm 2.

In the end of our new algorithm, we will find an index k such that $f(n, m, k)$ gives the length of an LCS of X and Y excluding P. Then, a function call $back(n, m, k)$ will produce the answer LCS accordingly.

Algorithm 2. $back(i, j, k)$

Comments: A recursive back tracing algorithm to construct the answer LCS

1: **if** $i = 0$ **or** $j = 0$ **then**
2:     **return**
3: **end if**
4: **if** $x_i = y_j$ **then**
5:     **if** $f(i, j, k) = f(i - 1, j - 1, k)$ **then**
6:         $back(i - 1, j - 1, k)$
7:     **else**
8:         **for each** $\bar{k} \in S$ **do**
9:             **if** $k = \delta(\bar{k}, x_i)$ **and** $f(i, j, k) = 1 + f(i - 1, j - 1, \bar{k})$ **then**
10:                 $back(i - 1, j - 1, \bar{k})$
11:                 **print** x_i
12:             **end if**
13:         **end for**
14:     **end if**
15: **else if** $f(i - 1, j, k) > f(i, j - 1, k)$ **then**
16:     $back(i - 1, j, k)$
17: **else**
18:     $back(i, j - 1, k)$
19: **end if**

Since the cost of $\delta(k, x_i)$ is $O(1)$ in the worst case, the time complexity of the algorithm $back(i, j, k)$ is $O(n + m)$.

Finally we summarize our results in the following theorem.

Theorem 2. *For the two input sequences $X = x_1 x_2 \cdots x_n$ and $Y = y_1 y_2 \cdots y_m$ of lengths n and m, respectively, and a set of d constraints $P = \{P_1, \cdots, P_d\}$ of total length r, the Algorithms 1 and 2 solve the M-STR-EC-LCS problem correctly in $O(nmr)$ time and $O(nmr)$ space, with preprocessing time $O(r|\Sigma|)$.*

References

1. Aho, A.V., Corasick, M.J.: Efficient string matching: an aid to bibliographic search. Commun. ACM **18**(6), 333–340 (1975)
2. Ann, H.Y., Yang, C.B., Tseng, C.T., Hor, C.Y.: A fast and simple algorithm for computing the longest common subsequence of run-length encoded strings. Inform. Process Lett. **108**(11), 360–364 (2008)
3. Ann, H.Y., Yang, C.B., Peng, Y.H., Liaw, B.C.: Efficient algorithms for the block edit problems. Inf. Comput. **208**(3), 221–229 (2010)
4. Apostolico, A., Guerra, C.: The longest common subsequences problem revisited. Algorithmica **2**(1), 315–336 (1987)
5. Arslan, A.N., Egecioglu, O.: Algorithms for the constrained longest common subsequence problems. Int. J. Found. Comput. Sci. **16**(6), 1099–1109 (2005)
6. Blum, C., Blesa, M.J., Lpez-Ibnez, M.: Beam search for the longest common subsequence problem. Comput. Oper. Res. **36**(12), 3178–3186 (2009)

7. Chen, Y.C., Chao, K.M.: On the generalized constrained longest common subsequence problems. J. Comb. Optim. **21**(3), 383–392 (2011)
8. Chin, F.Y.L., Santis, A.D., Ferrara, A.L., Ho, N.L., Kim, S.K.: A simple algorithm for the constrained sequence problems. Inform. Process. Lett. **90**(4), 175–179 (2004)
9. Crochemore, M., Hancart, C., Lecroq, T.: Algorithms on Strings. Cambridge University Press, Cambridge, UK (2007)
10. Deorowicz, S.: Quadratic-time algorithm for a string constrained LCS problem. Inform. Process. Lett. **112**(11), 423–426 (2012)
11. Deorowicz, S., Obstoj, J.: Constrained longest common subsequence computing algorithms in practice. Comput. Inform. **29**(3), 427–445 (2010)
12. Farhana, E., Ferdous, J., Moosa, T., Rahman, M.S.: Finite automata based algorithms for the generalized constrained longest common subsequence problems. In: Chavez, E., Lonardi, S. (eds.) SPIRE 2010. LNCS, vol. 6393, pp. 243–249. Springer, Heidelberg (2010)
13. Gotthilf, Z., Hermelin, D., Lewenstein, M.: Constrained LCS: hardness and approximation. In: Ferragina, P., Landau, G.M. (eds.) CPM 2008. LNCS, vol. 5029, pp. 255–262. Springer, Heidelberg (2008)
14. Gotthilf, Z., Hermelin, D., Landau, G.M., Lewenstein, M.: Restricted LCS. In: Chavez, E., Lonardi, S. (eds.) SPIRE 2010. LNCS, vol. 6393, pp. 250–257. Springer, Heidelberg (2010)
15. Gusfield, D.: Algorithms on Strings, Trees, and Sequences: Computer Science and Computational Biology. Cambridge University Press, Cambridge (1997)
16. Hirschberg, D.S.: Algorithms for the longest common subsequence problem. J. ACM **24**(4), 664–675 (1977)
17. Hunt, J.W., Szymanski, T.G.: A fast algorithm for computing longest common subsequences. Commun. ACM **20**(5), 350–353 (1977)
18. Iliopoulos, C.S., Rahman, M.S.: New efficient algorithms for the LCS and constrained LCS problems. Inform. Process. Lett. **106**(1), 13–18 (2008)
19. Iliopoulos, C.S., Rahman, M.S.: A new efficient algorithm for computing the longest common subsequence. Theor. Comput. Sci. **45**(2), 355–371 (2009)
20. Iliopoulos, C.S., Rahman, M.S., Rytter, W.: Algorithms for two versions of LCS problem for indeterminate strings. J. Comb. Math. Comb. Comput. **71**, 155–172 (2009)
21. Iliopoulos, C.S., Rahman, M.S., Vorcek, M., Vagner, L.: Finite automata based algorithms on subsequences and supersequences of degenerate strings. J. Discrete Algorithm **8**(2), 117–130 (2010)
22. Knuth, D.E., Morris, J.H., Pratt, V.: Fast pattern matching in strings. SIAM J. Comput. **6**(2), 323–350 (1977)
23. Maier, D.: The complexity of some problems on subsequences and supersequences. J. ACM **25**, 322–336 (1978)
24. Peng, Y.H., Yang, C.B., Huang, K.S., Tseng, K.T.: An algorithm and applications to sequence alignment with weighted constraints. Int. J. Found. Comput. Sci. **21**(1), 51–59 (2010)
25. Shyu, S.J., Tsai, C.Y.: Finding the longest common subsequence for multiple biological sequences by ant colony optimization. Comput. Oper. Res. **36**(1), 73–91 (2009)
26. Tang, C.Y., Lu, C.L.: Constrained multiple sequence alignment tool development and its application to RNase family alignment. J. Bioinform. Comput. Biol. **1**, 267–287 (2003)

27. Tsai, Y.T.: The constrained longest common subsequence problem. Inform. Process. Lett. **88**(4), 173–176 (2003)
28. Tseng, C.T., Yang, C.B., Ann, H.Y.: Efficient algorithms for the longest common subsequence problem with sequential substring constraints. J. Complex. **29**, 44–52 (2013)
29. Wagner, R., Fischer, M.: The string-to-string correction problem. J. ACM **21**(1), 168–173 (1974)
30. Wang, L., Wang, X., Wu, Y., Zhu, D.: A dynamic programming solution to a generalized LCS problem. Inform. Process. Lett. **113**(1), 723–728 (2013)

Improved Survey Propagation on Graphics Processing Units

Yang Zhao$^{(\boxtimes)}$, Jingfei Jiang, and Pengbo Wu

National University of Defense Technology, Changsha, Hunan, China
{zhaoyang10nudt,pengbo026}@163.com, jingfeijiang@126.com

Abstract. The development of graphic processing units (GPUs) ensures a significant improvement in parallel computing performance. However, it also leads to an unprecedented level of complexity in algorithm design because of its physical architecture. In this paper, we propose an improved survey propagation (SP) algorithm to solve the Boolean satisfiability problem on GPUs. SP is a CPU-based incomplete algorithm that can solve hard instances of k-CNF problems with large numbers of variables. In accordance with the analysis on NVIDIA Kepler GPU architecture, a more efficient algorithm is designed with methods of changing data flow, parallel computing, and hiding communication. For NVIDIA K20c and Intel Xeon CPU E5-2650, our proposed algorithm can obtain speed 4.76 times faster than its CPU counterpart.

1 Introduction

Boolean satisfiability problem (SAT) plays an important role across a broad spectrum of computer science areas, including computational complexity theory [5], coding theory [8], and artificial intelligence [6,13]. Obtaining substantial assignments is an important problem in this field. The well-known k-SAT problem is a classical NP complete problem [5] for all $k \geq 3$. The problem is challenging because of the difficulty in deciding if a random formula can obtain a satisfactory assignment for a random formula [9,15]. In statistical physics, Mézard, Parisi and Zecchina proposed a new algorithm *Survey Propagation* (SP) to solve k-SAT problems [12]. SP effectively solves large-scale random k-SAT problems. Based on this advantage, many studies have been proposed in statistical physics and computer science communities [1–4].

With the development of graphic processing units (GPUs), parallel computing on GPUs have promoted all kinds of algorithms in recent years [14,16]. For SAT problems, meaningful works have been proposed. In pSATO, Zhang et al. [18] proposed a parallel and distributed solver based on their previous serial solver SATO [17]. This solver uses a master-slave model where the master aims to balance the work of the slaves to achieve acceleration. Fujii and Fujimoto [7] used GPU to speedup clause analysis. Luo and Liu [10] implemented cellular genetic algorithm and local search for 3-SAT problem based on GPU. The performance of an appropriately-designed algorithm based on GPU can be ensured. However, not all works on SP can perform effectively even in serial computing.

© Springer International Publishing Switzerland 2016
X. Huang et al. (Eds.): GPC 2016, LNCS 9663, pp. 30–41, 2016.
DOI: 10.1007/978-3-319-39077-2_3

Most well-known studies involve parallelized SP from the LonestarGPU benchmark suite, which is automatically parallelized by Galois. Obviously, this version has not adequately considered GPU architecture. Manolios and Zhang [11] implemented SP on GPU; however, their work was performed on an NVIDIA GTX 7900 GPU and parallel computation was considered while the time-consuming part of data transfer was ignored.

Considering the lack of research in this area, we propose an improved SP based on GPU. We focus not only on parallel computation but also on hidden communication. We first design an appropriate data structure to store propagation information based on GPU, then divide tasks for the multicore GPU to balance the load. Furthermore, stream technology is used in hiding communication, which evidently improves performance.

The rest of this paper is organized as follows. We review the k-SAT problem and SP in Sect. 2. Then, we describe our proposed algorithm in Sect. 3. Section 4 shows the results of our experiments, and the last section is conclusion.

2   Background and Problem Set-Up

In this section, we introduce notation and terminologies required in the k-SAT problem and explain SP in detail.

2.1   The k-SAT Problem and Factor Graphs

We define C as index sets for the clauses, V as index sets for variables; they satisfy $|C| = m$ and $|V| = n$. We denote variables as letters i, j, k, and so on, and clauses as a, b, c, and so on. x_s denotes the subset of variables $\{x_i : i \in S\}$. In the k-SAT problem, the clause indexed by $a \in C$ is specified by the pair $(V(a), J_a)$, where $V(a) \subset V$ consists of k elements, and $J_a := (J_{a,j} : i \in V(a))$ is a k-tuple of $\{0, 1\}$-valued weights. The clause indexed by a is *satisfied* by the assignment x if and only if $x_{V(a)} \neq J_a$. Equivalently, $\delta(y, z)$ denotes an indicator function for the event $\{y = z\}$, if we define the function

$$\Psi_{J_a}(x) := 1 - \prod_{i \in V(a)} \delta(J_{a,i}, x_i), \tag{1}$$

then the clause a is satisfied by x if and only if $\Psi_{J_a}(x) = 1$. The overall formula consists of the AND of all the individual clauses, and is satisfied by x if and only if $\prod_{a \in C} \Psi_{J_a}(x) = 1$.

We call the graphical representation of any k-SAT problem provided by the formalism of constraints as factor graphs. As illustrated in Fig. 1, we use circular nodes to describe variables, square nodes to describe clauses. If variable i is in clause a, there is an edge (a, i). If variable i in clause a is a positive presentation, the edge (a, i) is a solid line, while for negative presentation, the edge is a dotted line.

For each $i \in V$, we define the set $C(i) := \{a \in C : i \in V(a)\}$, which corresponds to clauses that impose constraints on variable x_i. This set of clauses

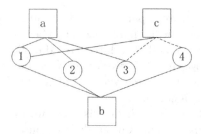

Fig. 1. An example of a factor graph with 4 variable nodes $i = 1, \ldots, 4$, 3 function nodes a, b, c. The formula which is encoded is : $F = (x_1 \vee x_2 \vee x_3) \wedge (x_1 \vee x_2 \vee x_4) \wedge (x_1 \vee \bar{x}_3 \vee \bar{x}_4)$.

can be decomposed into two disjoint subsets, according to whether the clause is satisfied by $x_i = 0$ or $x_i = 1$ respectively.

$$C^-(i) := \{a \in C(i) : J_{a,i} = 1\} \tag{2}$$

$$C^+(i) := \{a \in C(i) : J_{a,i} = 0\} \tag{3}$$

Moreover, for each pair $(a, i) \in E$, the set $C(i) \backslash a$ can be divided into two (disjoint) subsets, depending on whether their preferred assignment of x_i *agrees* (in which case $b \in C_a^s(i)$) or *disagrees* (in which case $b \in C_a^u(i)$) with the preferred assignment of x_i corresponding to clause a. More formally, we define

$$C_a^s(i) := \{b \in C(i) \backslash \{a\} : J_{a,i} = J_{b,i}\} \tag{4}$$

$$C_a^u(i) := \{b \in C(i) \backslash \{a\} : J_{a,i} \neq J_{b,i}\}. \tag{5}$$

2.2　Survey Propagation

In contrast to the naive BP approach, a marginalization-decimation approach based on SP appears to be effective in solving random k-SAT problems even close to the threshold. In this case, we provide an explicit description of what we refer to as the SP(ρ) family of algorithms, where setting the parameter $\rho = 1$ yields the pure form of survey propagation. For any given $\rho \in [0, 1]$, the algorithm involves updating messages from clauses to variables, as well as from variables to clauses. Each clause $a \in C$ passes a real number $\eta_{a \to i} \in [0, 1]$ to each of its variable neighbors $i \in V(a)$. In the other direction, each variable $i \in V$ passes three real numbers $\prod_{i \to a} = (\prod_{i \to a}^u, \prod_{i \to a}^s, \prod_{i \to a}^*)$ to each of its clause neighbors $a \in C(i)$ (that is the set of clauses that impose constraints on variable x_i). The precise form of the updates is given as follow:

Message from clause a to variable i:

$$\eta_{a \to i} = \prod_{j \in V(a) \backslash i} \left[\frac{\prod_{j \to a}^u}{\prod_{j \to a}^u + \prod_{j \to a}^s + \prod_{j \to a}^*} \right] \tag{6}$$

Message from variable i to clause a:

$$\prod_{i \to a}^u = [1 - \rho \prod_{b \in C_a^u(i)} (1 - \eta_{b \to i})] \prod_{b \in C_a^s(i)} (1 - \eta_{b \to i}) \tag{7}$$

$$\prod_{i \to a}^{s} = [1 - \rho \prod_{b \in C_a^s(i)} (1 - \eta_{b \to i})] \prod_{b \in C_a^u(i)} (1 - \eta_{b \to i}) \qquad (8)$$

$$\prod_{i \to a}^{*} = [\prod_{b \in C_a^s(i)} (1 - \eta_{b \to i})] \prod_{b \in C_a^u(i)} (1 - \eta_{b \to i}) \qquad (9)$$

The following are comments on these SP(ρ) updates:

1. Although the time-step index was omitted for simplicity, Eqs. (6–9) should be interpreted as defining a recursion on $(\eta, \prod)$. The initial values for ρ are chosen randomly in the interval $(0, 1)$.
2. The idea of the ρ parameter is to provide a smooth transition from the original naive belief propagation algorithm to the SP algorithm. In Eq. (6), setting $\rho = 0$ yields the belief propagation updates applied to the probability distribution [3], whereas setting $\rho = 1$ yields the pure version of SP.

Intuitive "Warning" Interpretation. To gain insight into these updates, the pure SP setting of $\rho = 1$ must be considered. As described by Braunstein et al. [3], the messages in this case have a natural interpretation in terms of probabilities of warnings. In particular, at time $t = 0$, we suppose that clause a sends a warning message to variable i with probability $\eta_{a \to i}^{0}$, and a message without a warning with probability $1 - \eta_{a \to i}^{0}$. After receiving all messages from clauses in $C(i) \backslash a$, variable i sends a particular symbol to clause a, which indicates that it cannot satisfy ("u"), that it can satisfy ("s"), or that it is indifferent ("*") depending on what messages it received from the other clauses. The following are the four cases:

1. If variable i receives a warning from $C_a^u(i)$ and no warning from $C_a^s(i)$, then it cannot satisfy a and sends a "u" message.
2. If variable i receives a warning from $C_a^s(i)$ but no warning from $C_a^u(i)$, then it sends an "s" message to indicate that it is inclined to satisfy the clause a.
3. If variable i receives no warnings from either $C_a^u(i)$ or $C_a^s(i)$, then it is indifferent and sends a "*" message.
4. If variable i receives warning from both $C_a^u(i)$ or $C_a^s(i)$, a contradiction has occurred.

Updates from clauses to variables are simple; in particular, any given clause sends a warning if and only if it receives "u" symbols from all the other variables.

In this context, real-valued messages involved in pure SP(1) all have natural probabilistic interpretations. In particular, the message $\eta_{a \to i}$ corresponds to the probability that clause a sends a warning to variable i. The quantity $\prod_{j \to a}^{u}$ and $\prod_{j \to a}^{*}$. Normalization by the sum $\prod_{j \to a}^{u} + \prod_{j \to a}^{s} + \prod_{j \to a}^{*}$ reflects the fact that the fourth case is a failure, and therefore is excluded a priori from the probability distribution. We suppose that all possible warning events were independent. In this case, the SP message update Eqs. (6–9) would be the correct estimates for the probabilities. This independence assumption is valid on a graph without cycles, and in which case the SP updates have a rigorous probabilistic interpretation. Whether or not the equations have a simple interpretation in the case $\rho \neq 1$ is not clear.

Decimation Based on SP. We suppose that these SP updates are applied and converged, and the overall conviction of a value at a given variable is computed from the incoming set of equilibrium messages as

$$\mu_i(1) \propto [1 - \rho \prod_{b \in C^+(j)} (1 - \eta_{b \to j})] \prod_{b \in C^-(j)} (1 - \eta_{b \to j}).$$

$$\mu_i(0) \propto [1 - \rho \prod_{b \in C^-(j)} (1 - \eta_{b \to j})] \prod_{b \in C^+(j)} (1 - \eta_{b \to j}).$$

$$\mu_i(*) \propto \prod_{b \in C^+(j)} (1 - \eta_{b \to j}) \prod_{b \in C^-(j)} (1 - \eta_{b \to j}).$$

To be consistent with their interpretation as (approximate) marginals, the three variables $\mu_i(0), \mu_i(*), \mu_i(1)$ at each node $i \in V$ are normalized to obtain a sum of one. We define the *bias* of a variable node as $B(i) := |\mu_i(0) - \mu_i(1)|$.

The marginalization-decimation algorithm based on SP [3] consists of the following steps:

1. Run SP(1) on the SAT problem. Extract fraction β of variables with the largest biases, and set them to their preferred values.
2. Simplify the SAT formula, and return to Step 1.

Once the maximum bias over all the variables falls below a pre-specified tolerance, the Walk-SAT algorithm is applied to the formula to find the remainder of assignment(if possible). Intuitively, the goal of the initial phases of decimation is to locate a cluster; once inside the cluster, the induced problem has a simple solution, which means that any "local" algorithm should perform effectively within a given cluster.

Algorithm Analysis. The algorithm is described as follow Algorithm 1:

The calculation in line [10] is irrelevant among different variables. The same condition applies that the calculation in line [7] is irrelevant among different clauses. However, the second part has a large number of iterations (from line [5] to line [19] except [17]), which consumes most of the execution time. All of the iterations are included in the total iteration procedure seeking for convergence. The execution time of different scales of datasets is shown in Table 1:

Optimization Target. As shown by Amdahl's law, given $n \in N$, the number of threads of execution, $B \in [0, 1]$, the fraction of the algorithm that we optimize. $T(n)$ is the time that an algorithm takes to finish execution of n threads, which corresponds to:

$$T(n) = T(1)(1 - B + \frac{1}{n}B) \tag{10}$$

Therefore, the theoretical speedup $S(n)$ that can be obtained by executing a given algorithm on a system capable of executing n threads of execution is:

$$S(n) = \frac{T(1)}{T(n)} = \frac{T(1)}{T(1)(1 - B + \frac{1}{n}B)} = \frac{1}{1 - B + \frac{1}{n}B} \tag{11}$$

Algorithm 1. Survey Propagation

procedure SURVEY PROPAGATION(n variables v, m clauses c, maximum iteration number $maxIteration$, stripe per cycle $stripe$, bias threshold $biasThreshold$)
    Initialize all messages variables received randomly
    $iterationNum \leftarrow 0$
    while not converge **and**
    $iterationNum < maxIteration$ **do**
        for all v **do**
            calculate the message $m_{c \rightarrow v}$
        end for
        for all c **do**
            update messages $m_{v \rightarrow c}$
        end for
        $iterationNum \Leftarrow iterationNum + 1$
        fix the $stripe$ most-biased variables
        $sofb \Leftarrow$ sum of the bias of all unfixed variables
        $sofv \Leftarrow$ sum of the number of all unfixed variables
        if $sofb/sofv < biasThreshold$ **then**
            use local algorithm and exit
        end if
    end while
end procedure

Table 1. Percentage of iteration time in execution time

Input variables	360	560	900	2000	4000	6000
Total time (s)	0.37	0.81	7.75	5.30	32.13	60.93
Iteration time (s)	0.36	0.78	7.02	4.94	29.86	56.20
(%) of iteration	97.3	95.3	90.5	93.2	92.9	92.2
Input variables	8000	10000	12000	14000	16000	18000
Total time (s)	86.20	142.81	196.13	283.58	346.67	422.59
Iteration time (s)	79.49	131.34	180.26	259.05	315.14	386.70
(%) of iteration	92.2	91.9	91.9	91.3	90.9	91.5

Speedup is directly proportional to the percentage rate of total execution time. According to the Table 1, taking the iteration procedure as the optimization target would produce the best speedup time. Thus, our group converted the two procedures to calculate messages into GPU.

3 Improved SP on GPU

In SP, iteration execution time is more than 90 % of total execution time, while iteration operations have the potential to run in parallel. Based on the analysis in Sects. 2.2 and 2.2, we present a framework of the improved SP on GPU.

3.1 Data Structure

In SP, each variable v_i may exist in several clauses, while each clause c_a may have many variables. For every v_i, its bias (i.e., true or false) needs to be calculated in all the clauses it exists in. Therefore, data correlation exists between different clauses. To avoid this problem, we use a method to make a copy of every variable in every clause and gather the messages after message collection. In the meantime, to quickly find the clauses that a certain variable exists in, we add the index of clauses to every variable.

In factor graph, we use two edges to present the indirected edge $e_{i \leftrightarrow a}$:

1. $e_{i \to a}$: edge from v_i to c_a also provides the index of variables in clause c_i.
2. $e_{a \to i}$: edge from c_a to v_i also provides the index of clauses that variable v_a exists in.

Every pair of edges in opposite directions creates a *one-to-one mapping* in massage-passing edges. By storing messages in edges, we can achieve the message-passing with no correlation using no extra memory and calculation as illustrated in Fig. 2.

3.2 Memory Hierarchy Optimization

Memory access latency is also a problem in high-performance calculation. Memory hierarchy can be classified as register, shared memory, local memory, texture and surface memory, constant memory, and global memory.

Global memory resides in device memory, which is the slowest memory on GPU.

Local memory space resides in device memory; thus, local memory access has the same high latency and low bandwidth as the global memory access and is subject to the same requirements for memory coalescence.

Texture and surface memory spaces reside in the device memory and are cached in the texture cache. Thus, a texture fetch or surface read costs one

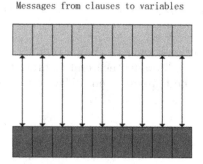

Messages from clauses to variables

Messages from variables to clauses

Fig. 2. In factor graph, for the indirected edge, we use two edges to present it with two directions: one is from variables to clauses, the other is from clauses to variables.

memory read from the device memory only on a cache miss. Otherwise, it only costs one read from the texture cache and is an alternative optimization option.

Shared memory is on-chip; therefore, it has significantly higher bandwidth and significantly lower latency than the local or global memory. Shared memory appears to be the best option to optimize our program. However, its disadvantage is its 48 KB capacity, which is insufficient for this program.

Consequently, we focus on maximizing the use of the register. A main difference between CPU and GPU is the method of mapping registers. CPU uses register renaming and stack to execute multiple threads. The context switch procedure must save data in registers and load new data. By contrast, GPU aims to allocate all registers to every thread. It only needs to change the pointer of the register group, which involves no cost.

3.3   Data Communication and Calculation

Communication influences parallel computing. Although communication is necessary to ensure the correctness of the program, it always consumes part of the speedup gained using multi-threads. Our group reduced communication costs by hiding communication, which clearly improves performance.

Cutting Down Communication. Transferring all data between CPU and GPU is not necessary when using GPU. We need all information on variables, clauses, and their copies in the optimization procedure, while we only need part of the information in other parts of the algorithm. Therefore, we can initialize the data of copies of clauses and transfer them to GPU *only once* and then leave it in GPU to reduce communication time.

Communication Hidden. After the messages from clauses to variable optimization procedure, the calculation of messages for every variable is performed. No change in this procedure in GPU occurs, while calculation is performed thereafter, which is needed in CPU. Copies of variables need to be transferred from GPU to CPU. Thus, we can perform parallel communication and GPU calculation as illustrated in Fig. 3.

4   Experiment

We applied our proposed methods to the data set of SAT2009. We evaluated the optimizing method using different data set sizes and achieved performance improvement. Specifically, hidden communication is different from preceding work and shows improvement, which leads to a new way of optimizing the algorithm.

4.1   Experimental Platform

We implement our improved survey propagation on an Intel Xeon CPU E5-26500 @ 2.00GHz 2.00GHz(double core) with a NVIDIA Tesla K20c GPU. The operating system consists of 64-bit Windows 7 with a total memory of 64 GB RAM. Both CPU and GPU run at high speed.

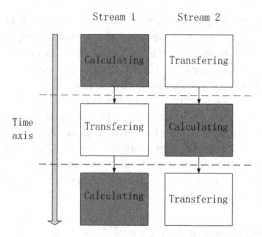

Fig. 3. Two streams can execute in parallel using one when one is calculating while the other is transfering data.

4.2   Data Structure Optimization Results

We use the data structure we previously defined to make the algorithm execute concurrently. Using parameters $BLOKS = 2, THREADS = 1024$, we obtain satisfactory results, as shown in Figs. 4 and 5.

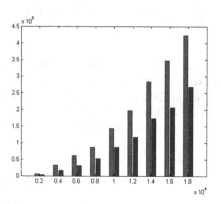

Fig. 4. The x-axis represents the number of variables, the y-axis represents the execution time(ms). The blue ones stand for CPU, the others stand for GPU only with data structure optimization. (Color figure online)

From the figures, the algorithm using our data structure running in GPU is faster than that in CPU using the entire data set. This task is only the beginning of our optimization process; speedup is highly significant because of the availability of high-speed CPU today.

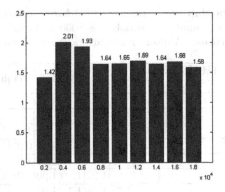

Fig. 5. The x-axis represents the number of variables, the y-axis represents the speedup of GPU to CPU.

Table 2. This table gives the influence of allocation of register by changing the combination of BLOCKS and THREADS.

Number of variables	2000	4000	6000	8000
Initial $THREADS \times BLOCKS$	2×1024	2×1024	2×1024	2×1024
Execution time of GPU (ms)	3736	15983	31539	52627
Best $THREADS \times BLOCKS$	64×128	64×256	256×64	128×128
Best execution time of GPU (ms)	1999	7686	14778	24971
Speedup to initial GPU	1.87	2.08	2.13	2.11
Number of variables	10000	12000	14000	18000
Initial $THREADS \times BLOCKS$	2×1024	2×1024	2×1024	2×1024
Execution time of GPU (ms)	86597	116021	172914	267539
Best $THREADS \times BLOCKS$	64×128	64×64	16×512	32×256
Best execution time of GPU (ms)	42097	60635	89458	127950
Speedup to initial GPU	2.06	1.91	1.93	2.09

4.3   Memory Hierarchy Optimization Results

We try different combinations of $BLOCKS$ and $THREADS$, in which GPU would change the allocation of registers to different threads.

The best performance is more surprising than the initial ones. Detailed data are reported in Table 2.

By choosing the proper allocation of registers, the entire data set performed faster, which means that memory hierarchy is necessary in optimization. The speedup to the initial combination ($BLOCKS * THREADS = 2 * 1024$) can reach up to 2.13, which cuts processing time in half, enabling the speed of our program to run at a new level.

Table 3. This is the speedup *using stream method hiding communication* to *without using stream method* when number of variables is 8000. It includes different BLOCKS and THREADS combinations. Almost all conditions are improving the performance.

BLOCKS \ THREADS	8	16	32	64	128	256	512	1024
4								1.11
8							1.05	0.93
16						1.25	1.169	0.94
32					1.11	0.92	1.04	1.12
64				1.30	1.27	1.08	1.09	1.15
128			1.27	1.20	1.06	1.08	1.21	
256		1.22	1.27	1.13	1.02			
512	1.09	1.13	1.05	1.14	1.03			

4.4 Data Communication Optimization Results

When the stream method on hidden communication is used as described in Sect. 3.3, the algorithm executes faster. Data communication optimization contributes to the data set as shown in Table 3.

Speed gain is not obvious as in other optimization methods. First, we have yet to investigate certain parallelism on data transfer and calculation. Second, hidden data transfer does not take a large amount of time. However, reducing data transfer time enables our program to run faster.

4.5 Final Optimization Results

By using all the methods we previously mentioned, we obtain satisfactory results. All the methods can be applied in one program, which improves SP to enable GPU to run faster than CPU. The final optimization results are shown in Table 4. The highest speed can reach 4.76 times faster on Intel Xeon CPU 5-2650.

Table 4. Speedup to CPU in final optimization

Number of variables	2000	4000	6000	8000	10000	12000	14000
Speedup to CPU	2.85	**4.76**	4.45	3.77	3.70	3.83	3.40

5   Conclusion

In this paper, we propose an improved SP-based GPU. According to the analysis of GPU architecture, a new data structure is defined to adapt the calculation. Then, we equally divide the tasks for every processor and use stream technology to save time on calculation and data transfer. As the experiments demonstrate, our proposed algorithm can achieve 4.76× speedup in NVIDIA K20c to Intel Xeon E5-2650.

Acknowledgements. This work is funded by National Science Foundation of China (number 61303070). Dr. Jingfei Jiang was an academic visitor at University of Manchester. We acknowledge TianHe-1A supercomputing system service.

References

1. Achlioptas, D., Moore, C.: Random k-SAT: two moments suffice to cross a sharp threshold. SIAM J. Comput. **36**(3), 740–762 (2006)
2. Braunstein, A., Mézard, M., Weigt, M., Zecchina, R.: Constraint satisfaction by survey propagation. In: Computational Complexity and Statistical Physics, p. 107 (2005)
3. Braunstein, A., Mézard, M., Zecchina, R.: Survey propagation: an algorithm for satisfiability. Random Struct. Algorithms **27**(2), 201–226 (2005)
4. Braunstein, A., Zecchina, R.: Survey propagation as local equilibrium equations. J. Stat. Mech. Theory Exp. **2004**(06), P06007 (2004)
5. Cook, S.A.: The complexity of theorem-proving procedures. In: Proceedings of the Third Annual ACM Symposium on Theory of Computing, pp. 151–158. ACM (1971)
6. Dechter, R.: Constraint Processing. Morgan Kaufmann, Burlington (2003)
7. Fujii, H., Fujimoto, N.: GPU acceleration of BCP procedure for SAT algorithms. IPSJ SIG Notes **8**, 1–6 (2012)
8. Gallager, R.G.: Low-density parity-check codes. IRE Trans. Inf. Theory **8**(1), 21–28 (1962)
9. Levin, L.A.: Average case complete problems. SIAM J. Comput. **15**(1), 285–286 (1986)
10. Luo, Z., Liu, H.: Cellular genetic algorithms and local search for 3-SAT problem on graphic hardware. In: IEEE Congress on Evolutionary Computation, CEC 2006, pp. 2988–2992. IEEE (2006)
11. Manolios, P., Zhang, Y.: Implementing survey propagation on graphics processing units. In: Biere, A., Gomes, C.P. (eds.) SAT 2006. LNCS, vol. 4121, pp. 311–324. Springer, Heidelberg (2006)
12. Mézard, M., Parisi, G., Zecchina, R.: Analytic and algorithmic solution of random satisfiability problems. Science **297**(5582), 812–815 (2002)
13. Pearl, J.: Probabilistic Reasoning in Intelligent Systems: Networks of Plausible Inference. Morgan Kaufmann, Burlington (2014)
14. Tao, T., Xuejun, Y., Yisong, L.: Locality analysis and optimization for stream programs based on iteration sequence. J. Comput. Res. Dev. **6**, 027 (2012)
15. Wang, J.: Average-case computational complexity theory. In: Complexity Theory Retrospective II, pp. 295–328 (1997)
16. Wen, M., Su, H., Wei, W., Wu, N., Cai, X., Zhang, C.: High efficient sedimentary basin simulations on hybrid CPU-GPU clusters. Cluster Comput. **17**(2), 359–369 (2014)
17. Zhang, H.: SATO: an efficient prepositional prover. In: McCune, W. (ed.) CADE 1997. LNCS, vol. 1249, pp. 272–275. Springer, Heidelberg (1997)
18. Zhang, H., Bonacina, M.P., Hsiang, J.: PSATO: a distributed propositional prover and its application to quasigroup problems. J. Symbolic Comput. **21**(4), 543–560 (1996)

ZooKeeper+: The Optimization of Election Algorithm in Complex Network Circumstance

Xinyan Zhang, Zhipeng Tan$^{(\boxtimes)}$, Meng Li, Yingfei Zheng, and Wei Zhou

School of Computer Science and Technology,
Wuhan National Laboratory for Optoelectronics,
Huazhong University of Science and Technology, Wuhan 430074, China
xyzhangcs@gmail.com, zhipengtan@163.com

Abstract. Dynamic configuration management brings challenge for the distributed file systems while keeping the normal service. In this paper, we describe a robust election algorithm based on ZooKeeper, we realize the dynamic addition and deletion of servers without service interruption. There is only one clustered mode for servers without switching between prior two modes, it also speeds up the leader election. The leader maintains an active server list which speeds up handling of the transaction. The algorithm also ensures the data consistency and system stability against all possible issues. Through the evaluation, it takes not much overhead to realize the addition and deletion of servers and the recovery of crashed servers under various complex network circumstances, and it takes little more election time and initialization time of service to obtain the greater scalability.

Keywords: Election algorithm · ZooKeeper · Consistency · Scalability

1 Introduction

The clustered file system with multivariate metadata servers is an inevitable trend for the growing needs of performance, capacity and scale. It is critical for the clustered file system to guarantee the data consistency when providing normal service, it usually takes the coordination service to harmonize the nodes in cluster and ensures data consistency.

The difficult of designing distributed file system is handling the partial failure, it means the network may happen failure when message transfers from one node to another. The message sender cannot ensure whether the receiver has received the message or not. The receiver may receive the message before the network failure or not, and the receiver thread may have been broken down.

ZooKeeper [1] is an architecture to resolve this partial failure, it is an open source distributed coordination services. It is a centralized service that encapsulates public services, such as naming, configuration management, synchronization and cluster service into a simple interface. All of these kinds of services are widely used in many distributed applications such as Hadoop, KafkaMQ [2], Storm [3], etc.

© Springer International Publishing Switzerland 2016
X. Huang et al. (Eds.): GPC 2016, LNCS 9663, pp. 42–60, 2016.
DOI: 10.1007/978-3-319-39077-2_4

ZooKeeper keeps data consistency through a set of guarantees, such as sequential consistency, atomicity, single system image, reliability and timeliness. It provides transparent services for outside distributed system through a cluster that consists of $2n + 1$ servers who know the existence of each other. Its service mechanism is summarized as following.

(1) Servers in ZooKeeper can communicate with each other. They maintain the server's status, save the operations' logs and generate periodic snapshots in memory. The ZooKeeper can work only if more than half servers are correct (i.e., with $2n+1$ servers we can tolerate n but not $n+1$ failures). All proposals should be subject to approval by the leader, the followers then are informed of the changes by using Zab protocol [4].
(2) Client can choose anyone of cluster servers to read or write data. Operations will be synced to all servers, and each server maintains the memory state image, snapshots, and transaction logs of persistent storage. Once connected to a server, client maintains a TCP connection to submit requests, get response, get monitoring events and send heartbeats. If the TCP connection gets broken, client will connect to another server to ensure service continuity.

This paper designs a robust leader election algorithm that can adapt to arbitrary topological changes in complex environments such as network partitions, servers crashed, etc. There is only one clustered mode for servers.

The rest of this paper is organized as follows. Section 2 presents the related works. Section 3 describes the robust consistent election protocol. Section 4 analyzes its data consistency guarantee under various complex situations and then proves correctness of the robust algorithm. In Sect. 5, we demonstrate the effectiveness of robust election algorithm versus Zookeeper through experiments. And the last section concludes the paper.

2   Related Works

For ensuring the high availability of ZooKeeper service, it needs to do the multiple redundant backups, the write operations to these multiple backups bring the consistent problem. It is critical to guarantee the data consistency between these redundant backups.

Eric Brewer proposed the CAP theorem [5,6] that there is a fundamental trade-off between consistency, availability, and partition tolerance when designing the distributed file system. According to the degree of consistency, the paper [7] divided it into three parts: strong consistency, weak consistency and eventual consistency. The consensus problem existed in the multiple backups can be dived into two parts: the consistency of any updates and multiple updates.

The cluster needs to reach a consensus by leader election so as to coordinate the servers. The existing studies of the leader election algorithm have proved that it cannot keep the consistency about the leader election without any assumption on the premise of the network environment [8]. Considering the speed of message delivery during the network communication, the current leader election algorithms can be divided into the following three sorts.

(1) The election algorithm of strong consistency. These election algorithms aim at the consistency of any updates. The election algorithm proposed in paper [9] ensures the voters can finish the updaing operation in a limited time. The paper [10] uses heap tree method to elect the leader with the lesser complexity. The Raft election algorithm [11] and the Ark algorithm [12] both guarantee the consistency of any updates.

(2) The election algorithm of weak consistency. These algorithms improve the high concurrency of single update and guarantee the consistency of multiple updates. The algorithm in paper [13] allows the network partition has its own leader when network partition occurs, it will elect the unique leader finally after system merges these partitions. The algorithm in paper [14] based on TORA guarantees the system can elect the unique leader finally after the partitions restore the connection. The algorithm in paper [15] tolerates frequent topology changes and finally elects the unique leader, but it cannot guarantee a unique leader at all times.

(3) The election algorithm of eventual consistency. It only needs to ensure the updates keep consistent finally. The paper [16] gives a complete network with N nodes, it tolerates up to $N/2 - 1$ links incident failure on each node, so the system tolerates up to $N^2/4 - N/2$ links failure. The algorithm in paper [17] eventually uses only n links to carry message and it ensures that a leader is elected in constant time when the system is stable. The Fast Leader Election algorithm [18] that used in ZooKeeper architecture set a half bound variable-*quorum*, only the number of active nodes are more than quorum can the network partition elects the leader.

The reconfiguration protocol for Primary/Backup replication systems exploits primary order [19], it needs to persist information about new configuration S' on stable storage at a quorum of current system S, deactivate the current configuration, then identify and transfer all committed state from S to S'. As this algorithm needs to write new configuration S' to a quorum of S at least, a quorum of S should execute these operations at least, it has low efficiency.

We analyze the Release_3.4.5 of ZooKeeper and we find it simplifies the configuration management strategy by using a static configuration to deploy both clients and servers. It needs to restart cluster multiple times to reconfigure the system, this leads to service interruptions unavoidably. Its scalability is limited and its weakness can be summarized as follows.

(1) Zookeeper uses two deployment modes: standalone mode and distributed mode. The standalone mode is usually used for test or demos. It is not flexible to switch between two modes.

(2) It limits the number of servers in cluster, only more than three servers can form the cluster to provide the service outside.

(3) It cannot add or delete any servers dynamically during runtime of the cluster, the multiple servers need to be shut down and restarted if it needs to reconfigure the cluster.

(4) The leader sends commands and broadcasts to the ensemble when handling transactions, the messages send to the crashed servers are unnecessary.

Based on the above weakness of ZooKeeper, we propose a robust consistent election algorithm with the following contributions.

(1) It takes the unique clustered mode to replace the original standalone and distributed modes. It avoids the overhead brought by the conversion between the prior two modes.
(2) The cluster scale is unrestricted, one or two servers can also elect the leader through election algorithm. It can speed up the leader election through configuring a single participant and multiple observes at startup.
(3) It realized the dynamic server addition and deletion when the cluster provides the normal service. It reduces the service interruptions brought by the restart operations, it also reduces the redundancy of the persistent server list.
(4) The proposals and commands are only send to the servers in the active server list which is maintained by the leader. It improves the efficiency by reducing the overhead that is send to the inactive servers.

For the complex environment that may have the split brain, data corruption and crashed servers, the algorithm guarantees the data consistency during the proceeding of server addition, deletion and recovery, and it improves the efficiency of handling transactions. The algorithm obtains better performance and gains greater availability and scalability.

3   The Consistent Election Algorithm

Specific implementation details are given in this section, such as the design of start mode, server addition and deletion, and how to ensure the consistency of the data during the ensemble dynamic changing procedure.

(1) The cluster's initial startup
    (1-1) If the administrator needs to start up n servers with initial mode, he should configure n servers' information in each server' persistent list so that all servers can keep consistent at startup.
    (1-2) Each server initializes its persistent server list version and zxid to 0, and sets quorum to $\lfloor n/2 \rfloor$.
    (1-3) Each server starts with the initial mode, and executes the leader election step 2.
(2) Leader election
    (2-1) Set each participant's status as *Looking*.
    (2-2) Each participant sends votes to those participants in its persistent server list one by one.

(2-3) It judges whether its own *version* of the persistent server list is bigger than the submitter's *version* and is the maximum among the known *version* when a participant receives one vote message. It will put self's server list, *version* and *zxid* into the next vote if the judgments above are true. The server will update self's persistent server list and restart a new vote according to the updated server list if self's *version* of the persistent server list is smaller than the *version* of the received votes and these received votes contain the information about the persistent server list.

(2-4) It judges whether more than $\lfloor n/2 \rfloor$ participant's *version* are the biggest and the same once it finishes traversing the n participant of the latest persistent server list. Execute the next step if it meets the conditions, otherwise jump to step (2-2).

(2-5) Every participant votes the server whose *zxid* is the biggest among all survived participants as the leader. It chooses the server with biggest ID number as the leader if all the *zxid* are the same. Then leader's epoch plus 1 and updates the quorum to the $\lfloor n/2 \rfloor$. The leader election finishes and then turns to the registration procedure (3).

(3) Server registration

(3-1) Learner sends registration request that includes information about the *zxid* and *version* to leader.

(3-2) Leader receives the registration request from learner and replies its own *zxid* to the learner.

(3-3) Learner replies the data synchronization type including *OK*, *SNAP*, *TRUNC*, and *DIFF* to leader after comparing its own *zxid* with leader's *zxid*.

(3-4) Leader sends the necessary *UpToDate* data according to the data synchronization and judges whether its own persistent server list to be sent according to learner's version information.

(3-5) Learner updates the *UpToDate* data, persistent servers' list, *version*, and *zxid*, then it returns an *ack* back to leader, and finally turns to heartbeat procedure (4).

(3-6) After receiving more than quorum participants' acks, Leader generates active server list and then turns to heartbeat procedure (4).

(3-7) When a learner recovers from failure, it executes leader election procedure (2) first, then sends registration request to leader, who will add the learner to its active server list after leader and learner execute the procedures from (3-1) to (3-5), and returns a registered success message to the learner, thus finishing the crashed servers' recovering procedure.

(4) Server heartbeat

(4-1) Leader sends ping message to all learners in the active server list every tickTime, it will delete the learner from the active list if no *ack* returns of successive three times. Once it finds that the quantity of participants in the active server list is less than the quorum, it will turn to the leader election procedure (2).

(4-2) Learner detects the ping message from leader and returns ack. If it hasnot received leader's ping message in three $tickTimes$, it will turn to the leader election procedure (2).

(4-3) Particularly, leader sends the detecting message which comes with its own server information (ID number, IP address, client port, role) to all inactive learners every two T times. When inactive learner recovers from the crash, it begins to register to leader once it received the detecting message from leader. This procedure guarantees special crashed servers' recovery, such as server that stays in failed section for a long time and other servers in its own server list have all been deleted.

(5) Data synchronization

Just like the original ZooKeeper system, learner sends request to leader, leader uses two-phase protocol which is similar to the Paxos algorithm. The adding and deleting operation of our algorithm do not impact on the data synchronization. It should be noted that because of the active server list is to be used once leader launches data synchronization proposal, so coupling between data synchronization and servers' addition and deletion is the change of the active server list. The new active server list can be used for synchronization at the next time to commit the proposal after changing active server list.

(6) Server addition

(6-1) The administrator needs to configure a latest persistent server list for NS (new server) when a new server wants to add into the cluster.

(6-2) The NS starts up with the adding mode.

(6-3) NS sends the participants in its persistent server list the message about whether it exists in the others' persistence server list and which server is the leader successively. It will execute the leader election procedure (2-2) if more than quorum of the participants returns the certain answer, otherwise turn to (6-4) if it just know the leader information.

(6-4) NS sends an add request to the leader.

(6-5) Leader broadcasts the proposal about adding a server to the active participant after receiving the add request from the NS, each participant returns an ack after receiving the proposal broadcast.

(6-6) If the leader receives more than quorum participants' ack, it will update itself persistent server list and plus 1 to its $version$, then sends performing operations to all the active participant.

(6-7) Participants update their persistent server list and version according to the information of NS in the proposal after receiving the commit message, then each returns an ack.

(6-8) The leader sends a successful message about addition to the NS after receiving more than quorum participants' acks.

(6-9) NS executes the registering procedure (3-7) after receiving the successful message about addition from the leader, or restarts executing the procedure (6-3).

(6-10) Leader updates the quorum number to the $\lfloor n/2+1 \rfloor$ according to the latest participants' number after receiving the NS's registering message at procedure (3-7).

(7) Server deletion

(7-1) Administrator just needs to call the deleting interface from any server (operation server, hereinafter referred to as the *OS*) in the cluster when he wants to delete one server from the current system.

(7-2) OS sends request about deleting *DS* (the server to be deleted) to the leader.

(7-3) Leader checks whether *DS* existed in its server list after receiving the deleting request, it returns 'X may be not existing' if *DS* does not exist in its server list, otherwise sends message of stopping service of *DS*, removes the *DS* from its own server list and updates quorum number to $\lfloor n/2-1 \rfloor$ and version. If the *DS* is an active server, it will shut down itself directly after receiving the message of stopping service from the leader, it will also turn to election procedure if it has not received the ping message from leader, then shut down itself through knowing itself do not exist in the current system from other servers' feedback; if *DS* is a crashed server, leader will delete it from its own persistent server list and stop send detecting message, which in order to prevent the crashed server recovering and adding in the cluster.

(7-4) Leader broadcasts the proposal to active participants, participants delete the *DS* and update its persistent server list, and then each returns an ack to leader.

(7-5) Leader sends message about deleting successfully to the *OS* if it receives more than quorum participants' acks.

(7-6) The delete operation is completed after the *OS* receiving the successful message about deletion from leader, otherwise *OS* restarts executing the procedure (7-2) if it receives the message about deleting failed or waits for a timeout.

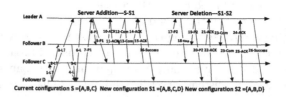

Fig. 1. Reconfiguration with server addition and deletion

Here is an example about the reconfiguration with the server addition and deletion which is shown in the Fig. 1. The current configuration S contains server A, B and C, A is the leader, B and C are followers.

A new server D begins to add into the cluster at a time and its persistent server list is $[A, B, C, D]$, it firstly sends messages whether it exists in the current cluster and the leader information to the server A, B and C, all of them returns leader information. Then it sends adding request to Leader A, Leader A broadcasts the proposal about adding D to the active server B and C, B and C return ACK back to leader A, Leader A updates its persistent list to $[A, B, C, D]$ after receiving more than quorum ACK, and sends committing message to server B and C, the server B and C updates to the latest persistent list $[A, B, C, D]$ and return ACK back, the leader A sends the addition success message to server D after receiving more than quorum ACK, server D turns to registers to leader A and leader A updates its quorum number from 2 to 3. Server D successfully adds into cluster.

The leader A sends message about stopping service to server C after receiving request to delete server C from server B. Server C shuts down itself directly after receiving the command to stop service from the leader A. Leader A removes server C from its own persistent list, updates quorum from 3 to 2 and changes the version, then broadcasts proposal about deleting server C to the active server B and D. Server B and D keep it in the local disk by the transaction log mode and return an ACK back after receiving the proposal broadcast, the leader A receives the ACK messages from server B and D, then sends commit commands to server B and D. The server B and D update their persistent list to $[A, B, D]$ after receiving the commit commands and plus 1 to their version, then return an ACK back. The leader A sends deletion successful message to server B after it receives more than quorum ACK.

4   Algorithm Analysis and Proof

4.1   Guarantee of Consistency

The algorithm in this paper will modify and synchronize the persistent server list when add and delete servers. The consistency of persistent server list is affected by the complex network circumstance (message loss, server crashes, and network partitions). We should know how consistency problem of the persistent server list happened before proving the correctness of algorithm, because it directly influences the motive and principle of the algorithm.

Fig. 2. The custom icons

The consistency problem that may occur during the execution of the algorithm, it can be boiled down to the following two categories:

(1) As servers in normal partition may enter into crashed partition at any times and servers in crashed partition cannot contact with the servers in normal

partition, the crashed partition cannot check the change of persistence server list in normal section, which leads to the disaccord between the crashed partition and normal partition.

(2) In normal partition, if the message losses or the leader exits during the process of synchronization about persistent server list when the leader executes the adding or deleting operations, the normal partition's inner persistent server list will not keep consistency.

There are three extreme cases of the consistency problem in the running process of cluster. First, we give the custom icons used in following steps in Fig. 2.

Consistency Guarantee in Server Addition. The following Fig. 3 shows how it keeps consistency of server list in server addition step when the leader goes down.

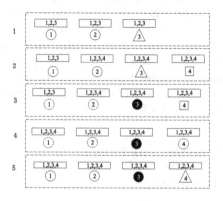

Fig. 3. Consistency guarantee in server addition

Step 1: There are three servers at startup of cluster, server 1, 2 are followers and server 3 is leader. All the persistent server lists are [1, 2, 3].

Step 2: Server 4 begins to add into cluster, it polls its persistent server list to look for the leader, then it sends adding request to server 3, server 3 updates its server list to [1, 2, 3, 4] and executes two-phase commit protocol after receiving adding request from 4. Server 2 updates its server list to the latest while server 1 does not update for some reasons such as unreliable network or dropped packets, etc.

Step 3: Leader server 3 crashes before it returns successful message back to server 4, server 1 and 2 restart leader election.

Step 4: For server 4, it waits for timeout and restarts to add into cluster, but it finds cluster is electing the leader, the server 1 and 2 have updated their server list to the latest [1, 2, 3, 4], server 4 joins into leader election.

Step 5: Server 4 is elected as the leader because of the biggest $zxid$, server 4 adds successfully.

Consistency Guarantee in Server Deletion. The following Fig. 4 expounds how it keeps consistency of server list in servers' deletion when leader fails.

Step 1: There are 3 servers in cluster, and 3 is leader, now server 4 adds into the cluster successfully.

Step 2: Leader 3 receives the request of deleting server 4, and sends message of stopping service to server 4. The message loses because of network malfunction or dropped packets, but server 3 updates its server list to [1, 2, 3].

Step 3: Leader server 3 sends deletion proposal to active servers, only server 2 responses and updates its server list to [1, 2, 3]. Server 4 restarts to leader election as losing heartbeat from leader 3.

Step 4: If server 3 crashes now, server 1, 2 will restart to leader election.

Step 5: Server 1, 2, 4 send votes to each other and update to the latest server list ([1, 2, 3]), server 4 finds itself is not in the latest server list and will shut down. Server 2 becomes the leader because of the bigger zxid among the active servers.

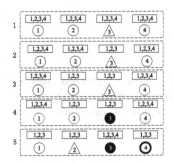

Fig. 4. Consistency guarantee in server addition

Consistency Guarantee in Server Recovery. The following Fig. 5 exposits how it keeps consistency of server list in servers' recovery when leader goes down.

Step 1: there are three servers in the cluster, server 1 was isolated due to network partition and it is in state of leader election, server 3 is elected as the leader.

Step 2: server 4, 5, 6 add into cluster successfully some time later.

Step 3: server 3 failed after deleting server 2 successfully, the rest servers restart to leader election.

Step 4: server 6 is elected as the leader, then cluster deletes server 3 successfully.

Step 5: server 1 recoveries from the crash as network partition disappears, it sends votes to server 2 and 3 but gets no reply. Server 1 receives the exploring message from leader 6, gets the latest server list and registers to server 6, and then it adds into cluster successfully. (For crashed server, leader sends exploring message to them every $3\,T$ times for detecting their recovery).

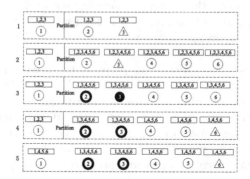

Fig. 5. Consistency guarantee in server addition

4.2   Algorithm Proof

The algorithm in this paper supports adding and deleting server dynamically when the system is running, and ensures the correct operation of the system under the complex network circumstance (message loss, server crashes, network partitions) at the same time. The algorithm meets the following two characters:

Property 1. For any two servers (A, B) of the cluster, if their versions of persistent list meet $Version(A) > Version(B)$, then the persistent server list of A must contain server B.

Illustration: Property 1 makes sure that any two participants can exchange their persistent server list according the election step (2-2) -(2-4) when partition contains any number of servers. So it will not happen that servers cannot communicate with each other because of the inconsistency of the persistent list, thus providing the safeguard for subsequent algorithm.

Proof.

(1) In procedure (1-1), all servers' persistent list keep consistency at startup, the version is 0, and each server's persistent list concludes all servers' information, so Property 1 is corrected.

(2) In procedure (6-1), before adding a new server, the new server should know all servers' information and obtain the biggest version of persistent server list from the leader after the success of the addition, thus Property 1 is corrected.

(3) In procedure (7), the service of the DS needs to be stopped first, leader then deletes it from its persistent list. It will not recover for a deleted server, so it will never happen that the deleted server is still working but not existing in other servers' persistent list, thus proving the correctness of the Property 1. □

Property 2. Let n denotes the number of participants in the system (including active and crashed servers), then the system will elect a unique leader eventually and provide the service in a network partition that its numbers of active participant are not less than $\lfloor n/2+1 \rfloor$.

Illustration: Property 2 guarantees that the algorithm can elect a unique leader to provide service when more than quorum of participants are active and they can communicate with each other inner one partition, so the consistency problem caused by multiple leaders that run concurrently.

Proof.

(1) The persistent list of all servers is consistent at the startup, so it can ensure the correctness of Property 2 by the quorum principle in the electing procedure (2).
(2) Only more than quorum of participants' persistent list keep consensus can the leader provide service in procedure (3).
(3) Only leader ensures that more than quorum of participants' persistent list keep consensus can it returns the successful message about server addition or deletion in procedure (6) or (7) of algorithm steps.
(4) There are more than quorum of participants inner current system have updated to the latest persistent list when the system returns the successful message about adding or deleting server, these participants make up set A, and because more than quorum of participants in current system are survival, these servers make up set B, so set A and set B have an intersection and set B must have some servers that own the latest persistent list, then participants inner set B will finally update to the latest persistent list according to procedure (2), this guarantees the correctness of the Property 2.
(5) There are two cases when system returns failed message about adding or deleting server:
  (5-1) Only less than quorum of ensemble inner system update to the latest persistent list;
  (5-2) There are more than quorum of participants updating to the latest persistent list, but the successful messages about adding or deleting server are lost in the procedure (6-8) or (7-5) of algorithm steps. The servers submitted request wait to time out.

So it can be concluded from the executor: successful addition or deletion is certain, but failed addition or deletion maybe not. If one sends message to the other when any two servers communicate with each other inner unreliable network circumstance, only one receives the reply message can we make sure the other have received the sending message, otherwise it is not sure whether the other receives the sending message.

Starting from this logic, when the system returns the failed message about server addition or deletion, the algorithm will retry constantly and not execute the next addition or deletion operations until it succeeds. This can finally make up system's consensus problem and provide guaranty for the Property 1 and 2. From the sight of the system, the system is problematic if it returns failed message about server addition or deletion, it makes no sense to execute the follow-up operation of addition and deletion.   □

Property 3. Let n denotes the number of participants in the current system (including active and crashed servers), it will not elect a leader inner one partition that its active participants are less than the $\lfloor n/2+1 \rfloor$.

Illustration: The Property 3 avoids more than one leader appearing in the system, it will not elect a leader when less than quorum of participants constitutes a partition because of the inconsistent problem of persistent list (It may reduce the quorum requirements because the server list in this partition may be old and participants in its persistent list are limited).

Proof.

(1) There is a set A consists of m active participants in a partition that has less than quorum of participants, $2 * m <= n$;

(2) Let a denotes the participant whose version of persistent list is the biggest in set A.

(3) According to the electing procedure (2), the persistent server list of active participants in set A will keep consistent with server a.

(4) By reduction to absurdity, assumes that the Property 3 is false: set A can elect a leader, then if persistent list of server a contains k servers, it must satisfy this conditions: $k < 2 * m$.

(5) Because $k < 2 * m$ and $2 * m <= n$, so $k < n$, which means that server a malfunctions at some point during the system running and it have not updated to the latest version that contains n servers' information.

(6) According to the Property 1, server a has the biggest version in the set A, so its persistent list inevitably contains all participants of set A, this means set A has m participants at least.

(7) There must contain serval servers' addition and deletion from the former system that it contains k participants when server a fails to the current system contained n participants, and only more than quorum of participants' update to the latest persistent list successfully can the leader returns the successful message. Let set B denotes the quorum of participants before server a fails, so only make sure more than servers in set B are survival at least before server a malfunctions can we ensure the successful execution of the follow-up servers' addition or deletion.

(8) As participants in set B execute servers' addition or deletion successfully after server a fails, so the versions of all the participants' persistent list in set B are certain bigger than the versions in set A. So the set A and set B must be no intersection.

(9) Combined with the above procedures (6), (7), (8), we have the following conclusions:

(9-1) Set A has m participants at least.

(9-2) Set B should have more participants than set A, so set B has $m + 1$ participants at least.

(9-3) The persistent server list of server a must contains set A and B, and set A and B must be no intersection.

It can conclude that $k \geq 2 * m + 1$, while this is the contradiction with the assumption about $k < 2m$ in procedure (4). Thus proving the correctness of Property 3. □

5   Evaluation

In this part, we mainly evaluate the robust election algorithm supporting dynamical reconfiguration from the following two parts: function test and performance. We used 9 servers to build a ZooKeeper cluster for the evaluation, each server has one Inter Xeon dualcore 2.4 GHz processor, 4 GB of RAM, 1 Gigabit Ethernet, and two SATA drives. The operating system is Red Hat Enterprise Linux Server release 5.4 (Tikanga), Linux Kernel version is 2.6.18 and the java version is 1.7.0_51.

5.1   Function Test

The function test aims at ensuring the cluster can work normally under various complex situations, we devided it into three parts: test for server addition, deletion and recovery. The cluster scale consists of three cases: single participant (P), two participants (P_2, PO) and multiple followers and observers $(P_m O_n)$. The moment for the server addition, deletion and recovery should consider the current cluster status (normal, electing, crashed). The operated server status includes follower and observer.

It needs to be considered for server addition and deletion is whether servers can be successfully added or deleted or not when the crashed servers happen to recover from the crash at the moment of server addition and deletion. And for the sever recovery, after multiple servers' addition and deletion, some crashed server may no longer have any current cluster's configuration information, but more than quorum active servers still keep the crashed server's information, the crashed server can add into the cluster by leader's exploring message when it is recovered from crash. In an extreme case, the persistent server list of crashed server contains $[1, \ldots m]$ while the current cluster is $[m, \ldots n]$. The crashed server is m. It can register to the leader and successfully add into the cluster after it recovers from the crash and receives the leader's exploring message.

SID	ZooKeeper+			ZooKeeper		
	num	>10	tim	num	>10	tim
65	230469	9	0.256044	236453	8	0.249761
66	209580	9	0.282553	235310	8	0.250865
67	leader			leader		
69	216969	9	0.272927	233788	7	0.252721
70	153491	9	0.386894	142352	8	0.417019
71	195853	8	0.302525	177402	7	0.333836
72	164944	10	0.359944	172545	8	0.343431
73	216253	11	0.273754	213678	8	0.276487
sum	1387559	65	414650.2633	1411528	54	414094.0719
ave		4.7E-05	0.298834329		3.8E-05	0.293365822

Fig. 6. The comparison on operations

5.2 Performance Test

We used the ZooKeeper Benchmark tool provided by the Computer Science department of Brown University which measures the perrequest latency of a ZooKeeper ensemble for a predetermined length of time [20] to the throughput.

The benchmark exercises the ensemble performance by handling znode reads, repeating writes to a single znode, znode creation, repeating writes to multiple znodes, and znode deletion. These tests can be performed with either synchronous or asynchronous operations. The benchmark connects to each server in the ZooKeeper ensemble using one thread per server. In synchronous operation, each client makes a new request upon receiving the result of the previous one. In asynchronous operation, each client thread has a globally configurable target for the number of outstanding asynchronous requests. If the number of outstanding requests falls below a configurable lower bound, then new asynchronous requests are made to return to the target level.

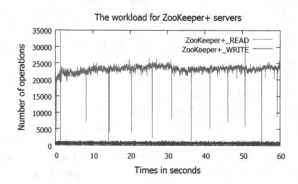

Fig. 7. Workload for ZK servers with znode read and creation

We use 9 machines to evaluate its performance, the server ID is from 65 to 73, 68 is used for running benchmark, we configure the cluster with three participants, five observers and one client server. The server 65, 66, 67 are configured as the participants, the rest are set as observers. We named the robust election algorithm ZooKeeper+ to facilitate the comparison test. We use the Release_3.4.5 of ZooKeeper as the comparison. We donot run benchmark on the leader. During the benchmark, the current rate of request processing is recorded at a configurable intermediate interval to one file per operation: READ.dat, SETSINGLE.dat, CREATE.dat, SETMULTI.dat, and DELETE.dat. the operation time is 600 s, and the request frequency is 800,000 requests per second for each client. We analyze the *.dat and count the number of operations per node. Meanwhile, we analyze the ZooKeeper.out under the bin directory of each node and calculate the election time and initialization time. We mainly make the comparison about znode reads and creation. We run each cluster for 10 min, and make the comparison between ZooKeeper and our robust algorithm.

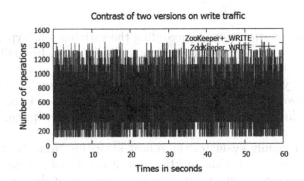

Fig. 8. Comparison between two versions on znode creation

The above Fig. 6 shows comparison on operations in *.dat, num represents the total number of operations, >10 represents the number of outliers that are more than 0.01, and tim represents the arithmetic average of the time. It can be not hard to see the operations in ten minutes between two versions do not have much difference, and the number of outliers are nearly the same compared with the huge number of operands. Meanwhile, there is little variation among these two version on the numbers of total operations.

The Fig. 7 shows the read and write traffic for the cluster during one hour, each point corresponds to the number of operations in that second. We observe that the read traffic is much higher compared to the write traffic, that because the read operations in this workload are getData(), getchildren(), and exists(), in increasing order of prevalence.

The Figs. 8 and 9 show the comparison between ZooKeeper+ and ZooKeeper on znode writes and reads during the cluster working normally in one hour, the ensemble operations are all in the same range, it is nearly the same with the ZooKeeper, which means ZooKeeper+ works stably as well as the ZooKeeper.

As shown in Fig. 10, it provides the leader election time and initialization time of two versions. The election and initialization time of ZooKeeper is little less than the ZooKeeper+, the reasons are as follows. Firstly, server needs to

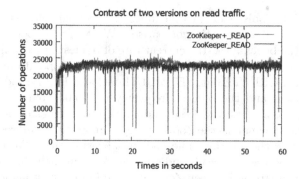

Fig. 9. Comparison between two versions on znode read

choose the different startup mode according the variable startType, and leader needs to monitor the adding request from the new server. In addition, servers need to judge value of the vote information of persistent server list contained in the votes, they may need to update the persistent server list if its vision is old. But the above all realize the dynamical server addition and deletion without restarting the cluster and causing the current service interruption, it gains the greater scalability.

This section mainly evaluates the robust algorithm from the function and performance parts. Through the function test, it concludes that the robust consistent election algorithm greatly realizes the expansion of cluster from the single node to the multiple nodes. It can add new server and delete the servers successfully, and it guarantees the recovery of the crashed servers, ensures the availability and improves the scalability of the cluster. Through the performance test, compared with the ZooKeeper, the number of operations of two versions in the same time have no difference nearly, the traffic of the reading and writing operations are essentially flat, the election and initialization time is little more than ZooKeeper, but it is acceptable as it gains greater scalability.

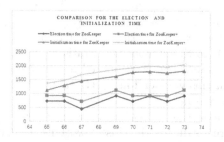

Fig. 10. Comparison for the election and initialization time

6   Conclusion

This paper is focus on the leader election problem in distributed file systems. Based on the architecture of ZooKeeper, a robust election algorithm supporting dynamic reconfiguration is proposed. The original standalone mode and distributed mode are replaced by the unique cluster mode without switching between prior two modes. The cluster scale is unrestricted, one or two servers can also elect the leader, it can speed up the leader election through configuring a single participant and multiple observers at startup. It realized the dynamic server addition and deletion without the service interruptions. It speeds up handling of the transaction as the release of proposals and commands is only send to the servers in the active server list which maintained by the leader. Then the robust algorithm and traditional ZooKeeper are fully implemented and tested under different circumstances. Test results demonstrate that the consistent election algorithm supporting dynamical reconfiguration has the same performance with the traditional model and gains greater availability and scalability. In conclusion, the robust algorithm is meaningful and it makes ZooKeeper more practicable and flexible.

Acknowledgments. This work is supported by 973 project 2011CB302301, the National Basic Research 973 Program of China under Grant by National University's Special Research Fee (2015XJGH010).

References

1. Hunt, P., Konar, M., Junqueira, F.P., Reed, B.: ZooKeeper: waitfree coordination for internet-scale systems. In: USENIX Annual Technical Conference, vol. 8, p. 9 (2010)
2. Kreps, J., Narkhede, N., Rao, J., et al.: Kafka: a distributed messaging system for log processing. In: NetDB (2011)
3. Ranjan, R.: Streaming big data processing in datacenter clouds. IEEE Cloud Comput. 1, 78–83 (2014)
4. Junqueira, F.P., Reed, B.C., Serafini, M.: Zab: high-performance broadcast for primary-backup systems. In: 2011 IEEE/IFIP 41st International Conference on Dependable Systems & Networks (DSN), pp. 245–256. IEEE (2011)
5. Gilbert, S., Lynch, N.: Brewer's conjecture and the feasibility of consistent, available, partition-tolerant web services. ACM SIGACT News 33(2), 51–59 (2002)
6. Gilbert, S., Lynch, N.A.: Perspectives on the CAP theorem. Institute of Electrical and Electronics Engineers (2012)
7. Vogels, W.: Eventually consistent. Commun. ACM 52(1), 40–44 (2009)
8. Garcia-Molina, H.: Elections in a distributed computing system. IEEE Trans. Comput. 100(1), 48–59 (1982)
9. Huang, S.T.: Leader election in uniform rings. ACM Trans. Program. Lang. Syst. (TOPLAS) 15(3), 563–573 (1993)
10. EffatParvar, M., Yazdani, N., EffatParvar, M., Dadlani, A., Khonsari, A.: Improved algorithms for leader election in distributed systems. In: 2010 2nd International Conference on Computer Engineering and Technology (ICCET), vol. 2, pp. V2–6. IEEE (2010)

11. Ongaro, D., Ousterhout, J.: In search of an understandable consensus algorithm. In: 2014 USENIX Annual Technical Conference (USENIX ATC 14), pp. 305–319 (2014)
12. Kasheff, Z., Walsh, L.: Ark: a real-world consensus implementation. arXiv preprint arXiv:1407.4765 (2014)
13. Fetzer, C., Cristian, F.: A highly available local leader election service. IEEE Trans. Softw. Eng. **25**(5), 603 (1999)
14. Malpani, N., Welch, J.L., Vaidya, N.: Leader election algorithms for mobile ad hoc networks. In: Proceedings of the 4th International Workshop on Discrete Algorithms and Methods for Mobile Computing and Communications, pp. 96–103. ACM (2000)
15. Vasudevan, S., Kurose, J., Towsley, D.: Design and analysis of a leader election algorithm for mobile ad hoc networks. In: Proceedings of the 12th IEEE International Conference on Network Protocols, 2004, ICNP 2004, pp. 350–360. IEEE (2004)
16. Singh, G.: Leader election in the presence of link failures. IEEE Trans. Parallel Distrib. Syst. **3**, 231–236 (1996)
17. Aguilera, M.K., Delporte-Gallet, C., Fauconnier, H., Toueg, S.: Stable leader election. In: Welch, J.L. (ed.) DISC 2001. LNCS, vol. 2180, pp. 108–122. Springer, Heidelberg (2001)
18. Lamport, L.: Fast paxos. Distrib. Comput. **19**(2), 79–103 (2006)
19. Shraer, A., Reed, B., Malkhi, D., Junqueira, F.P.: Dynamic reconfiguration of primary/backup clusters. In: Presented as Part of the 2012 USENIX Annual Technical Conference (USENIX ATC 12), pp. 425–437 (2012)
20. Ferguson, A., Liang, C.: ZooKeeper-benchmark (2012). https://github.com/brownsys/zookeeper-benchmark

Cloud Computing

An Efficient Dynamic Provable Data Possession Scheme in Cloud Storage

Ge Yao[1], Yong Li[1,2]([✉]), Linan Lei[1], Huaqun Wang[3], and Changlu Lin[2,4]

[1] School of Electronic and Information Engineering, Beijing Jiaotong University,
Beijing 100044, People's Republic of China
liyong@bjtu.edu.cn
[2] Fujian Provincial Key Laboratory of Network Security and Cryptology,
Fujian Normal University, Fuzhou 350007, People's Republic of China
[3] Dalian Ocean University, Dalian 116023, People's Republic of China
[4] College of Mathematics and Computer Science, Fujian Normal University,
Fuzhou 350117, People's Republic of China

Abstract. Cloud storage provides clients with flexible, dynamic and cost effective data storage service. This new paradigm of data storage service, however, introduces new security challenges. Since clients can no longer control the remote data, they need to be convinced that their data are correctly stored in the cloud. Moreover, supporting dynamic data updates is a practical requirement of cloud storage. It is imperative to provide an efficient and secure dynamic auditing protocol to check the data integrity in the cloud. In this paper, we first analyze the dynamic performance of some prior works and propose a new *Dynamic Provable Data Possession* (DPDP) scheme. We introduce a secure signature scheme and the Large Branching Tree (LBT) data structure in our scheme. LBT structure simplifies the process of updates and the signature scheme is used to authenticate both the value and the position of data blocks, which greatly improves the efficiency in communication. The security and performance analysis show that our DPDP scheme is provably secure and efficient.

Keywords: Cloud storage · Provable data possession · Large branching tree · Dynamic update

1 Introduction

Cloud computing has been envisioned as the next-generation architecture of IT enterprise [1]. It enables users to access to the infrastructure and application services on a subscription basis. This computing service can be categorized into Infrastructure-as-a-Service (IaaS), Platform-as-a-Service (PaaS) and Software-as-a-Service (SaaS) [2]. Due to the advantage characteristics including large scale computation and data storage, virtualization, high scalability and elasticity, cloud computing technologies have been developing fast, of which the

© Springer International Publishing Switzerland 2016
X. Huang et al. (Eds.): GPC 2016, LNCS 9663, pp. 63–81, 2016.
DOI: 10.1007/978-3-319-39077-2_5

important branch is cloud storage system. Cloud storage service is a new paradigm for delivering storage on demand, over a network and billed for just what is used. Many international IT corporations now offer cloud storage service on a scale from individual to enterprise, such as Amazon Simple Storage Service (S3) and EMC Atoms Cloud Storage.

Although cloud storage is growing in popularity, data security is still one of the major concerns in the adoption of this new paradigm of data hosting. For example, the cloud service providers may discard the data which has not been accessed or rarely accessed to save the storage space or keep fewer replicas than promised [3]. And the storage service provider, which experiences Byzantine failures occasionally, may decide to hide the data errors from the client for the benefit of their own [1]. Furthermore, disputes occasionally suffer from the lack of trust on cloud service provider (CSP) because the data change may not be timely known by the cloud client, even if these disputes may result from the users own improper operations [4]. Therefore, clients would like to check the *integrity* and *availability* of their stored data. However, the large size of the outsourced data and the limited resource capability present an additional restriction: the client should perform the integrity check *without downloading all stored data*.

To date, extensive researches are carried out to address this problem [5–14,18–20]. Early work concentrated on enabling *data owners* to check the integrity of remote data, which can be denoted as *private verifiability*. Although schemes with private verifiability can achieve higher scheme efficiency, *public verifiability* (or *public auditability*) allows *anyone* not just the client (data owner), to challenge the cloud server for correctness of data storage while keeping no private information [1]. In cloud computing, data owners are able to delegate the verification of data integrity to a trusted third party auditor (TPA), who has expertise and capabilities to audit the outsourced data on demand. This is because the client themselves are not willing to perform frequent integrity checks due to the heavy overhead and cost.

Recently, public auditability has become one of the basic requirement of proposing a data storage auditing scheme. However, there are still some major concerns need to be solved before put the auditing schemes into practical use. Many big data applications keep clients' data on the cloud and offer frequently update operations. A most typical example is Twitter. Data stored in cloud may not only be accessed but also updated by the clients through either modify an existing data block, or insert a new block, or delete any block. To support the most general forms of update operation is important to broaden the scope of practical application of cloud storage. Therefore, it is imperative to extend the auditing scheme to support provable updates to outsourced data. Unfortunately, traditional data integrity verification schemes are mainly designed for *static* data storage. The direct extension of these schemes may lead to functional defect or security vulnerability. In this paper, we will focus on better support for *dynamic* data operation for cloud storage applications. We employ a secure signature scheme from bilinear maps [15] and the Large Branching Tree (LBT) to achieve that aim. Our contribution can be summarized as follows:

(1) We formally define the framework of dynamic provable data possession scheme and provide an efficient construction, which supports fully dynamic updates including modification, insertion and deletion.

(2) We analyze the existing schemes and point out the disadvantages of the Merkle Hash Tree (MHT) used as the data structure for dynamic updates. For better efficiency, we replace MHT with LBT. This multiple branching data structure enables reduction in size of auxiliary information, thereby causes less communication cost compared to MHT-based schemes.

(3) We employ a secure signature algorithm for LBT data structure. The characteristics of bilinear pairings in the signature algorithm only cause $O(1)$ computation cost on CSP for each dynamic update. Besides, the client no longer needs to construct LBT structure to support dynamic operation. Consequently, this algorithm greatly reduces computation cost both on CSP and client as well as simplifies the update process.

(4) We prove the security of our proposed construction and justify the performance of our scheme through comparisons with existing data integrity verification schemes [1,5–7,11,12].

The rest of this paper is organized as follows. Section 2 discusses related works. In Sect. 3, we introduce main techniques, system model and security model. Then, Sect. 4 presents the specific description of our proposed scheme. Section 5 provides security analysis. We further analyze the experimental results in Sect. 6. Section 7 concludes the paper.

2   Related Works

Recently, the integrity verification for data outsourced in cloud has attracted extensive attention. The existing provable data integrity schemes can be classified into two categories: *proof of retrievability* (POR) and *provable data possession* (PDP). POR scheme was first proposed by Juels *et al.* in 2007 [5]. In their scheme, the client can not only check their remote data integrity, but also recover outsourced data in its entirety by employing erasure-correcting code. The following researches of POR focused on providing security analysis [7] and improving the construction. However, most of existing POR schemes can only be used to the static archive storage system, e.g., libraries and scientific data sets [5,7–9]. The reason is that the erasure-correcting codes using in POR system bring a problem: the *whole* outsourced data is required to perform a small update. This is the main issue towards making POR dynamic.

In cloud computing, the dynamic update is a significant issue for various applications which means that the outsourced data can be dynamically updated by the clients such as: modification, deletion and insertion. Therefore, an efficient dynamic auditing protocol is essential in practical cloud storage systems [10].

In 2007, Ateniese *et al.* [6] proposed PDP framework. Compared to POR scheme, PDP did not use erasure-correcting codes, and hence was more efficient. Although PDP did not provide the retrievability guarantee, the dynamic techniques of PDP are developed well in follow-up studies. Ateniese *et al.* [11]

gave a dynamic PDP scheme based on their prior work [6], in which the client pre-computes and stores at the server a limited number of random challenges with the corresponding answers. This scheme cannot perform insertion since that would affect all remaining answers.

The first fully dynamic PDP protocol was proposed by Erway *et al.* [12] in 2009. They considered using dynamic data structure to support data updates, so they constructed the rank-based authenticated dictionaries based on the skip list. However, the skip list requires a long authentication path and large amount of auxiliary information during the verification process. Wang *et al.* [1] employed homomorphic signature and MHT data structure to achieve supporting fully dynamic updates. Zhu *et al.* [4] proposed a dynamic auditing system based on fragment, random sampling and Index-Hash Tree (IHT) that supports provable updates and timely anomaly detection. Later on, researches are focus on supplying additional properties [16], distribute and replicate [13] or enhance efficiency and using other data structure [17]. For instance, Wang *et al.* [18] firstly proposed a proxy provable data possession (PPDP) system. Their protocol supports the general access structure so that only authorized clients are able to store data to public cloud servers. Lin *et al.* [19] proposed a novel provable data possession scheme, in which data of different values are integrated into a data hierarchy, and clients are classified and authorized different access permissions. Their scheme also allows the data owner to efficiently enroll and revoke clients which make it more practical in cloud environment.

Recently, Gritti *et al.* proposed an efficient and practical PDP system by adopting asymmetric pairings [20]. Their scheme outperforms other existing schemes because there are no exponentiation and only three pairings are required. However, this scheme is vulnerable to three attacks as they later pointed out [21]. Several solutions are proposed by Gritti *et al.* corresponding to all the vulnerabilities of scheme [20]. They used IHT and MHT techniques to resist the replace attack and replay attack. They also employed a weaker security model to achieve data privacy. Although system security can be guaranteed, the performance of the system still needs improvement.

To solve the above problems, we employ a new data structure Large Branching Tree (LBT) into PDP system. The difference between LBT and MHT is that each none-leaf node yields out multiple children, taking q as an example. This multiple branching data structure enables the client to increase the number of a node's children and decrease the depth of the tree without inflating the signature length. For further improving the system efficiency, we introduce a secure signature scheme to verify the value of the data blocks. In fact, the improvement is achieved by the difference of the way the sibling nodes are authenticated. We will discuss this in detail in Sect. 4.

3 Preliminaries

3.1 Large Branching Tree

Compared to MHT, LBT is concise in structure. Each node of the tree except leaves has more than 2 children nodes. For concreteness, we take the outdegree of the node to be q, and the height of the tree is l. An authentication LBT scheme produces signatures that represent paths connecting data blocks to the root of the tree. The authentication mechanism works inductively: the root authenticates its children nodes, these nodes authenticate their children nodes, and the authentication proceeds recursively down to the data blocks authenticated by its parent [15]. In our scheme, the way the sibling nodes are authenticated is different. Since every node has multiple brother nodes, we label them with a number to denote its position among siblings. And an unique authentication value that can be verified independently has been generated for the verification.

3.2 Dynamic PDP System

The dynamic PDP system for outsourced data in cloud consists of three entities: *Client*, who has limited storage resource and computational ability but large amount of data to be stored in the cloud; *Cloud Storage Server* (CSS), an entity which has huge storage space and is able to provide data maintenance and computation; *Third Party Auditor* (TPA), who specializes in verifying the integrity of outsourced data in cloud when received a request from the client. The system model is shown in Fig. 1.

We assume the communication between any two of these three entities is reliable. The whole auditing scheme is on a *challenge-response* protocol, which contains three phases: first, the client completes initializing work and then hosts his/her data files in cloud; second, the client makes an update operation by communication with CSS; third, TPA and CSS work together to provide data auditing service through exchanging the challenge and proof messages. TPA would report the audit results to the client.

Definition 1. *In a DPDP system, the client, CSS and TPA cooperate with each other to accomplish the challenge-response procedure. A DPDP scheme consists of the following algorithms:*

- *$KeyGen(1^k) \rightarrow \{sk, pk\}$. This probabilistic algorithm is run by the client. It takes as input security parameter 1^k, and returns private key sk and public key pk.*
- *$TagGen(F, sk) \rightarrow \{T\}$. This algorithm is run by the client to generate the metadata. It takes as input the data file F and private key sk and outputs the tag sets T, which is a collection of signatures $\{\tau_i\}$ on $\{m_i\}$.*
- *$Update(F, Info, \Omega, pk) \rightarrow \{F', P_{update}\}$. This algorithm is run by CSS in response to an update request from TPA. As input, it takes the data file F, update information Info, the previous auxiliary information Ω and the public key pk. The output is the new version of the data file F' along with its proof P_{update}. CSS sends the proof to TPA.*

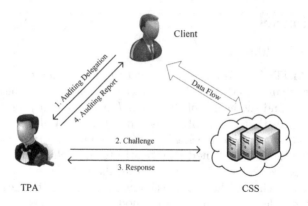

Fig. 1. System model

- $VerifyUpdate(P_{update}, sk, pk) \rightarrow \{accept, reject\}$. *This algorithm is run by TPA to verify CSS updated the data correctly. The input contains the proof P_{update} from CSS, the new file F' with its corresponding metadata T', and the private and public keys. The output is accept if the proof is valid or reject otherwise.*
- $Challenge(\cdot) \rightarrow \{chal\}$. *TPA runs this algorithm to start a challenge and send the challenge information chal to CSS.*
- $GenProof(F, T, chal, pk) \rightarrow \{P\}$. *This algorithm is run by CSS. It takes data file F, metadata T, the challenge information chal and the public key as inputs, and outputs the proof for the verification.*
- $VerifyProof(P, pk) \rightarrow \{accept, reject\}$. *TPA run this algorithm to verify the response P from CSS. It outputs "accept" if the proof is correct, or "reject" otherwise.*

3.3 Security of Dynamic PDP

Following the security model defined in [12,20], we define the security model for our proposed DPDP scheme by a data possession game between a challenger C and a adversary A. The detailed data possession game is described in Appendix A.

Definition 2. *We say that a DPDP scheme is secure if for any probabilistic polynomial time (PPT) adversary A (i.e., malicious CSS), the probability that A wins the data possession game is negligible.*

4   Construction

The main building blocks of our scheme include LBT, a secure signature scheme proposed by Boneh *et al.* [15] and Homomorphic Verifiable Tags (HTVs) [6]. LBT data structure is an expansion of MHT, which is intended to prove that a set of elements are undamaged and unaltered [1]. Naturally, we consider employing the hash algorithm used in MHT structure to authenticate the values of nodes in LBT, but this algorithm brings undesirable effects on the performance. During the update process, that the client modify, insert, or delete the data if only for one block will affect the whole data structure, causing $O(n)$ computation overhead for both the client and CSS. Therefore, it is imperative to find a better method to authenticate LBT data structure. Instead of using hash functions, we employ the signature scheme [15] to improve the efficiency of verifying the elements in LBT. The computation complexity decreases to $O(1)$ in the update process. As for the public auditability, we resort to the homomorphic verifiable tags. The reason is that HVTs make it possible to verify the integrity of the data blocklessly.

The procedure of our scheme is summarized in three phase: Setup, Dynamic Operation and Periodical Auditing. The details are as follows:

4.1   Setup

In this phase, we assume the data file F is segmented into $\{m_1, m_2, ..., m_n\}$, where $n = q^l$ and q, l are arbitrary positive integers. Bilinear map $e : G \times G \rightarrow G_T$ is secure. Group G has a prime order p. Let g be the generator of G. $H : \{0,1\}^* \rightarrow G$ is a family of collision-resistant hash functions. Note that all exponentiations in following algorithms are performed modulo p on G, and for simplicity we omit writing "(mod p)" explicitly.

KeyGen (1^k). The client runs this algorithm to generate a pair of private and public keys. Choose a random $x \leftarrow Z_p$ and compute $y = g^x$. Pick $\alpha_1, \alpha_2, ..., \alpha_q \leftarrow Z_p$ and $\lambda \leftarrow G$. Compute $\lambda_1 \leftarrow \lambda^{1/\alpha_1}, \lambda_2 \leftarrow \lambda^{1/\alpha_2}, ..., \lambda_q \leftarrow \lambda^{1/\alpha_q} \in G$. Pick $\mu \leftarrow G$, $\beta_0 \leftarrow Z_p$, then compute $\nu = e(\mu, \lambda)$ and $\eta_0 = e(\mu, \lambda)^{\beta_0}$ where η_0 denotes the root of LBT (the root of MHT is the hashes of all the nodes). And for every node in LBT tree, the client chooses $\{\beta_j\}_{1 \leq j \leq n}$. The client also generates a random signing key pair (spk, ssk). The public key is $pk = \{y, \lambda, \nu, \mu, \{\alpha_i\}_{1 \leq i \leq q}, \{\beta_i\}_{1 \leq i \leq n}, spk\}$ and the private key is $sk = \{x, \beta_0, ssk\}$.

TagGen (F, sk). For each data block m_i $(i = 1, 2, ..., n)$, the client chooses a random element $\omega \leftarrow G$, and computes a signature tag $\tau_i \leftarrow (H(m_i) \cdot \omega^{m_i})^x$. The set of all the tags is denoted by $T = \{\tau_i\}, 1 \leq i \leq n$. Then the client computes $\gamma = Sig_x(\eta_0)$ and sends $Ini = \{F, T, t, \gamma\}$ to CSS. Let $t = name \parallel n \parallel \omega \parallel Sig_{ssk}(name \parallel n \parallel \omega)$ be the tag for file F. The client will then compute $sig = Sig_{ssk}(t)$ and sends sig along with the auditing delegation request to TPA for it to compose a challenge later on.

Upon receiving the initialize information Ini, CSS first stores all the data blocks, and then construct a LBT as follows: for the ith data block m_i $(i = 1, 2, ..., n)$, CSS generates the i-th leaf of LBT together with a path from the leaf to the root. We denote the leaf by $\eta_l \in G$, where l is the layer of the leaf and the nodes on its path to the root are $(\eta_l, i_l, \eta_{l-1}, i_{l-1}, ..., \eta_1, i_1)$, where η_j is the i_j-th child of $\eta_{j-1}, 1 \leq j \leq l$. The authentication values for these nodes are computed as follow steps:

- Step 1: For every node on the path from leaf η_l to the root, CSS generates $\eta_j \leftarrow e(\mu, \lambda_{i_j})^{\beta_j}$.
- Step 2: The authentication value of node η_j, the i_jth child of η_{j-1}, is $f_j \leftarrow \mu^{\alpha_{i_j}(\beta_{j-1}+H(\eta_j))}$.
- Step 3: The authentication value of $H(m_i)$, the child of the leaf node η_l, is $f \leftarrow \mu^{\beta_l+H(m_i)}$.

Therefore, the signature on data block m_i is $\Omega_i = (f, f_l, i_l, ..., f_1, i_1)$, which is also the auxiliary information for authentication in the dynamic update process. The construction of LBT is illustrated in Fig. 2.

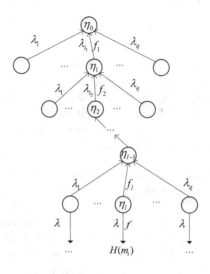

Fig. 2. Construction of LBT

4.2 Dynamic Operation

(1) **Modification.** The client composes an update request $Info = (m, i, m'_i, \tau'_i)$, it denotes that the client wants to modify m_i to m'_i, and $\tau'_i = (H(m'_i) \cdot \omega^{m'_i})^x$ is the signature of m'_i. Then he/she sends the update information $Info$ to CSS.

Update $(F, Info, \Omega, pk)$. Upon receiving the update request, CSS first modifies the data block m_i to m'_i, and replaces the $H(m_i)$ wth $H(m'_i)$ in LBT. As shown in the Fig. 3, CSS generates the new authentication value

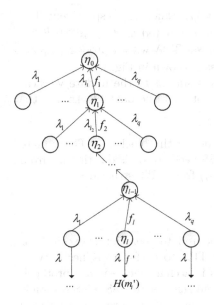

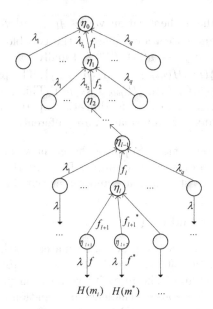

Fig. 3. LBT update under modification

Fig. 4. LBT update under insertion

$f' \leftarrow \mu^{\beta_l + H(m_i')}$ and update the signature Ω into Ω'. Note that, CSS only consumes $O(1)$ computation overhead. Finally, CSS responds

$$P_{update} = (H(m_i'), \Omega', \gamma),$$

to TPA.

VerifyUpdate $(Pupdate, sk, pk)$. TPA generates root η_0' based on $(H(m_i'), \Omega_i')$ as follows:

- Step 1: Compute $\eta_l' \leftarrow e(f', \lambda) \cdot \nu^{-H(m_i')}$.
- Step 2: Computes $\eta_{j-1}' \leftarrow e(f_j', \lambda_{ij}) \cdot \nu^{-H(\eta_j')}$ for $j = l, ..., 1$.
- Step 3: The proof is accepted if $e(\gamma, g) = e(\eta_0', y)$ or otherwise rejected.

(2) **Insertion.** As the insert operation would change the structure of LBT. This process is different from data modification. We assume the client wants to insert block m^* after the ith block m_i. First, the client generates a tag $\tau^* \leftarrow (H(m^*) \cdot \omega^{m^*})^x$. Then the client chooses two parameters $\beta_{l+1}, \beta_{l+1}^*$ and sends an update request $Info = (i, m^*, \tau^*, \beta_{l+1}, \beta_{l+1}^*)$ to CSS.

Update $(F, Info, \Omega, pk)$. Upon receiving the update information, CSS updates data files and turns the leaf node η_l into a father node whose first child node is η_{l+1} and the second one is η_{l+1}^*. Data blocks m_l and m^* are authenticated with respect to the leaves η_{l+1} and η_{l+1}^*. As shown in the Fig. 3, CSS computes the authentication values f_{l+1} and f^*_{l+1} by η_{l+1} and η^*_{l+1} respectively. The authentication values of the two blocks are computed as $f \leftarrow \mu^{\beta_{l+1}+H(m_i)}$ and $f^* \leftarrow \mu^{\beta^*_{l+1}+H(m^*)}$. Finally, CSS responses TPA with a proof $P_{update} = \{(\Omega'_i, H(m_i)), (\Omega^*, H(m^*)), \gamma\}$. The process is shown in Fig. 4.

VerifyUpdate (P_{update}, sk, pk). This process is similar to the update verification process in modification operation except that the data blocks and the auxiliary information are different.

(3) **Deletion.** Suppose the client wants to delete the block m_i. The update process is very simple. The only thing CSS needs to do is deleting m_i from its storage space and taking out the $H(m_i)$ from LBT structure.

4.3   Auditing

After the Setup process, no mater whether the update operation is executed or not, the integrity verification is available for TPA to perform his/her duty as an auditor. The integrity verification process is a challenge-response protocol, TPA generates a challenge information *chal* and sends it to CSS. CSS responds with a proof P. Then TPA verifies the correctness of the proof and outputs *accept/reject*.

Challenge $(\cdot)$. Before challenging, TPA first use ssk to verify the signature on t to recover ω. Suppose TPA wants to challenge c blocks. The indexes of these blocks are randomly selected from $[1, n]$. Namely, let $I = \{i_1, i_2, ..., i_c\}$ be the indexes of the challenged blocks. For each $i \in I$, TPA chooses a random element $\pi_i \leftarrow Z_p$. TPA then sends $chal = \{(i, \pi_i)_{i \in I}\}$ to CSS.

GenProof $(F, T, chal, pk)$. Upon receiving the challenge, CSS takes the data F, tags T and challenge information *chal* as inputs, and outputs: $\varphi = \sum_{i \in I} \pi_i m_i$ and $\tau = \prod_{i \in I} \tau_i^{\pi_i}$.

Moreover, CSS also provides TPA with the auxiliary information $\{\Omega_i\}_{i \in I}$, which denotes the authentication path from the challenged data blocks to the root. CSS sends proof $P = \{\varphi, \tau, \{H(m_i), \Omega_i\}_{i \in I}, \gamma\}$ to TPA.

VerifyProof (P, pk). For each challenged block m_i, $i \in I$, TPA first use the auxiliary information to reconstruct the nodes $\eta_l, \eta_{l-1}, ..., \eta_0$ in a bottom-up order by the following steps:

- Step 1: Compute $\eta_l \leftarrow e(f, \lambda) \cdot \nu^{-H(m_i)}$.
- Step 2: For $j = l, l - 1, ..., 1$, compute $\eta_{j-1} \leftarrow e(f_j, \lambda_{i_j}) \cdot \nu^{-H(\eta_j)}$.
- Step 3: Verify $e(\gamma, g) = e(\eta_0, y)$.

If the equality in step 3 holds, TPA continues to verify $e(\tau, g) = e(\prod_{i \in I} H(m_i)^{\pi_i} \cdot \omega^\varphi, y)$.

If so, the proof is accepted, otherwise rejected.

5   Correctness and Security

Correctness. The correctness of our scheme is that both the proof generated for dynamic auditing and integrity checking passes the verification algorithm. The correctness of the proof for dynamic auditing is easy to prove. Indeed, Step 1 of the verification algorithm results in

$$e(f, \lambda) \cdot \nu^{-H(m_i)} = e(\mu^{\beta_l + H(m_i)}, \lambda) \cdot e(\mu, \lambda)^{-H(m_i)} = (\mu^{\beta_l}, \lambda) = \eta_l.$$

For any $j \in \{l, l-1, \ldots, 1\}$, the result of computation in step 2 of the verification algorithm is

$$e(f_j, \lambda_{i_j}) \cdot \nu^{-H(\eta_j)} = e(\mu^{\alpha_{i_j}(\beta_{j-1} + H(\eta_j))}, \lambda^{1/\alpha_{i_j}}) \cdot e(\mu, \lambda)^{-H(\eta_j)}$$
$$= e(\mu^{\beta_{j-1} + H(\eta_j)}, \lambda) \cdot e(\mu^{-H(\eta_j)}, \lambda) = e(\mu^{\beta_{j-1}}, \lambda) = \eta_{j-1}.$$

The proof for integrity checking is also based on the properties of bilinear maps.

$$e(\tau, g) = e(\prod_{i \in I}(H(m_i) \cdot \omega^{m_i})^{x\pi_i}, g) = e(\prod_{i \in I}(H(m_i)^{\pi_i} \cdot \omega^{m_i \pi_i}), g^x) = e(\prod_{i \in I} H(m_i)^{\pi_i} \cdot \omega^{\varphi}, y).$$

Now we show that our proposed scheme is secure in the random oracle model. The security of our scheme is depending on responding correctly generated proof. We divide the security analysis of our scheme into two parts:

(1) Prove that if the challenger accepts the proof $P = \{\varphi, \tau, \{H(m_i), \Omega_i\}_{i \in I}, \gamma\}$, where τ denotes the tag proof which aggregates some forged tags for all the challenged blocks, the Computational Diffie-Hellman (CDH) problem is tractable within non-negligible probability.
(2) Prove that if the challenger accepts the proof $P = \{\varphi, \tau, \{H(m_i), \Omega_i\}_{i \in I}, \gamma\}$, where φ denotes the data proof generated by the adversary with all the challenged blocks $\{m_i\}_{i \in I}$, the Discrete Logarithm (DL) problem is tractable within non-negligible probability.

Security. During the analysis of existing schemes, we found that different schemes have different security levels. We classify some typical schemes' security level by their key techniques. Most of MAC-based schemes are semantically secure. RSA-based schemes and BLS-based schemes are both provably secure since they rely on public keys. Like most homomorphic tag-based schemes, our scheme is provably secure in the random oracle model.

Theorem 1. *If the tag generation scheme we use is existentially unforgeable, CDH problem and DL problem is intractable in bilinear groups in the random oracle model, there exist no adversary against our provable data possession scheme could cause the verifier to accept a corrupted proof in the challenge-verify process, within non-negligible probability, except by responding the correctly computed proof.*

Proof. The full proof of this theorem can be found in Appendix B.

6   Performance

In this section, we analyze the performance of our scheme in the terms of storage overhead, computation cost and communication complexity.

6.1   Storage Overhead

Through analysis of the state-of-the-art, we find that what affects the storage overhead most is the metadata. For example, in [5], the verifier (the client) has to store the sentinels for verification. In [14], the verifier (the client) needs to store MACs.

In our scheme, the metadata is stored in CSS instead of the verifier (TPA). The client sends the metadata together with data to CSS during the setup phase. For each challenge, CSS responds both the data proof and the tag proof to TPA.

Table 1 shows the comparison of the storage overhead of different schemes. In the table, k denotes the total number of the sentinels, n denotes the total number of the data blocks, λ is the security parameter, p denotes the order of the group G and N is RSA modulus.

Table 1. Comparison of the storage overhead

Schemes	Storage overhead	
	CSS	Verifier
[5]	$k \cdot \mid sentinel \mid$	$k \cdot \mid sentinel \mid$
[6]	$O(\lambda)$	$n \cdot \mid N \mid$
[12]	$O(\lambda)$	$n \cdot \mid N \mid$
[7](BLS)	$O(\lambda)$	$n \cdot \mid p \mid$
[1]	$O(\lambda)$	$n \cdot \mid p \mid$
Our scheme	$O(\lambda)$	$n \cdot \mid p \mid$

6.2   Computation Complexity

There are three entities in our scheme: the client, CSS and TPA. We discuss their computation cost respectively in different phase. In the setup phase, the client needs to compute 2 pairings, $2n + 2$ exponentiations and n multiplications on G.

For better comparison, we implemented both our scheme and MHT-based scheme [1] in Linux. All experiments are conducted on a system with an Intel Core i5 processor running at 2.6 GHz, 750 MB RAM. Algorithms such as paring and SHA1 are employed by installing the Paring-Based Cryptography (PBC) library and the crypto library of OpenSSL. All experimental results represent the mean of 10 trials. Figure 5 shows the pre-processing time as a function of block

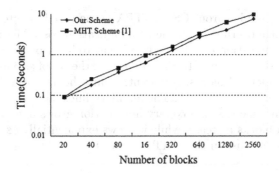

Fig. 5. Comparison of pre-processing time

numbers for client. The MHT-based scheme [1] exhibits slower pre-processing performance. Our scheme only performs an exponentiation on every data block in order to create the metadata. However, in scheme [1], client needs to perform the exponentiation as well as constructing a MHT to generate the root.

Besides, in the dynamic update phase, TPA only needs to compute 1 exponentiation in modification, 2 exponentiations in insertion and causes no computation in deletion. Note that the computation complexity of CSS in scheme [1] is $O(n)$ in all three update operations, where n is the number of data blocks. Therefore, the secure signature scheme based on bilinear maps [15] introduced in our scheme has greatly reduced the computation overhead during the dynamic update phase. In the auditing phase, TPA needs to do $2c$ summations and $2c$ multiplications, where c is the number of challenged data blocks. The computation complexity of TPA is $O(n)$.

6.3   Communication Cost

The main communication cost we concern is the communication cost between CSS and TPA during each challenge-response query. Since the metadata is stored

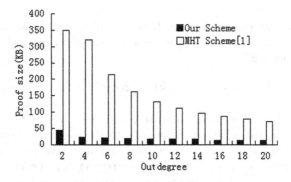

Fig. 6. Comparison of communication cost

in CSS, the proof sended from CSS to TPA is increased. There is a trade-off between the storage overhead and the communication cost. The major component of the communication cost is the proof sent to TPA by CSS. We compare our scheme with MHT scheme [1]. Figure 6 shows the proof size as a function of the number of challenged blocks. Apparently, our scheme causes less communication cost between CSS and TPA. The auxiliary information accounts for that gap. In our scheme, the size of auxiliary information grows linearly as the number of challenged blocks increase, while it grows exponentially as the number of challenged blocks increase in the MHT scheme [1].

7   Conclusion

In this paper, we propose an efficient dynamic auditing scheme based on a secure signature scheme [15] and LBT data structure. We formally give the system model and security model. Then, we present the concrete process of the proposed scheme. LBT data structure enables reduction in size of auxiliary information, thereby causes less communication cost compared to MHT-based schemes. Moreover, the characteristics of bilinear pairings in the signature algorithm only cause computation cost on CSP for each dynamic update. And the client no longer needs to construct LBT structure to support dynamic operation. Therefore, our scheme greatly reduce computation cost both on CSP and client as well as simplify the update process. Through security analysis and performance analysis, our scheme is provably secure and efficient.

Acknowledgements. The authors would like to thank the anonymous referees for useful comments. This research is supported in part by "the Fundamental Research Funds for the Central Universities" (No. 2015YJS005), National Natural Science Foundation of China under Grant Nos. 61472032, 61272522, 61572132 and Fujian Provincial Key Laboratory of Network Security and Cryptology Research Fund (Fujian Normal University)(No. 15007).

Appendix A. Data Possession Game

The security of a data possession game between a challenger C and a adversary A is presented as follows. The challenger plays the role of verifier and the adversary acts as a malicious CSS.

KeyGen: The challenger runs $(pk, sk) \leftarrow KeyGen(1^k)$, then sends pk to the adversary.

ACF Queries: The adversary can make adaptively chosen file (ACF) queries as follows. First, the adversary interact with the tag generation oracle $\mathcal{O}_{TG}$. For each query, A chooses a data block m_i and sends it to $\mathcal{O}_{TG}$. Then the oracle responds each query with a corresponding verification metadata $\tau_i \leftarrow (H(m_i) \cdot \omega^{m_i})^x$. The adversary keeps making n times queries. Then, it enables to create an ordered collection of metadata $T = \{\tau_i\}_{1 \leq i \leq n}$ for all the selected data blocks $F = \{m_1, m_2, ..., m_n\}$. Second, the adversary is given access to a data update oracle $\mathcal{O}_{UP}$. A chooses a data block m_i $(i=1,2,...,n)$ and generates corresponding update information $Info_i$ indicating what operation the adversary wants to perform. Then the adversary runs $Update$ algorithm and outputs a new version of data file F' and an update proof P_{update}. After receiving these information submitted by the adversary, the oracle $\mathcal{O}_{UP}$ verifies the proof P_{update} by running algorithm $VerifyUpdate$. The output is $accept$ or $reject$. The adversary can repeat the above interaction in polynomial times.

$\textbf{\textit{Setup}}$: The adversary decides on data block m_i^* and corresponding update information $Info_i^*$ for all $i \in I \in [0, n+1]$. The ACF $Queries$ are performed again by the adversary, with the first $Info_i^*$ specifying a full re-write (this corresponds to the first time the client sends a file to CSS). The challenger verifies the update information and update his local metadata.

$\textbf{\textit{Challenge}}$: The final version of data file F is created according to the data update requested by A, and verified then accepted by the challenger. Now the challenger generates a challenge $chal$ and sends it to the adversary.

$\textbf{\textit{Forge}}$: The adversary computes a data possession proof P based on $chal$. Then the challenger runs algorithm $VerifyProof$ and outputs the result belonging to $accept/reject$. If the output is $accept$, then the adversary wins.

Appendix B. Proof of Theorem 1

Theorem 1. *If the tag generation scheme we use is existentially unforgeable, CDH problem and DL problem is intractable in bilinear groups in the random oracle model, there exist no adversary against our provable data possession scheme could cause the verifier to accept a corrupted proof in the challenge-verify process, within non-negligible probability, except by responding the correctly computed proof.*

Proof. We firstly prove that the tag generation scheme is existentially unforgeable with the assumption that BLS short signature scheme is secure. We prove this by reduction. Assume BLS signature scheme is secure and its public key is $pk = g^x$. If there exists an adversary who can win the challenge game with non-negligible probability, then the adversary must be able to forge a signature in BLS scheme. Pick $x \leftarrow Z_p$, and compute $u = g^x$. When the adversary queries about a data block m_i, he/she sends the block to BLS signature oracle, and the oracle responds with the signature $s_i = H(m_i)^x$. The adversary queries the oracle about the same block in our scheme, and be replied with the tag $\tau_i = (H(m_i) \cdot \omega^{m_i})^x$. Let $\omega = g^\alpha$, then $\tau_i = s_i \cdot \mu^{\alpha m_i}$. Suppose that the adversary can forge a new tag $\tau_j = (H(m_j) \cdot \omega^{m_j})^x$ for the block m_j that has never been queried. Therefore, the adversary can compute BLS signature on m_j as $s_j = \tau_j / \mu^{\alpha m_j}$. This completes the proof of the security of the tag generation scheme.

Now we prove the Theorem 1 by using a sequence of games.

Game 1. The first game is the data possession game we defined in Appendix A.

Game 2. Game 2 is the same as Game 1, with one difference. When the challenger responds the *ACF Queries* made by the adversary, he/she keeps a list of all his/her responses. Then the challenger observes each instance of the challenge-response process with the adversary. If in any of these instances the adversary responds a valid proof which can make the challenger accept, but the adversary's tag proof is not equal to the $\tau = \prod_{i \in I} \tau_i^{\pi_i}$, which is the expected response that would have been obtained from an honest prover, the challenger declares *reject* and aborts.

Analysis. Before we analyzing the difference in probabilities between Game 1 and Game 2, we firstly describe the notion and draw a few conclusions. Suppose the data file that causes the abort is divided into n blocks, and the tags of data blocks are $\tau_i = (H(m_i) \cdot \omega^{m_i})^x$ for $i \in [1, n]$. Assume $chal = \{i, \pi_i\}_{i \in I}$ is the query that causes the challenger to abort, and the adversarys response to that query was $P' = \{\varphi', \tau', \{H(m_i), \Omega_i\}_{i \in I}, \gamma\}$. Let the expected response be $P = \{\varphi, \tau, \{H(m_i), \Omega_i\}_{i \in I}, \gamma\}$. The correctness of $H(m_i)$ can be verified through $\{H(m_i), \Omega_i\}_{i \in I}$ and γ. Because of the correctness of the scheme, the expected response can pass the verification equation, that is

$$e(\tau, g) = e(\prod_{i \in I} H(m_i)^{\pi_i} \cdot \omega^{\varphi}, y).$$

Because the challenger aborted, we know that $\tau \neq \tau'$ and that τ' passes the verification equation $e(\tau', g) = e(\prod_{i \in I} H(m_i)^{\pi_i} \cdot \omega^{\varphi'}, y)$. Observe that if $\varphi' = \varphi$, it follows from the verification equation that $\tau' = \tau$, which contradicts our assumption above. Therefore, it must be the case that $\Delta\varphi$ is nonzero, here we define $\Delta\varphi = \varphi' - \varphi$.

With this in mind, we show that if the adversary win Game 2 and causes the challenger to abort, we can construct a simulator to solve CDH problem.

Given the values $g, g^x, h \in G$ as inputs, the goal of the simulator is to output h^x. The simulator behaves like the challenger in Game 2 and interacts with the adversary as follows:

(1) To generate a tag key, the simulator sets the public key y to g^x, and then forwards y to the adversary.

(2) The simulator programs the random oracle H and keeps a list of queries to respond consistently. Upon receiving the adversarys queries, the simulator chooses a random $r \leftarrow Z_p$ and responds with $g^r \in G$. It also responds queries of the form $H(m_i)$ in a special way, as we will see below.

(3) When requested to store the data file which is divided into n blocks $\{m_i\}_{1 \leq i \leq n}$, the simulator responds as follows. It firstly chooses a random block m_i. For each $1 \leq i \leq n$, the simulator chooses a random value $r_i \leftarrow Z_p$ and sets $\omega = g^a h^b$ for $a, b \leftarrow Z_p$, then it outputs $H(m_i) = g^{r_i} h^{-m_i}$. Therefore, the simulator can compute the tag $\tau_i = (H(m_i) \cdot \omega^{m_i})^x = (g^{r_i} h^{-m_i} \cdot (g^a h^b)^{m_i})^x$.

(4) The simulator continues interacting with the adversary until the adversary succeeds in responding with a tag τ' that is not equal to the expected tag τ. After receiving the valid proof P' from the adversary, the simulator is able to compute $e(\tau'/\tau, g) = e(\omega^{\Delta\varphi}, g) = e((g^a h^b)^{\Delta\varphi}, g)$.

Rearranging terms yields $e(\tau'\tau^{-1}y^{-a\Delta\varphi}, g) = e(h, y)^{b\Delta\varphi}$.

Since $y = g^x$, we obtain $h^x = (\tau'\tau^{-1}y^{a\Delta\varphi})^{\frac{1}{b\Delta\varphi}}$. To analyze the probability that the challenger aborts in the game, we only need to compute the probability that $b\Delta\varphi = 0 \pmod{p}$. Because b is chosen by the challenger and hidden from the adversary, the probability that $b\Delta\varphi = 0 \pmod{p}$ will be only $1/p$, which is negligible.

Therefore, if there is a non-negligible difference between the adversarys probabilities of success in Game 1 and Game 2, we can construct a simulator that solves CDH problem by interacting with the adversary.

Game 3. Game 3 is the same as Game 2, with one difference. When the challenger responds the *ACF Queries* made by the adversary, he keeps a list of all his responses. Then the challenger observes each instance of the challenge-response process with the adversary. If in any of these instances the adversary responds a valid proof which can make the challenger accept, but the adversary's data proof is not equal to the $\varphi = \prod_{i\in I} \pi_i m_i$, which is the expected response that would have been obtained from an honest prover, the challenger declares *reject* and aborts.

Analysis. Again, let us describe some notation. Suppose the data file that causes the abort is divided into n blocks. Assume $chal = \{i, \pi_i\}_{i\in I}$ is the query that causes the challenger to abort, and the adversary's response to that query was

$$P' = \{\varphi', \tau', \{H(m_i), \Omega_i\}_{i\in I}, \gamma\}.$$

Let the expected response be $P = \{\varphi, \tau, \{H(m_i), \Omega_i\}_{i\in I}, \gamma\}$, among which the data proof should be $\varphi = \prod_{i\in I} \pi_i m_i$. Game 2 already guarantees that we have $\tau' = \tau$. It is only the values of φ' and φ that can differ. Define $\Delta\varphi = \varphi' - \varphi$, again, it must be the case that $\Delta\varphi$ is nonzero.

We now show that if the adversary causes the challenger in Game 3 to abort with non-negligible probability, we can construct a simulator to solve DL problem.

Given the values $g, h \in G$ as inputs, the goal of the simulator is to output α such that $h = g\alpha$. The simulator behaves like the challenger in Game 2 and interacts with the adversary as follows:

(1) When requested to store the data file which is divided into n blocks $\{m_i\}_{1\leq i\leq n}$, the simulator first sets $\omega = g^a h^b$ for $a, b \in Z_p$. Then, it responds to the adversary according to the *TagGen* algorithm.

(2) The simulator continues interacting with the adversary until the adversary succeeds in responding with a data proof φ' that is not equal to the expected φ. After receiving the valid proof P' from the adversary, the simulator is able to compute

$$e(\prod_{i \in I} H(m_i)^{\pi_i} \cdot \omega^{\varphi'}, y) = e(\tau', g) = e(\tau, g) = e(\prod_{i \in I} H(m_i)^{\pi_i} \cdot \omega^{\varphi}, y).$$

From this equation, we have $1 = \omega^{\Delta\varphi} s = (g^a h^b)^{\Delta\varphi}$.

Thus, the solution to DL problem has been found, that is $h = g^{-\frac{a\Delta\varphi}{b\Delta\varphi}}$, unless the denominator is zero. However, $\Delta\varphi$ is not equal to zero, and the value of b is chosen by the challenger and hidden from the adversary, the probability that $b\Delta\varphi = 0 \pmod{p}$ will be only $1/p$, which is negligible.

Therefore, if there is a non-negligible difference between the adversary's probabilities of success in Game 2 and Game 3, we can construct a simulator that solves DL problem by interacting with the adversary.

Wrapping Up. As we analyzed above, there is only negligible difference probability of the adversary between game sequences Game i ($i = 1, 2, 3$), if the tag generation scheme is existentially unforgeable, CDH problem and DL problem are hard in bilinear groups. This completes the proof of Theorem 1. $\square$

References

1. Wang, Q., Wang, C., Li, J., Ren, K., Lou, W.: Enabling public verifiability and data dynamics for storage security in cloud computing. In: Backes, M., Ning, P. (eds.) ESORICS 2009. LNCS, vol. 5789, pp. 355–370. Springer, Heidelberg (2009)
2. Liu, C., Chen, J., Zhang, X., Yang, C., Ranjan, R., Kotagiri, R.: Authorized public auditing of dynamic big data storage on cloud with efficient verifiable fine-grained updates. IEEE Trans. Parallel Distrib. Syst. **25**(9), 2234–2244 (2014)
3. Yang, K., Jia, X.: An efficient and secure dynamic auditing protocol for data storage in cloud computing. IEEE Trans. Parallel Distrib. Syst. **24**(9), 1717–1726 (2013)
4. Zhu, Y., Ahn, G.-J., Hu, H., Yau, S.S., An, H.G., Chen, S.: Dynamic audit services for outsourced storages in clouds. IEEE Trans. Serv. Comput. **6**(2), 227–238 (2013)
5. Juels, A., Kaliski, B.S.: PORs: proofs of retrievability for large files. In: Proceedings of CCS 2007, pp. 584–597. ACM (2007)
6. Ateniese, G., Burns, R., Curtmola, R., Herring, J., Kissner, L., Peterson, Z., Song, D.: Provable data possession at untrusted stores. In: Proceedings of CCS 2007, pp. 598–609. ACM (2007)
7. Shacham, H., Waters, B.: Compact proofs of retrievability. In: Pieprzyk, J. (ed.) ASIACRYPT 2008. LNCS, vol. 5350, pp. 90–107. Springer, Heidelberg (2008)
8. Dodis, Y., Vadhan, S., Wichs, D.: Proofs of retrievability via hardness amplification. In: Reingold, O. (ed.) TCC 2009. LNCS, vol. 5444, pp. 109–127. Springer, Heidelberg (2009)
9. Ateniese, G., Kamara, S., Katz, J.: Proofs of storage from homomorphic identification protocols. In: Matsui, M. (ed.) ASIACRYPT 2009. LNCS, vol. 5912, pp. 319–333. Springer, Heidelberg (2009)

10. Yang, K., Jia, X.: Data storage auditing service in cloud computing: challenges, methods and opportunities. Proc. WWW 2012 **15**(4), 409–428 (2012). Springer, Heidelberg

11. Ateniese, G., Di Pietro, R., Mancini, L.V., Tsudik, G.: Scalable and efficient provable data possession. In: Proceedings of SecureComm 2008, pp. 1–10. ACM (2008)

12. Erway, C., Küpçü, A., Papamanthou, C., Tamassia, R.: Dynamic provable data possession. In: Proceedings of CCS 2009, pp. 13–222. ACM (2009)

13. Wang, H.: Identity-based distributed provable data possession in multicloud storage. IEEE Trans. Serv. Comput. **8**(2), 328–340 (2015)

14. Shah, M.A., Swaminathan, R., Baker, M.: Privacy-preserving audit and extraction of digital contents. Cryptology ePrint Archive, 2008/186 (2008). http://eprint.iacr.org/2008/186

15. Boneh, D., Mironov, I., Shoup, V.: A secure signature scheme from bilinear maps. In: Joye, M. (ed.) CT-RSA 2003. LNCS, vol. 2612, pp. 98–110. Springer, Heidelberg (2003)

16. Barsoum, A., Hasan, A.: Enabling dynamic data and indirect mutual trust for cloud computing storage systems. IEEE Trans. Parallel Distrib. Syst. **24**(12), 2375–2385 (2013)

17. Wang, C., Wang, Q., Ren, K., Cao, N., Lou, W.: Toward secure and dependable storage services in cloud computing. IEEE Trans. Serv. Comput. **5**(2), 220–232 (2012)

18. Wang, H., He, D.: Proxy provable data possession with general access structure in public clouds. In: Proceedings of Inscrypt 2015. Springer, Heidelberg (2015)

19. Lin, C., Luo, F., Wang, H., Zhu, Y.: A provable data possession scheme with data hierarchy in cloud. In: Proceedings of Inscrypt 2015. Springer, Heidelberg (2015)

20. Gritti, C., Susilo, W., Plantard, T.: Efficient dynamic provable data possession with public verifiability and data privacy. In: Foo, E., Stebila, D. (eds.) ACISP 2015. LNCS, vol. 9144, pp. 395–412. Springer, Heidelberg (2015)

21. Gritti, C., Susilo, W., Plantard, T., Chen, R.: Improvements on efficient dynamic provable data possession protocols with public verifiability and data privacy. Cryptology ePrint Archive, 2015/645 (2015). http://eprint.iacr.org/2015/645

iGEMS: A Cloud Green Energy Management System in Data Center

Chao-Tung Yang[1,2(✉)], Yin-Zhen Yan[1], Shuo-Tsung Chen[1],
Ren-Hao Liu[1], Jean-Huei Ou[2], and Kun-Liang Chen[2]

[1] Department of Computer Science, Tunghai University,
Taichung 40704, Taiwan
{ctyang,shough33}@thu.edu.tw,
r541754175@gmail.com,
ryan125125@gmail.com
[2] Computer Center, Tunghai University, Taichung 40704, Taiwan
{randall,kala}@thu.edu.tw

Abstract. Today the growing demand for reducing the power is not limited to household electricity saving. For businesses, it is the more important issue to effectively reduce the cost of electricity and the excess consumption under the huge electricity. In order to achieve energy saving and energy requires, the development of energy monitoring systems to obtain information related to consumption is necessary. Accordingly, this work proposes a cloud green energy management system. Because of the data size and the computational efficiency of data analysis, we add the big data technology and cloud computing to upgrade the system performance. By building cloud infrastructure and distributed storage cluster, we adopt the open source, Hadoop, to implement the two main functions: storage and computation. Based on these two functions, the proposed system speeds up the analysis and processing of big data by using Hadoop MapReduce to access HBase. The systemic risk is thus reduced too. Both real-time data and historical data are analyzed to obtain electricity consumption behavior for real-time warning and early warning. Moreover, carbon reduction and environmental protection are also considered in the analysis. Finally, a virtualized user-interface is designed to show the proposed system functions and analysis results. The experimental results indicate the performance of the proposed system.

Keywords: Cloud computing · Power management · Energy saving · Big Data · Hadoop MapReduce

1 Introduction

How to save electricity costs has been a very important issue today. Not just in the family, for businesses this issue is more important, particularly in the manufacturing-related industries. Manufacturing now has high automation by using a lot of automated

This work is supported in part by the Ministry of Science and Technology, Taiwan, under grants number MOST 104-2221-E-029-010-MY3, MOST 104-2622-E-029-008-CC3, and MOST 103-2622-E-029-012-CC3.

X. Huang et al. (Eds.): GPC 2016, LNCS 9663, pp. 82–98, 2016.
DOI: 10.1007/978-3-319-39077-2_6

manufacturing machines. However, the manufacturing machine consumes energy so that the cost of electricity costs a big proportion for manufacturing industries account. To be able to control and manager electricity costs, we must clearly and completely understand electricity. Therefore, power monitoring is a very important issue. Many energy monitoring or energy management systems have been proposed in recent years. In addition to providing real-time monitoring, these systems provide data recording function.

Han and Lim [1] suggested a Smart Home Energy Management System (SHEMS) based on IEEE802.15.4 and ZigBee. The proposed smart home energy management system divides and assigns various home network tasks to appropriate components. It can integrate diversified physical sensing information and control various consumer home devices, with the support of active sensor networks having both sensor and actuator components by using Disjoint Multi Path based Routing. Park et al. [3] proposed a Smart Energy Management System (SEMS) which functions as a control using a motion sensor and setting time of power usage to reduce power consumption. The SEMS not only supplies power as the way the common power strips do but also controls sockets of the SEMS using ZigBee wireless communication. Yardi [4] designed a Home Energy Management (HEM) system comprises an HEM unit that provides monitoring and control functionalities for a homeowner, and load controllers that gather electrical consumption data from selected appliances and perform local control based on command signals from the HEM system. A gateway, such as a smart meter, can be used to provide an interface between a utility and the data base for the electrical consumption is also maintained through internet.

According to assessment of the necessary conditions energy based on Leadership in Energy and Environmental Design (LEED), using above 300RT of the central air-conditioning chiller systems in IT room, PUE value must be less than 1.52 which can meet the basic threshold of LEED. In contrast, the domestic IT room PUE average actual measurement results above about 1.9, shows that IT room with more than 30 % energy-saving space. If it can integrate the use of international technology, design techniques and related standards, the new domestic IT room should be able to achieve the carbon reduction targets of LEED standard [5, 6].

However, most systems only monitor the rough region to estimate total electricity consumption so that they do not measure the detail electricity consumption for each device and analyze the big historical data. Accordingly, this work apply the cloud infrastructure and virtualization technology to develop a cloud green energy management system. The proposed system has many useful functions including: historical electricity data analysis, single device abnormal warning, system electricity abnormal warning, estimation of pipeline failure by using tree-network electricity layer checking, power restoration, power adjustment in contract capacity of electricity, prediction for machine breakdown and renewal. In order to have these functions in the proposed cloud green energy management system, we first adopt electric sensor, namely WPM-100 Wireless Multifunction Power Meter, to collect data including electric voltage, electric current, power factor, machine status, etc. Next, we adopt the open source Hadoop [8–12] consisting of many components including MapReduce [11, 13] and HBase [9, 10, 13–16, 22] to build a decentralized architecture to efficiently store and assess the big data including real-time data and historical data. Then, both real-time data and historical data are analyzed to obtain electricity consumption behavior for real-time warning and early warning. Moreover, carbon reduction and environmental protection are also considered in the analysis. Finally, a graphical user-interface is designed by graphical presentation to facilitate data analysis including Power Usage Effectiveness (PUE), power consumption, and so on. For a demonstration, we implement the proposed system in IT room of our school. The experimental results indicate the performance of the proposed system.

The rest of this work is as follows. Section 2 gives background and some preliminaries. In Sect. 3, we introduce the proposed system design and implementation. Section 4 shows our experiment environment and results. In Sect. 5, some conclusions are given.

2 Background and Preliminaries

This section reviews some background knowledge and preliminaries [17–21] including Hadoop, HDFS, HBase, MapReduce. We will implement the proposed system based on these background knowledge and preliminaries in next section.

2.1 Hadoop

Hadoop is an open source project under the Apache Software Foundation. The initial prototype of Hadoop-Nutch was developed for web searching by Doug Cutting and Mike Cafarella. In 2006, Doug Cutting joined Yahoo and set up a professional team to continue research and development of this technology, officially named as Hadoop. Hadoop is written in java; it can provide a distributed computing environment for huge data. The Apache Hadoop software library is a framework that allows for the distributed processing of large data sets across clusters of computers using simple programming models. It is designed to scale up from single servers to thousands of machines, each offering local computation and storage. Rather than rely on hardware to deliver high-availability, the library itself is designed to detect and handle failures at the application layer, so delivering a highly-available service on top of a cluster of computers, each of which may be prone to failures. The project includes following modules:

- Hadoop Common: The common utilities that support the other Hadoop modules.
- Hadoop Distributed File System (HDFS): A distributed file system that provides high-throughput access to application data.
- Hadoop YARN: A framework for job scheduling and cluster resource management.
- Hadoop MapReduce: A YARN-based system programming model for massive data processing of large data.

2.2 HDFS

The Hadoop Distributed File System (HDFS) is a distributed file system designed to run on commodity hardware. It has many similarities with existing 1distributed file systems. However, the differences from other distributed file systems are significant. HDFS is highly fault-tolerant and is designed to be deployed on low-cost hardware. HDFS provides high throughput access to application data and is suitable for applications that have large data sets. HDFS relaxes a few POSIX requirements to enable streaming access to file system data. HDFS was originally built as infrastructure for the Apache Nutch web search engine project. HDFS is now an Apache Hadoop subproject. HDFS has a master/slave architecture.

An HDFS cluster consists of a single NameNode, a master server that manages the file system names-pace and regulates access to files by clients. In addition, there are a number of DataNodes, usually one per node in the cluster, which manage storage attached to the nodes that they run on. HDFS exposes a file system names-pace and allows user data to be stored in files. Internally, a file is split into one or more blocks and these blocks are stored in a set of DataNodes. The NameNode executes file system namespace operations like opening, closing, and renaming files and directories. It also determines the mapping of blocks to DataNodes. The DataNodes are responsible for serving read and write requests from the file systems clients. The DataNodes also perform block creation, deletion, and replication upon instruction from the NameNode. Figure 1 shows the architecture of HDFS.

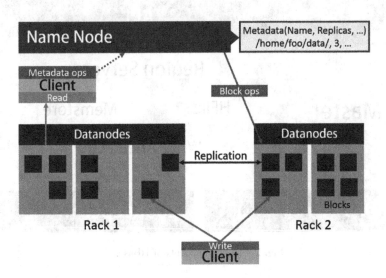

Fig. 1. HDFS architecture.

2.3 HBase

HBase, is an open source, high reliability, high performance, scalable, and not based on the relational model based on distributed repository for storing large scale unstructured data.

HBase is a distributed, versioned, non-relational database (i.e., NoSQL) modeled after Google's Bigtable: A Distributed Storage System for Structured Data. Just as Bigtable leverages the distributed data storage provided by the Google File System, Apache HBase provides Bigtable-like capabilities on top of Hadoop and HDFS. HBase data is actually stored in HDFS. Figure 2 shows the different components of HBase, and how it works with existing systems. The features of HBase are listed in the following:

- Strongly consistent reads/writes: HBase is not eventual consistent data storage; thus, it is ideal for the task of gathering, such as for high-speed counter.
- Automatic sharing: HBase tables are distributed over the cluster through regions that can be automatic separated and allocated as data grow.
- Hadoop/HDFS Integration: HBase is in support of HDFS as its distributed file system.
- MapReduce: HBase supports massively parallel processing through MapReduce by using HBase as sources and sinks.
- Java Client API: HBase supports easy-to-use Java APIs for programming.
- Thrift/REST API: HBase supports REST and Thrift as non-Java front ends.
- Block Cache and Bloom Filters: HBase supports block caches and Bloom filters for high-capacity query optimization.
- Operational Management: HBase provides insight into the operation and JMX metrics by the built-in web page.

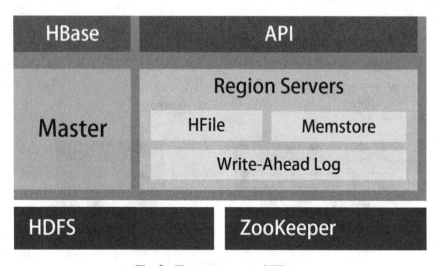

Fig. 2. The components of HBase.

3   System Design and Implementation

This section introduces the design of the proposed cloud green energy management system and its implementation. We first introduce the proposed system architecture design and then present the system implementation.

3.1 System Architecture Design

The proposed cloud green energy management system has three phases: Cloud infrastructure, Cloud platforms, Cloud services. Cloud infrastructure is the basis of the proposed system. It consists of the deployment and management of virtual machines which can be used to increase the scalability of the proposed system [23]. Based on this infrastructure, both real-time data and historical data collected from electric meters are collected and processed to obtain electricity consumption behavior for real-time warning and early warning. In addition, carbon emission and environmental data are also collected and stored. All these data will form big data. To store and process the big data, some high-availability platforms including Big Data Distributed Database Platform and Cloud Computing Platform are established based on this infrastructure. Four cloud services are provided for users in our system. They are Data Collection Service, Data Monitoring Service, Data Analysis Service, and Web Applications Service. In order to increase the feasibility of our system, we adopt open source to implement above three phase as shown in Fig. 3.

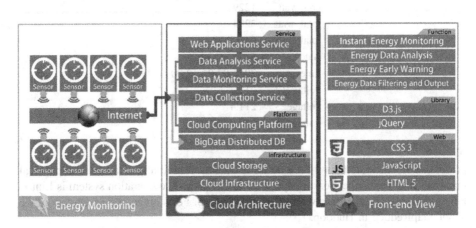

Fig. 3. Architecture design of the proposed system.

3.2 System Implementation

The first step to implement our system is the deployment of sensors. Without wiring, we adopt the electric sensor, namely WPM-100 Wireless Multifunction Power Meter, to collect data including voltage, electric current, power, etc. These collected data are then transmitted to the proposed Big Data Distributed Database in our cloud system. The format and amount of the collected data is listed in Table 1. It is expected that the data will be big data in the future since each sensor transmit 120 Byte data every minute. To store and process big data, we design a cloud infrastructure as shown in Fig. 4. In order to have better environmental data monitoring, data storage, and data

Table 1. The format and amount of the collected data

Name	Data example
meter_id	13243
location	L040
tool_id	HC705
ch1_pf	0.807
ch1_voltage	121.6
ch1_current	10.343
ch1_watt	1015
ch2_pf	0.878
ch2_voltage	122.2
ch2_current	9.786
ch2_watt	1050
ch3_pf	0.88
ch3_voltage	121.8
ch3_current	11.466
ch3_watt	1229
total_watt	3294
total_kwm	0.055998
state	PRD-PROD
time_stamp	2014-02-01 12:00
voltage12	211.2
voltage23	211.4
voltage31	210.9

processing in our system, in this cloud infrastructure we initially create several physical machines and 1 Gb/s networking speed to be a cluster. The operation system is Linux. For storing, we adopt Hbase with HDFS in Hadoop. For storage and computation, we adopt MapReduce in Hadoop.

In addition, four services, Data Collection Service, Data Monitoring Service, Data Analysis Service, and Web Applications Service are provided for users in our system. These four services are introduced as follows. As shown in Fig. 5, Data Collection Service is a Java Web Service which receives and checks the sensor data through Java. If the sensor data is from our sensor, then they will be put into Hbase by using ZooKeeper and then distributed in physical machines by HDFS. Data Monitoring Service filters and operates the collected data according to user's request while Data Analysis Service analyzes the collected data according to user's request. Figures 6 and 7 show the detail of these two services. Finally, Web Applications Service shows the results obtained from Data Monitoring Service and Data Analysis Service.

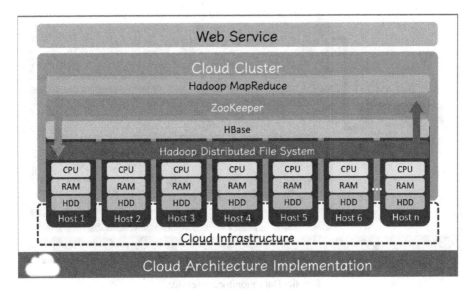

Fig. 4. Architecture of cloud.

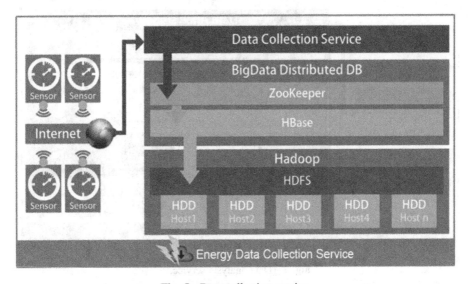

Fig. 5. Data collection service.

4 Experimental Environment and Results

This section first presents the experimental environment for the proposed system design. Next, we implement the proposed energy management system and obtain several useful experimental results based on this experimental environment.

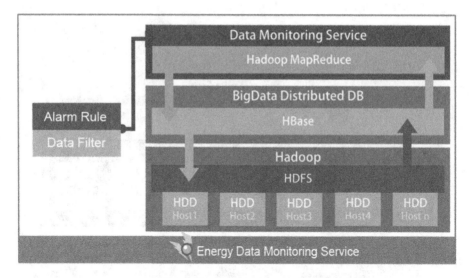

Fig. 6. Data monitoring service.

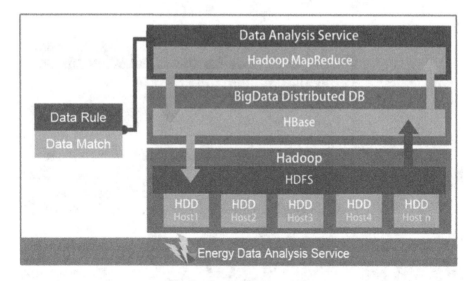

Fig. 7. Data analysis service.

4.1 Experimental Environment

To implement the proposed system, our experimental environment is introduced as follows. We adopt Intel Xeon 8-core E5-2640 V2@2.0 GHz as the CPU of the physical machine. Ubuntu 12.04 with 64 bit is adopted as our operating system. In addition, we use the electrical sensor WPM-100 Wireless Multifunction Power Meter.

4.2 Experimental Results

In this section, we present three results of our power-saving concept. First, we show the function which provides the real-time information of all machines and the air conditioning in IT room. This function is shown on an interface so that users can monitor all information we obtained. Second, PUE is calculated to help us have an energy-saving basis. Finally, we develop an interface function for historical information monitoring.

4.3 Real-Time Information of Electricity

For the proposed system performance, a monitoring platform for environmental status, air conditioning and power consumption is first established. Users can survey the real-time information related to environmental status, air conditioning, and power consumption obtained from each machine. Accessing environmental information is to make the system a better way for power saving. When user is connected to the home page, the view of the monitoring function is shown as Fig. 8. Moreover, users can observe the detail information of voltage, current, and others. In addition, the information updates automatically per second so that one can see the proportion of server power consumption and air conditioning, as shown in Fig. 9.

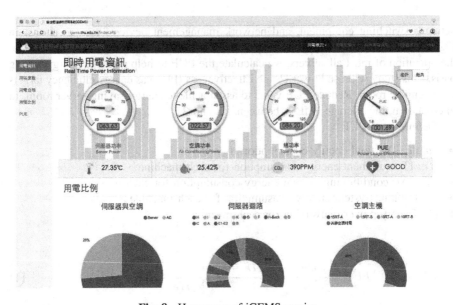

Fig. 8. Homepage of iGEMS service

4.3.1 PUE Calculation

The main server room power consumption required for the operation from the server power consumption, energy-consuming air conditioning system for cooling, power

Fig. 9. The proportion of server power consumption and air conditioning

network switching equipment, and network management devices, etc., as shown in Fig. 10. For excellent energy efficiency in the server room, the energy consumption for the operation of most all servers, we calculate the PUE to help us make energy-saving basis. This study will use Power Usage Effectiveness (PUE) as energy efficiency targets of the engine room. Reduce PUE value to assist achieve energy-saving server room. In international, the average PUE is between 1.8 and 2.1.

Definition of PUE

- *Totale:* The total energy consumption room
- *ITe:* IT equipment energy consumption for each machine
- *ACs:* Air-conditioning system energy consumption for each machine
- *Ls:* Lighting system energy consumption for each machine
- *Ec:* Energy power conversion for each machine

$$PUE = \frac{Totale}{\sum ITe} = \frac{\sum ITe + \sum ACs + \sum Ls + \sum Ec}{\sum ITe}. \tag{1}$$

4.3.2   Observation of Historical Information

We can show the interface of our power environment monitoring for historical data information. In Fig. 11, through the exploration of the historical data, we can record the amount of the monthly server power, air conditioning, environmental status, and power

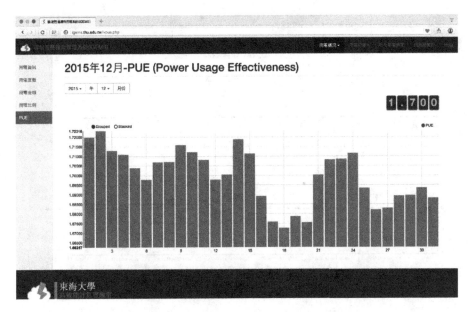

Fig. 10. PUE calculation results on interface

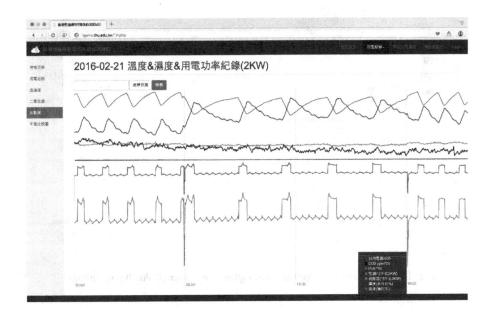

Fig. 11. Comparison of various historical data.

consumption each month. Due to the fact that our IT server is not closed all day long, we can predict the electric power changes this month. The data will update and calculate the average electricity costs each time when it gets a new data. It is shown in Fig. 12.

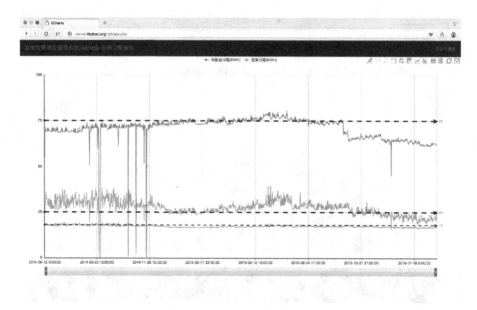

Fig. 12. Comparison of electrical data.

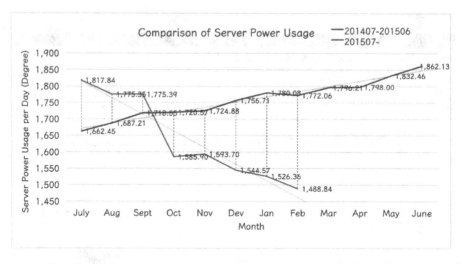

Fig. 13. Improvement of power consumption for server (Color figure online)

By presenting server location and providing each server's status including operation loading, networking loading, etc., one can observe the relation between any two factors and conclude some results to adjust system. For example, based on the analysis

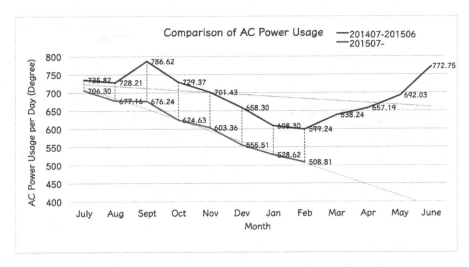

Fig. 14. Improvement of power consumption for air conditioner (Color figure online)

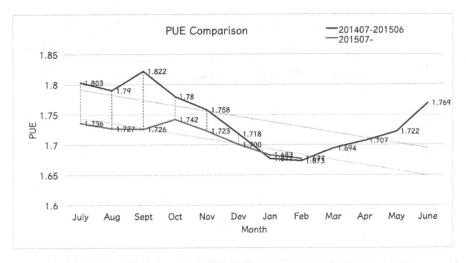

Fig. 15. Improvement of power consumption for PUE. (Color figure online)

results of the historical data, we know the proper location of air conditioners and find out the servers with high power consumption. Thus, we move the air conditioners to the location close to servers and change the servers with high power consumption to VMware virtual platforms so as to obviously reduce PUE and power consumption, as shown in Figs. 13, 14, 15, 16 and 17.

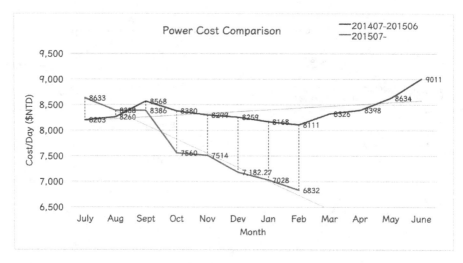

Fig. 16. Improvement of total power cost per day for each month. (Color figure online)

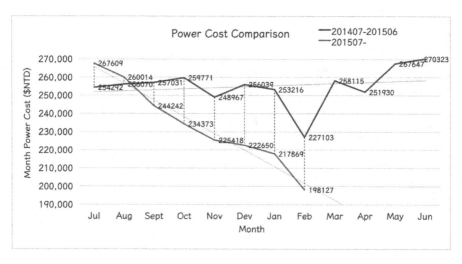

Fig. 17. Improvement of total power consumption cost for each month. (Color figure online)

5   Conclusions

This work applied the cloud infrastructure and virtualization technology to develop a cloud green energy management system. The proposed system has many useful functions including: historical electricity data analysis, single device abnormal warning, system electricity abnormal warning, estimation of pipeline failure by using tree-network electricity layer checking, power restoration, power adjustment in contract capacity of electricity, prediction for machine breakdown and renewal. The analysis of all information allows us to understand the factors relative to power consumption of IT room. Moreover, it helps us to know how to reduce power consumption.

Acknowledgements. This work is supported in part by the Ministry of Science and Technology, Taiwan ROC, under grants number MOST 104-2221-E-029-010-MY3, MOST 104-2622-E-029-008-CC3, and MOST 103-2622-E-029-012-CC3.

References

1. Han, D.-M., Lim, J.-H.: Design and implementation of smart home energy management systems based on ZigBee. IEEE Trans. Consum. Electron. **56**, 1417–1425 (2010)
2. Huang, L.-C., Chang, H.-C., Chen, C.-C., Kuo, C.-C.: A ZigBee-based monitoring and protection system for building electrical safety. Energ. Build. **43**, 1418–1426 (2011)
3. Park, S., Choi, M.-i., Kang, B., Park, S.: Design and implementation of smart energy management system for reducing power consumption using ZigBee wireless communication module. Procedia Comput. Sci. **19**, 662–668 (2013)
4. Yardi, V.S.: Design of smart home energy management system. Int. J. Innovative Res. Comput. Commun. Eng. **3**(3), 1851–1857 (2013)
5. Park, W.-K., Choi, C.-s., Jang, J.: Energy efficient multi-function home gateway in always-on home environment. IEEE Trans. Consum. Electron. **56**, 106–111 (2010)
6. Yang, I.-K., Jung, N.-J., Kim, Y-I.: Status of advanced metering infrastructure development in Korea. In: Korea Electric Power Research Institute IEEE T&D, pp. 1–3, Asia (2009)
7. Han, J., Choi, C.-S., Park, W.-K., Lee, I., Kim, S.-H.: Smart home energy management system including renewable energy based on ZigBee and PLC. IEEE Trans. Consum. Electron. **60**(2), 198–202 (2014)
8. O'Driscoll, A., Daugelaite, J., Sleator, R.D.: 'Big data', Hadoop and cloud computing in genomics. J. Biomed. Inform. **46**(5), 774–781 (2013)
9. Taylor, R.C.: An overview of the Hadoop/MapReduce/HBase framework and its current applications in bioinformatics. BMC Bioinform. **11**(Suppl. 1), S1 (2010)
10. QIU, Z., Lin, Z.-w., Ma, Y.: Research of Hadoop-based data flow management system. J. China Univ. Posts Telecommun. **18**(Suppl. 2), 164–168 (2011)
11. Dittrich, J., Quian, J.A.: Efficient big data processing in Hadoop MapReduce. Proc. VLDB Endowment **5**(12), 2014–2015 (2012)
12. O'Driscoll, A., Daugelaite, J., Sleator, R.D.: 'Big data', Hadoop and cloud computing in genomics. J. Biomed. Inform. **46**(5), 774–781 (2013)
13. Taylor, R.C.: An overview of the Hadoop/MapReduce/HBase framework and its current applications in bioinformatics. BMC Bioinform. **11**(Suppl. 12), S1 (2010)
14. Zhang, C., De Sterck, H.: Supporting multi-row distributed transactions with global snapshot isolation using bare-bones HBase. In: 2010 11th IEEE/ACM International Conference on Grid Computing, pp. 177–184 (2010)
15. Vashishtha, H., Stroulia, E.: Enhancing query support in HBase via an extended coprocessors framework. In: Abramowicz, W., Llorente, I.M., Surridge, M., Zisman, A., Vayssière, J. (eds.) ServiceWave 2011. LNCS, vol. 6994, pp. 75–87. Springer, Heidelberg (2011)
16. Sun, J., Jin, Q.: Scalable RDF store based on HBase and MapReduce. In: ICACTE (2010) 3rd International Conference on Advanced Computer Theory and Engineering, vol. 1 (2010)

17. Yang, C.-T., Liao, C.-J., Liu, J.-C., Den, W., Chou, Y.-C., Tsai, J.-J.: Construction and application of an intelligent air quality monitoring system for healthcare environment. J. Med. Syst. **38**(2), 15 (2014)
18. Yang, C.-T., Shih, W.-C., Chen, L.-T., Kuo, C.-T., Jiang, F.-C., Leu, F.-Y.: Accessing medical image file with co-allocation HDFS in cloud. Future Gener. Comput. Syst. **43–44**, 61–73 (2015)
19. The Hadoop distributed file system: architecture and design (2007). http://hadoop.apache.org/docs/r0.18.0/hdfs_design.pdf
20. Hadoop. http://hadoop.apache.org/
21. Vora, M.N.: Hadoop-HBase for large-scale data. In: 2011 International Conference on Computer Science and Network Technology (ICCSNT), vol. 1, pp. 601–605 (2011)
22. Yang, C.-T., Shih, W.-C., Huang, C.-L., Jiang, F.-C., Chu, William, C.C.: On construction of a distributed data storage system in cloud. Computing **98**(1–2), 93–118 (2016)
23. Yang, C.-T., Liu, J.-C., Huang, K.-L., Jiang, F.-C.: A method for managing green power of a virtual machine cluster in cloud. Future Gener. Comp. Syst. **37**, 26–36 (2014)

The Macro-DSE for HPC Processing Unit: The Physical Constraints Perspective

Yuxing Tang[✉], Lei Wang, Yu Deng, Xiaoqiang Ni, and Qiang Dou

School of Computer, National University of Defense Technology, Changsha, China
{tyx,leiwang,dengyu,xiaoqiangni,douqiang}@nudt.edu.cn

Abstract. Because of the popularity of big data and cloud computing, the evolution of microarchitecture has to concentrated on raw computing ability, throughput, low power and cost at the same time. Due to the huge Non-recurring engineering costs, computer architects and processor designers rely on the simulation tools and models to optimize the main processing unit. Design space exploration (DSE) methodology is responsible to filter all the possible choices. However, thousands of parameters for current multi-core processor make it too expensive to complete the exhausting search. The future high performance computing (HPC) no longer insist on peak double precision performance (DFP) only, but also on high throughput and light-weight. Depending on the various details from the number of cores to the individual pipeline buffer size, we can divide the DSE problem into macro and micro level.

In this paper, we focus on the macro-DSE problem around choosing the right style for the processing core design. Firstly, we extended McPAT, the de facto DSE tools to support from 65 nm to 16 nm technology and up to 256 Cores. Based on the physical design constraints: chip area, power and balance design request, we examine and explore the design of future processing unit of high performance. Although traditional HPC pursued the peak performance only, our DSE results show the physical constrain will direct the processing unit of future HPC to limited choice. The experiment results show that with only 74.8 % increasing in chip die area and 3.8 % increasing in power, one many-core design can archive 4 times peak performance both in INT and FP, and 285.6 % increasing in performance/power efficiency than another. The key insight of our experiment indicates that unique type of processing core can be the best choice depending on the specific physical design plan.

Keywords: Processor · Design space · HPC · Cloud

1 Introduction

Driven by the emergency application of big data, machine learning, as long as the traditional endless demands in weather forecast, physical simulation, chemical and bio-information computing, the HPC community is still eager for higher performance [1]. But unlike the last century, today's top.10 supercomputers

© Springer International Publishing Switzerland 2016
X. Huang et al. (Eds.): GPC 2016, LNCS 9663, pp. 99–112, 2016.
DOI: 10.1007/978-3-319-39077-2_7

in top500.org are restricted further by physical constrain, such as power, energy and cost. The challenges of big data and cloud computing force the traditional HPC processor to adapt various scales [20]. Throughput and extreme low power can be the good example, such as AMD/SeaMicro's SM15000 [21], Cavium's TunderX [22] and even Intel's new Xeon D.

How to build or assemble the future processing unit in HPC is still an open question. Even the most of previous RISC processors have lost their positions from Top500 List. In the list of Nov 2015, the world most powerful top500 HPCs are using 19 types of processor from 5 vendors and 29 types of accelerator from 4 vendors.

The limited market capability and budget also make the popularity of choosing the affordable, typically off-the-shelf processing unit, like the commercial CPU, GPU and FPGA. This trend means the importance of reusable, general purpose design for HPC processing unit. Also the microarchitecture must take the chip size into account. Because the unique bigger silicon area leads to lower yield and huge cost, resembling multiple appropriate size die may be the right choice.

The silicon technology is one of the most important implemental driven for HPC processing unit. As the example, we can consider dual-core x86 design, which is the main choice of old HPC Red Storm (No. 2 in Top500 of Nov. 2006) and Jaguar (No. 2 in Top500 of Jun. 2007). Due to 65 nm was the state-of-the-art silicon technology in 2006, we use McPAT to predict the piled 16-Core x86 design results in Fig. 1. The prediction is based on physical and microarchitecture parameters like dual core Xeon 5160, extending McPAT tech-model to support 16 nm and enlarging the on-chip cache for underlying balancing requirement.

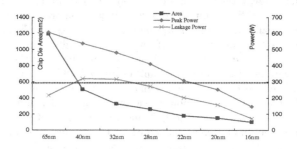

Fig. 1. Extending 2006 dual-core Xeon into 2015 popular 16-Core in various silicon technologies

Because it is difficult to dissipate the heat and the limited budget for cooling, even the processing unit of HPC won't break the 300 W power per chip easily. The package cost and yield limit won't promise the chip size too far away from 625 mm² (25 mm × 25 mm). The dot line in Fig. 1 means the 16 core design can be the reality only after the reality of 32 nm. According to the real CPU DB data [2], due to the improving microarchitecture, SOI, High-K gate and other silicon technology, the 16-Core Sandy Bridge or Interlagos can control the chip's peak power (or TDP: Thermal Design Power) below 300 W.

In the era of traditional HPC, the driven of endless processing power will remain all the time. But the NRE cost for high-end silicon, and the problem of program porting or usability will prevent the most ambitious microarchitecture design. Based on proved core design, multi-core or many-core became the tradeoff answer for performance and cost. In this paper, we present the DSE (Design Space Exploration) results and key findings of multicore/manycore design for HPC under the physical constrain. The result key insights are:

- Traditional High Performance processing core, which has 4-way (or even above 4) out-of-order pipeline, large multi-level cache and plenty of integer and float-point function units, is the best choice by using advance package technology, like MCM, 2.5D or 3D stack. (the example cores are current Xeon, Opteron and Power or traditional Alpha21164 EV5, AMD K5).
- Standard Performance processing core, which has 2-way out-of-order pipeline, proper multi-level cache and function units, is the best choice for homogeneous manycore. (just like traditional PowerPC 603e).
- Low Power (low performance) processing core, which has 2-way in-order pipeline, simple cache system, would be the best choice to apply SIMD extension for special accelerator. (Much like GPGPU core or traditional Alpha EV4 core).

The rest of the paper is organized as follows. In Sect. 2, we present the methodology of preferred HPC processing unit, covering the choices in core, chip die and package. The modeling and Experiments is described in detail in Sect. 3. Related works is presented in Sect. 4, and Sect. 5 gives our conclusion.

2   Macro-DSE and Methodology

The choice of homogeneous multi-core or heterogeneous accelerator is still an open issue, and sometimes they can be treated as application dependable question. The most popular GPU accelerator is becoming more and more general purposed [3]. At the same time, resent research in general purpose CPU shows the choice of different ISA would not play an intrinsic role in performance or energy efficiency [4]. All these make an ISA irrelevant DSE possible and valuable. We may consider the macro-aspect of microarchitecture, architecture, silicon and package features only in following discuss.

In the following experiment we consider the power dissipation and die size as the main physical constrain of multi-core or many core design. As the statistics from CPU-DB [2], after 2005 almost every new processor is using new deep sub-micro technology from 65 nm to most recently 16/14 nm. Although the most advance silicon technology means better power and chip size, it also means huge NRE cost. With the present of advance MCM or stacked 2.5D/3D package, old mature technology may still be attractive. The DSE in this paper will scan all the possible technology feature size from 65 nm to 16 nm.

2.1   Processing Core Choice

Without consider the choice of ISA, we classify the main general processing cores into three different types: high performance core (HP), standard performance core (SP), and low power core (LP), which from the best single core performance to the lowest performance. Vice versa for better power, energy and die area spend.

Table 1 show the configuration of these three cores in brief. The HP core is the popular 4-way out of order execution engine, which needs better memory (cache system) support and usually high frequency. The LP core is the simple 2-way superscalar in-order design, which theoretically can achieve much higher frequency than HP or SP core. But for 2 GHz target frequency, LP core will consume twice the power than the same LP core running in 1 GHz (5.68 W vs. 2.9215 W @65 nm). Much higher frequency will need deeper pipeline and better cache structure, which means much more power and larger die area. The LP core's low power feature will benefit the following processor architecture and chip package. The SP core is the trade of between HP and LP core configuration.

Table 1. The main configuration of three core's types

Core	Microarchitecture feature	L1	Freq.	Perf.	Die area	Power/energy
HP	4-W Out-of-Order, 4 INT and 4 FP/Cycle	32K/32K	2GHz	4Gops 4GFlops	Big	High
SP	2-W Out-of-Order, 2 INT or 4 FP/Cycle	32K/16K	2GHz	2Gops 4GFlops	Normal	Normal
LP	2-W inorder, 2 INT or 2 FP/Cycle	16K/16K	1GHz	2Gops 2GFlops	Small	Low

Although the DSE in this paper is tend to not exploring in micro-detailed parameters, there were plenty of processing core design in history and future. We think these three types of core design (in Table 1) will be enough to discover main directions in the choosing of processing unit. According to popular SIMD extended style, the Macro-DSE methodology is expended to all three types of core in following experiments.

2.2   Architecture Choice

For multi-core and many-core design, the main designing and researching targets are switch from the processing core to cache-memory subsystem and the network on chips (NoC). In order to explore the design space of more than 100+ core, the simple cache monitoring coherence and bus system will not fit the scalability.

Based on popular data center or Cloud processor design such as ThunderX 48 core [22], and traditional High performance design suach as Xeon E7 or Power8, we figure out that the SP and HP many-core design will be built on small SMP cluster which may share Level-2 cache, and equipped with large or multi-level NoC and cache. However, today's real 1000+ core such Nvidia's gk110 [25] or tile64 uses small processing core and simple cache.

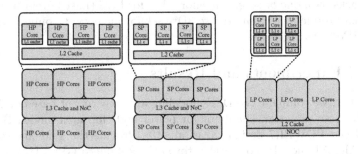

Fig. 2. Scale these three different cores to manycore architecture

As illustrated in Fig. 2, for small number of multiple HP or SP cores (typically 4–8 Core), the hierarchical cache system will be enough. But for larger manycore design, HP and SP cores will need L3 Cache and NoC system. And also because higher performance, the many HP cores need more sophisticated and larger L3 and NoC Router than SP. For simplicity and reflect the current architecture of GPGPU, the many LP core design won't introduce the complex 3-Level coherence and sophisticated NoC.

2.3   Possible Silicon Package Choice

Early than 2001, MultiChip Module (MCM) had been used to integrate multiple adjacent die into a single SMP system [5]. Most recently the 2.5D and 3D stack package have be consider as an easy way to insist on integration speed of Moore's Low. For a silicon chip die, the bigger area size means lower yield, higher cost. With the help of advance package and some extension in circuits and architecture, we can use multiple cheaper smaller die to achieve same design purpose of big die. Based on Xilinx Virtex-7 2000T [23] and the Center3De [24] prototype, we predict the future many-core design with advance packaging technology illustrated in Fig. 3.

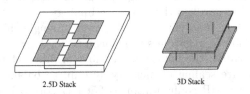

2.5D Stack   3D Stack

Fig. 3. Possible 2.5D and 3D advance package extend the die size limitation

The substrate or interposer would support the interconnection among several dies. Comparing to 3D-TSV package, the MCM or 2.5D package will not increase the power density. Because power is becoming the No. 1 physical design constrain, it's rare to stack several processor dies, but rather one layer of processor die stacks with one or several memory dies for LLC (Last Level Cache). The commercial products now tend to use 3D stack for memory die only, such as the HBM or HMC [8].

3   DSE Experiments and Results

In this paper, we complete the DSE modeling and experiment based on McPAT [9], the de facto processor simulator for power and chip area model. Based on the privileged POWER7 design, Xi et al. [10]. Provide the guideline to create accurate McPAT models. For accelerator such as modern GPGPU, Leng et al. present the modified model in GPUWattch [11]. Inspired by these works, we can extend the current source code of McPAT, and complete the design space exploration.

Power efficiency (Eq. 1) is already a well known metric and used in Green500 list. In order to represent NRE and foundry cost, we use die-Area efficiency (Eq. 2) metric too. For traditional HPC application such as the Linpack benchmark, the emphasis performance is the double precision float point operation (DFP, or flop/s in top500.org). Today's text searching or graph applications also concern the performance integer operation (INT, or op/s). In following experiment, we use power efficiency and area efficiency metric to evaluate every design configuration under the silicon technology from 64 nm to 16 nm.

$$Pe = \frac{ChipPerformance}{PeakPower} \tag{1}$$

$$Ae = \frac{ChipPerformance}{HorizontalChipSize} \tag{2}$$

Just as GPUWattch modeling Nvidia Fermi/GT2000 which may have 1000+ CUDA cores, we treat the current thousand level manycore as a special cluster of SIMD extended low power core without sophisticated multi-level coherence cache system. Based on the information from CPU DB, and the physical data of state-of-arts commercial GPU and Accelerator (MIC), the following physical constraints will be check all through the experiment:

1. **Area Constraint**: the area of singe die should not larger than 625 mm^2 (25 mm × 25 mm), regardless the silicon technology.
2. **Power Constraint**: the dynamic peak power of single chip package should not higher than 300 W, regardless the silicon technology.
3. **Balance Constraint**: the increasing number of different type cores should need the proper size scaling of memory system, to balance the data transfer with processing. HP configuration is 256 KB/core private L2 cache and 1024 KB/Core share L3 Cache. SP is 128 KB/Core private L2 cache and 512 KB/Core shared L3 cache. LP is 64 KB/Core shared L2 cache only.

Of course, these three physical limits are not the real firm constrain. They can be adjusted by various trade-off in technology, budget and other resources. For example, the advance cooling method will permit several die been stacked to high power density. But these adjustments won't give a deep effect on the DSE in this paper. For Ae and Pe metric, the high value will be considered as much more valuable design choice.

3.1 Homogeneous Design

To minimize the redundancy, we present the experiment result of homogeneous multicore or manycore design in the beginning from octa-core (8-Core), and at the stop in the 100+ configuration (128-Core). In actual DSE experiment, we explore the space from 2-Core to 128/256-Core, with the stepping of the integrated power of 2.

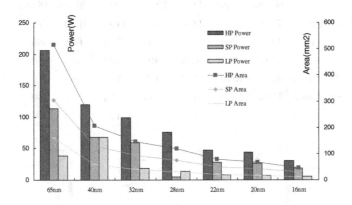

Fig. 4. The Die area and power data for 8-Core design in different technology

Figure 4 presents the results of 8-Core design. Although even in 65 nm technology, the three types of 8-Core designs follow all constraints. Because our methodology limits the HP/SP/LP's core frequency to 2/2/1 GHz, the peak performance of whole 8-Core chip will be limited in 64/32/16 GOPS or 64/64/32 Gflops. From the Fig. 5 data, the advance technology almost improves both the power efficiency and area efficiency.

Because in-order pipeline and small size of cache, LP core design is much more power efficiency than HP Core and SP core in Integer performance. Due to the same DFP SIMD design as HP core, SP core with larger cache size still beat HP core and LP core both in Power efficiency and Area Efficiency for DFP.

Table 2 and Fig. 6 present the area and power data for 128-Core. Due to the large number of Core, HP design breaks the power and area constraint both in every technology. The 128-SP-Core can be realized in 16 nm foundry technology only. For 128-Core LP design, we can apply 32 nm and further technology without break the physical constraints.

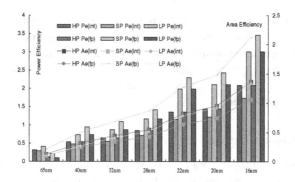

Fig. 5. The INT and FP efficient data for 8-Core design in different technology

Table 2. The DIE area and power data for 128-Core design in different technology

Date	65 nm	40 nm	32 nm	28 nm	22 nm	20 nm	16 nm
HP area	7818	3218	2250	1779	1194	1020	712
SP area	4875	2065	1410	1132	771	661	465
LP area	2593	935	625	491	324	275	188
HP power	3204	1872	1547	1179	727	680	470
SP power	1755	1059	904	17	425	401	280
LP power	552	331	279	207	121	115	80

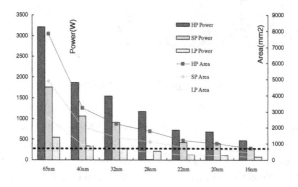

Fig. 6. The Die area and power data for 128-Core design in different technology

Figure 7 confirms the same efficiency trends as Fig. 5. Because of the balance design constraint, according the specific type of core design, the efficiency data is dominated by silicon technology node. For Power efficiency, SP core is the best choice for DFP, but LP core for INT. Although break the chip area constraint, HP core's area efficient is slightly better than LP core. HP core is the best choice for INT, but SP core is the best choice for FP. If we recall the unchangeable performance need in HPC, the 128-SP-Core design will be the best, because of

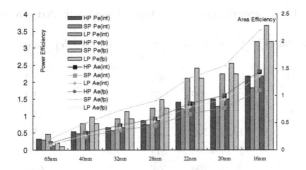

Fig. 7. The INT and FP efficient data for 128-Core design in different technology

its peak performance (512Gops and 1Tflops) is much better than 128-LP-Core design (256Gops and 256Gflops).

3.2 SIMD and Discrete Accelerator Design

In some part, the homogeneous manycore DSE experiment just confirm the silicon design rules for HPC, which is using the silicon as function unit for execution, not for memory and pursuing for low power design. Besides the balance needs for memory, SIMD functional extension would be the perfect technology, because it double or quad the performance but only increasing some part of power and area (as illustrated in Fig. 8). This type of manycore design has been treated as accelerator, a application speed up processing unit like GPGPU, not suitable for main processing. The SIMD extension design is most suitable for HP core, because HP core is equipped with multi-port register file and abundant function units. The SIMD extension will only increase the area size by 18.74 % on average, and increasing the power by 16.5 %. But for LP core, it is a whole different story. The increasing rate number is 56.83 % and 52.38 % for area and power.

Under the advanced 16 nm technology, and 512bit-SIMD extension (-SE in Table 3 for short), the power efficiency 64-HP-SE design has a better score than 256-LP-Core which has quarter number of cores. Comparing to 256-LP-Core,

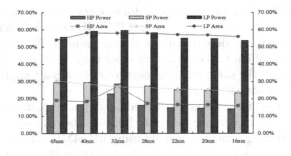

Fig. 8. The increasing rate by double SIMD extension in 64-Core design

Table 3. The largest design for each type of simd extended core in 16 nm

Type	Cores	Int	FP	Gops	Gflops	Area (mm^2)	Power (W)	Gops/W	Gflops/W
HP	64	4	4	512	512	361	237	2.16	2.16
SP	128	2	4	512	1024	465	280	1.83	3.66
LP	256	2	2	512	512	376	160	3.20	3.20
HP-SE	64	8	8	1024	1024	419	270	3.79	3.79
SP-SE	128	8	8	2048	2048	577	346	5.92	5.92
LP-SE	256	8	8	2048	2048	586	246	8.33	8.33

64-HP-SE doubles the peak performance, with a little large die size, but not breaking the area constraint.

The most powerful SP manycore design (128 Core) cannot be SIMD extended, because of the violation in power constraint. Except for Area size, the 256-LP-SE-Core has all the best scores in peak performance, total power and power efficiency. Comparing to 64-HP-Core, with 74.8 % increasing in chip die area and 3.8 % increasing in power, 256-LP-SE-Core archives 4 times peak performance both in INT and FP, and 285.6 % increasing in performance efficiency.

There still needs a coupled main processor with the accelerator, to perform the task scheduling, data preparing and communication with neighbor nodes. This main processor would prefer the HP style multi-core design, which is good for the legacy application. There is no violation of 16-Core HP design with technology node from 32 nm. So the main processor does not need macro-DSE again.

3.3   Merged Heterogeneous Design

The data communication between the main processor and accelerator is the biggest hazard in previous discrete accelerator design. The merged on-chip heterogeneous design, such IBM Cell [13] or AMD Fusion [14], is proposed to deal with such bottleneck.

The same as the main processor plus discrete accelerator, merged heterogeneous design prefer to use the same HP + LP SIMD extended combine. Unlike it, merged heterogeneous design can not change ratio of different type of core by using various combinations of main processor chip and accelerator chip. Also because produced in the same die, heterogeneous cores can't apply for different silicon technology node.

In HPC side, the main reason for merged on-chip heterogeneous design is for possible best performance in one chip, which means the most part of silicon will be used for chasing performance, usually using LP SIMD extension many core. For the least heterogeneous, the small number of HP or SP cores (dual or quad) design is common, like Cell or Fusion for low power.

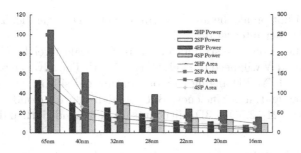

Fig. 9. The Die area and power data for 2 or 4 HP/SP Core in merge heterogeneous design

Figure 9 shows that even for 4-HP-Core design, in 28 nm the area size is only 59.93 mm² and the power is only 38.88 W. Compared with original power and area constraints, although it depresses the space for LP-SE many core, the number of LP-SE-cores will not worse too much in advance tech node.

3.4 Advance Package Implementation

The advance package technology, such MCM, 2.5D, and 3D stack will permit the designer to break the area constraint. These technologies enhance the integration with the cost of further circuits design and expensive package. The designer can apply the least advance silicon technology to counteract the package and cooling cost. Table 4 shows we can use 32 nm in HP or even 40 nm for SP and LP to archive the same performance in 16 nm, with 4-die be packaged horizontal together.

The horizontal package like MCM and 2.5D won't increase the power density, but only request for large cooling area cover. 3D stack will worse the power density. So we can only stack the cache memory with the core to minimize the depravation of power density. But even for 128-HP-Core design, which has the largest size of L3 Cache (256 MB), the cache size is only 16.56 % of the whole chip. Although the 3D stack will make the 128-HP-Core possible, the 591 mm²

Table 4. Horizontal advance multi-die

Type	Cores/chip	nm	Area mm²	Power (W)	AeI	PeI	AeF	PeF
HP	64	16	361	237	1.42	2.16	1.42	2.16
HP-2.5	16	32	292*4	196*4	0.44	0.65	0.44	0.65
SP	128	16	465	280	1.1	1.83	2.2	3.6
SP-2.5	32	40	537*4	268*4	0.24	0.48	0.48	0.96
LP	256	16	577	346	1.36	3.19	1.36	3.19
LP-2.5	64	40	475*4	167*4	0.27	0.77	0.27	0.77

size core would not break the area constraint as in 2D single die. There is little space left for further integration.

Recalling the design constraints in future ExaScale level HPC, to support 1000Pflops in 20 MW will need the PeF at least 50 [1]. The advance package won't help for such goal. And changing to more mature old silicon technology would worse the power and area efficiency. But for high density cloud computing or datacenter server [21], 2.5D or 3D still counts for high bandwidth and integration.

4   Related Works

For traditional HPC cpu design like Xeon, Opteron or Power, Dubach et al. have proposed a microarchitecture and pipeline DSE model based on machine learning [18]. Besides GPGPU or other accelerator like Xeon Phi, embedded core like ARM has also be considered as the main HPC processing unit. Rajovic et al. have presented the possibility and bright future to apply real ARM processor in HPC system [17].

Normally the design space exploration will face the challenge to filter thousands possible architecture parameters, and pick up the optimized configuration among millions combination. The multicore, manycore or MP-SOC design will enlarge the design space. Statistic method or prediction model is used to reducing the simulation time and the number of design point that need to check [15]. Lee et al. proposed the RpStack methodology to accelerate DSE by critical path analysis [16]. Based on critical path analysis directed DSE (CPADSE), Wang et al. [19] also proposed two different algorithms to speedup the identification and analysis of critical path in relative proceedings.

The DSE in this paper are focused on selecting the right many-core design style in deep sub-micro silicon technology node. The results and key insight of this paper can be used to guide the choice of the number of cores, the technology node, the possible package method etc. For detail processing core DSE and sophisticated NoC or application directed DSE, the traditional DSE analysis is still needed.

5   Conclusion and Future Works

In this paper we use three types of processing core to present the multicore and manycore design space exploration in all seven possible deep sub-micrometer silicon technology nodes. Combined with homogeneous and heterogeneous architecture design, and SIMD extended accelerator or advance package technique, we get the following insight:

1. The standard performance core with reasonable 2-way out-of-order pipeline, and proper size of multi-level cache is the best choice for homogeneous many-core design;
2. For SIMD extended accelerator, the in-order low power core is best for peak performance, power efficiency and area efficiency.

3. Although advance package will not improve efficiency, the high performance core with aggressive 4-way out-of-order pipeline, plenty function units and large balance is the best choice for multi-die horizontal package.

The physical constrains in this paper are from the power and die size. However, the thermal maybe another critical constrain in deep-submicron technologies. The future McPAT model and DSE methodology should be adjusted to thermal effect and constraint.

Another future work is to figure out the efficient way to combine the macro DSE with micro DSE. For more advanced silicon technology node and sophisticated realized processor core, the McPAT simulator should be adjusted again.

Acknowledgements. We thanks the other cpu@nudt team numbers that provide architecture, microarchitecture and physical design parameters of various processor. This work is supported in part by NSFC grants No. 61272139 and National Science and Technology Major Project HGJ-2015ZX01028001-001.

References

1. Bergman, K., Borkar, S., Campbell, D., Carlson, W., Dally, W., Denneau, M., Franzon, P., Harrod, W., Hill, K., Hiller, J., Karp, S., Keckler, S., Klein, D., Lucas, R., Richards, M., Scarpelli, A., Scott, S., Snavely, A., Thomas Sterling, R., Williams, S., Yelick, K.: ExtraScale Computing Study: Technology Challenges in Achieving Exascale System. Kogge, P. (ed. and study lead) (2008)
2. Danowitz, A., Kelley, K., Mao, J., Stevenson, J.P., Horowitz, M.: CPU DB: recording microprocessor history. Commun. ACM **55**(4), 55–63 (2012)
3. Lee, V.W., Kim, C., Chhugani, J., Deisher, M., Kim, D., Nguyen, A.D., Satish, N., Smelyanskiy, M., Chennupaty, S., Hammarlund, P., Singhal, R., Dubey, P.: Debunking the 100X GPU vs. CPU myth: an evalution of throughput computing on CPU and GPU. In: Proceedings of the 37th Annual International Symposium on Computer Architecdture (ISCA 2010), pp. 451–460 (2010)
4. Blem, E., Menon, J., Vijayaraghavan, T., Sankaralingam, K.: ISA wars: understanding the relevance of ISA being RISC or CISC to performance power and energy on modern architecture. ACM Trans. Comput. Syst. **33**(1), 3 (2015)
5. Tendler, J.M., Dodson, J.S., Fields, J.S., Le, H., Sinharoy, B.: POWER4 System microarchtecture. IBM J. Res. Dev. **46**(1), 5–15 (2001)
6. Sampson, R., Yang, M., Wei, S., Chakrabarti, C., Wenisch, T.F.: Sonic Millip3De: a massively parallel 3D-stacked accelerator for 3D ultrasound. In: Proceedings of the 19th IEEE International Symposium on High Performance Computer Architecture, pp. 318–329 (2013)
7. Akin, B., Franchetti, F., Hoe, J.C.: Data reorganization in memory using 3D-stacked DRAM. In: Proceedings of the 42nd International Symposium on Computer Architecture, pp. 131–143 (2015)
8. Koyanagi, M.: Heterogeneous 3D integration - technology enabler toward future super-chip. In: Proceedings of IEEE International Electron Devices Meeting (IEDM), pp. 1.2.1–1.2.8 (2013)
9. Li, S., Ahn, J.H., Strong, R.D., Brockman, J.B., Tullsen, D.M., Jouppi, N.P.: The McPAT framework for multicore and manycore architecture: simultaneously modeling power, area, and timing. ACM Trans. Archit. Code Optim. **10**(1), 5 (2013)

10. Xi, S.L., Jacobson, H., Bose, P., Wei, G.-Y., Brooks, D.: Quantifying sources of error in McPAT and potential impacts on architecture studies. In: Proceedings of 21st Internaional Symposium on High Performance Computer Architecture, pp. 577–589 (2015)

11. Leng, J., Hethering, T., ElTantawy, A., Gilani, S., Kim, N.S., Aamodt, T.M., Reddi, V.J.: GPUWattch: enabling energy optimizations in GPGPUs. In: Proceedings of the ACM/IEEE International Symposium on Computer Architecture (ISCA 2013), pp. 487–498 (2013)

12. Serafy, C., Srivastava, A., Yeung, D.: Unlocking the true potential of 3D CPUs with micro-fluidic cooling. In: Proceedings of the 2014 International Symposium on Low Power Electronics and Design, pp. 323–326 (2014)

13. Johns, C.R., Brokenshire, D.A.: Introduction to the cell broadband engine architecture. IBM J. Res. Dev. **51**(5), 503–520 (2007)

14. Gutta, S.R., Foley, D., Naini, A., Wasmuth, R., Cherepacha, D.: A low-power integrated X86-64 and graphics processor for mobile computing devices. In: 2011 IEEE International Solid-State Circuits Conference (ISSCC) Digest of Technical Papers, pp. 270–272 (2011)

15. Davy, G., Deckhout, L.: Chip multiprocessor design space exploration through statistical simulation. IEEE Trans. Comput. **12**(58), 1668–1681 (2009)

16. Lee, J., Jang, H., Kim, J.: RpStacks: fast and accurate processor design space exploration using representative stall-event stacks. In: Proceedings of 47th Annual IEEE/ACM International Symposium on Microarchitecture (MICRO), pp. 255–267 (2014)

17. Rajovic, N., Carpenter, R.M., Gelado, I., Puzovic, N., Ramirez, A., Valero, M.: Supercomputing with commodity CPUs: are mobile SoCs Ready for HPC? In: Proceedings of 2013 International Conference of Supercomputing (SC 2013), pp. 1–12 (2013)

18. Dubach, C., Jones, T., O'Boyle, M.: Microarchitectural design space exploration using an architecture-centric approach. In: Proceeding of the 40th Annual IEEE/ACM International Symposium on Microarchitecture (MICRO 40), pp. 262–271 (2007)

19. Wang, L., Tang, Y., Deng, Y., Qi, F., et al.: A Scalable and fast microprocessor design space exploration methodology. In: Proceedings of McSoC (2015)

20. Gibbons, P.B.: Big data: scale down, scale up, scale out. The Keynotes in 29th IEEE International Parallel and Distributed Processing Symposium (IPDPS 29) (2015)

21. Dhodapkar, A., Aauterbach, G., Li, S., et al.: SeaMicro SM10000-64 server: building datacenter servers using cell phone chips. In: Proceedings of 23rd IEEE HotChips Symposium (2011)

22. Gwennap, L.: ThunderX rattles server market: cavium develops 48-Core ARM processor to challenge Xeon. MicroProcessor report, 9 June 2014

23. Gwennap, L.: 3D packaging gains momentum: xilinx FPGAs to use stacked silicon - will processors follow suit? MicroProcessor report 12/27/10-01 December 2012

24. Dreslinski, R.G., Fick, D., Giridhar, B., Kim, G., Seo, S., Fojtik, M., Satpathy, S., Lee, Y., Kim, D., Liu, N., Wieckowski, M., Chen, G., Sylvester, D., Blaauw, D., Mudge, T.: Centip3De: a many-core prototype exploring 3D integration and near-threshold computing. Commun. ACM **56**(11), 97–104 (2013)

25. Nickolls, J., Dally, W.J.: The GPU computing era. IEEE Micro **30**(2), 56–69 (2010)

A Scalable Cloud-Based Android App Repackaging Detection Framework

Jinghua Li$^{(\boxtimes)}$, Xiaoyan Liu, Huixiang Zhang, and Dejun Mu

School of Automation, Northwestern Polytechnical University, Xi'an, China
jovistar@gmail.com, liuxyleo@163.com,
{zhanghuixiang,mudejun}@nwpu.edu.cn

Abstract. The problem of app repackaging has become a huge threat to the security of Android ecosystem. The massive amount of existing and developing apps makes a high demand on scalability of app repackaging detectors. In this paper, we propose a cloud-based app repackaging detection framework. It is designed to analyze and detect repacked Android apps in a large-scale way. The framework consists of three primary components: market monitor, app feature extractor and app similarity computer. Market monitor crawls all new and updated apps in specific alternative app markets periodically. Then, the multi-level features of apps are extracted by app feature extractor. App similarity computer computes the similarity score of two apps based on these features. A prototype system is implemented. The evaluation results demonstrate that the proposed cloud-based framework is highly scalable and effective for large-scale Android app repackaging detection.

Keywords: Android · App markets · Repackaging detection · Cloud computing

1 Introduction

In recent years, the industry of mobile device grows rapidly. Android has become the most popular mobile operating system in the world after years of developing. The emerging of millions of apps have changed the way people use their mobile devices.

However, it's easy to decompile and repack Android apps with existing decompiling tools. Taking advantage of this feature, hackers can easily decompile and inject malicious codes into existing popular apps. Those apps will be repacked and submitted to alternative app markets. Contrast to iOS ecosystem in which apps can be downloaded only from the official "App Store" [1], Android apps can be downloaded anywhere, including the official "Google Play" [2] and countless alternative app markets. Lots of users (especially those from China) install apps downloaded from various alternative markets on their Android devices. Thus, the repacked popular (yet malicious) apps will be downloaded and installed on users' devices. This situation results in lots of economic losses and privacy leaks. The problem of app repackaging has become a huge threat to the Android ecosystem.

A number of Android security researchers have flung themselves into the field of app repackaging detection. Some detection approaches [17, 18, 20] have been proposed

© Springer International Publishing Switzerland 2016
X. Huang et al. (Eds.): GPC 2016, LNCS 9663, pp. 113–125, 2016.
DOI: 10.1007/978-3-319-39077-2_8

and claimed to be effective. But few of them take consideration into the problem of scalability. As the number of Android apps in markets grows rapidly, the practicality of those approaches are questionable.

In this paper, a scalable cloud-based detection framework is presented, which utilizes a hierarchical similarity-based app repackaging detection approach. The framework monitors specific alternative app markets and searches for new or updated apps. Then, the metadata and binary apk (application package) files of those matched apps will be crawled for multi-level feature extraction. A hierarchical multi-level based approach will be applied to generate a similarity score for two apps. Firstly, the similarity scores of apps is applied to smali [3] files in packages. Then, the similarities of packages will be computed according to the files similarity scores. Finally, the similarity score of apps will be calculated based on the packages similarity and app-level metadata. The presented approach takes consideration of similarities of files, packages and app-level metadata.

Upon the proposed framework and detection approach, we implemented a simplified prototype system. All components run in containers. The implemented system was deployed in the Aliyun cloud [4] on purpose of performance evaluation. The experiment results demonstrate that the proposed app repackaging detection framework is able to analyze and detect large-scale apps in an effective, efficient and flexible way.

The main contributions of this paper are summarized in the following:

- A scalable cloud-based Android app repackaging detection framework is presented. It takes the power of flexible cloud computing to monitor alternative app markets, extracting app features and compute similarities of apps in a large-scale way.
- A hierarchical similarity-based repacked app detection approach is proposed. It computes the similarity of apps with app-level metadata, packages similarity and smali files similarity results.
- A prototype system is implemented and deployed in a real cloud computing environment with all components running in containers. The evaluation results prove the effectiveness and efficiency of the proposed framework.

The rest of this paper is structured as follows. In Sect. 2, the proposed framework and its components are introduced. In Sect. 3, the implementation of prototype system is described. In Sect. 4, we evaluate the prototype system. In Sect. 5, we discuss the limitations of our work and the future improvement. In Sect. 6, we introduced the related work on Android app repackaging detection. Finally, we conclude our work in Sect. 7.

2 Design

2.1 Architecture Overview

As the market share of Android grows, the number of Android apps newly released every day also increases. Moreover, lots of existing apps update periodically. Thus, the total number of Android apps in official and alternative markets is quite considerable. Under this circumstances, the scalability is rather important for Android repacked app detection.

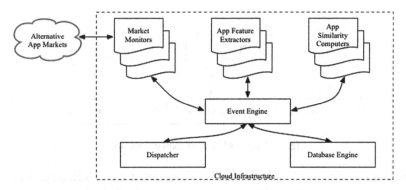

Fig. 1. The architecture overview of proposed framework.

The architecture overview of the proposed cloud-based framework for large-scale Android app repackaging detection is shown in Fig. 1. The market monitor checks the alternative app markets in watch list. When an app is added or updated in those markets, the market monitor crawls the app's metadata and downloads the corresponding apk file from the market. The app feature extractor takes the metadata and apk file as inputs for multi-level app features extraction. The app similarity computer computes the similarity scores of apps with these extracted features. The dispatcher distributes tasks to corresponding components. Besides, it monitors running load of the framework. The app metadata and extracted features are stored in a database engine. As the framework is designed to be event driven, there exists an event engine for events producing and consuming.

All components in the proposed framework are low-coupled, as all inter-components communications are accomplished through the event engine. Each component runs in respective computing instances in cloud.

2.2   Market Monitor

The key to fast app similarity computing is effective feature extraction in advance. To achieve this goal, all newly emerged or recently updated apps should be found and processed in time. Thus, the market monitor is constructed to monitor alternative app markets in the framework. Thinking of the resource limitation and spider politeness, currently, the market monitor scans all app markets only once a day. This frequency can be changed dynamically to meet different demands. As shown in Fig. 2, the workflow of market monitor consists of category monitoring, app metadata crawling and apk file downloading.

Category Monitoring. Category is defined as an app list in app markets. Market monitor is category-based, not market-based. This means each monitor just scans one app category in one market in the same time. With this mechanism, market monitor is able to scan different categories in the same market simultaneously without interference.

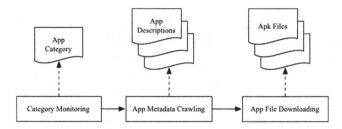

Fig. 2. The workflow of market monitor.

Every monitoring result will be kept as a screenshot of the category. When the screenshot changes, it means there are some newly uploaded apps in this category. After comparing with the previous screenshot, market monitor will mark these new apps as "NEW".

App Metadata Crawling. After scanning the app category, market monitor crawls each app's metadata (name, version, description, etc.) as an app screenshot to judge whether it is updated. Once the screenshot is found to be changed, the app will be marked as "UPDATED".

Apk File Downloading. In this step, the apk files of all apps marked as "NEW" and "UPDATED" will be downloaded from app markets. After that, all these binary files with all metadata will be sent to app feature extractor.

2.3 App Feature Extractor

A hierarchical similarity-based app repackaging detection approach is proposed. It consists of two steps: feature extracting and similarity computing. App feature extractor is used to extract multi-level features: app-level features, package-level features and file-level features in six steps as illustrated in Fig. 3.

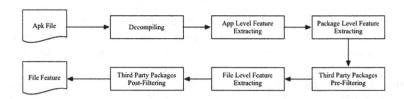

Fig. 3. The workflow of app feature extractor.

Decompiling. All downloaded apk files will be decompiled to get the file of "AndroidManifest.xml" and the file of author's signature certification. "Classes.dex" will be decompiled into smali files.

App Level Feature Extracting. App level feature includes app name, main activity, author signature and some other necessary elements.

Package Level Feature Extracting and Third Party Packages Pre-Filtering. Package-level feature consists of the name of package used in the app. The existing of third party packages may interfere the similarity computing result. Thus, we build a whitelist with a number of known third party packages. All those packages will be filtered during the pre-filtering step.

File Level Feature Extracting. There are three kinds of file-level features including the counts of specific methods, the counts of fields and the counts of opcodes in each smali file. Table 1 lists the main elements of file feature.

Third Party Packages Post-Filtering. We construct a post-filter to filter unknown third party packages according to the compound of some elements in file-level features.

Table 1. Main elements of file-level features.

Method related	private, public, static, final, Z, B, S, C, I, J, F, D, L, [
Field related	private, public, static, final, Z, B, S, C, I, J, F, D, L, [, V
Opcode related	goto, packed-switch, sparse-switch, if-eq, if-ne, if-lt, if-ge, if-gt, if-le, if-eqz, if-nez, if-ltz, if-gez, if-gtz, if-lez, cmpl-float, cmpg-float, cmpl-double, cmpg-double, cmp-long, add-type, sub-type, mul-type, div-type

2.4 App Similarity Computer

In the app repackaging detection approach, there are three thresholds: app similarity threshold, package similarity threshold and file similarity threshold. Once the similarity score of two apps/packages/files exceeds the corresponding threshold, the apps/packages/files are deemed to be similar. As shown in Fig. 4, there are three steps in app similarity computing.

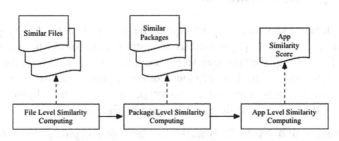

Fig. 4. The workflow of app similarity computer.

File Level Similarity Computing. All elements in the file feature will be transformed into integral values. These values make up of a file feature vector. The similarity score of two files is the cosine distance of the vectors:

$$Sim_F(File_a, File_b) = \text{cosine}(File\_Vec_a, File\_Vec_b) \qquad (1)$$

Here, $File\_Vec_a$ and $File\_Vec_b$ represent the file feature vector. If the score exceeds the file similarity threshold, the two files are similar.

Package Level Similarity Computing. The package similarity score is computed based on all the similarity scores of files in two packages:

$$Sim_P(Package_a, Package_b) = \frac{File\_Num_{P,sim}}{\min(File\_Num_{P,a}, File\_Num_{P,b})} \qquad (2)$$

Here, $File\_Num_{P,sim}$ is the number of similar files in two packages, while $File\_Num_{P,a}$ and $File\_Num_{P,b}$ are the number of files in respective packages. Two packages with a similarity score of exceeding the package similarity threshold are similar.

App Level Similarity Computing. After all packages similarity in two apps have been computed, the final similarity score of two apps are:

$$Sim_A(App_a, App_b) = \frac{File\_Num_{A,sim}}{\min(File\_Num_{A,a}, File\_Num_{A,b})} + \alpha \qquad (3)$$

Here, $File\_Num_{A,sim}$ is the number of actual similar files (only those similar files in similar packages) in two apps. $File\_Num_{A,a}$ and $File\_Num_{A,b}$ are the total file numbers in each app (not considering those files in packages filtered as third party packages). α is the weighted similarity result of app metadata. If the similarity score exceeds the app similarity threshold, the two apps are similar. Currently, the app similarity threshold is just for reference.

3 Prototype Implementation

We have implemented a simplified prototype of the proposed Android app repackaging detection framework. Redis [5] is used as an event engine for events producing and consuming. By utilizing the container technology, the prototype system can be easily and quickly deployed on any kind of cloud computing infrastructures. For evaluation purpose, we have deployed the whole prototype system in the Aliyun cloud. The architecture of the prototype system is illustrated in Fig. 5.

Database Engine and Event Engine. Redis, an in-memory data structure store, is used both as database engine and event engine.

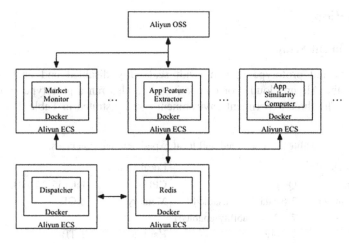

Fig. 5. The architecture of implemented prototype.

Dispatcher. All tasks are partitioned and distributed to the corresponding components. Celery [6], the distributed task queue, is the foundation of dispatcher. It also monitors running load of the prototype.

Market Monitor. This component crawls specific markets' web pages to search for newly added or updated apps periodically (like a day). All metadata and apk files of the qualified apps will be downloaded and stored. Currently, this component builds upon the outstanding open source spider: Scrapy [7].

App Feature Extractor. Once added or updated apps are crawled and downloaded, this component decompiles the corresponding apk files to extract metadata and smali files' features.

App Similarity Computer. Unlike other components, this component is external event-driven. It provides a simple interface for apps similarity computing demands.

Containerization. In consideration of simplicity and speed of system deployment, container technology is applied in the prototype implementation. More specifically, Docker [8], the most popular container is used. All system components: Redis, market monitor, app feature extractor and app similarity computer run in respective containers.

Scalability. Once the dispatcher finds the system has been under high load for a period of time, more computing instances of primary components will be started to accelerate the processing. Vice versa, some instances will be shut down while the load is continuously low.

Deployment. We have deployed our prototype system in the Aliyun cloud. While Aliyun Container Service [9] is still testing, several computing instances of Aliyun ECS [10] are used to host all containers running system components. To ease the sharing of apk files and decompiled files, Aliyun OSS [11] is used to host all files.

4   Evaluation

4.1   Experiment Setup

Two implemented prototype system (with scalability disabled and enabled) were deployed in the Aliyun cloud. For comparison, we also ran a prototype system in a local laptop. The three experiment environments are illustrated in Table 2.

Table 2. The cloud and local experiment environments.

Aliyun cloud		Local laptop	
Region	Qingdao	CPU	Intel i5 2.7 GHz
ECS number	7 (scalability disabled)	Memory	8 GB
	7–12 (scalability enabled)		
ECS CPU	2 Cores	Hard drive	1 TB
ECS memory	2 GB		
ECS hard drive	20 GB		
OS	Ubuntu 14.04 64Bit	OS	Ubuntu 14.04 64Bit
Docker number	8 (scalability disabled)	Docker number	5
	8–13 (scalability enabled)		

Table 3. The app markets in the watch list.

App markets	Gfan, Appchina,
	Anzhi, Pc6,
	3310, Hiapk,
	Liqu, Cnmo

Table 4. The number of apps crawled.

Category	Number of apps
Entertainment	14204
Finance	13986
Shopping	13873

The watch list of market monitor contains eight app markets shown in Table 3. Considering the purpose of evaluating, only three categories were monitored and crawled: entertainment, finance and shopping.

During the experiment, there were a total number of 42063 apps crawled by the system as shown in Table 4.

4.2   Results

Table 5 lists the average time consuming of several operations of the prototype system in cloud and at local. Actually, the performances of one CPU core in both environments are close, which is proven by the result of operation No.3. Only one CPU core will be used when app level feature is being extracted. However, since the other operations are all CPU-bound, the systems deployed in cloud are much faster.

Furthermore, Table 5 shows that the implemented framework is quite scalable. While the system with scalability enabled is working hard on time-consuming tasks

Table 5. The average time consuming of several operations.

No	Operation	Aliyun cloud (Scalability disabled)	Aliyun cloud (Scalability enabled)	Local laptop
1	Crawling all three app categories in all eight markets	59.38 s	60.13 s	300.21 s
2	Crawling metadata of all 42063 apps in all eight markets	1634.59 s	1038.30 s	12030.43 s
3	Extracting app level feature of one app	0.32 s	0.30 s	0.34 s
4	Extracting package level features of all packages in one app	1.42 s	1.20 s	11.34 s
5	Extracting file level features of all files in one app	28.98 s	19.32 s	160.39 s
6	Computing the similarity score of two apps	4.95 s	3.44 s	21.89 s

(like operation No.2 and No.5), more computing instances are activated. With more computing resources, the total time of processing decreases a lot.

We manually analyzed hundreds of crawled apps crawled and collected 100 groups of highly similar (same or repacked with minor modifications) to evaluate the hierarchical similarity-based app repackaging detection approach. Another 100 groups were also selected, each of which consists of eight totally different apps.

Since the app similarity threshold is just for reference, we use a two-tuples: <package similarity threshold, file similarity threshold> in the experiment. Currently, the default app similarity threshold is set to be 0.8. As shown in Fig. 6, with <0.8, 0.9>,

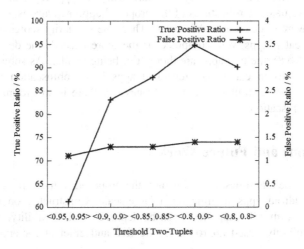

Fig. 6. The true positive ratios and false positive ratios of the proposed approach with different thresholds.

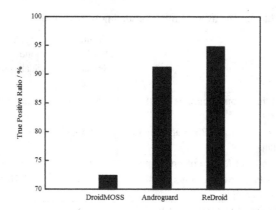

Fig. 7. The contrasting detection rates.

Table 6. The result of obfuscation resilient measurement.

Number of original apps	50
Number of obfuscated apps	50
Number of similar app pairs	47
Average similarity score	0.8349

the proposed approach achieved true positive ratio of 94.8 % and false positive ratio of 1.4 %. Actually, the false positive ratio is rather stable.

For comparing purpose, Fig. 7 shows the detection rates of "Androguard" [12], "DroidMOSS" [13] (implemented by ourselves) and our approach (with <0.8, 0.9>) called "ReDroid". As seen in Fig. 7, "ReDroid" outperforms the other approaches.

Obfuscation resiliency is a key measurement for app repackaging detection approach. To evaluate the robustness of the proposed approach against obfuscation, 50 different apps were selected and obfuscated. Then, the similarity scores of the original apps and obfuscated apps were computed. If the score exceeds the default app similarity threshold (0.8), the two apps are thought of being similar. As shown in Table 6, the proposed approach can detect repacked apps in an obfuscation resilient way. Moreover, the average similarity score indicates that there is still room for improvement against obfuscation.

5   Limitations and Future Work

Benefiting from the cloud-based architecture, the proposed framework is able to crawl and process Android apps in time on a large-scale. Constructed on the container cloud-based platform, all components can be deployed with flexibility. The proposed hierarchical similarity based approach is effective and efficient for app repackaging detection.

Nevertheless, during evaluation of the implemented prototype, a few limitations have come up which may influence the practicality of the framework. Thus, here lists some future work to avoid those limitations.

Under specific occasions, our framework fails to recognize some third-party packages which interfere the result of similarity computing. To solve this problem, an optimized third-party package self-learning and recognizing method is under developing. With the help of machine learning, the method is able to learn and recognize unknown third-party packages.

Currently, the similarity computing result comes just with similarity score, which is not intuitive for researchers. Thus, we are trying to present the result in a visual way with full details of computing procedure.

The biggest limitation is that the current implemented prototype is unsuitable for real-time app similarity computing. With the massive amount of existing apps in markets and in consideration of the explosion growth of new apps, the current similarity computing method requires too many computing resources. Though it can be achieved with continuous cloud resources investment, the cost is too high. A real-time cluster-based similarity computing method with proper cost is the key to solve this cloud resources black hole problem.

6 Related Work

ANDRUBIS [14] is an automated Android apps analysis system with both static and dynamic analysis. It is designed to provide Android security researchers a large-scale platform to analyze Android malwares. Users can submit Android apps through web site and mobile app provided by ANDRUBIS. ANDRUBIS has analyzed more than 1 million Android apps. A lot of details including network behavior of Android malwares are also presented.

A lightweight real-time Android malware detection framework: AndRadar [15] is proposed and implemented to identify potential malware in alternative Android app markets. It takes advantage of the metadata of apps (including the package name and developer's certificate fingerprint) to build a powerful app tracking framework. With AndRadar, the researchers are able to monitor the third-party markets efficiently in a real-time way.

DNADroid [16] is a large-scale Android clone apps searching tool against app cloning in app markets. Based on specific app attributes, suspicious cloned app candidates are selected and grouped for next robust clone code searching. The results claimed that the false positive rate of DNADroid is very low with a relatively high detection performance.

PiggyApp [17] is a fast and scalable system intended to find repacked apps in app markets. A module decoupling approach with semantic features extraction is introduced to decouple the primary modules of apps. The search approach for apps with similar modules is fast and efficient. However, the extracted feature fingerprint is not quite representative. Thus, the accuracy of detection system may be interfered.

ViewDroid [18] is also an app repackaging detection system. It extracts birthmarks as features from user interface components of apps. With these features, view graphs are constructed for next repackaging detection. The evaluation results show that ViewDroid is robust, effective and highly resilient to code obfuscation. However, the graph comparison time grows much with the increment of the number of graph pairs..

DIVILAR [19] is a virtualization-based approach for Android app's self-protection. By hooking into the Dalvik VM, DIVILAR is able to composite the virtual instruction and Dalvik bytecode execution. DIVILAR is robust enough for both static and dynamic analysis, thus, effective for preventing app repackaging. However, the hooking mechanism severely limits the usage of DIVILAR since it requires a huge change in the underlying system.

DroidSim [20] is mainly designed to detect code reuse in Android Apps, especially for repackaged apps and malware variants detection. Compared to the other approaches, it's more accurate and robust. Component-based control flow graph (CB-CFG) is extracted to compute similarity score by DroidSim. An App can be uniquely represented with CB-CFG and author information. The evaluation results show that DroidSim is effective and robust for both repacked apps and malware variants detection. Yet, as it is claimed to be effective, the efficiency of DroidSim is almost not mentioned. The consuming time of construction of CB-CFG and graph-based pair-wise comparison is unclear.

As so many app repackaging detection and analysis approaches have been proposed, a framework for evaluating those algorithms [21] was presented. It is mainly designed to evaluate the performance of anti-obfuscation of detection algorithms. The experiment results show that the framework is able to evaluate detection algorithms broadly and deeply. The framework will present a full view about the strength and weakness of the evaluated algorithm after the evaluation.

7 Conclusion

In this paper we present a scalable cloud-based Android app repackaging detection framework. It is composed of three primary components: market monitor, app feature extractor and app similarity computer. Market monitor observes specific alternative app markets. Once there are apps newly added or updated in these markets, the metadata of apps will be crawled with the downloading of corresponding apk file for feature extraction and similar apps searching. App feature extractor extracts multi-level features. App similarity computer computes the similarities of apps as demanded.

Taking the advantages of cloud computing, the proposed framework is appropriate for large-scale app markets monitoring, features extracting and similarity computing. By using the cloud-based container technology, the implemented prototype is built to be scalable. The evaluation results demonstrate that this framework is able to detect repacked apps in a scalable, fast and effective way.

References

1. Apple App Store, December 2015. https://itunes.apple.com/us/genre/ios/
2. Google Play, December 2015. https://play.google.com/store/

3. Smali, December 2015. https://github.com/JesusFreke/smali/
4. Aliyun, December 2015. http://www.aliyun.com/
5. Redis, December 2015. http://redis.io/
6. Celery, December 2015. http://www.celeryproject.org/
7. Scrapy, December 2015. http://scrapy.org/
8. Docker, December 2015. http://docker.com/
9. Aliyun Container Service, December 2015. http://www.aliyun.com/product/containerservice/
10. Aliyun ECS, December 2015. http://www.aliyun.com/product/ecs/
11. Aliyun OSS, December 2015. http://www.aliyun.com/product/oss/
12. Androguard December 2015. https://github.com/androguard/androguardd
13. Zhou, W., Zhou, Y., Jiang, X., Ning, P.: Detecting repackaged smartphone applications in third-party Android marketplaces. In: Proceedings of the 2nd ACM Conference on Data and Application Security and Privacy (CODASPY), pp. 317–326. ACM (2012)
14. Lindorfer, M., Neugschwandtner, M., Weichselbaum, L., Fratantonio, Y., van der Veen, V., Platzer, C.: ANDRUBIS-1,000,000 apps later: a view on current Android malware behaviors. In: Proceedings of 3rd International Workshop on Building Analysis Datasets and Gathering Experience Returns for Security (BADGERS) (2014)
15. Lindorfer, M., et al.: AndRadar: fast discovery of Android applications in alternative markets. In: Dietrich, S. (ed.) DIMVA 2014. LNCS, vol. 8550, pp. 51–71. Springer, Heidelberg (2014)
16. Crussell, J., Gibler, C., Chen, H.: Attack of the clones: detecting cloned applications on Android markets. In: Foresti, S., Yung, M., Martinelli, F. (eds.) ESORICS 2012. LNCS, vol. 7459, pp. 37–54. Springer, Heidelberg (2012)
17. Zhou, W., Zhou, Y., Grace, M., Jiang, X., Zou, S.: Fast, scalable detection of "Piggybacked" mobile applications. In: Proceedings of the 3rd ACM Conference on Data and Application Security and Privacy (CODASPY), pp. 185–196. ACM (2013)
18. Zhang, F., Huang, H., Zhu, S., Wu, D., Liu, P.: ViewDroid: towards obfuscation-resilient mobile application repackaging detection. In: Proceedings of the 2014 ACM Conference on Security and Privacy in Wireless and Mobile Networks (ACM WiSec), pp. 25–36. ACM (2014)
19. Zhou, W., Wang, Z., Zhou, Y., Jiang, X.: DIVILAR: diversifying intermediate language for anti-repackaging on Android platform. In: Proceedings of the 4th ACM Conference on Data and Application Security and Privacy (CODASPY), pp. 199–210. ACM (2014)
20. Sun, X., Zhongyang, Y., Xin, Z., Mao, B., Xie, L.: Detecting code reuse in Android applications using component-based control flow graph. In: Cuppens-Boulahia, N., Cuppens, F., Jajodia, S., Kalam, A.A.E., Sans, T. (eds.) SEC 2014. IFIP AICT, vol. 428, pp. 142–155. Springer, Heidelberg (2014)
21. Huang, H., Zhu, S., Liu, P., Wu, D.: A framework for evaluating mobile app repackaging detection algorithms. In: Huth, M., Asokan, N., Čapkun, S., Flechais, I., Coles-Kemp, L. (eds.) TRUST 2013. LNCS, vol. 7904, pp. 169–186. Springer, Heidelberg (2013)

Virtualisation

Chameleon: Virtual Machine Migration Supporting Cascading Overload Management in Cloud

Ying Liu[✉]

Services Computing Technology and System Lab, Cluster and Grid Computing Lab,
School of Computer Science and Technology, Huazhong University of Science and Technology,
Wuhan 430074, Hubei, People's Republic of China
yliu1106@gmail.com

Abstract. Virtualization makes the resources management easily in cloud datacenters by enabling virtual machine (VM) migration to eliminate the hotspots. Many migration strategies have been adopted in order to mitigate the resources competition and maintain the VM performance. However, the hotspots are not all accurately flagged without delay in the recent cloud workload and the cascading overloads are probably triggered after VM migration at the same time. In this paper, we present a workload-aware migration strategy called Chameleon targeting the recent cloud workload. Chameleon constructs a novel indicator and the corresponding threshold to flag the hotspots accurately. Chameleon also predicts the resource provision of VM in the complex workload pressure to avoid the secondary overload in the physical machine (PM), which the migrated VM moves to. We performed our evaluation on a virtual datacenter simulated by Xen. Our evaluation results show that Chameleon can flag the hotspots accurately and timely. Furthermore, the policy of resources estimation for the VMs helps Chameleon to make the decision of selecting the under-load PM, in order to mitigate the risk of secondary hotspot.

Keywords: Cloud computing · Resources management · Hotspot · Cascading overload

1 Introduction

Cloud computing is being increasingly used for easing deployment and management of all kinds of computing resources. Many cloud datacenters (such as GAE [1], Amazon cloud service [2]) have adopted virtualization technology (such as Xen [3] and KVM [4]) to multiplex computing resources and facilitate system management. Further, for the clients, in order to obtain the stringent performance guarantees of VMs that they use, the dynamic workload fluctuations should be handled by remapping the computing resources to the corresponding VMs flexibly and timely. The heavily-loaded VMs are allocated more resources if idle resources are available in their PMs or migrated to another PMs, rich in computing resources [5]. Therefore, effective resources management, accurately detecting the hotspots caused by the workload fluctuations and

© Springer International Publishing Switzerland 2016
X. Huang et al. (Eds.): GPC 2016, LNCS 9663, pp. 129–145, 2016.
DOI: 10.1007/978-3-319-39077-2_9

preventing the secondary resources competition after the overload VM migrated, is an important task in the cloud datacenters.

The mainstream virtual machine monitors (VMM), such as Xen, KVM, and VMware ESX server [6], all provide the support the ability of transparent migration [7] for the VMs. VM migration can reduce the resources management complexity in cloud data-centers. However, monitoring the hotspots and initiating VM migration to mitigate the resources shortage are only handled manually in these VMMs. It lacks the enough agility to respond to sudden workload changes.

Further, researchers have studied various kinds of VM migration policies, in aim to load balance [5] or server consolidation [8]. These policies directly support the perform-ance guarantee of VMs against the dynamic workload fluctuations. One of the typical intelligent, autonomous and performance-aware VM migration policies is [5]. It provides an effective model for detecting resources hotspots, determining a new mapping and initiating the necessary migrations that could make the tradeoff between mitigating resources competition and the cost of VM migration.

The existing strategies shed a light on how computing resources can be fully used in cloud. However, there are still some challenges for us to solve. The root cause of these challenges is that the new characteristics of the workload that commonly happen in the recent cloud datacenters [9]. The existing kinds of VM migration policies mentioned before may not better respond to the new characteristics in cloud. To be more specific:

- The resource hotspots are not all accurately detected without delay by the existing approach [5] - a hotspot is flagged if the predefined index (e.g., resource utilization or response time) exceeds an empirical threshold. Based on the recent studies on the trace of cloud [9], the preferred cloud jobs come from web services (search queries, and online document editing and translations). The main characteristics of this kind of job are that their resources requirements vary quickly due to big workload fluc-tuations and at the same time their performance requirements are stringent due to real-time or interactive commercial requirements. Therefore, the approach of flag-ging a hotspot by a fixed predefined value is not reasonable. Firstly, the big workload fluctuations easily produce some small transient resources spikes and a fixed threshold may trigger more needless migrations. Secondly, the empirical threshold determines how aggressively hotspots are flagged. The higher level of threshold implies aggressive migrations at expense of lower resources utilization, while the lower level threshold implies higher resources utilization with the risk of performance violations. In the absence of reliable evaluation method, it is difficult to use a fixed threshold to protect these commercial applications in the complex load pressure. In conclusion, it is not quite clear what would be the right policy to detect the hotspot accurately.

- VM migration might cause the cascading overload on the destination PM. This type of overload may be triggered when the VM migration is performed haphazardly and further resources shortage will occur on the destination PMs. For an existing VM migration policy [10], the effectiveness of migration is validated by the statuses of VMs hosting in the source and destination PMs. That means the destination PM can provide the sufficient resources to welcome the newcomer VM. However, the resources requirements of VMs vary quickly in big workload fluctuation and the resources cost is produced by performance interference among the co-hosting VMs [11]. Finally, the risk of cascading overload on the destination PM increases due to the poor estimation of the spare resources in destination PM. At last, the new hotspot might be detected in the destination PM caused by the migration.

To address the above issues, we propose a workload-aware migration strategy, named Chameleon, for commercial web service in cloud. Comparing with the existing migration strategies, the core differences of Chameleon are: (1) the hotspots are flagged by the request waiting queue of the web service and the value of this threshold is varied as the workload pressure and performance requirements; (2) the risk of cascading overload is mitigated by estimating the resource entitlement of the migrated VMs and other ones hosting in the destination PM according to the workload fluctuation, performance requirements and performance interference [12]. We enable migration strategy, in aim to load balance, through detecting the hotspots accurately (not aggressive or conservative migrations) without delay and seeking the appropriate destination PM (the migrated VMs and the existing ones working regularly) to eliminate the resources competition. The waiting queue presents the pause for client's request and indicates that how busy the web service VM is. The hotspot will be highly sensitive to the manipulation of this variable, comparing with resource utilization or throughput. This variable needs to satisfy within the client's tolerance range and then outside of this range means the hotspot appears. The estimation of resources provision is based on the workload fluctuation and client's performance requirements. We provide an accurate and flexible solution to avoid the secondary overload.

In this paper, in order to eliminate the resources competition among VMs, we propose a migration strategy in dynamic threshold to meet different workload pressure. We plan to define some parameters to derive the client's requests, request waiting queue, resources and performance requirements, and then use the profiling method to find the relationship among these parameters. We will go through a quantitative calculation of the threshold to flag the hotspots based on client's requests and performance requirements and then estimate the resource provision of the related VMs based on their own workload pressure, performance requirements and mutual performance interference. At last, we should choose the appropriate PM in terms of the above estimation to eliminate the first overload and avoid the secondary overload at the same time.

The main features of Chameleon and the contributions of this paper are summarized below:

- Chameleon finds the appropriate monitoring metric to better support hotspot detection. In order to avoid resources waste or performance loss caused by the aggressive or conservative migrations, the limitation of request wait queue is tuned with the status of the corresponding workload pressure and client's performance requirement. It implies how busy the VM is without delay.
- Chameleon provides a scheme to find out the resource provision of VM in the complex workload pressure, which can satisfy interests of both cloud service providers and clients. The accurate resources estimation is benefit to seek the destination PM for the overloaded VMs.

- This paper provides a formal proof that the resource provision can support the corresponding VMs under the circumstance of performance interference from neighbor VMs based on the tolerance level set by clients and finally avoid the secondary hotspots.

The rest of this paper is organized as follows. Section 2 talks the motivation of our design and analysis of related problems. Section 3 presents a statistic method to quantify resources characteristics. Section 4 describes the details of our method for proposing a novel hotspot indicator and how to avoid the secondary hotspot. Section 5 shows the implementation and experimental results. Section 6 discusses the related work of existing migration strategies. Section 7 concludes the paper.

2   Design Motivation and Problem Analysis

In this section, we first introduce what the new characteristics of workload in cloud environment. Next, we discuss why the existing migration policy, in aim to eliminate hotspots, does not work for the novel workload and even might improve the risk of the cascading overload. Finally, we present challenges in practice about implementing the workload-aware VM migration.

2.1   The New Characteristics of the Cloud Load

The statistical properties of cloud load refer to a detailed trace of over 25 million tasks across over 12500 hosts during one month period by Google Inc. [9], which provides several cloud services to clients, such as email and web search. We believe this trace is representative of real-world cloud workloads.

It is generally recognized that cloud computing has been progressively adopted in different scenarios, such as scientific computation and data analysis experiments, etc. [13, 14]. These kinds of applications or experiments are usually composed of a certain number of tasks, with various computation and data needs. In contrast, the preferred cloud loads come from web services and the jobs (such as searching keywords or checking email) are commercial and interactive. The user job is relatively compact and self-contained. Based on above analysis, we can summarize some differences between two kinds of loads from in four aspects:

- Working length (the duration between its submission time and its completion time): about 55 % of web services loads are finished within 10 mins and over 80 % of them only need shorter than 18 mins. On the other hand, the execution time of scientific computation lasts for several days or weeks. Therefore, the first characteristic of new load is short working.
- Submission frequency: the average number of loads submission is 552 per hour for web services and then the frequency of the scientific computation is 126 per hour at most. Additionally, it is noted that web services does not have the strong diurnal periodicity according to the data analysis. Therefore, the second characteristic of new

load is high and stable submission frequency. It implies that the workload fluctuation is big comparing with scientific computation.

- Success rate: about the new load tasks, nearly 60 % of them are abnormal and not finishing the initial goals. The reasons include task failure, killed by its user and losing the source data. It indicates that the performance guarantee is not satisfactory for the client and we need to provide more effective performance guarantee.
- Resource requirements: according to the resource usage data of cloud, the requirements of CPU change greatly for kinds of web service, but memory demand is steady. It indicates that the core concern of resources competition is the hotspot of CPU.

2.2 Existing Migration Policy for Load Balance

VM migration is used to help the cloud service provider to implement load balance and improve the resource utilization of the whole datacenters. This kind of migration policy generally includes three parts: (1) detecting hotspots; (2) selecting the migrated VMs from the overload PM; (3) finding the appropriate destination PM to eliminate the resource competition.

The first part is detecting hotspots. It is responsible for signaling a need for VM migration when the resource competition or performance violation is detected. The universal way of flagging a hotspot is to construct an indicator and the corresponding threshold for each VM or PM. The most common indicators are resource utilization, such as CPU utilization, response time and throughput. For example, the strategy states that if the CPU utilization exceeds 75 %, the hotspot is flagged. However, this method has several drawbacks for the new workload introduced above. First, as the indicator, its prediction is delayed. For example, when we monitor the resource requirements of Apache web service exceed the threshold, the client requests have been already queued for the later execution due to resources competition. The similar situation is for the response time and throughput. Second, the high frequency workload pressure easily produces some small transient resources spikes and then a stricter level threshold may trigger more needless migrations and a more relaxed threshold may cause performance violation. It indicates that a fixed threshold is hard to describe how busy the web service is.

The second part is determining which VM to be migrated from the overload PM. In the existing load balance algorithms, migration overhead and other difficulties (e.g., which VM is the most overload) are fully considered [5] and these researches are also suitable for the new load, so this part is not my concern in this paper.

The third part is selecting the destination PM to end the whole migration. The basic idea of this part is moving VM from the most overloaded PM to the least-overloaded PM. If sufficient resources are not available, then the platform examines the next least-overloaded PM and so on. However, this method has several drawbacks. First, the resources provisions of VMs are hard to confirm due to the high frequency workload pressure. It greatly improves the risk of the secondary hotspot in the destination PM. Second, it has been proven that VM performance is affected by other VMs hosting in the same PM [11]. We should consider the performance interference among co-hosting

VMs into the strategy of PM selection. The neglected resources estimation caused by performance interference also improves the risk of the cascading overload.

According to the above analysis, existing approaches have their own limitation to solve resource competition of new load. We propose a novel migration strategy to detect the hotspot and mitigate the resource competition.

2.3   Challenges

There are several challenges in designing and implementing our migration strategy.

- How to figure out an indicator and the corresponding threshold to flag the hotspot: Each application has its own performance requirements and the workload pressure. The indicator enables to show how busy the detected VM is at any moment and the threshold enables to present the range of client's tolerance in the current workload. So we should design an appropriate method to find the relationship with the client's performance tolerance and the corresponding workload and then construct the indicator and its threshold to guide us for detecting the hotspot.
- How to estimate the appropriate (neither more nor less) resources entitlement for VM in big workload fluctuation: each application has its own resources usage characteristic. Even when the client's performance requirements for the same application are different, the resources requirements are naturally different too. In addition, workload pressure and performance interference both produce the effects on the resources entitlement too. So we should establish a map between workload pressure and the resource entitlement under the circumstance of performance interference from neighbor VMs based on the tolerance level set by clients. The accurate resources estimation can provide a guarantee of decreasing the risk of the secondary hotspot.

3   Strategy Design, Parameters Definition and Profiling

In this section, we first describe Chameleon, our migration strategy design. We then propose a set of parameters to describe the resource characteristics, performance requirements, and workload pressure. Finally, we propose a profiling method to present the relationship between a variety of kernel event and resource characteristics that conform to the observed client's request and performance requirements.

3.1   Strategy Design

The goal of Chameleon is to efficiently maintain the cloud load balance. The whole strategy can be divided into three steps: (1) flagging the hotspots by monitoring the indicator; (2) selecting the migrated VM from the overload PM; (3) confirming the destination PM to end the whole migration and mitigate the resources competition.

The general framework of Chameleon is depicted in Fig. 1. Our system uses Xen to implement such architecture. Each VM runs a component called monitor engine to provide real-time resource usage and client's request information to the hotspot detector and migration management. The hotspot detector uses some types of information to predict the status of each VM. The profile module, working for the migration management, receives the periodic reports of resources usage and maintains a history log file, which is used to compute a VM profile. When a hotspot is flagged, the related VMs' profiles are transmitted to migration management. The VM control is responsible for selecting the migrated VM and the PM control is responsible for confirming the destination PM.

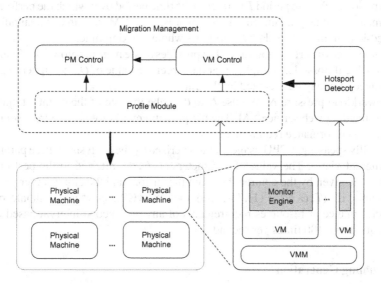

Fig. 1. Architecture of migration strategy. Some VMs run in one PM and share resources with each other.

According to the analysis of the cloud trace mentioned before, the requirements of CPU change greatly for kinds of web service, but memory demand is steady. So in this paper, we focus on managing CPU competition between the co-hosting VMs. To avoid interference between applications, it is assumed that each VM only allows one application to use.

3.2 Parameter Definition

In this section, we propose five parameters to comprehensively define the resources characteristics, performance requirements and workload pressure. These parameters can be used to quantitatively describe the VM profile. For each VM, we describe its characteristics from two aspects: the virtual CPU (vCPU) capacity and the tolerance for resource supply delay. The former aspect represents the vCPU entitlement based on the clients' performance requirements for VMs and the latter one is to show these performance requirements as given by the clients. We define a bigram (α, β) to describe the resources demand: vCPU utilization α and vCPU maximum burst time β. In addition, we also use a bigram (T, O) to demonstrate the tolerance for supply delay: the period of

VM desiring performance guarantees T and the tolerance of performance loss O. In addition, we define a parameter N to present the workload pressure of each VM.

The vCPU demand bigram (α, β): The first and second parameters capture the basic characteristics of vCPU usage by modeling them as a token bucket (α, β) [15]. The parameter (α, β) respectively denote the vCPU utilization and the length of maximum burst time of vCPU consumption provided by the PM.

The period T: We use period T to refer to the time period over which the performance requirements must be guaranteed. In other words, for a VM, resource is available over any fixed-length time interval of T during its whole working time.

The tolerance of performance loss O: It provides a safe margin below 100 % performance available if possible. It implies that the larger the value of O, the higher degree of performance loss may be accepted by the clients.

The workload pressure N: We use N to describe the rate of the client's requests to the corresponding web service VM. The big pressure means we need more resources to maintain the performance requirements.

Generally speaking, vCPU usage is characterized by the analysis of these parameters from different views. The value of parameters (T, O, N), referred to the performance guarantees, is given by the contract between the custom and the cloud server provider. For example, if $(T, O, N) = (1s, 1\%, 100)$, then the vCPU entitlement should be met 99 % performance or resources requirements of any one second interval based on the client request rate 100 times per second.

3.3 Profiling Generation

The profiling model for VM based on the specific workload pressure in this paper is the same as our earlier work [22]. This model can profile the vCPU utilization for each VM based on its performance requirements parameters (T, O) and present the relationship between utilization α and the best value of maximum burst time β.

We define the trace as a pattern of $F = \{(t_i, l_i) | 1 \leq i \leq n\}$ (see Fig. 2), indicating that, the starting moment t_i and duration l_i of process execution for the ith time. We use Linux Trace Toolkit Next Generation as our kernel profiling mechanisms [16] that monitor application behaviors in the VMs.

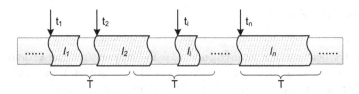

Fig. 2. An example of working trace. Note that t_i is the starting moment of process execution for the ith time, and l_i is the length of the corresponding busy period.

Based on the existing profiling method, the relationship between utilization α and the best value of maximum burst time β is described as:

$$\beta_{opt}(\alpha) = \max\left\{ \sum_{i=u}^{v} l_i - \alpha \cdot (t_v - t_u) \right\} \tag{1}$$

These parameters are used to estimate the resources requirements of the overload VM to decrease the risk of the secondary hotspot.

4 Hotspot Detection and Mitigation

In this section, we first introduce that how to figure out an indicator to flag the hotspots. Next, we propose a method of remapping the overload VM.

4.1 Hotspot Detection

This section shows the novel indicator for hotspot flagging based on the web service workload. It is keenly perceptive for the business of the VM in the recent load and benefits for maintaining the client's performance.

When a group of client's requests ask for the services (e.g., Apache web service or Mysql database service), if the computing resources are inadequate, part of the requests are got into the waiting-queue status, which means that these requests are not able to be immediately scheduled as they are submitted. This mechanism can be used for constructing the indicator.

Firstly, for each $VM_i(O_i, T_i, N_i)$, the rate of maximum tolerable waiting queue is $N_i \cdot O_i$ requests per second. If the number is detected beyond this value, it means the recent resources entitlement cannot guarantee the client's performance requirements. The hotspot is flagged timely. Secondly, we define the time interval of two nearby waiting requests as Δt and it is treated as the hotspot indicator in our strategy. In order to protect the performance requirements, the constraint expresses that:

$$2/\Delta t \leq N_i \cdot O_i \tag{2}$$

Then

$$\Delta t \geq 2/(N_i \cdot O_i) \tag{3}$$

Therefore the hotspot indicator is the time interval of any two nearby waiting requests, and the corresponding threshold η is $2/(N_i \cdot O_i)$. When the time interval is less than the threshold ($\Delta t < \eta$), it means that the hotspot is detected.

From this inequality (3), we can find two shining points to help resources management in cloud datacenters: (1) when load pressure is none $(N_i = 0)$, it shows that there is no requests are got into the waiting-queue status ($\Delta t \geq +\infty$). Therefore, even the resource utilization presents a short peak in this moment, the migration is still needless, because there are no work requests for this detected VM after the recent loads are done. This indicator successfully evades the needless migrations in this situation; (2) when the performance loss is unbearable $(O_i = 0)$, the waiting queue should be empty too $(\Delta t \geq +\infty)$. It means that once a client's request is got into the wait-queue status, the migration should be triggered for eliminating resources competition whether how much resources are being used.

4.2 Hotspot Mitigation

It is clear that the resources shortage can be detected by the hotspot indicator. Therefore, we should propose a method to find the appropriate PM to host the overload VM and we wish the new hotspot is not flagged in this PM as long as possible.

In order to avoid the secondary resources competition, we should estimate the resources requirements of migrated VM and the spare resources of the candidate underload PM accurately. We consider the performance interference among the co-hosting VMs into the resources estimation. A PM can accept new VMs as long as the existing co-hosting VMs work normally. There are still sufficient remaining resources existing to meet the requirements of the new VMs. We express the constraint that a viable configuration must respect as follows.

Firstly, for each $VM_i(\alpha_i, \beta_i, T_i, O_i, N_i)$, the allocated vCPU working time is $(\alpha_i \cdot t + \beta_i)$ in any period t. Then, the system should allocate $(\alpha_i \cdot T_i + \beta_{opt}(\alpha_i)) \cdot (1 - O_i)$ resources to the ith VM during period T_i. So the resource entitlement of VM_i is $(\alpha_i + \beta_{opt}(\alpha_i)/T_i) \cdot (1 - O_i)$ for normal work alone.

Secondly, the vCPU requirements of the existing and new VMs must be satisfied by the PM. The mathematical description of the VM placement constraint is that: the aggregate of all the vCPU requirements including the new one cannot exceed the physical capacity. It is clear that the PM must provide performance guarantee to all the VMs in it. Therefore, the constraint expresses as that:

$$\sum_{i=1}^{k+1} (\alpha_i \cdot t + \beta_{opt}(\alpha_i)) \cdot (1 - O_i) \leq C \cdot t \tag{4}$$

$$\min(T_1, \ldots, T_{k+1}) \leq t \leq \max(T_1, \ldots, T_{k+1})$$

Where C denotes the number of processing units of the PM owned, k denotes the number of the existing VMs, $k + 1$ is the new one. The constraint inequality can optimize as follow:

$$\sum_{i=1}^{k+1} \left(\alpha_i + \max\left\{\sum_{i=u}^{v} l_i - \alpha_i \cdot (t_v - t_u)\right\} \middle/ T_{\min}\right) \cdot (1 - O_i) \leq C \tag{5}$$

$$T_{\min} = \min(T_1, \ldots, T_{k+1})$$

From this inequality (5), we can find that the resource entitlement of VM_i is $(\alpha_i + \beta_{opt}(\alpha_i)/T_i) \cdot (1 - O_i)$, and $T_{\min} = \min(T_1, \ldots \ldots, T_{k+1})$ represents the most stringent performance guarantee among the VMs, which host in the same PM with VM_i. Based on the above analysis, for each of VM_i, its resource entitlement contains the resources cost produced by performance interference and resources requirements for normal work. The PMs, which conform to the inequality (5), are all qualified for the destination of the migrated VM, but the best one is that the remaining resources are the largest after the migration is operated.

5   Experimental Evaluation

In this section, we validate the soundness of our strategy and the related formulas. The test bed for our profiling and follow-up experiments consists of a cluster of five DELL PowerEdge R710 physical servers, each with two 2.27 GHz Intel Xeon E5620 quad-core processors and 128 GB memory running Red Hat Enterprise Linux AS release 6 [17]. We use Xen 4.5.0 as the virtual machine monitor on each physical server, and all VMs run the 3.19 version of the Linux kernel [18] patched with the Linux Trace Toolkit Next Generation version 2.4.2. The processing unit of each VM is one core with a memory of 512 MB.

To profile an application hosting in the VM, we run it on a VM and use the remaining VMs to generate the workload for profiling. We use the RUBiS 1.4 [19] benchmark to generate the workload for the Apache web server (version 2.2.21) and Mysql database server (version 5.1.62). To avoid confusion in terminology, we use "Apache web server VM" and "Mysql database server VM" to refer to the two VMs that are used to host the Apache web server and Mysql database server software respectively.

The first part of experiment presents the profiling of two commonly used web service, hosting in the VMs. Our experimental results show the relationship between performance requirements and resources characteristics. The second part of experiment focuses on testing the formula of resources entitlement for a VM, and proves that our method of resources estimation benefits for mitigating the first hotspot and avoiding the second one. The third part of experiment presents the advantages of our hotspot indicator: (1) flagging the hotspot accurately and timely; (2) reducing the unnecessary migration.

5.1   Profiling vCPU Usage

In this section, we profile two kinds of commonly web service VMs (Apache web server VM and Mysql database server VM). We now present some results from our experiments.

Figure 3(a) depicts the vCPU probability function $U(x)$ of an Apache web server VM. The corresponding workload is generated by the RUBiS benchmark using 200 concurrent clients and the value of parameter $T = 1s$. As shown, the Y-axis (Probability) represents performance requirement of the profiled VM. For example, if the value of Y-axis is one ($O = 0\%$), it means the performance requirements should be met 100 % at any time. Figure 3(b) describes the valid $(\alpha, \beta_{opt}(\alpha))$ pairs for the vCPU usage. Obviously, depending on the specified tolerance of performance loss O for each VM, the corresponding (α, β_{opt}) pair can be chosen from this figure. Similarly, Fig. 3(c) describes (α, β_{opt}) pairs of another VM, hosting Mysql database server. Its workload and performance requirement are the same as that of the Apache web server VM. For our test environment, it is easy to find that the main job of our Apache web server is responding the clients' requests in RUBiS. These requests are more involved in CPU but not I/O.

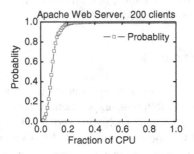

(a) Probability distribution function

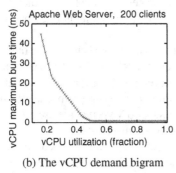

(b) The vCPU demand bigram

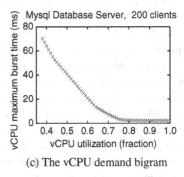

(c) The vCPU demand bigram

Fig. 3. Profile of the VMs using the RUBiS benchmark. The number of concurrent clients is 200.

On the contrary, the main job of Mysql database server is accessing to kinds of data, so it is more referred to I/O. Through the test (Y-axis of Fig. 3(b) and (c)), I/O wait of the database server is longer than the Apache web server. The test results are verified by the theoretical analysis.

5.2   Resources Estimation for VM

In this section, our experiments prove the method for resources estimation is feasible for the VM. We select the appropriate destination PM to mitigate the hotspots and avoid the secondary overload, provided that we estimate the sufficient resources to the corresponding VMs. The first step is examining the single VM and the second step is about multiple VMs co-hosting together. These multiple VMs can be interpreted as the migrated VM and other VMs hosting in the candidate destination PM.

In the first step, we compare the performance metric under different conditions with the VM performance on an unlimited mode (allocate resources to the VM as much as possible). The rationality of these performance gaps shows the precision of resource estimation for a single VM.

The subject of the first group experiment is the Apache web server. We examine its performance metric (by measuring throughput in requests/s) for the default RUBiS workload, using 200 concurrent clients. We test the throughputs in four sets of performance requirements defined by the performance parameters (T, O): $(1s, 0\%), (1s, 1\%), (1s, 5\%), (1s, 30\%)$. The detailed results are shown in the second column of Table 1. As shown, provisioning based on 100 % ($O = 0\%$) requirements yields performance that is comparable to running the VM on an unlimited mode. Provisioning based on 99 % ($O = 1\%$) and 95 % ($O = 5\%$) requirements results in a small degradation in throughput. The resource estimation based on performance requirements can cause throughput degradation, but it is tolerable within the permissible range of 1 % or 5 %. The results demonstrate that the idea of our profile method and the resource entitlement formula for single VM are feasible. We estimate the resources provisions are fully based on the client's performance requirements. Table 1 also shows that provisioning based on the requirements ($O = 30\%$) results in a substantial fall in throughout, indicating that our resources allocation strategy is reasonable and the assignment of resources is neither more nor less. We repeat the second group of the experiments the same as the first group, except that the subject of experiments is Mysql database server. The third column of Table 1 plots all the results.

Table 1. Performance of two web service VM based on different degree of performance requirements

Application	Apache	Mysql
Metric	Throughput (req/s)	Throughput (transactions/s)
Unlimited	36.36	28.42
$O = 0\%$	36.02	28.15
$O = 1\%$	35.78	28.01
$O = 5\%$	33.16	27.79
$O = 30\%$	18.73	11.37

In the second step, we verify the method of resources estimation among multiple co-hosting VMs by examining their average performance. The test procedure is that: We deploy the VMs one by one in the same PM. Before a new VM coming, we note the average throughput of the existing VMs in this PM. But it is noteworthy that in this test, even the fifth and follow-up VMs join this PM, we still note the average throughput of the first three VMs.

The subject of the first group experiment is the Apache web server. We examine its performance metric (by measuring throughput in requests/s) for the default RUBiS workload, using 200 concurrent clients. The first three VMs based on the performance requirements $(T, O) = (2s, 5\%)$. From the fourth VM, we adjust the performance requirements $(T, O) = (1s, 5\%)$. The results presents in the Fig. 4. The horizontal coordinates show the number of VMs hosted in the PM and the vertical coordinates show the average throughput of VMs in this PM (only compute the first three VMs). In the solid dot line, the resources estimations for these tested

VMs are not considering performance interference. In contrast, the resources are allocated more against performance interference in the soft dot line. It is clearly that the throughput is down due to interference (the solid dot line). The two lines coincide in the first three VMs because the most stringent performance guarantee among the VMs changes from the fourth VM coming $(T_1 = T_2 = T_3 > T_4 = T_5 = \dots = T_{k+1} = 1s)$. We repeat the second group of the experiments the same as the first group, except that the subject of experiments is Mysql database server. The results presents in the Fig. 5. It is proved that we should allocate more resources against the performance interference among co-hosting VMs. Therefore when the new destination PM is being selected, we can give a good guide for resource estimation and then secondary overload may be avoided as long as possible in the destination PM.

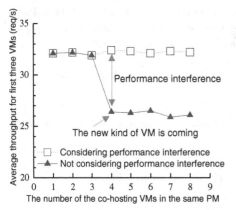

Fig. 4. The average throughput for the first three VMs, running the Apache web server.

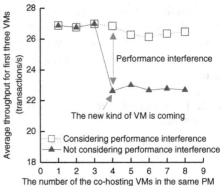

Fig. 5. The average throughput for the first three VMs, running the Mysql database server.

5.3 Hotspot Indicator Effectiveness

In this section, our experiments demonstrate the effectiveness of our novel hotspot indicator. The test procedure is that: We deploy two Apache web service VMs for the default RUBiS workload and the corresponding performance requirements both are $(T, O) = (1s, 0\%)$. The only difference is that the workload pressure of VM_1 is 100 concurrent clients and the other VM_2 is 150 concurrent clients. To build a situation where a VM gets heavily-load unpredictably, we change the workload of VM_1 to 200 concurrent clients. In order to present the resource competition in the PM due to workload fluctuation, we create a certain number of VMs running CPU-bound workloads to achieve the goal of CPU competition. At last, we need to migrate VM_1 to mitigate hotspot.

The results are shown in Fig. 6. The horizontal coordinates are the elapsed time and the vertical coordinates are the throughput of the VMs. When we execute the VM_1 only, it successfully handles the workload even after is increased (situation 1 in Fig. 6(a)). When we execute two VMs $(VM_1 \, and \, VM_2)$, the normal work lasts until the workload of

VM_1 changed (situation 2 in Fig. 6(b)). It means that the hotspot is flagged and we need VM migration (Fig. 6(c)). In red zone of the Fig. 6(a) and green zone of Fig. 6(b), the throughput are both keeping rising trend. If we use the throughput as the hotspot indicator, the needless migration may trigger in red zone and the hotspot detecting may be delayed in green zone. In contrast, our indicator can flag the hotspot when the workload is changed in situation 2 not in situation 1.

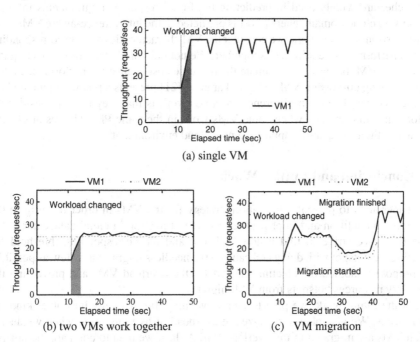

Fig. 6. Profile of the web server VM using the RUBiS benchmark. The number of concurrent clients is 200 (Color figure online).

6   Related Work

Firstly, we present existing research about migration strategy and analyze the detailed difference with our work. Secondly, we show existing work that predicts future resource usage of VMs based on the historic data as it is an important aspect of avoiding the secondary hotspots.

The existing migration strategy: Timothy et al. [5] present how to detect and eliminate the hotspots in cloud datacenters. In this paper, the hotspot indicator is defined as CPU utilization and the threshold is the empirical value 75 %. It uses the historical data to predict the resources provision for VMs to support VM migration. It also defines the VSR to describe the resources shortage and migration overhead. This parameter is used to seek which VM should be migrated. In our paper, we first follow the strategy of VM selection. It fully considers the migration cost during the load balance. Secondly, we propose a novel hotspot indicator to flag the resource competition. Our indicator detects the hotspot accurately and timely and more importantly, it can avoid triggering the needless migration in some cases mentioned in Sect. 4. Thirdly, we estimate the resources provision based on the client's performance and workload pressure. Furthermore, we consider the resources cost produced by performance interference among co-hosting VMs. It decreases the risk of secondary hotspots in destination PM.

The existing method of estimating resources requirements: machine learning-based approaches are widely used in predicting the future resources requirements in many domains. In cloud domain, energy cost is predicted in the interference-aware VMs [20]. In comparison with our work, we consider the VM characteristics and the corresponding client's performance requirements together. We not only predict the resources requirements for a VM, but also can estimate the resource cost against the performance interference among co-hosting VMs. Urgaonkar et al. [21] presents a predicting method for resource saving. The main difference from our work is that they do not consider the performance interference when some VMs work in the same PM. The result of such resource estimation cannot support the new cloud environment.

7   Conclusion and Future Work

This paper aims to present a migration strategy for the VMs in order to mitigate the resources competition and improve the resource utilization in cloud datacenter at the same time. We strive to find a new indicator and the corresponding threshold for detecting the hotspot with delay and causing the needless migrations as few as possible. We propose a method of selecting the PM for the overload VMs and preventing the secondary resources hotspots from VM migration.

For the future work, we plan to merge our migration strategy into other kinds of applications. We also plan to analyze the overhead of live migration when we decide which VMs are migrated in the overload PM. At last, we plan to compare the hotspot indicator presented in this paper to the ones available in the other related paper.

References

1. Google App Engine. http://appengine.google.com
2. Amazon Elastic Compute Cloud. http://aws.amazon.com/ec2/
3. Barham, P., Dragovic, B.K., Fraser, B., et al.: Xen and the art of virtualization. In: 19th ACM Symposium on Operating Systems Principles, pp. 164–177. ACM Press, New York, USA (2003)
4. Habib, I.: Virtualization with KVM. Linux J. **2008**, 8 (2008)
5. Wood, T., Shenoy, P., Venkataramani, A., et al.: Black-box and gray-box strategies for virtual machine migration. In: 4th USENIX Conference on Networked Systems Design & Implementation, pp. 229–242. USENIX Association, Cambridge, MA, USA (2007)
6. VMware ESX. http://www.vmware.com/products/esx
7. Clark, C., Fraser, K., Hand, S., et al.: Live migration of virtual machines. In: 2nd USENIX Symposium on Networked Systems Design and Implementation (NSDI 2005), pp. 273–286. ACM Press, Boston, MA, USA (2005)

8. Hermenier, F., Lorca, X., Menaud, J.M., et al.: Entropy: a consolidation manager for clusters. In: 2009 ACM SIGPLAN/SIGOPS International Conference on Virtual Execution Environments, pp. 41–50. ACM Press, Washington DC, USA (2009)
9. Di, S., Kondo, D., Cirne, W.: Characterization and comparison of cloud versus grid workloads. In: 2012 IEEE International Conference on Cluster Computing, pp. 230–238. IEEE Computer Society, Beijing, China (2012)
10. Ghribi, C., Hadji, M., Zeghlache, D.: Energy efficient VM scheduling for cloud data centers: exact allocation and migration algorithms. In: 13th IEEE/ACM International Symposium on Cluster, Cloud and Grid Computing, pp. 671–678. IEEE Press, Delft, Netherlands (2013)
11. Nathuji, R., Kansal, A., Ghaffarkhah, A.: Q-clouds: managing performance interference effects for Qos-aware clouds. In: 5th European Conference on Computer Systems, pp. 237–250. ACM Press, New York, USA (2010)
12. Koh, Y., Knauerhase, R.C., Brett, P., et al.: An analysis of performance interference effects in virtual environments. In: IEEE Symposium on Performance Analysis of Systems and Software, pp. 200–209. IEEE Press, SAN JOSE, CA, USA (2007)
13. Etinski, M., Corbalan, J., Labarta, J., Valero, M.: Optimizing job performance under a given power constraint in HPC centers. In: 1st International Conference on Green Computing, pp. 257–267. IEEE Computer Society, Hangzhou, China (2010)
14. Bouchenak, S., De Palma, N., Hagimont, D., Taton, C.: Autonomic management of clustered applications. In: 2006 IEEE International Conference on Cluster Computing, pp. 230–238. IEEE Computer Society, Barcelona (2006)
15. Tang, P., Tai, T.: Network traffic characterization using token bucket model. In: IEEE International Conference on Computer Communications, pp: 256–268. IEEE Press, New York, USA (1999)
16. LTTng Project. http://lttng.org
17. Love, R.: Linux Kernel Development, 2nd edn. Novell Press, USA (2005)
18. Tickoo, O., Iyer, R., Illikkal, R., et al.: Modeling virtual machine performance: challenges and approaches. ACM SIGMETRICS Perform. Eval. Rev. **37**, 55–60 (2010)
19. RUBiS benchmark. http://rubis.ow2.org/
20. Berl, Andreas, et al.: Energy-efficient cloud computing. Comput. J. **53**(7), 1045–1051 (2010)
21. Urgaonkar, B., Shenoy, P., Roscoe, T.: Resource overbooking and application profiling in shared hosting platforms. In: 5th Symposium on Operating Systems Design and Implementation (OSDI 2002), pp. 239–254. ACM Press, Boston, MA, USA (2002)
22. Liu, Y.: Sponge: an oversubscription strategy supporting performance interference management in cloud. Commun. China **12**(11), 1–14 (2015)

Heterogeneous Computation Migration on LLVM

Tyng-Yeu Liang[✉] and Yu-Jie Lin

Department of Electrical Engineering, National Kaohsiung University of Applied Sciences,
Kaohsiung, Taiwan
lty@mail.ee.kuas.edu.tw, jaredlin@hpds.ee.kuas.edu.tw

Abstract. In past decades, the development of mobile applications was limited due to lack of enough computational power. To resolve this problem, the framework of mobile cloud computing (MCC) was proposed for offloading the massive computation tasks of mobile applications onto cloud centers for execution. However, the computational power of mobile devices recently has received a great promotion, and the bandwidth and reliability of wireless networks has been significantly improved. These development advances make it practical for mobile devices to share the computational tasks of cloud centers. In other words, the direction of resource supply chain can be from clouds to mobile devices but also from mobile devices to clouds. This is useful for integrating the computational power of mobile devices and cloud resources to serve mobile or cloud users. To achieve this goal, this paper is aimed at the development of an efficient scheme of computation migration based on LLVM for addressing the problem of resource heterogeneity and dynamicity in MCC. With the support of the proposed scheme, user programs can dynamically move between mobile devices and cloud servers for the load balance, QoS and reliability of MCC.

Keywords: Mobile cloud computing · Mobile devices · Computation migration · LLVM · Reliability

1 Introduction

Nowadays, mobile devices such as smart phones and tablets have replaced PCs and laptops to become the main equipment for users to handle their daily staffs including communication, information searching, shopping, working, learning and gaming under the support of an enormous number of devise APPs. However, because of lack of enough computational capability and electrical power, the past application development of mobile devices was not effectively extended to the area of high performance computing. To address this issue, the framework of mobile cloud computing was proposed to support mobile devices for performing high performance computing applications.

The basic idea of MCC is to offload the massive computation tasks of applications from mobile devices to cloud servers for execution. This solution indeed successfully releases the application development of mobile devices from the problem of lacking enough computational power. Many mobile applications such as M-learning [1] and M-healthcare [2] have been developed based on the MCC framework. In these applications, mobile devices usually are resource consumers while clouds play resource

© Springer International Publishing Switzerland 2016
X. Huang et al. (Eds.): GPC 2016, LNCS 9663, pp. 146–162, 2016.
DOI: 10.1007/978-3-319-39077-2_10

providers. Nonetheless, this relationship of resource demand and supply has become not always one directional because the computational capability and electrical power of mobile devices have been greatly promoted.

Generally speaking, most of modern mobile devices have 1–4 GB RAM, quad core ARM CPU, and many-core GPU such as Adreno, PowerVR, and NVIDIA Tegra. They become comparable with common PCs in computational capability, and can continuously work for more than a dozen hours by the support of long-termed battery and mobile power supply. On the other hand, the bandwidth of wireless network technology has reached to hundreds Mbps through LTE. Consequently, many mobile APPs has been proposed for resolving research problems by using the computational power of mobile devices. For example, BOINC [3] allows users to donate the spare time of their mobile devices for different science research projects. Addi [4] and Octave [5] allows users to perform mathematical computation and plotting by means of MATLAB instructions and scripts in mobile devices. CCTools [6] and C4droid [7] supports a C/C++ programming for users to develop and execute scientific-computing applications on mobile devices. This development trend shows that mobile devices have drawn high attention from researchers. It also implies that mobile devices can play not only resource consumers but also providers in the architecture of MCC. Since the number of mobile devices has reached to billions, the computation power hidden in mobile devices is amazing and waiting for exploration. For clouds, they can offload tasks to mobile devices for reducing load pressure in rush hours. For mobile devices, they can share their own resources with others, and thereby do not always rely on the assistance of clouds any more.

To achieve this goal, the first challenge is to overcome the problem of resource heterogeneity in task migration. For this issue, many past studies [8, 9] were focused on JVM since Java is frequently used for developing portable applications, and Java bytecodes are executable on heterogeneous resources through JVM. However, Java programs cannot directly access system information and hardware through JVM. Consequently, Java is not as good as C/C++ in the performance of I/O. Although Java Native Interface (JNI) is effective for resolving this problem, it increases the programming complexity and execution cost of user applications. On the other hand, most of scientific and high performance computing (HPC) applications are developed by C/C++ instead of Java because of execution performance consideration. Even they are developed by Java. They are not always executable on any mobile devices because of different Java or JVM versions.

By contrast, Low Level Virtual Machine (LLVM) [10] has not the above problems existing in JVM. LLVM is a lightweight virtual machine. It can be divided into frontend compiler and backend executor. The front-end compiler, i.e., Clang is responsible to translate user programs into LLVM IRs while the backend executor converts and LLVM IRs into optimized native codes at runtime according to the architecture of target processor first and then executes the native codes by the target processor by means of MCJIT. Because the native codes generated by LLVM are easily linked with external libraries and able to directly access hardware, LLVM does not degrade the performance of CUDA and OpenCL API while JVM does. This advantage is very important for cloud and mobile computing because more and more clouds and mobile devices has supported GPU for HPC and big data applications.

As previously discussed, this paper is aimed at design and implementation of an efficient heterogeneous computation migration (simply called HCM) scheme based on LLVM. With the support of this scheme, the programs of mobile and cloud users can roam around the MCC architecture according to network bandwidth, electrical power, or computational capability for obtaining a good execution performance and fault tolerance. We have evaluated the efficiency of proposed scheme in this paper. Our experimental results have shown that the cost of proposed scheme is acceptable or negligible for the performance of tested applications.

The rest of this paper is organized as follows. Section 2 discusses related work. Sections 3 and 4 describe the framework and implementation of HCM, respectively. Section 5 evaluates and discusses the efficiency of HCM. Section 6 gives a number of conclusions for this paper and our future work.

2 Related Work

In 1980s, process migration [11–13] was a hot research topic for addressing the issues of load balance and reliability of distributed systems. The main advantage of process migration is transparent for user applications since it is implemented at the system level [14, 15]. However, this approach suffers from the problem of residual dependencies that is a migrated process relies on a host for data structures or functional supports such as opened file descriptors and shared memory segments after this process moves away from the host. Consequently, it is difficultly applied to real applications.

By contrast, virtual machine (VM) migration [16, 17] can avoid the problems of process migration because it moves an entire OS, and all of its applications as one unit from one physical machine to another. It is frequently applied for the resource and energy management of cloud computing since VM software such as Xen, KVM and VMware is the main solution used for resource virtualization and sharing in data centers. Nonetheless, the time cost of virtual migration is so long as to degrade the performance of applications especially when the number of memory pages copied to the new VM is large or network speed is extremely slow. For this problem, live VM migration [18] is an effective solution for reducing the negative impact of migration cost because it allows applications to continue running during migration process.

The process of live VM migration can be classified into three phases: push, stop-and-copy and pull [19]. In the push phase, the original virtual machine continues to run on source node while simultaneously copies the recently used pages to the new virtual machine on destination node. For data consistency, the pages modified during migration process must be sent to the new virtual machine. In the stop-and-copy phase, the original virtual machine stops to copy the remaining dirty pages to the new virtual machine, and then the new virtual machine starts. In the pull phase, the new virtual machine executes and fetches necessary pages from the old one when it accesses the pages and the pages are not present in local memory. Most of proposed VM migration algorithms consist of one or two of these phases to reduce down time and total migration time. For example, the Pre-copy algorithm [20] mixes the push phase and the stop-and-copy phase. It adds a threshold condition to limit the time cost of sending data pages and estimates the cost of data consistency maintenance and the update rate of dirty pages to decide when to stop the original virtual machine for sending all the dirty pages to the new virtual machine. It resolves the problem of frequent page re-transmission in the push phase, and reduces down time and total migration time. In contrast, the Post-copy algorithm [21] mixes the pull phase and the stop-and-copy phase in order to delay the copy of memory pages until they are accessed. Compared to the Pre-copy algorithm, the advantage of the Post-copy algorithm is to avoid page re-transmission. Each page is transmitted at most once while the performance of user applications suffers from a large amount of page faults as the new virtual machine frequently is faulty on accessing the absent memory pages.

On the other hand, a stack-on-demand solution based on JVM [22] was proposed for offloading massive computation tasks from mobile devices to clouds to speed up the completion of these tasks. This solution only sends the top stack frame and the currently called object method to clouds for execution. Consequently, it can reduce the communication cost of task migration to the minimal. However, it requires the client keeps connection with the server for exchanging the parameter data and execution result of the migrated object method.

Apparently, VM migration is not suitable for task migration between mobile devices and clouds because the migration cost is too expensive to be compensated in wireless networks. The worse is the memory space of mobile devices is not big enough for storing the image of VM. Although the Pre-copy and Post-copy algorithms can effectively reduce downtime or/and total migration time, they are not realistic for task migration between mobile devices and clouds because the operating system of mobile devices does not allow users to define the page-fault handler. On the other hand, the requirement of the stack-on-demand approach is difficult to be satisfied because the connection between client and server is easily broken due to the movement of mobile devices in wireless networks. In addition, it produces a lot of data communication when user applications are implemented by iteratively calling object methods.

By contrast, the proposed scheme is a lightweight process migration while it is independent to hardware or operating system because it is implemented based on LLVM. Although pure stop-and-copy migration increases down time as well as the number of copied memory pages, it is easy to be implemented without data-consistency maintenance. In addition, the number of memory pages transmitted for task migration on LLVM is much less than that of VM migration. Therefore, the proposed migration scheme adopts the pure stop-and-copy algorithm. For reducing migration cost, the proposed scheme compresses transferred data to minimize the amount of data transferred over wireless networks.

3   Framework

The framework of HCM is as shown in Fig. 1. This framework is mainly composed of sensor, server, and broker. The HCM sensor aims at monitoring resources, cyclically reporting resource states such as load or remaining electrical-power capability to the HCM broker, and sending a migration semaphore to the HCM server when it finds the local resource states has satisfied the migration condition set by resource owner or administrator. The HCM server is mainly used to execute user programs, and backup or restore the runtime contexts of user programs on LLVM for task migration. Since mobile devices and cloud servers are regarded as the same in the framework of HCM, both of these two different resources can play source or destination nodes in task migration. The registered information mainly consists of their network location, and condition of accepting migrated tasks. On the other hand, the HCM broker is responsible to allocate resources for task migration and play an agent for mobile devices or cloud servers to migrate their tasks to new resources for execution, and cache the execution results of migrated tasks.

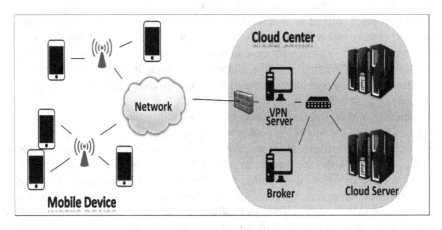

Fig. 1. Framework of HCM

In the HCM framework, any user program is compiled into an executable file of LLVM IRs. When the program is executed, the executable file of this program is loaded and executed by LLVM by means of MCJIT. All the HCM servers and the HCM broker are connected with a virtual private network for secure and communication across different network domains. The direction of task migration can be mobile device to cloud (M2C), cloud to mobile device (C2M) and mobile device to mobile device (M2M) no matter where source and destination node are located in networks. Because HCM currently supports only batch but interactive tasks, the I/O of user programs is redirected into file accesses. The user scenario and the process of task migration in the HCM framework are described as follows.

As shown in Fig. 2, when a HCM server is initialized at a mobile device or cloud server, it joins into the virtual private network of HCM first, and then collects and registers local resource information to the HCM broker. After the resource registration is finished, the HCM server waits for executing local tasks or remote tasks migrated from other cloud servers or mobile devices. On the other hand, it creates a background thread to perform the HCM sensor in order to cyclically detect local load state or electrical power capability. If the HCM sensor finds the resource state satisfies the migration condition set by resource owner or administrator, it will set a migration flag as true; otherwise, it will set the flag as false. When the HCM server accepts a task of executing a program submitted by the local node, it automatically modifies the executable of the program by inserting a number of checkpoints into the entry and departure points of basic blocks or function calls in the program first, and then dispatches the user program onto LLVM for execution. When LLVM executes the user program, it checks the migration flag at the checkpoints inserted by the HCM server. If it finds the migration flag is set as true, it will immediately invoke the HCM server to retrieve and backup the context of the execution stack and memory segments including data and heap of the program from local memory into an image file. Then, it sends the image, executable and I/O files of the user program to the HCM broker for task migration. After receiving a migration request and the files of the migrated program, the HCM broker selects a new execution node from the pool of registered resources according to the task-acceptance conditions and the current states of resources. Next, it relays the files of the migrated program to the HCM server of the new execution node, and then the new HCM server rebuilds the context of execution stack and memory segments in the local memory and resumes the execution of the user program on LLVM. After the execution of the migrated program is finished, the new HCM server sends the output file of the user program to the HCM broker. Finally, the HCM broker caches the output file in the local file system until the old HCM server on the original execution node fetches the output file of the program.

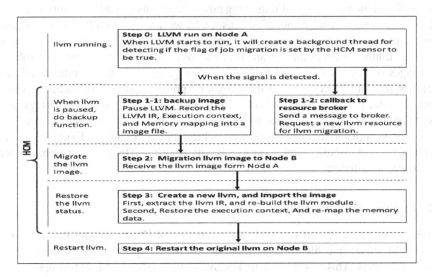

Fig. 2. Flow of task migration in the HCM framework

It is worthy to say that this study adds three command parameters into LLVM LLI for the HCM scheme as shown in Table 1. "–remote-mode" is used to set the local node as HCM server. The "–broker-ip" and "–broker-port" parameters is used to set up the network location of HCM broker for the HCM server. The HCM broker must have a public IP for connection with the HCM servers and sensors on mobile devices and cloud servers.

Table 1. Commands of HCM

Command parameter	Description
–remote-mode=?	Maybe CLIENT or SERVER
–broker-ip=?	HCM broker public IP
–broker-port=?	HCM broker binding port

4   Implementation

The main jobs of implementing the proposed scheme consists of resource monitoring, program recompilation and standard I/O redirection. The details of these things are described as follows.

4.1   Resource Monitoring

Currently, the proposed scheme allows resource owners to set the conditions of performing task migration according to remaining power capability, CPU/Memory usages. When the percentage of remaining power capability or CPU/Memory usages is below or above a threshold, the HCM sensor will set the migration flag as TRUE, and then the process of task migration will be performed. To simplify our work, we made use of the Linux system primitives and files such as mpstat and /proc/meminfo to obtain the usages of current CPU and memory of user programs. On the other hand, we exploited the acpi function to get the remaining power capability of mobile devices. Since the information of these resource states is represented by means of strings, it is easy to implement the HCM sensor by Shell script. However, Android does not support bash, mpstat, acpi and the string tools such as head, tail, awk and wc. To overcome this problem, we ported these functions and tools with Android SDK for the implementation of resource monitoring.

4.2   Program Recompilation

In this paper, we developed a LLVM-IR re-compiler for HCM to automatically rewrite the LLVM executable files of user programs by inserting checkpoints, backup and restore functions. This re-compiler makes use of the toolkit of LLVM to operate the syntax trees of user programs. The process of executing a user program on LLVM is divided into five phases as shown in Fig. 3. The first phase is to load the executable of the user program, which is compiled by Clang into LLVM IRs. The second phase is to create a module, and then pass the LLVM IRs of the user program to the module. The third is to translate the LLVM IRs of the user programs into native codes based on the architecture of execution processor. The last two phases are to build a MCJIT execution engine and execute the native code with the MCJIT engine. Accordingly, the proposed

LLVM-IR re-compiler is used to rewrite the executable of the user program between the second phase and the third one.

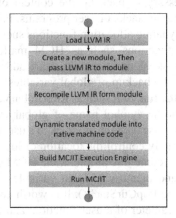

Fig. 3. Modified execution flow of user programs on LLVM

The recompilation flow of a user program is as shown in Fig. 4. First, the re-compiler register the functions and symbols of HCM to the LLVM parser in order for making these functions and symbols linkable with user programs. Second, it partitions the user program into a number of basic blocks, which are insert by checkpoints. Third, it collects the all of local variables including static or dynamic in each function, and inserts a log function for storing these local variable in a stack. Forth, it scans and stores all the function pointers and global variables of the user program into a symbol table. Finally, it inserts a backup and store function for basic blocks to back up and restore the context of the program in task migration.

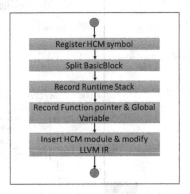

Fig. 4. Flow of program recompilation

Although the proposed re-compiler is to rewrite the LLVM IRs of user programs, here we use an example program presented by means of C but LLVM IRs in order to make it easy to understand the process of program recompilation, as shown in Fig. 5.

The first step of program recompilation is to insert the functions of storing the information of the memory image of the user program executed on LLVM. For live migration on LLVM, it is necessary to back up the content of heap, global variables,
function points and the runtime stacks of user programs. For the backup of heap, the
HCM server replaces the dynamic allocation functions such as malloc(), calloc() and
realloc() with the HCM functions such as HCM_malloc(), HCM_calloc() and
HCM_realloc() to keep track of the sizes and start addresses of memory spaces
dynamically allocated. For the backup of global variables and function pointers, the
HCM server makes use of the function such as RegGlobalVar() or RegFuncPoint() to
track the mapping between the symbol name of global variables or functions and
their memory addresses. Because the runtime stack of a user program is inside LLVM,
the HCM server cannot directly control the location of local variables or parameters
in the runtime stack. To overcome this problem, the HCM server maintain a shadow
stack to track the names and memory of local variables in each user function by
inserting PushCurStack() and PopCurStack(). It is worth noting that LLVM declares
a local variable for each parameter of a user function, and replaces the parameter in
any statement with the declared local variable, as shown in the ALLOC label. In
general cases, LLVM cannot keep the memory addresses of global and local variables in the destination node as same as in the source node of task migration. Therefore, it is necessary to copy out the data of global and local variables from the
memory of the source node before migration and copy the data values into the
memory of the destination node after migration based on the mapping of names and
memory addresses of variables.

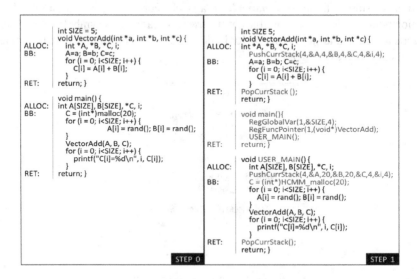

Fig. 5. Step 1 of program recompilation

The second step of program recompilation is to insert checkpoints in user programs for
checking if the migration flag, i.e., MigrationFlag, is set by the HCM sensor to be "BAC".

If it is true, LLVM jumps to invoke the backup routines added in user functions by looking back upon the calling sequence of user functions, as shown in Fig. 6. For reducing backup cost, the HCM server currently insert checkpoints only in front and rear of function calls, and the most outer layer of nest loops in any function. If a user program has no function call and loops, the HCM server add a checkpoint for each basic block in the user program. On the other hand, the backup routine is aimed at recording which pointer variable must be redirected to a new memory address after migration process, and storing the stack frame of each user function in the calling sequence into the image file. For example, assume the execution flow of the example program arrives at the CP1 label of VectorAdd(), and the migration flag is set as "BAC". LLVM jumps to the BACKUP label to call BackupCurr-Stack() for storing the stack frame of the VectorAdd() first. Next, it returns to the CP3 label of USER_MAIN(), and then jumps to the BACKUP label for calling BackupCurrStack() for storing the stack frame of USER_MAIN(). Finally, it returns to main() and then jumps to the BACKUP label for invoking BackCurrStack() to store the content of heap and global variables into the image file.

```
                //0:NML 1:BAC 2:RES                        void USER_MAIN() {
                extern int MigrateFlag;            ALLOC:  Int A[SIZE], B[SIZE], *C, I, Jump;
                int SIZE = 5;                              PushCurrStack(4,&A,20,&B,20,&C,4,&i,4);
                void VectorAdd(int *a, int *b, int *c) {  BB:  C = (int*)HCM_malloc(20);
ALLOC:          int *A, *B, *C, I, Jump;                   for (i = 0; i<SIZE; i++) {
                PushCurrStack(4,&A,4,&B,4,&C,4,&i,4);            Jump = 1;
BB:             A=a; B=b; C=c;                     CP1:        if(MigrateFlag=="BAC") goto BACKUP;
                for (i = 0; i<SIZE; i++) {                       A[i] = rand(); B[i] = rand();
                    Jump = 1;                                  }
CP1:                if(MigrateFlag=="BAC") goto BACKUP;     Jump = 2;
                    C[i] = A[i] + B[i];            CP2:     if(MigrateFlag=="BAC") goto BACKUP;
                }                                           VectorAdd(A, B, C);
RET:            PopCurrStack();                             Jump = 3;
                return;                            CP3:     if(MigrateFlag=="BAC") goto BACKUP;
BACKUP:         BackupCurrStack(3,&A,&B,&C);                for (i = 0; i<SIZE; i++) {
                goto RET; }                                     Jump = 4;
                                                  CP4:        if(MigrateFlag=="BAC") goto BACKUP;
                void main(){                                     printf("C[i]=%d\n", i, C[i]);
                RegGlobalVar(1,&SIZE,4);                       }
                RegFuncPointer(1,(void*)VectorAdd);  RET:   PopCurrStack();
                USER_MAIN();                               return;
                if(MigrateFlag=="BAC") goto BACKUP;  BACKUP:  BackupCurrStack(1,&C);
RET:            return;                                    goto RET; }
BACKUP:         BackupCurrStack();
                goto RET; }
                                                                                      STEP 2
```

Fig. 6. Step 2 of program recompilation

It is worth noting there is a local variable called Jump in VectorAdd() and USER_MAIN(). This variable is used to control the flow of recovery process later. When LLVM performs BackupCurrStack(), it also stores the value of the Jump variable in the image file. For our example, the values of the Jump variables in VectorAdd() and USER_MAIN() are 1 and 2, respectively.

The third step of program recompilation is to insert restore routines for recovering the context of the migrated program on destination node, and resuming the execution of the program from the checkpoint starting the migrated process. As shown in Fig. 7, the HCM server adds a RestoreCurrStack() in each user function for rebuilding the stack frame of the user function. The Jump parameter of RestoreCurrStack() is used to guide LLVM jump to which statement in the user function after finishing RestoreCurrStack().

After receiving the image file of the migrated program, the HCM server on destination node sets MigrateFlag as "RES", and then recovers the content of heap, global variable and stack in the local memory of the destination node from the image file by invoking each RestoreCurrStack() based on the calling sequence of the migrated program.

```
           //0:NML 1:BAC 2:RES                            void USER_MAIN(){
           extern int MigrateFlag;                ALLOC:    int A[SIZE], B[SIZE], *C, i, Jump;
           int SIZE = 5;                                    PushCurrStack(4,&A,20,&B,20,&C,4,&i,4);
           void VectorAdd(int *a, int *b, int *c) {          if(MigrateFlag=="RES") goto RESTORE;
ALLOC:      int *A, *B, *C, i, Jump;              JUMP:     switch(Jump){
           PushCurrStack(4,&A,4,&B,4,&C,4,&i,4);            case 1: goto CP1;
           if(MigrateFlag=="RES") goto RESTORE;             case 2: goto CP2;
JUMP:      switch(Jump){                                    case 3: goto CP3;
           case 1: goto CP1; }                              case 4: goto CP4; }
BB:        A=a; B=b; C=c;                         BB:       C = (int*)HCMM_malloc(20);
           for (i = 0; i<SIZE; i++) {                       for (i = 0; i<SIZE; i++) {
           Jump = 1;                                        Jump = 1;
CP1:       if(MigrateFlag=="BAC") goto BACKUP;   CP1:       if(MigrateFlag=="BAC") goto BACKUP;
           C[i] = A[i] + B[i];                              A[i] = rand(); B[i] = rand();
           }                                                }
RET:       PopCurrStack();                                  Jump = 2;
           return;                                CP2:      if(MigrateFlag=="BAC") goto BACKUP;
BACKUP:    BackupCurrStack(3,&A,&B,&C);                    VectorAdd(A, B, C);
           goto RET;                                        Jump = 3;
RESTORE:   RestoreCurrStack(&Jump);              CP3:       if(MigrateFlag=="BAC") goto BACKUP;
           goto JUMP; }                                    for (i = 0; i<SIZE; i++) {
                                                            Jump = 4;
           void main(){                           CP4:      if(MigrateFlag=="BAR") goto BACKUP;
           RegGlobalVar(1,&SIZE,4);                        printf("C[i]=%d\n", i, C[i]);
           RegFuncPointer(1,(void*)VectorAdd);              }
           if(MigrateFlag=="RES") goto RESTORE;  RET:      PopCurrStack();
           USER_MAIN();                                     return;
           if(MigrateFlag=="BAC") goto BACKUP;  BACKUP:    BackupCurrStack(1,&C);
RET:       return;                                         goto RET;
BACKUP:    BackupCurrStack();                    RESTORE:  RestoreCurrStack(&Jump);
           goto RET;                                       goto JUMP; }
RESTORE:   RestoreCurrStack();
           goto JUMP; }

                                                                              STEP 3
```

Fig. 7. Step 3 of program recompilation

For the previous assumed case, the recovery process is described as follows. First, LLVM re-executes the program from main() while it only invokes RegGlobalVar(), RegFunctionPointer() and RestoreCurrStack() to obtain the new memory addresses of global variables and VectorAdd(), and to restore the content of heap and global variables from the image file to the memory of the destination node, respectively. Second, LLVM jumps to USER_MAIN() while it only calls PushCurrStack() and RestoreCurrStack() to get the new memory locations of local variables in this function, and to copy the values of the local variables from the image file to the new memory locations of these variables, respectively.

Finally, LLVM jumps to the CP2 label of invoking VectorAdd(). After it jumps to VectorAdd(), it calls PushCurrStack() and RestoreCurremStack() to do the same things as done in the USER_MAIN(), and then jumps to the CP1 label to continue the execution of the for loop.

4.3   Redirection of Standard I/O

In the HCM framework, the standard I/O of user programs is redirected to files. Because of security consideration, we developed an adapter library for HCM to direct any file functions called by user programs into a dedicated file directory in order for preventing the programs from accessing other file directories. Whenever user programs access files out of this dedicated file directory, HCM will catch the file accesses and terminate the execution of the programs right away. In addition to user files, HCM automatically open a file in the same directory for the standard output such of each user program before it starts to run. However, users must direct the standard input of their programs to the files specified by themselves. Before a user program is moved from one node to another, the descriptors of the files opened by the user program will be logged, and the opened files will be automatically closed. Then, the HCM server will send the files with the image file of the user program to the destination node. After receiving the files, the new HCM server will write these files into disks with the same file path, and will automatically open these files, and seek the access headers of the files to the logged positions according to the file descriptors.

4.4   Optimization

Although the cost of task migration on LLVM is much less than that of VM migration, in order to further reduce migration cost, the proposed scheme compress any files transmitted from source nodes to destination nodes for task migration, and then decompress the files in destination nodes for rebuilding the context of user programs. Since the computational power of mobile devices recently has been greatly improved, the benefit from saving communication cost usually is larger than the loss from compressing and decompressing file data because the bandwidth of wireless networks is not stable especially in outdoors.

5   Performance Evaluation

We have primarily evaluated the performance of proposed scheme in this paper. We implemented an application called Matrix Multiplication for this performance evaluation. For building our test bed, we used two Xiaomi MiPAD to play mobile client and server, and two PCs to play broker and cloud server, respectively. The specification of these mobile devices and PCs is depicted in Table 2. On the other hand, the broker and the cloud server are connected with a 100 Mbps Ethernet. The gateway between PCs and mobile devices was ZyXEL USG20W, i.e., an access point supporting 802.11n. The mobile devices communicated with the PCs through Wi-Fi or 4G.

We have finished three experiments in the test bed. The first experiment is to estimate the cost of checkpoints in HCM. The second and the third ones are to measure the costs of task migration under three different paths including mobile device to cloud server (M2C), cloud server to mobile device (C2M) and mobile device to mobile device (M2M) through Wi-Fi and 4G, respectively. In fact, the task migration between mobile device and cloud server is delegated to the HCM broker (denoted as B). Therefore, the three different paths of task migration physically are M-B-C, C-B-M and M-B-M.

Table 2. Device specification

Device	CPU	RAM	Network	OS	Amount
Xiaomi Mipad	NVIDIA Tergra K1	2G-LPDDR3	Wi-Fi 802.11n	Android 4.4.2	2
X86 Server	AMD A10-5800 k	8G-DDR3	Ethernet 100 Mbps	Ubuntu 14.04	1
Broker	Intel i5-760	4G-DDR3	Ethernet 100 Mbps	Ubuntu 14.04	1

5.1   Checkpoint Cost of HCM

In this experiment, we aimed at evaluating the impact of checkpoint cost on the execution performance of the test application executed on the mobile client. To achieve this goal, we recompiled the LLVM executable of the test application, and evaluated the execution performance of the test applications with and without program recompilation. In addition, we also recompiled the test program by inserting a checkpoint in each LLVM IR to compare this exhaustive checkpoint way with the lazy checkpoint way of HCM in terms of time cost. Our experimental result is depicted in Fig. 8.

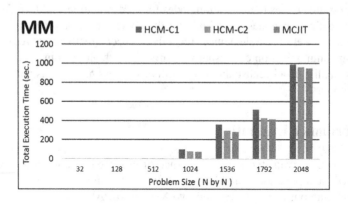

Fig. 8. Checkpoint cost of the test applications

In this figure, HCM-C1 and HCM-C2 represent the exhaustive checkpoint way and the lazy checkpoint way of HCM, respectively. In contrast, MCJIT denotes no checkpoint in the test application. The performance comparison between the HCM-C2 case and the MCJIT case shows that the checkpoint cost of HCM is negligible for the execution performance of the test application. Conversely, the cost of exhaustive checkpoint way is significant for the execution performance of the test application. The applications must spent extra 20~33 % execution time for checkpoints. Although performing checkpoint for each instruction is useful to reduce the delay of activating the mechanism of task migration, the overhead apparently is too expensive to be tolerated.

5.2 Cost of Task Migration Through Wi-Fi

This experiment is to evaluate the efficiency of task migration under Wi-Fi. We performed task migration for the MM application in three different migration paths (i.e., M2C, C2M and M2M) with or without compressing transferred data, and then evaluated and the cost of task migration. In addition, we estimated the transmission rate of these three paths in advance for different data sizes as depicted in Fig. 9. It shows that the transmission rate increases as well as the size of each transmitted data. The C-B-M path has the largest transmission rate while the M-B-M path has the smallest one no matter what size of transmitted data.

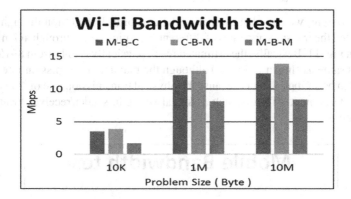

Fig. 9. Transmission rates of different migration paths.

Figure 10 is the cost of task migration for the MM application under three different migration paths. The breakdown of task migration cost includes backup, transmit and restore. The backup and restore costs are the time used to save and restore memory data, program codes and execution context to/from the image file of the test application, respectively. In contrast, the transmit cost is the time spent on transmitting the image,

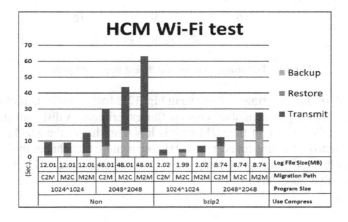

Fig. 10. Migration cost of MM through Wi-Fi

executable, I/O files from the source node of task migration to the destination node. The total cost of task migration is increased with the size of the files no matter what migration path is. Both of the transmit cost and the backup cost are obvious while the restore cost is negligible. In addition, the transmit cost is effectively reduced after applying data compression. This result makes it confirmed that compressing the image files of migrated programs is useful and necessary for reducing the cost of live migration especially when the migration path is M2M because the transmission rate of the M2M path is much smaller than those of the other two paths.

5.3   Cost of Task Migration Through 4G

In this experiment, we aimed at evaluating the cost of task migration through 4G. We also estimated the transmission rates of different migration paths through 4G in advance as shown in Fig. 11. Basically, the estimated result physically is only from 8~15.8 Mbps which is as same as shown in Fig. 10 although the maximal transmission rate of 4G is announced to be 1 Gbps. That is because the physical transmission rate of 4G is affected by many environmental factors such as signal strength, sender/receiver location, and outdoor/indoor.

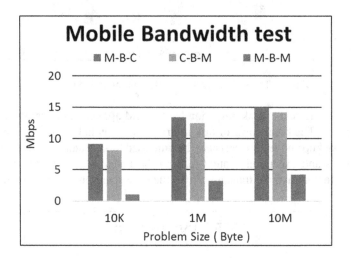

Fig. 11.   Transmission rates of different migration paths.

The result of this experiment is shown in Fig. 12. Most of the situations observed from the previous experiment also occurs in this experiment. A different situation is that the transmission rate of the C2M path is less than that of the M2C path under 4G. Consequently, the transmit cost the C2M path is more than that of the M2C path. On the other hand, the impact of compressing transfer data under 4G becomes more obvious than that under Wi-Fi.

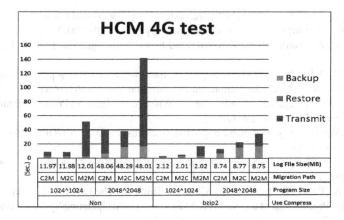

Fig. 12. Migration cost of MM through 4G

6   Conclusions and Future Work

In this paper, we have successfully developed an efficient heterogeneous computation migration scheme for mobile cloud computing. With the proposed scheme, user programs can dynamically move among mobile devices and cloud servers while they can obtains an execution performance as good as native code on any execution node. Consequently, the proposed scheme is effective for integrating the computational power of mobile and cloud resources to serve mobile and cloud users as well as possible. In this paper, we only focused on the development of live migration mechanism on LLVM. We will develop an advance scheduling algorithm based on the proposed migration scheme for mobile cloud computing.

Acknowledgment. This work is supported by Ministry of Science and Technology of the Republic of China under the project number: MOST 103-2221-E-151-044.

References

1. Seppälä, P., Alamäki, H.: Mobile learning in teacher training. J. Comput. Assist. Learn. **19**(3), 330–335 (2003)
2. Varshney, U.: Pervasive healthcare and wireless health monitoring. Mobile Netw. Appl. **12**(2–3), 113–127 (2007)
3. Anderson, D.P.: BOINC: a system for public-resource computing and storage. In: Fifth IEEE/ACM International Workshop on Grid Computing, pp. 4–10 (2004)
4. Champion, C.: Addi (2015). https://play.google.com/store/apps/details?id=com.addi
5. Quarteroni, A., Saleri, F., Gervasio, P.: Scientific Computing with MATLAB and Octave. Springer, Heidelberg (2010)
6. Chukov, A.: CCTools (2015). https://play.google.com/store/apps/details?id=com.pdaxrom. cctools
7. n0n3m4: C4droid - C/C++ compiler & IDE (2015). https://play.google.com/store/apps/details?id=com.n0n3m4.droidc

8. Zhu, W., Wang, C.-L., Lau, F.: JESSICA2: a distributed Java virtual machine with transparent thread migration support. In: Cluster Computing, pp. 381–388 (2002)
9. Bouchenak, S., Hagimont, D.: Zero overhead Java thread migration. Technical report 0261 (2002)
10. Lattner, C., Adve, V.: LLVM: a compilation framework for lifelong program analysis and transformation. In: Code Generation and Optimization, pp. 45–86 (2004)
11. Milojičić, D.S., Douglis, F., Paindaveine, Y., Wheeler, R., Zhou, S.: Process migration. ACM Comput. Surv. **32**(3), 241–299 (2000)
12. Smith, J.M.: A survey of process migration mechanisms. ACM SIGOPS Oper. Syst. Rev. **22**(3), 28–40 (1988)
13. Zayas, E.: Attacking the process migration bottleneck. ACM SIGOPS Oper. Syst. Rev. **21**(5), 13–24 (1987)
14. Walker, B., Popek, G., English, R., Kline, C., Thiel, G.: The LOCUS distributed operating system. In: Proceedings of the Ninth ACM Symposium on Operating Systems Principles, pp. 49–70 (1983)
15. Miller, B.P., Powell, M.L., Presotto, D.L.: DEMOS/MP: the development of a distributed operating system. Softw. Pract. Exp. **17**(4), 277–290 (1987)
16. Piao, J.T., Yan, J.: A network-aware virtual machine placement and migration approach in cloud computing. In: Grid and Cooperative Computing, pp. 87–92 (2010)
17. Stage, A., Setzer, T.: Network-aware migration control and scheduling of differentiated virtual machine workloads. In: Proceedings of the ICSE Workshop on Software Engineering Challenges of Cloud Computing, pp. 9–14 (2009)
18. Clark, C., Fraser, K., Hand, S., Hansen, J.G., Jul, E., Limpach, C., Pratt, I., Warfield, A.: Live migration of virtual machines. In: USENIX Symposium on Networked Systems Design and Implementation, pp. 273–286 (2005)
19. Perez-Botero, D.: A brief tutorial on live virtual machine migration from a security perspective. University of Princeton (2011). http://www.cs.princeton.edu/~diegop/data/580_midterm_project.pdf
20. Theimer, M.M., Lantz, K.A., Cheriton, D.R.: Preemptable remote execution facilities for the V-system. ACM SIGOPS Oper. Syst. Rev. **19**, 2–12 (1985)
21. Hines, M.R., Deshpande, U., Gopalan, K.: Post-copy live migration of virtual machines. ACM SIGOPS Oper. Syst. Rev. **43**(3), 14–26 (2009)
22. Ma, R.K.K., Wang, C.-L.: Lightweight application-level task migration for mobile cloud computing. In: Advanced Information Networking and Applications, pp. 550–557 (2012)

A Flow Scheduling Algorithm Based on VM Migration in Data Center Networks

Xingyan Zhang[✉]

School of Computer Science and Technology, Huazhong University of Science and Technology,
Wuhan, Hubei, China
zhangxingyan@hust.edu.cn

Abstract. Data centers employ virtualization to organize thousands of servers. Applications such as MapReduce and Hadoop are deployed in virtual machines (VMs). However, with the development of client requirements, the traffic among VMs, which host different types of applications, becomes irregular and unpredictable. This traffic may cause congestion links and performance violations in applications. In this study, we first analyze the performance impact of changes in flow distribution and then attempt to migrate VMs with large traffic flows to a suitable destination server to decrease the number of congestion links. We design a multi-level bloom filter to detect large flows and propose a flow scheduling algorithm based on VM migration (FSVMM) for data centers to optimize network performance. The FSVMM is evaluated with real trace data. Results show that the FSVMM can reduce the number of congestion links and improve user experience.

Keywords: VM migration · Flow scheduling · Counting bloom filter · Link congestion · Goodput

1 Introduction

Cloud providers organize large numbers of servers and leverage virtualization technology to support various applications for tenants [1], e.g., large-scale computing, data storage, database, and data analysis. Tenants rent virtual machines (VMs) with dedicated sources, including CPU, memory, and storage, among others. However, as common resources, underlying networks are shared by customers. Therefore, ensuring sufficient bandwidth at any given time is difficult. Uneven traffic distribution may produce congestion links, which can degrade application performance. Hence, the timely flagging of an uneven flow distribution in data centers is extremely important. In other words, flow scheduling is a significant topic in the area of data center networks.

From the perspective of topology, Fat-tree [2] employs multi-rooted tree to overcome the high oversubscription of traditional single-rooted tree for high bisection bandwidth. VL2 [3] adopts valiant load balancing to spread traffic across all available paths between core switches and aggregate switches. In case of incoming flow, servers independently choose random paths to achieve uniform high capacity. From the perspective of VM placement, Oktopus [1] tries to deploy intra-tenant VMs in physical servers as close as

© Springer International Publishing Switzerland 2016
X. Huang et al. (Eds.): GPC 2016, LNCS 9663, pp. 163–179, 2016.
DOI: 10.1007/978-3-319-39077-2_11

possible to overcome traffic bottlenecks and provide aggregation throughput. However, the changes in applied patterns and the emergence of various new applications make the traffic between VMs increasingly irregular and unpredictable. Such traffic conditions cause congestion links and affect application performance. Unfortunately, this problem cannot be avoided when VMs are deployed. In this regard, VM migration is an efficient solution because of the following reasons.

Applied Traffic Patterns have Changed. Most flow scheduling approaches are designed for applications that require big data processing, e.g., MapReduce and Hadoop. The rule lengths of flow is easily predicted and controlled by administrators. However, applications with new traffic patterns increase the difficulty of dealing with flow. The traffic patterns of these applications contain fixed-size data, such as data chunks, and indicate unpredictable flow among VMs, such as Twitter [4] and Facebook [5]. The data transmission between two users of these social applications, including the transmission of messages and videos via various tools, may cross several switches and lead to flow collision with the flow of other applications. Furthermore, certain applications require cooperation among VMs, thereby generating heavy traffic among such machines [6]. Intuitively, these VMs with heavy traffic transmission are preferably deployed close to one another. However, stochastic flow distribution makes this process difficult. The best approach is the migration of VMs to a server within an edge switch.

The Expansion of Data Centers in Terms of Scale has Changed. Data centers are exponentially growing in terms of scale. Network topology [2] has thus changed from a symmetrical structure to a partial structure. Such change enhances the possible emergence of new network bottlenecks. Furthermore, a hybrid cloud [7] necessitates the deployment of several VMs from a private cloud to a public cloud. This type of traffic between VMs from different locations complicates flow scheduling. The selection of potential VMs for migration is a key point for high-efficiency traffic engineering.

Traffic Distribution is Uneven. A large number of flows generate several congestion links because of the uneven flow distribution in data centers [8]. Previous studies on data center traffic [9] showed that over 50 % and 25 % of the flow traffic of education and production data centers, respectively, traverses different rack switches. Simultaneously, data center flows feature a long-tail distribution, and some large flows easily cause flow collision [10], which degrades network throughput.

The scheme proposed in the present study involves collecting traffic volume between VM pairs, determining the largest cumulated traffic, and migrating some VMs to a different location. We design an improved bloom filter called the multi-level counting bloom filter (MCBF), which easily checks large flows and computes data volume. The MCBF requires a small storage space and is suitable for commodity switches. We normalize the traffic volume between VMs and define the cost of VM migration. Finally, a flow scheduling algorithm based on VM migration (FSVMM) for data centers is proposed to optimize network performance. The FSVMM finds the best VM for migration on the basis of flow volume and network topology to reduce the aggregate flow. We evaluate the performance of the FSVMM with real trace data. The results and analysis show that a reasonable VM migration can help reduce highly utilized links and avoid congestion nodes. This work offers the following contributions:

- Design of the MCBF based on the standard bloom filter to check VM pairs with large flows and to calculate data volume
- Definition of the cost of VM migration and identification of potential VMs for migration based on cumulative data volume
- Proof of the effectiveness of the FSVMM in reducing congestion links and improving user experience

The rest paper of the paper is organized as follows: Sect. 2 describes the background and motivation of dynamic VM migration. Section 3 presents the designs of the MCBF and FSVMM. Section 4 describes the evaluation and analysis of the FSVMM results. Section 5 summarizes the related works. Section 6 discusses the conclusion and identifies our future work.

2 Background and Motivation

In this section, we introduce the concept of network congestion caused by uneven traffic distribution. Subsequently, the motivation for migrating VMs to reduce congestion nodes is described. Finally, we conclude with the requirements for efficient VM migration.

2.1 Flow Distribution in Data Center Networks

Data center networks comprise hundreds of thousands of large-scale servers for cloud data centers or enterprise data centers. These servers simultaneously transmit data and thus cause heavy traffic. Hence, traffic distribution has been extensively studied [8, 11, 12]. Data center flows feature an uneven distribution in terms of flow size and the number of flows. A small number of large flows contribute large data volume. For example, the literature [8] shows that less than 10 % of a large flow contributes to 80 % of the data volume. A large number of mice flows may actually equate to a low data volume. Meanwhile, highly utilized links commonly form, e.g., 86 % of links observe congestion that lasts for at least 10 s, whereas 15 % of links observe congestion that lasts for at least 100 s. Long-lasting congestion periods tend to be localized to a small set of links, as shown in Fig. 5 of Ref. [8]. The fixed traffic between special VMs consumes a significant portion of bandwidth. Large flows easily cause congestion links and obstruct the mice flows transmission. Most applications, including online social networks, generate large mice flows. These large numbers of mice flows can produce partial congestion links and affect user experience [13].

The purpose of a reasonable flow scheduling is to reduce congestion links as soon as possible. Hedera [10] proposed a flow redirection method to avoid congestion resulting from large flow collision and consequently improve aggregate flow. Unfortunately, not all flow collisions can be redirected to another path, e.g., some congestion links are difficult to eliminate in partial topology, or all core switches are unavailable.

Therefore, the migration of VMs with large flows can benefit non-congestion links and avoid performance degradation.

2.2 VM Migration for Decreasing Flow Collision

Several studies have proposed relevant methods for VM placement [14, 15], with the common approach involving the placement of VMs with heavy traffic in close proximity. However, existing methods rarely consider the effect of the dynamic flow between VMs. Thus, new congestion may emerge with dynamic flows, although the original VM placement is reasonable.

Next, we show the motivation for VM migration and utilize an example to introduce the performance loss caused by an unreasonable VM placement. As shown in Fig. 1, four servers (Server$_1$, Server$_2$, Server$_3$, and Server$_4$) are connected by several switches (S$_1$, S$_2$, and S$_3$); the VMs (VM$_1$, VM$_2$, VM$_3$, and VM$_4$) are deployed in these servers. This partial network can be seen as part of a fat-tree network while all the other core switches are busy. The traffic between VM$_1$ and VM$_3$ creates a large flow for a long period; the same is true for the traffic between VM$_2$ and VM$_3$. We assume that the traffic between VMs is overloaded in switch S$_1$ and that such congestion cannot be avoided via flow redirection. Therefore, we can only resolve this problem via VM migration.

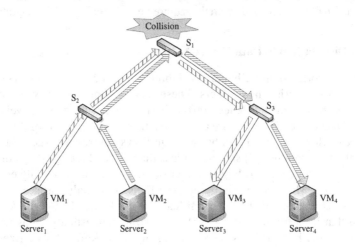

Fig. 1. Large flow collision in a core switch

We assume that the traffic volume between different VMs is different and that it is calculated into normalized data. The details of the traffic volume between VMs are shown in three triples <from, to, volume>. Therefore, all the traffic between VMs can be represented as <VM$_1$, VM$_3$, 4>, <VM$_2$, VM$_4$, 6>, <VM$_1$, VM$_2$, 1>, and <VM$_3$, VM$_4$, 2>. Here, the data volume from VM$_1$ to VM$_3$ is 4, and the largest traffic volume is the traffic from VM$_2$ to VM$_2$. The second largest traffic volume is from VM$_1$ to VM$_3$. We assume that congestion occurs in switch S$_1$. The efficient and easy solution in this case is the migration of the VM for the best quality of service (QoS).

The straightforward method for ensuring the QoS of VM pairs involves migrating one of the VMs to another location to decrease the traffic across switch S_1. The next issue is the selection of the most suitable VM for migration. With regard to the volume size between VMs, migrating VM_2 to the right child node of S_1 or migrating VM_4 to the left child node of S_1 can degrade the traffic volume across S_1. However, the values of these schemes differ; that is, the traffic volume value between the VMs of the first scheme is $4 + 1 = 5$, whereas the value for the second scheme is $2 + 4 = 6$. If any other conditions are equal, the first scheme is better than the second scheme.

2.3 Requirements for Efficient VM Migration

VM migration is the best complement for the optimization of data center performance. However, VM migration also generates additional traffic between VMs. The best VM migration must consider the following issues:

- **Defining VM migration cost.** A VM can be migrated only with sufficient traffic volume between VMs. The first influencing factor of VM migration cost is the traffic volume between two VMs. We choose all the flows crossing VM pairs as the cumulated traffic volume. The second factor is the data size of the VM demo [16]. If the traffic volume is lower than the demo of the migrating VM, VM migration is obviously unnecessary. Moreover, changing the location of VM placement may cause new traffic. Therefore, the final factor to be considered is the additional traffic generated as the VM location changes.
- **Calculating the traffic volume between VMs.** As the traffic of data center networks exhibits a long-tail distribution, we cannot record the details of all packets in data centers. Therefore, we calculate traffic according to the recorded number of packets between VMs and according to packet size. Considering the trend in which data center networks comprise commodity switches to replace expensive and professional switches [2], we chose an improved bloom filter to check the packet size between different VM pairs. The greatest advantage of the bloom filter is its small holding space and time efficiency.
- **Timing of VM migration.** For simplicity, we focus on the maximum cost of VM pairs. When the demo of the migrating VM is of the same size, we can find the potential VM starting from the VM pairs with maximum traffic. When the effect of VM migration on other VMs is acceptable, we can start the process of VM migration.

We design a bloom filter called the MCBF to record and calculate the traffic volume between VMs for the application of the FSVMM. We describe the FSVMM and MCBF in detail in the following sections.

3   FSVMM Methodology

In this section, we introduce the principle of the MCBF for large flow detection. Subsequently, we introduce the methodology of the FSVMM. Finally, we analyze the performance of our design.

3.1 Flow Detection with Improved Bloom Filter

The counting bloom filter (CBF) [20] was proposed to record and count elements. In the case of an incoming element, several hash functions are used to calculate the mapped counter, and the corresponding counters are incremental. When an element is deleted, the corresponding counters are decremented. The CBF can easily calculate the number of elements, the value of which is the minimum value of the corresponding counters.

However, the disadvantage of the CBF is the presence of false positives, wherein some elements are often mistaken for a different set of elements. If most counters exceed fixed counts, the false positive rate becomes too large such that the wrong element count is easily calculated. Inspired by the multi-level cache design [17], we adopt the MCBF to detect large flows and to estimate the numbers of flow packets. The design of the MCBF is shown in Fig. 2.

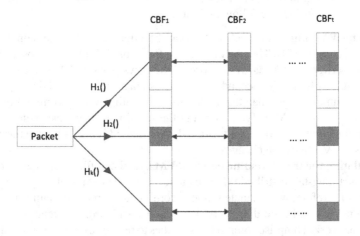

Fig. 2. Design of a multi-level counting bloom filter

Figure 2 shows the design of the MCBF. When a packet arrives, two tuples of <source address, destination address> from the packet header are mapped into CBF_1 with the hash function h_1, that is, h_2 to h_k, and the k responding counters are incremental. Subsequently, the corresponding counters are checked. When all values exceed a predefined threshold *len_threshold*, this flow can be mapped to the next CBF, and all the responding counters minus *len_threshold*. In the same manner, CBF_2 can be mapped to the next CBF when the corresponding counter exceeds the *len_threshold*.

The process of the MCBF is described as follows. CBF_1 handles the two triples <src, dst>, where src and dst are the source IP address and destination IP address of the packet, respectively. The two triples are mapped into counters with k hash functions, and all the k mapped counters are incremental. Subsequently, CBF_1 checks whether the value of the recently mapped counters is smaller than the *len_threshold*. If the answer is yes, all the mapped counters are incremental. Otherwise, all the mapped counters are subtracted with the *len_threshold*, and the two triples with the previous k hash functions are mapped to CBF_2. The CBF_t process is similar to that of the previous CBF_{t-1} and can be expressed in a recursive manner. We select the MCBF to check for large flows instead of the single

CBF because we must verify whether the enough packets reaching gigabyte amounts of data can be recorded and easily to calculate. The CBF is naturally deficient in terms of correctness, hence our analysis of the characteristics of the MCBF.

We set one-tenth of the demo size [16] of a migrating VM as the standard value. In our design, we set the standard value to 200 MB; thus, the MCBF simply searches VM pairs with a traffic volume of more than 200 MB. The standard packet size of TCP/IP is 1,500 B, and the least number of packets is 1.33×10^5. Therefore, we set the value of k to 3, which is as small as possible to save holding space. These parameters can support the large flow volume of $500^3 \times 1,500$ B $= 187$ GB, which is large enough to support large flow detection. Therefore, the minimum space required is just $500 \times 4 \times 3/8 = 750$ B, which is a small proportion of the switch space. In addition, the large number of flows features a long-tail distribution in the data center; thus, we ignore the effect of these flows.

3.2   Search for VM Pairs with Minimum Cost

The purpose of the FSVMM is traffic degradation via VM migration, but the process of VM migration generates new traffic between VMs and other VMs in the new location. We define $Cost_{ij}$ as the change in traffic as VM_i is migrated to the server closer to VM_j; the equation is

$$Cost_{ij} = M_{ij} - T_{ij} + D_{ij} \tag{1}$$

where M_{ij} is the traffic volume of the VM_i migration demo; its value is easily obtained from the system configuration. T_{ij} is the decreasing traffic volume after VM migration; its value is the sum of the traffic from VM_i to VM_j and the traffic from VM_j to VM_i. The traffic between VMs can be obtained from the MCBF. D_{ij} is the traffic difference as the VM location changes. The computational methods are shown later in this paper.

$$H = \begin{bmatrix} 0 & 1 & 3 & 6 \\ 1 & 0 & 1 & 1 \\ 1 & 2 & 0 & 2 \\ 7 & 1 & 2 & 0 \end{bmatrix}$$

For simplicity, we calculate $Cost_{ij}$ by establishing a matrix of the traffic between all VMs. We provide specific examples to illustrate the computing process for $Cost_{ij}$. We assume that four VMs exist in a network and that the traffic between these VMs is detected and shown as normalized data. Therefore, the matrix H denotes the matrix, and H_{ij} denotes the traffic volume from VM_i to VM_j.

Take for example the special traffic between some VMs, the topology of which is shown in Fig. 1 as a matrix H. H_{21} represents the traffic volume from VM_2 to VM_1 and carries the value of 2. Once VM_2 migrates, the original traffic between VM_1 and VM_2 is unnecessary. Therefore, the repression of T_{21} is $H_{21} + H_{12}$, and its value is 3. Given the heavy traffic between VM_2 and VM_3, such traffic is added into switch S_1 after the migration of VM_2. Simultaneously, the traffic between VM_2 and VM_0 and the traffic between VM_2 and VM_1 are eliminated from switch S_1. Therefore, the expression of D_{21}

is $H_{23} + H_{32} - H_{21} - H_{21} - H_{20} - H_{02}$, and its value is -3. As previously described, the value of M_{21} is 10; thus, the expression of $Cost_{21}$ is $10 - 3 + (-3)$, and its value is 4.

VM migration with minimum cost entails comprehensive network information, including the topology and traffic between VMs. The flow traffic matrix is easily established on the basis of the MCBF, which is deployed on the switches. As shown in Fig. 3, the four triples <SW_ID, VM_SRC, VM_DST, Flow_VOL> are computed from the distributed switches, where SW_ID is the exact ID number for the switch, VM_SRC is the resource IP address of the flow, VM_DST is the destination IP address of the flow, and FLOW_VOL denotes the traffic volume from VM with VM_SRC to VM with VM_DST; the value is regarded as normalized data.

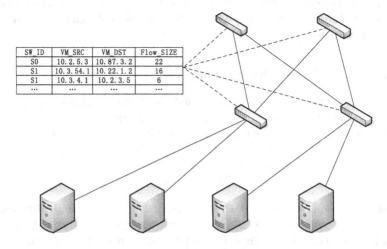

SW_ID	VM_SRC	VM_DST	Flow_SIZE
S0	10.2.5.3	10.87.3.2	22
S1	10.3.54.1	10.22.1.2	16
S1	10.3.4.1	10.2.3.5	6
...	...	...	...

Fig. 3. Flow recording table in the switch

The matrix H can be easily established while traffic information is collected. For simplicity, the problem of selecting a VM for migration is resolved with a greedy algorithm. The optimized algorithm is shown in Fig. 4.

Initially, the FSVMM finds the VM pair with a large traffic volume in Line 1 to Line 4. If $Cost_{ij}$ is negative, then VM_i can be migrated to the server close to VM_j. If $Cost_{ji}$ is negative, then VM_j can be migrated to the server close to VM_i. In addition, the minimum cost of VM_{ij} should be calculated, and the prospective VM for migration must be chosen from both VMs. However, VM migration is worthless if the minimum cost is not large enough. Therefore, the parameter *cost_threshold* is adopted as the description for the trigger of VM migration in Line 7 to Line 10.

The function $Cost(i, j)$ is calculated according to $Cost_{ij}$ from Line 11 to Line 16. The data volume, M_{ij}, which is required for VM migration, is normalized in Line 11. The traffic volume between VM_i and VM_j, T_{ij}, is calculated in Line 12. Line 13 and Line 14 exhibit all the original VMs in the same pods with VM_i and VM_j, respectively. Independent traffic, D_{ij}, is the difference of the sums of the traffic between a given VM and the VMs in the same pods. D_{ij} is calculated in Line 15, and $Cost_{ij}$ is calculated in Line 16.

We assume that the destination server is an additional resource (e.g., CPU, memory, or storage) for the migrated VM; thus, we only consider the situation of the networks. By comparing the network resource of each VM, the resource-like CPU or memory is easily adjusted [18]; in this study, we adopt the VM migration method with memory compression [16].

3.3 Algorithm Analysis

We first analyze the effect of various parameters on the ratio of false positives of the MCBF and set the correct parameter values to improve system performance. We assume that the number of hash functions is k in the MCBF and that the number of counters is m. In addition, n is the number of elements; hence, the probability of a false positive for the bloom filter [19] is

$$P_{bf} = (1 - (1 - 1/m)^{kn})^k \approx (1 - e^{-kn/m})^k \tag{2}$$

The principle of the CBF is the same as that of a bloom filter for checking elements from a specific set. Thus, the probability of false positives in the CBF is similar to that in a bloom filter. The probability of false positives for the CBF changes minimally from P_{bf}. However, the CBF can minus the constant *len_threshold* when all the mapped counters of an element are below the constant. Therefore, the false positive ratio of the

```
Require: Topology tree, <VM_SRCₖ,VM_DSTₖ> pairs with large
flow
Ensure: Minimum cost of VM migration
1:Search maximum flow volume H₁ⱼ from matrix H
2:if Cost(i, j)<=0 or Cost(j, i)<=0
3:   migrate VMᵢ to the server containing VMⱼ or migrate
VMⱼ to the server containing VMᵢ
4:   return true
5:else
6:   min= minimize(Cost(i, j), Cost(j, i))
7:   if min<cost_threshold
8:      migrate VM with minimal cost to another location
9:      return true
10:end
Function Cost(i, j)
11:Mᵢ=normalized volume of VMᵢ
12:Tᵢⱼ=Hᵢⱼ+Hᵢⱼ
13:VMₓ,ᵢ→Pod
14:VMᵧ,ⱼ→Pod
15:Dᵢⱼ=∑(Hᵢₓ+Hₓᵢ) -∑(Hⱼᵧ+Hᵧⱼ)
16:return Mᵢ-Tᵢⱼ+Dᵢⱼ
```

Fig. 4. Pseudo-code description of the FSVMM

CBF must be calculated in the case in which the probability of one element is mapped into one counter for *len_threshold* times.

Let $c(i)$ be the count associated with the ith counter. The probability that the ith counter is incremented j times is a binomial random variable given by

$$P\{c(i) = j\} = \binom{nk}{j}(\frac{1}{m})^j(1 - \frac{1}{m})^{nk-j} \tag{3}$$

Thus, the probability that the ith counter is equal to j is

$$P\{c(i) \geq j\} = \sum_{j=1}^{nk} P\{c(i) = j\} \tag{4}$$

We assume that the carry-over threshold is j and that the counter is m. The question is how to calculate the probability of the minimum value of the k mapped counter being. Given that m counters are independent of each other and that a single count is equal to j, the probability of the MCBF is the kth power of the probability of the ith counter being equal to j; that is,

$$P_k[c(i) \geq j] \leq (\frac{enk}{jm})^{kj} \tag{5}$$

The right part of equation is the false positive of CBF_1, that is,

$$P_{CBF_1} = (\frac{enk}{jm})^{kj} \tag{6}$$

The MCBF is the multi-level mapping in the basic equation of CBF_1. The false positive ratio of the t-level MCBF is

$$P_{CBF_t} = 1 - (1 - (\frac{enk}{jm})^{kj})^t \tag{7}$$

The MCBF is adopted to calculate the number of packets. The parameter *len_threshold* denotes the threshold value for every multi-level CBF. Thus, the value of j is *len_threshold*. We assume that each counter holds 4 bits and set the value of m to 1,000. On the basis of our experience [19], the best value of *len_threshold* is set to half of m, that is, 1,000.

The MBCF implements k hash functions to map elements; thus, the time complexity of every access is $O(k)$. When each mapped counter is over *len_threshold*, each carry-over operation is implemented. Therefore, the whole time complexity of the MCBF is $O(nk + kn/c)$, where c is a constant.

The FSVMM is a centralized algorithm for finding the largest traffic volume between VM pairs within a period of time. The number of VMs enlarges the matrix and increases its complexity. Therefore, the VM pairs should be handled as we record a large traffic volume of over 200 MB. From the observed traffic distribution [8], few VMs pairs meet the requirement; thus, the matrix H is sparse and not too complicated to handle.

The FSVMM allows centralized scheduling for all flows in VM pairs. Once the minimum $Cost_{ij}$ or $Cost_{ji}$ is found, we can determine the best VM for migration to optimize the data center networks. Therefore, the time complexity of the FSVMM is the same as that of the function $Cost(i, j)$. Lines 11 and 12 are both $O(1)$. Lines 13 and 14 map the VM_i or VM_j to the pod of a fat tree; thus, the time complexity of both lines is $O(n)$, where n is the number of switch ports [2]. Line 15 is also $O(n^2)$, and the last line is $O(1)$; thus, the time complexity of the FSVMM is $O(n^2)$. This value is easily acceptable because the parameter n is the number of switch ports.

4   Evaluation and Result Analysis

The performance of the FSVMM algorithm is evaluated in this section. Our objective is to not only migrating VMs with large flows by communicating with VMs far from others but also to improve user experience. Therefore, we seek to answer these questions for estimating the FSVMM: (1) How does the FSVMM affect the reduction of congestion? (2) How does the FSVMM affect system performance? (3) How is VM migration itself affected? This section introduces the evaluation environment, proposes the evaluation method and metrics, and analyzes the results.

4.1   Simulation Setup

The main purpose of the FSVMM is to improve network performance, especially the performance of data center networks; thus, we adopt the ns-2 simulator [20] to estimate our algorithm. We construct integrated fat-tree topology [2] networks with 48 ports. Therefore, we need 576 core switches and $48 \times 24 = 1,152$ aggregate switches. The number of edge switches is also 1,152. The networks can support $48^3/4 = 27,648$ servers, and all VMs are configured with a VPN address of 10/8.

In the simulation environment, the MCBF algorithm is used to detect large flows. The FSVMM is used to search large flows and find the best VM for migration to decrease aggregated traffic. The process of VM migration can be represented as a large flow, in which the volume size is equal to the data size of the VM demo. When the whole traffic of the VM demo is completely transferred, the VM is deemed to have completely migrated. In this work, we focus not on the VM capacity of the migration destination but on the network impact of VM migration.

For simplicity, we assume that all VMs are independent in networks; thus, our estimation focuses on network usage and VM migration completion time. We set 96 ports for the edge switches, which can thus access 72 servers in addition to the 24 uplink ports. In this case, every server can support 3 VMs. We evaluate the FSVMM algorithm with the synthetic data, which are improved from real networks [21]. The job completion time refers to the distribution of these flows and is similar to the flow completion time of data center networks [8]. We estimate and calculate the effect in a day and in a week.

4.2   Metrics

We evaluate the FSVMM in terms of network performance and user experience. We define the links with an occupancy bandwidth ratio below 70 % as the hot-spot links. The value of this parameter is similar to that in previous research [8]. The actual occupancy bandwidth is easily obtained by monitoring the networks. The first metric is the number of hot-spot links (**NHL**). The other metric is **goodput**, which is the real throughput and real capacity for job handling. Goodput is the metric that investors care most about. Notably, the goodput metric does not need to consider traffic from VM migration because this traffic can be seen as an additional load in system scheduling.

These two metrics are related to system performance. The third metric is the number of promptly completed jobs (**NCJ**). We can calculate the NCJ and compare this value with that for an ideal situation. For simplicity, we set the ideal NCJ as the number of jobs completed when the network is not congested. In a data center, most jobs are delay-intensive and need to be completed on time [22].

4.3   Result Analysis

In the simulation, we run the FSVMM in a fat-tree topology and record the detail of all flows. Subsequently, we calculate the NHL, goodput, and NCJ of the networks. We then compare the resulting values of the default flow scheduling of the fat-tree topology against those of the FSVMM in hours and days.

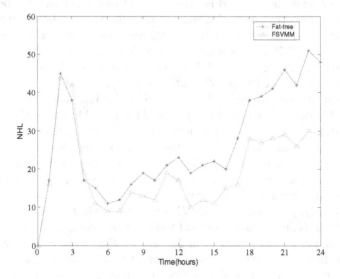

Fig. 5.   Number of hot-spot links in a day

Figures 5 and 6 show the number of hot-spot links of the FSVMM and the default fat-tree routing in days and weeks, respectively. As shown in Fig. 5, the hourly NHL of the FSVMM in one day is obviously less than that of the fat-tree topology, which means that the FSVMM effectively reduces the hot-spot links. The number of hot-spot links in a week is statistically shown in Fig. 6. The numbers of hot-spot links in one day and one night are separated statistically. The number of hot-spot links from 18:00 to 06:00 is obviously greater than that from 06:00 to 18:00. Regardless of whether the data were observed during the day or during the night, the NHL of the fat-tree topology is greater than that of the FSVMM. As indicated by the statistical analysis of the NHL for a whole week, our algorithm decreases the NHL by 14 % during the day and by 18 % at night.

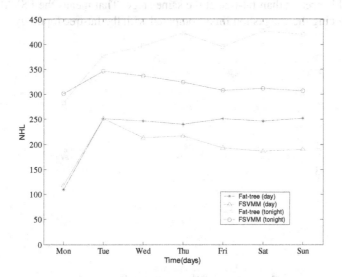

Fig. 6. Number of hot-spot links in a week

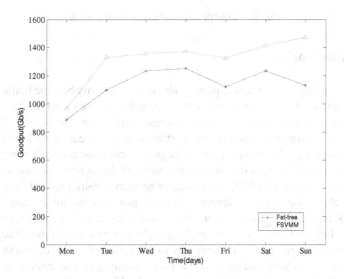

Fig. 7. Goodput for a week

The hot-spot links easily cause packet delays for some VMs and further damage the bandwidth resources for other VMs. Therefore, we must check the goodput, which is a reliable metric that supports user access. We calculate the goodput from the daily trace. The results are shown in Fig. 7.

The number of promptly completed jobs in a week is shown in Fig. 8. The three different lines respectively represent the ideal situation, fat-tree and FSVMM performance. The NCJ of fat-tree and FSVMM are both smaller than the ideal NCJ, and the NCJ of FSVMM is greater than fat-tree at the same stage. That means the FSVMM is well done in reducing the congestion links compared with the fat-tree topology.

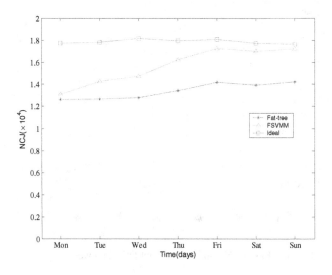

Fig. 8. Number of completed jobs in a week

5   Related Works

With the increasing scale of data centers, nodes and links easily become bottlenecks that prevent the expansion of network capacity, especially in core switches [23]. The elimination of these bottlenecks has thus become a research hotspot. The fat-tree [2] topology uses a multi-root structure to scatter traffic at original single core switch nodes. On the basis of this topology, Hedera [10] detects large flow collision and finds new paths with the simulated annealing algorithm to improve network throughput. Several works focus on bandwidth allocation for VMs in data center networks. FairCloud [24] mainly solves bandwidth allocation for inter-tenant VMs and provides minimum bandwidth and proportional bandwidth allocation for intra-tenant VMs to achieve maximum network utilization. Hadrian [25] solves the bandwidth sharing problem in the mixed VMs of inter-tenants and intra-tenants and appends various constraints on networks to ensure bandwidths between VMs and maximize network throughput. These solutions optimize the bandwidth allocation for VMs in networks and seldom consider the dynamic traffic between VMs.

Several works on VM placement ensure network bandwidth for VMs. Piao and Yan [26] deployed VMs on the basis of data storage and network conditions to decrease the effects of network delays or congestion. Li et al. [27] predicted network performance to determine the feasibility of VM migration. The leverage algorithm called optimal singular value decomposition is used to analyze current network performance and predict future network performance. The algorithm is also used to determine the VM to be migrated and the migration location, thereby avoiding congestion and implementing load balancing. A live migration strategy for VMs has also been proposed on the basis of a performance predicting algorithm. Jin et al. [16] presented an adaptive memory compression approach for live VM migration. The designed algorithm is a zero-aware memory compression algorithm for VM migration to implement lossless compression with minimal overhead for VM migration.

The abovementioned schemes improve network performance and decrease the cost of VM migration, but few of these schemes consider the effect of the dynamic traffic change between VMs and large network flows. To compensate for such deficiencies, our work aims to decrease the performance impact of huge flows and improve network availability.

6   Conclusion and Future Work

Uneven flow distribution may cause link congestion in data centers when applications similar to online social networks are running. We design the MCBF to capture large flows between VMs and attempt to migrate VMs to reduce congestion links. We define the cost function of VM migration and propose a greedy algorithm called the FSVMM, which can search a suitable destination for VM migration in a data center. Our objective is to reduce the number of congestion links and consequently improve network throughput and job completion efficiency. We evaluate the algorithm using real trace data and find that the FSVMM is better than the original flow scheduling in terms of throughput and user experience.

At the next step is to verify the performance of different parameters combination and obtain the best parameters set for more application patterns. Our ultimate goal is building a smart platform to support various new applications.

References

1. Ballani, H., Costa, P., Karagiannis, T., Rowstron, A.: Towards predictable datacenter networks. ACM SIGCOMM Comput. Commun. Rev. **4**, 242–253 (2011). ACM Press
2. Al-Fares, M., Loukissas, A., Vahdat, A.: A scalable, commodity data center network architecture. ACM SIGCOMM Comput. Commun. Rev. **38**(4), 63–74 (2008). ACM Press
3. Greenberg, A., Hamilton, J.R., Jain, N., Kandula, S., Kim, C., Lahiri, P., Maltz, D.A., Patel, P., Sengupta, S.: VL2: a scalable and flexible data center network. ACM SIGCOMM Comput. Commun. Rev. **4**, 51–62 (2009). ACM Press
4. Kwak, H., Lee, C., Park, H., Moon, S.: What is Twitter, a social network or a news media? In: 19th International Conference on World Wide Web, pp. 591–600. ACM Press, Raleigh, North Carolina (2010)

5. Ellison, N.B., Steinfield, C., Lampe, C.: The benefits of Facebook "friends:" social capital and college students' use of online social network sites. J. Comput.-Mediated Commun. **12**(4), 1143–1168 (2007). Wiley Online Library Press

6. Lu, T., Stuart, M., Tang, K., He, X.: Clique migration: affinity grouping of virtual machines for inter-cloud live migration. In: 9th IEEE International Conference on Networking, Architecture, and Storage (NAS) 2014, pp. 216–225. IEEE Press, Tianjin, China (2014)

7. Chopra, N., Singh, S.: Survey on scheduling in hybrid clouds. In: 5th International Conference on Computing, Communication and Networking Technologies (ICCCNT) 2014, pp. 1–6. IEEE Press, Hefei, China (2014)

8. Kandula, S., Sengupta, S., Greenberg, A., Patel, P., Chaiken, R.: The nature of data center traffic: measurements & analysis. In: 9th ACM SIGCOMM Conference on Internet Measurement Conference (IMC), pp. 202–208. ACM Press, Chicago, Illinois (2009)

9. Benson, T., Anand, A., Akella, A., Zhang, M.: Understanding data center traffic characteristics. In: 1st ACM Workshop on Research on Enterprise Networking, pp. 65–72. ACM Press, Barcelona, Spain (2009)

10. Al-Fares, M., Radhakrishnan, S., Raghavan, B., Huang, N., Vahdat, A.: Hedera: dynamic flow scheduling for data center networks. In: 7th USENIX Symposium on Networked Systems Design and Implementation (NSDI) 2010, pp. 19–19. ACM Press, San Jose, California (2010)

11. Benson, T., Akella, A., Maltz, D.A.: Network traffic characteristics of data centers in the wild. In: 10th ACM SIGCOMM Conference on Internet Measurement Conference (IMC), pp. 267–280. ACM Press, Melbourne, Australia (2010)

12. Aghdai, A., Zhang, F., Dasanayake, N., Xi, K., Chao, H.J.: Traffic measurement and analysis in an organic enterprise data center. In: 14th International Conference on High Performance Switching and Routing (HPSR) 2013, pp. 49–55. IEEE Press, Taipei, Taiwan (2013)

13. Xu, T., Chen, Y., Jiao, L., Zhao, B.Y., Hui, P., Fu, X.: Scaling microblogging services with divergent traffic demands. In: Kon, F., Kermarrec, A.-M. (eds.) Middleware 2011. LNCS, vol. 7049, pp. 20–40. Springer, Heidelberg (2011)

14. Dias, D.S., Costa, L.H.M.: Online traffic-aware virtual machine placement in data center networks. In: 4th Global Information Infrastructure and Networking Symposium, pp. 1–8. IEEE Press, Choroni, Venezuela (2012)

15. Beloglazov, A., Buyya, R.: Optimal online deterministic algorithms and adaptive heuristics for energy and performance efficient dynamic consolidation of virtual machines in cloud data centers. Concurrency Comput. Pract. Experience **24**(13), 1397–1420 (2012). Wiley Online Library Press

16. Jin, H., Deng, L., Wu, S., Shi, X.H., Pan, X.D.: Live virtual machine migration with adaptive memory compression. In: IEEE International Conference on Cluster Computing and Workshops, CLUSTER 2009, pp. 243–252. IEEE Press, New Orleans, Louisiana (2009)

17. Salwan, H.: Global conflict avoidance using block placement strategies in multi-level caches. In: IEEE Conference on Information and Communication Technologies (ICT) 2013, pp. 1221–1226. IEEE Press, Beijing, China (2013)

18. Jiang, Y., Perng, C.-S., Li, T., Chang, R.N.: Cloud analytics for capacity planning and instant VM provisioning. IEEE Trans. Netw. Serv. Manage. **10**(3), 312–325 (2013). IEEE Press

19. Broder, A., Mitzenmacher, M.: Network applications of bloom filters: a survey. Internet Math. **1**(4), 485–509 (2004)

20. The Network Simulator - ns2. http://www.isi.edu/nsnam/ns/

21. Logs of Real Parallel Workloads from Production Systems. http://www.cs.huji.ac.il/labs/parallel/workload/logs.html

22. Wilson, C., Ballani, H., Karagiannis, T., Rowtron, A.: Better never than late: meeting deadlines in datacenter networks. ACM SIGCOMM Comput. Commun. Rev. **4**, 50–61 (2011). ACM Press

23. Cisco Data Center Infrastructure 2.5 Design Guide. http://www.cisco.com/c/en/us/products/switches/data-center-switches/index.html#~products-services

24. Popa, L., Kumar, G., Chowdhury, M., Krishnamurthy, A., Ratnasamy, S., Stoica, I.: FairCloud: sharing the network in cloud computing. In: ACM SIGCOMM 2012 Conference on Applications, Technologies, Architectures, and Protocols for Computer Communication, pp. 187–198. ACM Press, Helsinki, Finland (2012)

25. Ballani, H., Jang, K., Karagiannis, T., Kim, C., Gunawardena, D., O'shea, G.: Chatty tenants and the cloud network sharing problem. In: 10th USENIX Symposium on Networked Systems Design and Implementation (NSDI 2013), pp. 171–184. ACM Press, Lombard, Illinois (2013)

26. Piao, J.T., Yan, J.: A network-aware virtual machine placement and migration approach in cloud computing. In: 9th International Conference on Grid and Cooperative Computing (GCC), 2010, pp. 87–92. IEEE Press, Nanjing, China (2010)

27. Li, Z., Luo, W., Lu, X., Yin, J.: A live migration strategy for virtual machine based on performance predicting. In: International Conference on Computer Science and Service System (CSSS), 2012, pp. 72–76. IEEE Press, Nanjing, China (2012)

Optimizing I/O Intensive Domain Handling in Xen Hypervisor for Consolidated Server Environments

Venkataramanan Venkatesh and Amiya Nayak[(✉)]

School of Electrical Engineering and Computer Science, University of Ottawa, Ottawa, Canada
{vvenk090,nayak}@uottawa.ca

Abstract. Consolidation of servers through virtualization, facilitated by the use of hypervisors, allows multiple servers to share a single hardware platform. Xen is a widely preferred hypervisor, mainly, due to its dual virtualization modes, virtual machine migration support and scalability. This paper involves an analysis of the virtual CPU (vCPU) scheduling algorithms in Xen, on the basis of their performance while handling compute intensive or I/O intensive domains in virtualized server environments. Based on this knowledge, the selection of CPU scheduler in a hypervisor can be aligned with the requirements of the hosted applications. We introduce a new credit-based vCPU scheduling strategy, which allows the vCPUs of I/O intensive domains to supersede other vCPUs, in order to favor the reduction of I/O bound domain response times and the subsequent bottleneck in the CPU run queue. The results indicate substantial improvement of I/O handling and fair resource allocation between the host and guest domains.

Keywords: Xen hypervisor · Server consolidation · Virtual machine monitor (VMM) · CPU scheduling

1 Introduction

According to a report [1] by Natural Resources Defense Council (NRDC), the overall data centre efficiency is still at 12 %–18 % with most of the servers remaining idle while drawing precious energy. Proliferation of data stored in the cloud has sprung the construction of a high number of server farms by organizations. This 'server sprawl' problem has been many years in the making, thus serving as the root cause for induction of virtualization into the server environment. Hussain and Habib in [2] have addressed the 'server sprawl' problem by using virtualization-based server consolidation and storage unification through storage area network (SAN). But, the risks that come with virtualization must also be considered to avert a crisis when an unprecedented event occurs, since consolidating servers also means introducing a single point of failure for all the applications running on the hosted virtual machines. Additionally, there is the problem of virtualized legacy applications not being able to deliver near-native performance as that of a dedicated application server.

While the Xen hypervisor [3] addresses some of the post-virtualization issues like security by providing isolation among virtual machines and provisions for adapting different resource allocation schemes to cater to the needs of the hosted applications, a

© Springer International Publishing Switzerland 2016
X. Huang et al. (Eds.): GPC 2016, LNCS 9663, pp. 180–195, 2016.
DOI: 10.1007/978-3-319-39077-2_12

near-native performance for every hosted application remains the ultimate goal of the developers in the Xen open source community. The motivation for this work originates from the reasoning that, since CPU scheduling algorithms are accounted for majority of the factors affecting a hypervisor's performance, this component of the hypervisor's architecture must be subjected to intensive research, so as to arrive at sustainable solutions to performance issues. Understanding the limits of a scheduling algorithm is of paramount importance when consolidating server hardware and this work provides an essential insight into the CPU scheduling characteristics and their impact on VM performance.

1.1 Xen Hypervisor Architecture

The architecture of Xen consists of two elements, namely the hypervisor and the driver domain. The function of the hypervisor layer is to provide abstraction between the guest operating systems and the actual hardware by creating virtual counterparts of the physical hardware components. The driver domain or host domain or Domain 0 ("dom0") is a privileged VM which manages other guest VMs or unprivileged domains or user domains ("domU"), enumerated as Domain 1, Domain 2 and so on. The term driver domain for dom0 is mainly due to its responsibility of coordinating the I/O operations on behalf of the user domains, since the guest domains do not have direct access to the I/O hardware. In initial versions of Xen, the hypervisor managed the I/O operations by creating simple device abstractions for the guest domains to access. This functionality has been transferred to the dom0 and the current methodology of I/O management by Xen works more efficiently, as the host domain handles all of the virtual I/O interrupts. In addition, this delegation of responsibility to dom0, allows the hypervisor to focus more on virtualizing other hardware components such as CPU, disk drives and network interfaces.

1.2 Domain States in Xen

Analogous to processes in operating systems, a domain in Xen can be present in, and transition into or out of, any of the following states:

Paused. The domain's execution is paused and it still consumes allocated resources like memory, but remains ineligible for scheduling.

Saved. A running domain is saved to a state file for it to be restored later, but TCP timeouts can severe live network connections; memory allocated for the domain will be released for other domains to use.

Running. Domain is running or runnable on the CPU.

Blocked. Domain is waiting on an I/O or in idle mode. It is currently neither running nor runnable.

Shutdown. Domain enters this state on a hard shutdown or shutdown command, terminating all the processes of the guest OS.

Terminated. The domain's processes are killed instantly and the domain id is deleted (Fig. 1).

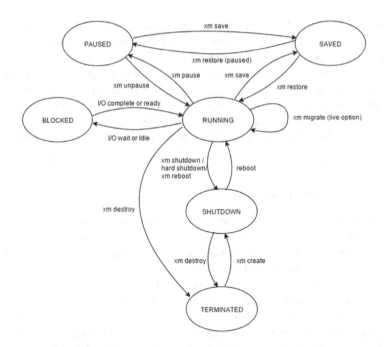

Fig. 1. Domain states in Xen hypervisor showing the five states a running domain can transition into, either manually using 'xm' commands or as part of an I/O cycle.

2   CPU Scheduling in Xen

The Xen hypervisor, since its inception, has employed a number of scheduling algorithms namely Borrowed Virtual Time [4], Atropos [5], Simple Earliest Deadline First [6], ARINC 653 [7], Credit and Credit2 [8]. Scheduling parameters of individual domains can be adjusted by management software running in Domain0. After the architectural change brought by Xen 3.0, the new model of I/O operations increased the complexity of CPU resource usage. The earlier algorithms such as Borrowed Virtual Time and Atropos have been phased out due to the I/O structural change and the lack of non-work-conserving mode (NWC) [11], which means that the running domain is able to exceed its CPU share in the absence of competition from other domains.

Borrowed Virtual Time. BVT is a weighted or proportional fair-share scheduler based on the concept of virtual time, dispatching the runnable VM with the earliest effective virtual time first. This concept of virtual time allows latency-sensitive or I/O intensive domains to "warp" [4] back in virtual time by temporarily promoting themselves a higher scheduling priority. The amount of virtual time equivalent which was spent for warping is compensated by depleting the domain's CPU allocation in the future. Minimum Charging Unit (MCU) [4], which is derived from the frequency of clock interrupts, is used as basic unit of accounting for a running domain. The decision for a context switch is made based on the parameter context switch allowance 'C', a multiple of MCU, which denotes the actual time comparable with another VM competing for the CPU. The proportional fair-sharing is implemented by allocating each domain, a share of the CPU based on the weights configured in the domains. Optimal fairness is ensured by BVT in allocation of CPU since the error value cannot exceed the sum of context switch allowance 'C' and one 'MCU'. BVT can operate only in work conserving (WC) mode which means that a domain cannot exceed its CPU share even if a portion of the CPU remains unused by other domains. This is one of the major draw-backs of BVT scheduler which severely restricts CPU utilization and hence, BVT was gradually phased out in the later stages of Xen development.

Atropos. The Atropos scheduler allocates shares on the basis of an application dependent period, determined by the slice 's' and period 'p', which together represent the processor bandwidth of that particular domain. Each domain is guaranteed to receive a minimum of 's' ticks of CPU time and if available, several slices of CPU time in each period of length 'p'. A domain is allocated a slack CPU time, only if it is configured to receive that extra time as indicated by the Boolean parameter 'x'. To ensure timely servicing of I/O from domains, a latency hint 'l' is specified as one of the parameters for differentiating I/O intensive or latency-sensitive domains [5].

The Atropos scheduler provides an additional degree of freedom by enabling the user to control both the absolute share of the domains and the frequency at which they are to be scheduled. Say if the domain's present state is on a scheduler queue, then based on the deadline 'd', which denotes the end of current period 'p' for the domain, a value 'r' is calculated in real-time and passed to the scheduler as the time remaining for the domain in that current period. Queues 'Q_r' and 'Q_w' [5], representing the list of ready-to-run and waiting domains respectively, are sorted according to deadline 'd', in addition to another queue of blocked domains. The values d_x and p_x denote the deadline and period of the domains at the head of the respective queues. The Atropos scheduler due to its significant overhead and inability to balance loads in a SMP has been replaced by more sophisticated load-balancing algorithms.

ARINC 653. It is based on the standard Real Time Operating System (RTOS) interface for partitioning of computer resources in the time and space domains. The resulting software environment is capable of handling isolated domains of applications, executing independently of each other. The partitioning of memory into sub-ranges for creating multiple application levels also leads to a spatial and temporal isolation of the domains, thus maintaining them under the impression of complete possession of the underlying hardware.

This methodology of domain isolation, wherein each independent block is called a 'partition' [7], provides ARINC 653 with the capacity to deterministically schedule the Xen domains. The CPU time is allocated in the form of 'credits' in frames which are consumed by the domains. When the domains have reached their credit limit for a given frame they are considered as 'out of credits' or 'expired' and correspondingly placed in a wait queue called 'expiry list'. When the credits are available via the next frame the domains can resume executing again. In case, a domain is made to yield the CPU or if a domain is blocked, prior to consumption of the allocated credits in a given major frame, execution for these domains is resumed later in the major frame.

On the event of completion of a major frame, the domains in the expired list are restored to their preset credit allocations. These preset values and other parameters of the ARINC 653 are configurable from within the dom0 or the driver domain. The parameters to be set include run time for each domain and the major frame for the schedule. Calculation of the length of the major frame depends on the condition that all the domains must be able to expend all of their configured credits. Current implementation of the ARINC 653 lacks support for multi-processor environments and hence, preferred mostly for special case usage.

Simple Earliest Deadline First. The SEDF scheduler is a proportional or weighted sharing algorithm which employs real-time information feedback to guarantee CPU time and deal with latency-sensitive domains. The SEDF scheduler may be considered to inherit its structure from the Atropos schedule, from the perspective of parameters and specifications. For example, a combination of the CPU bandwidth parameters denoted by a tuple <Slice (s_i), Period (p_i), Extra-time (x_i)> is used to specify the amount of CPU time requested by the domain. Like Atropos, there is a minimum guarantee of s_i time slices in every period of length p_i and a domain is allocated extra-time, if the Boolean flag x_i is set. This tendency of allowing domains to exceed their CPU limits forms the non-work conserving property of SEDF. More importantly, this slack time which is re-distributed as extra-time on demand, follows a best-effort and fair approach. The slack time is a by-product of under-utilized timeslices and is not borrowed from other domains' CPU time.

The optimization of fair allocation is impacted to a great extent by the granularity used in defining the tuple of a domain. Deadline d_i and remaining time r_i of a domain in the current period p_i are passed to the scheduler in real-time [6], thereby, facilitating the scheduler to make real-time decisions based on the status of the domains. The feature where SEDF differs from Atropos is that the SEDF scheduler chooses the domain with the earliest d_i, from the waiting queue, to be scheduled next.

Though the response time to latency-sensitive domains is better in SEDF, the lack of load balancing on SMPs proves to be a major drawback. This paper focuses on improving scheduling scheme to support soft real-time workloads in virtualization systems. Some of the latest research in Xen has been focussed towards adapting the hypervisor for deployment in real-time workload environments. In [14], Cheng et al. have proposed an enhanced scheduler named SRT-Xen which focuses on improving the Xen scheduling framework for handling domains with soft real-time tasks. In the paper they have also discussed about a scheduling mechanism which ensures fair and non-detrimental handling of both real-time and non-real-time tasks.

Credit. Credit is a proportional share scheduler in which the automation of global load balancing of virtual CPUs among the physical cores was introduced to Xen Hypervisor.

When a CPU completes execution of the domains assigned to it, the queues of other CPUs are surveyed for any ready-to-run vCPUs. This load balancing, to an extent, prevents CPUs from being overwhelmed and promotes optimized CPU utilization. The queue maintained by each physical CPU is sorted based on the priority of the vCPU and the priority may either be OVER or UNDER [8].

OVER: the initial allocation of the vCPU, based on proportional share scheduling, has been exceeded;
UNDER: the initial allocation for the vCPU is yet to be consumed completely.

Every 10 ms, or for every scheduler tick, the credits of the domain are decremented and when a vCPU has consumed all of its allocated credits, the value of the credit crosses the zero mark and the state of its priority is converted from UNDER to OVER, and prevented from being scheduled. A vCPU or VM has 30 ms before it is pre-empted by another VM, unless it has enough credits to stay UNDER. At the end of every 30 ms, the credit for each domain is replenished and the domains which were in OVER state are allowed to execute again.

In addition to the two priority states, an additional BOOST priority ensures that domains which are awoken after an idle I/O wait are placed ahead in the run queue to reduce latency. The scheduler is triggered when an I/O event occurs in the event channel and the domains with the BOOST priority are fast tracked to the head of the queue. Two parameters govern the credit allocation of a domain: Weight denotes proportion or percentage of CPU to be allocated; Cap denotes limit of extra credit which cannot be exceeded. Value of Cap set at '0', means there is no limit to the amount of CPU time that a domain can exceed. Non-zero value for Cap limits the amount of CPU a domain receives by restricting the extra credits to that particular percentage.

Credit2. The Credit scheduler, besides its favourable characteristics, has a few problems like below average performance in handling I/O intensive domains, lack of fairness in scheduling latency-sensitive or interactive domains (multiuser applications) and hyper-thread dependency issues. The revamped version of the Credit scheduler is Credit2, designed to overcome some of the shortcomings of its predecessor. The Credit scheduler implements fair scheduling based solely on the OVER, UNDER or BOOST priorities and organizing the run queue in a round-robin fashion for domains with equal priority state. The domains which burn through their allocated credits in a single schedule are more likely to be positioned ahead in the queue than those domains which yield the CPU every so often, only to consume a small portion of their credits before pre-emption. This inherent nature of round-robin scheduling combined with a credit based allocation policy, results in the unintentional, but preferential treatment towards compute heavy domains. The Credit2 attempts to solve these issues by removing the three priority states altogether and sorting the CPU run queue based on the credit balance of the domains.

From Xen 4.2 onwards, an option for scheduling rate limit has been added which sets the minimum amount of time, in microseconds, a domain is made to run before being preempted. This value limit ensures that the domains are performing some minimum amount of work rather than waking up only to be scheduled off without burning any credits. Based on the nature of the workload, for instance, a value of 10 ms for compute intensive workloads and a value of 500us or lower for latency sensitive workloads are advised. In addition, a timeslice parameter for varying the vCPU run time, in milliseconds, has also been introduced to meet the latency needs of the domains being executed.

3   Equalizer Scheduler for I/O Intensive Workloads

In case of virtualized high definition video streaming and compute servers, the CPU-intensive domains will occupy the CPU for longer periods since they require more computational time on the processor, ergo starving I/O bound domains. While the I/O bound vCPUs wait for the allocation of CPU the onset of the next accounting period replenishes the credits, thus further enriching the compute intensive vCPUs. Further, the option of scheduler rate limiting to reduce the time quanta to address this problem requires manual intervention at every instance a different workload is received and does not bode well for a consolidated workload environment. In [15], the authors Hongshan Qu et al. have discussed about the importance of analyzing the resource requirements of individual domains to perform predictive scheduling and have proposed a work-load aware scheduling method for heterogeneous VM environments.

With the purpose of enhancing I/O intensive domain performance in a multi-faceted workload setting, we propose a new credit-based vCPU scheduling scheme, where in, the credit remaining for each vCPU after every accounting plays an important role in making the scheduling decision. The starved vCPUs with the most remaining credits are allowed to supersede others to favor the reduction of the I/O bottleneck in the processor run queue. Since most I/O bound vCPUs need only 1 ms to 10 ms to complete their short CPU burst cycles, there will be no adverse effects in CPU-bound domain performance. The priority states of OVER and UNDER are used to determine if the domain is eligible to be scheduled and the scheduling decision is performed based on a combination of scheduling eligibility and credit availability of the domains.

The vCPU scheduling scheme proposed here has the potential to introduce context switch overhead because of additional validations in the scheduling decision path of code. Though some context switch overhead will exist, the benefits of rapid response-time scheduling for I/O bound domains are observed to outweigh the negative aspects of the Equalizer scheduler.

```
ALGORITHM:
equalizer_schedule (current time);
begin
perform vCPU validation at run queue head
if
vCPU`s priority is OVER OR vCPU_credit less than
max_credit
then
  check other PCPU run queue
      if
        at least one PCPU run queue empty
      then
        Dequeue from current PCPU run queue
        Insert vCPU into PCPU with empty run queue
      else
        deschedule running vCPU
        perform vCPU validation at run queue head
      endif
else
  update max_credit (vCPU_credit)
  return (vCPU); %vCPU to run next%
endif

deschedule running vCPU:
if
  running vCPU is runnable AND run queue non-empty
then
  insert vCPU at rear end of current PCPU run queue
else
      if run queue is empty
      then
        yield pcpu
        set PCPU idle flag
      endif
endif

update max_credit:
if
  passed vCPU_credit greater than zero
then
  set max_credit = vCPU_credit
endif
```

4   Simulation and Performance Analysis

In this section, we describe the benchmarking environment and parameter setting established for comparison between the scheduling algorithms in Xen. The version of Xen hypervisor under study is Xen 4.4.1 which employs Credit, SEDF and Credit2 as the main scheduling algorithms. The hardware specifications of the system, used for conducting the experiments, are as follows: Intel Core i3-370 M processor with two cores of 2.4 GHz each, 64-bit architecture, 3 GB RAM and 320 GB hard disk.

The driver domain ran Ubuntu 13.04 with linux kernel 3.8.0-19 and the user domain ran Ubuntu 12.04 with linux kernel 3.5.0-23 on Xen 4.4.1 stable release. The test suites used to simulate VM workloads in this experiment are as follows:

IBS. The Isolation benchmark suite [9] which incorporates a CPU intensive test is capable of creating simulated workloads by performing a series of integer and floating point calculations. The intense computational operations performed on the CPU resemble compute-intensive applications such as HD video playback or 3D graphics rendering.

IOzone. A file system benchmark [10] which allows performing of multiple Disk-I/O operations and monitor the rate of read/write operations. The sequential and random read/write operations collectively induce stress on the file system.

Netperf. A network monitoring tool [11], aids in measuring low-level network performance by exchanging bulk files with a remote host.

Sysbench. A performance benchmark tool [12], includes an OLTP test for simulating database server transactions from a Mysql database.

4.1   Disk I/O Benchmarking Using IOzone

We employ IOzone test suite, which performs a series [10] of sequential read/write (S-Read/S-Write) and random read/write (R-Read/R-Write) operations, followed by the measurement of the read/write rate in KBytes per second. We choose a combination of 512 Mb file size with 1 Mb record length for avoiding a system freeze, when hosting multiple guests while also keeping in mind, the cumulative operation time of the experiment. In order to avoid files being written or read from the cache memory or RAM, IOzone is set to perform only Direct I/O operations, which ensures that only the physical disk is used in the file operations. Figure 2a shows credit scheduler's dom0 disk I/O performance when dom0 is idle and when dom0 is performing heavy CPU operations facilitated by IBS's CPU intensive test. In the first case, the domU is able to achieve 93 % of dom0's I/O performance and when dom0 is under stress, domU's I/O execution rate degrades by 4 %–5 % of its earlier performance when dom0 was idle.

In Fig. 2b, the disk I/O performance of SEDF scheduler's domU (dom0 idle) is shown. Under the SEDF's scheduling the domU was able to run I/O operations at 97 % of dom0's I/O execution rate. This might seem better than the Credit scheduler's near-native performance but there is a tradeoff in overall I/O performance, where the Credit scheduler has an edge, as the SEDF scheduler lags due to the overhead induced by its real-time processes.

When the dom0 is subjected to heavy CPU operations in the SEDF scheduler, the domU's disk I/O performance is found to be drastically affected. As illustrated in Fig. 2b, the disk I/O performance of domU degrades by 41 %–45 % of its performance when dom0 was idle. Figure 3a shows the disk I/O performance of the Credit2 scheduler; domU, when the other domain is executing compute operations. With Credit2 scheduler the domU was able to achieve from 94 % up to 99 % of dom0's I/O execution rate. These

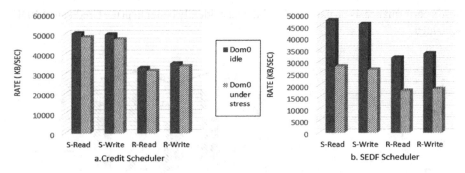

Fig. 2. Evaluation of Disk I/O performance of the Credit and SEDF schedulers using IOzone depicting the guest domain's throughput when host is idle and under computational stress

readings show a marked improvement in handling guest domain I/O requests from Credit scheduler and the overall I/O execution rate is also justifiably better.

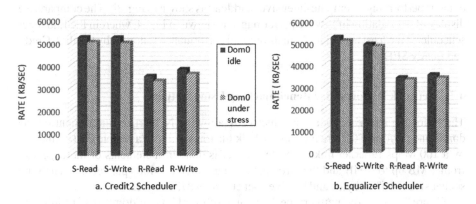

Fig. 3. Evaluation of Disk I/O performance of the Credit2 and Equalizer schedulers

The handling of I/O from domU by dom0 when under stress in Credit2 scheduler is better when compared to Credit and SEDF. As shown by Fig. 3a, the disk I/O performance by domU when dom0 is performing CPU intensive operations, produces results which show that Credit2 scheduler is capable of providing near-native I/O support in a compute intensive environment too. The results show that the domU is capable of restricting the throughput degradation to only 4 %–6 % and given the superior overall I/O execution rate, this fall in read/write rate is only of negligible magnitude. Figure 3b shows that Equalizer scheduler's domU reaches 98 %–99 % near-native disk I/O performance when Dom0 is idle, which exhibits the scheduling fairness among the vCPUs promoted by the new scheduling scheme. A clear improvement is seen over the Credit scheduler that could only reach a maximum of 93 % of near-native disk I/O performance.

The comparison shown in Fig. 4 shows that the Equalizer scheduler has a near- native performance index, which means performance of guest domain as a percentage of the host's performance, is on par with Credit2 and evidently better than the Credit and SEDF scheduler.

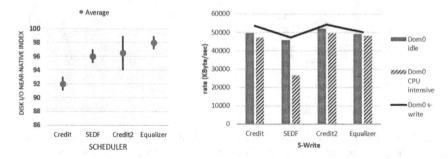

Fig. 4. Comparison of the proposed scheduler with Credit, SEDF and Credit2 schedulers

The Equalizer Scheduler suffers 2 %–4 % degradation in disk I/O performance when dom0 is performing a compute-intensive workload as shown in Fig. 3b. The comparative display of degradation in S-write performance is shown in Fig. 4, wherein the Equalizer scheduler is the least to deviate from its optimal performance followed by Credit2, Credit and finally SEDF.

4.2   Network Performance Benchmarking Using Netperf

The following experiments are conducted by allowing Netperf to run a client on the domU and perform TCP stream tests via bulk file transfers with a remote host connected by a 100 Mbps Ethernet link. The file transfer is done in increments of message size from 1 MB up to 4 MB and the throughput is measured in Mbits per second. The send socket size is 16384 bytes and receive socket size is 87380 bytes.

Figure 5 shows the network performance of domU when dom0 is kept idle and when dom0 is made to perform CPU intensive operations facilitated by IBS CPU stress tests. The results exhibit a clear drop in throughput from an average of 87.85 Mb/s to 72.71 Mb/s. The Credit scheduler has an average performance when the CPU is under contention and an above average performance when CPU is not performing any compute intensive tasks.

When SEDF is put under the same test, the results show that the real-time scheduler fails to handle I/O tasks promptly when the CPU is placed under stress. Figure 5 shows the performance of SEDF's bandwidth intensive test and we can observe a fall in throughput from an average of 89.30 Mb/s to 63.55 Mb/s when CPU is under contention.

The Credit2 scheduler exhibits significant improvement from Credit scheduler in network performance tests. As shown in Fig. 5, the average throughput of 91.05 Mb/s, when dom0 was idle, dropped to an average of 79.15 Mb/s, when CPU is under stress, which is better than the Credit scheduler's 72.71 Mb/s.

The comparative chart for network intensive benchmarking of the four schedulers indicates that the Equalizer scheduler has the minimal performance drop when a network

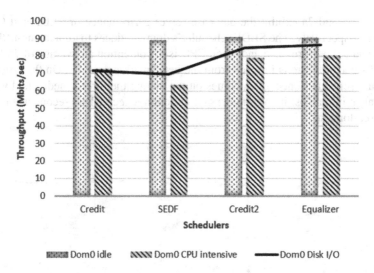

Fig. 5. Comparison of the network throughput of domU measured using Netperf, under different workload states of dom0

I/O intensive domain is competing with a compute-intensive domain or an I/O intensive domain.

4.3 OLTP Database Server Performance Benchmarking Using Sysbench

The performance of the schedulers when hosting database server applications can be measured using Sysbench. As a prelude to simulating the database server we create a Mysql test table with rows of data starting 1000 rows and continue scaling up to 1000000 rows. As illustrated in Fig. 6a, the Credit scheduler's number of transactions/second, which is an important merit for seamless database querying, suffers a performance drop when a user Domain is hosting the database server. And when the host domain is placed under computing stress the OLTP transaction rate further degrades due to the unavailability of the CPU for the server's I/O requests.

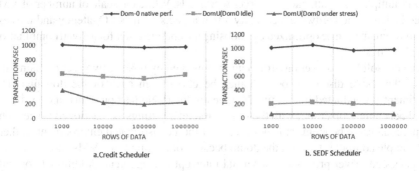

Fig. 6. Rate of transaction in dom0 and domU when simulating OLTP server using Sysbench-Credit and SEDF

Figures 6b and 7a exhibit the database server performance of SEDF and Credit2 schedulers respectively. The SEDF scheduler's domU reduces to almost one-fifth of its native domain's performance and when CPU is in contention an average of 75 % drop in domU's performance is inferred from the benchmarking results. On the other hand the Credit2 scheduler once again comes on top among the three schedulers, by showcasing only minimal loss in the number of transactions executed per second when hosted by the user domain.

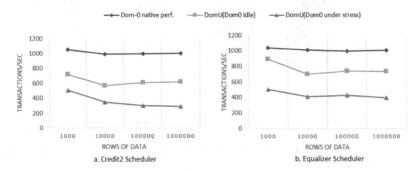

Fig. 7. Rate of transaction in dom0 and domU when simulating OLTP server using Sysbench-Credit2 and Equalizer

The Equalizer scheduler exhibits superior handling of database server requests, shown in Fig. 7b, with the native domain performance similar to that of Credit and Credit2. The loss of number of Transactions per second when domU is handling is lower than Credit2 exhibiting the high I/O throughput rate which is characteristic of the design.

4.4   Consolidated Server Environment

One of the solutions for server sprawl in data centers is the consolidation [13] of hardware, thus promoting resource optimization, while masking the shared server architecture from the users by ensuring negligible or unnoticeable deterioration in QoS. Any hypervisor which is claimed to be a candidate for server virtualization has to be qualified to host multiple and multi-faceted server workloads. While the scale of number of VMs hosted is tied to the hardware's capacity, other aspects such as I/O latency and fairness towards domains can be optimized by choosing the apt scheduler for a given combination of applications.

The consolidated server environment is simulated by hosting two user domains and one of the above discussed performance benchmarks in each of the domains. The experiment is conducted by running IOzone on dom0, Netperf on dom1 and Sysbench Mysql benchmark on dom2, with the same parameter settings as mentioned earlier. The compute intensive benchmark is not preferred for a consolidated environment as there exists ample compute stress on the dom0 because of hosting three VMs and the associated back-end driver processes for virtual interrupt management. Additional compute stress resulted in erratic behavior of the VMs and benchmarking results turned out to be inconsistent and unreliable.

The extent to which the virtual counterpart of a dedicated server has performed can be gauged by using the Domain0 or host's native performance. As shown in Fig. 8, the performance indexing based on dom0 gives a comprehensive picture of the schedulers in a typical server environment.

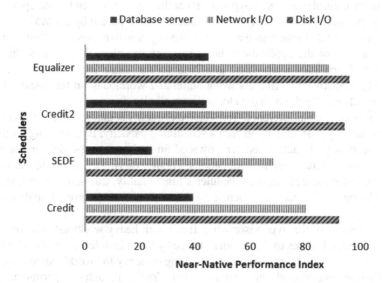

Fig. 8. Consolidated server environment, simulated by hosting two user domains and running IOzone on dom0, Netperf on dom1 and Sysbench Mysql benchmark on dom2

The consolidated workloads generate I/O requests on a frequent basis thus causing an I/O bottleneck, which has evidently caused the setback in the schedulers. The results obtained are not far from the observations made, when the CPU as a resource was under contention. This shows that servicing of I/O requests or interrupts is just as important as CPU allocation. The servicing of Disk I/O has not been interfered by the I/O bottleneck and this suggests the consolidation of disk intensive domains with I/O heavy workload servers such as a webserver.

The experiments provide a glimpse of the Credit2 scheduler's exceptional performance in a high frequency I/O environment and the adept I/O handling capacity which was lacking in Credit scheduler. The results obtained collectively form substantial evidence to the assertion that choice of CPU scheduling algorithm used by Xen hypervisor impacts the performance of the applications hosted on the server. The Equalizer scheduler's handling of I/O heavy domains marginally surpasses the Credit2 scheduler in a consolidated workload experimental setup. As shown in Fig. 8, the proposed scheduler has a slight edge over the Credit2 while performing database transactions and Network intensive I/O handling.

5   Conclusion and Future Work

We have discussed about the server sprawl problem and examined consolidation as a solution, which has shed light on the VM manageability and migration troubles which can rise in the control plane. Xen hypervisor's architecture has been looked upon briefly following the challenges in the VM environment to be expected by a VMM.

The choice of CPU scheduling algorithm used by Xen hypervisor evidently impacts the performance of the applications hosted on the machine. We analysed the CPU scheduling algorithms incorporated into Xen so far, since its earliest version and conducted exhaustive experiments using simulated workloads on the latest batch of schedulers released by the Xen developers' community.

The most significant inference from the experiments is that servicing of I/O by the driver domain depends heavily on Xen's scheduling capacity. By focussing on the I/O handling tendency of each scheduler provided an insight into the right usage of the hypervisor for workload specific applications. Though varying the scheduler parameters could even out some odds in the scheduler's functionality, true scheduling fairness is achieved by optimal performance across all domains without disproportionate usage of resources.

The behaviour of the hypervisor when faced with heavy workloads was discussed and the challenge it poses to the resource usage by the scheduler in charge. Credit and Credit2 have proven to be robust in their handling of heavy I/O workloads such as disk, bandwidth intensive network and database server. Credit2, though in experimental phase has been observed to exhibit and deliver the promised improvement in I/O handling over the Credit scheduler. The older SEDF scheduler has been observed to fall behind in contention with both the Credit scheduler versions. ARINC 653 is a special case scheduler built for uniprocessor architectures and hence cannot be compared with the other schedulers in this version of Xen.

The Equalizer scheduler designed and implemented has been put under different scenarios and benchmarked. The results indicate that the motives of design which are improved handling of compute-intensive domains and to improve effective I/O throughput have been realized although overlooking a small percentage of context switch overhead. Though the performance of the scheduler in idle conditions is not on par with the credit scheduler due to the overhead accumulated because of context switching, the behavior of the scheduler indicates that when competing with compute intensive or I/O intensive domains, every domain is ensured scheduling fairness.

Our future work involves further study on the capabilities of Xen's scheduling algorithms when employed as a hypervisor in collaboration with an open standard cloud computing platform such as Openstack. The live VM migration features of Xen and efficient VM management in a cloud environment seem to be the logical and viable step forward.

Furthermore, the application potentials of Xen as a Network Function Virtualization (NFV) solution for current SDN based networks are to be explored. Another focus area for supplementing the efforts of this research, in terms of green computing, is the study of VM migration strategies for energy efficient data center management.

Acknowledgement. The authors would like to thank the anonymous reviewers for their comments and suggestions. This work is partly supported by NSERC Grant CRDPJ 445731-12.

References

1. Natural Resources Defense Council (NRDC). Data Center Energy Assessment Report (2014). https://www.nrdc.org/energy/files/data-center-efficiency-assessment-IP.pdf
2. Hussain, T., Habib, S.: A redesign methodology for storage management virtualization. In: IFIP/IEEE International Symposium on Integrated Network Management (IM), pp. 676–679 (2013)
3. Barham, P., Dragovic, B., Fraser, K., et al.: Xen and the art of virtualization. In: 19th ACM Symposium on Operating Systems Principles, pp. 164–177 (2003)
4. Duda, K.J., Cheriton, D.R.: Borrowed-virtual-time (BVT) scheduling: supporting latency-sensitive threads in a general-purpose scheduler. In: 17th ACM SIGOPS Symposium on Operating Systems Principles, pp. 261–276 (1999)
5. Leslie, I.M., McAuley, D., Black, R., Roscoe, T., Barham, P., Evers, D., Fairbairns, R., Hyden, E.: The design and implementation of an operating system to support distributed multimedia applications. IEEE J. Sel. Areas Commun. **14**(7), 1280–1297 (1996)
6. Jansen, P.G., Mullender, S.J., Havinga, P.J., Scholten, H.: Lightweight EDF scheduling with deadline inheritance. University of Twente (2003). http://doc.utwente.nl/41399/
7. VanderLeest, S.H.: ARINC 653 hypervisor. In: 29th IEEE/AIAA Digital Avionics Systems Conference (DASC), pp. 5.E.2-1–5.E.2-20 (2010)
8. Credit Scheduler. http://wiki.xensource.com/xenwiki/CreditScheduler
9. Isolation Benchmark Suite. http://web2.clarkson.edu/class/cs644/isolation/index.html
10. IOzone Filesystem Benchmark. http://www.iozone.org/
11. IOzone Documentation. http://www.iozone.org/docs/IOzone_msword_98.pdf
12. Netperf. http://www.netperf.org/netperf/training/Netperf.html
13. Sysbench Benchmark Tool. https://dev.mysql.com/downloads/benchmarks.html
14. Uddin, M., Rahman, A.: Energy efficiency and low carbon enabler green IT framework for data centers considering green metrics. Renew. Sustain. Energy Rev. **16**(6), 4078–4094 (2012)
15. Cheng, K., Bai, Y., Wang, R., Ma, Y.: Optimizing Soft real-time scheduling performance for virtual machines with SRT-Xen. In: 15th IEEE/ACM International Symposium on Cluster, Cloud and Grid Computing (CCGrid), pp. 169–178 (2015)
16. Qu, H., Liu, X., Xu, H.: A workload-aware resources scheduling method for virtual machine. Int. J. Grid Distrib. Comput. **8**(1), 247–258 (2015)

User-Centric and Real-Time Activity Recognition Using Smart Glasses

Joshua Ho and Chien-Min Wang[(✉)]

Institute of Information Science, Academia Sinica,
115 Taipei, Taiwan
hojoshuacs@gmail.com,
cmwang@iis.sinica.edu.tw

Abstract. In this paper, we present a personalized and real-time prototyping solution on smart glasses targeting activity recognition. Our work is based on the analysis of sensor data to study user's motions and activities, while utilizing wearable glasses bundled with various sensors. The software system collects, trains data, and builds the model for fast classification, which emphasizes on how specific features annotate and extract head-mounted behavior. Based on our feature selection algorithm, the system reaches high accuracy and low computation cost in the experiments. Other than some previous works in data mining on sensors of smart phones or smart glasses, and related works of activity recognition on smartphones, our results show the accuracy achieves 87 %, and the responsive time is less than 3 s. The proposed system can provide more insightful and powerful services for the glass wearers. It would be possibly expected to carry out more user-centric and context-aware wearable applications in the future.

Keywords: Smart glasses · Context-awareness · Head tracking · Classification · Activity recognition

1 Introduction

Recently, wearable devices such as Apple Watch [19], smart glasses, and many others are coming to many peoples' lives. Especially, after the Explorer Edition of Google Glass released, people are paying more attention to the '*head-mounted*', '*versatile*', and '*augmented reality*' devices, such as Epson [20], Sony devices [21], and other manufactures are still working on many latest and innovative devices.

The wearable computers of smart glasses are able to detect voice commands, to identify the objects, to take pictures as well as to record video clips, etc. While wear-ing the smart glasses, the sensors such as Accelerometer, Gravity, Linear Acceleration, Gyroscope, and Rotation Vector, are able to produce logging data during various users' activities. Meanwhile, wearable services are based on more reliable and insightful information for immediate interactions, Machine Learning analysis, personalized context-aware recommendations and activity based recognitions. Thus, wearable computers are gaining more attentions as possibly more natural, intuitive, hands-free, and user-friendly for our mobile experiences.

© Springer International Publishing Switzerland 2016
X. Huang et al. (Eds.): GPC 2016, LNCS 9663, pp. 196–210, 2016.
DOI: 10.1007/978-3-319-39077-2_13

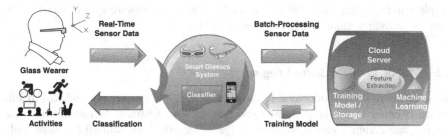

Fig. 1. The proposed system aims to classify user's head motions to recognize activities according to wearable sensor data from the smart glasses.

Our regular lives consist of many activities, such as working, exercising, socializing, shopping, sleeping, and so on. Contextual information of our behavior possibly provides us with more intelligent and suitable services in the future. Obviously, smart glasses bring users unique '*head-mounted*' and '*eye-wearing*' experiences, as well as fixed '*on- body*' position of face wearing while exploring the external world, by comparing with using smartphones, which are often put in the pocket, backpack, or held in user's hands. Thus, we currently focus on user's personal sports and entertainment activities via an eye-wearing wearable computer, searching accuracy of real-time personal activity recognitions via Machine Learning approaches, and looking for how '*head-tracking*' might matter in activity recognition, which are designed, evaluated, experimented, studied and discussed in our arguments.

Most early works are either lack of further discussions in '*on-body*' characteristic, or ignoring the realistic usage of the smartphones; (e.g. jogging/walking with smartphones in hands/tied to the arm? It might be put in the pocket, backpack, or just personal preferences due to some conditions.) Furthermore, by considering user's head motions, the results of accuracy and real-time reaction in activity recognition are achieved in the experiments. Based on our motivations to present the proposed system, shown in Fig. 1, we will anticipate that more context-aware wearable services are demanded in the coming future.

2 Related Works

Earlier works have discussed about context-awareness and user's mobile activity recognition on smartphones. More recent works also introduce using Accelerometer sensor and wearable computers to achieve some results of activity recognition.

2.1 Context Awareness

In the past decades, research works conducted to understand human context have been significantly achieved. They lead us into exploring the ways of communication between men and machines [3]. Context-aware applications in mobile computing help people's lives intelligently and conveniently. The context-aware system can react to humans' activities more dynamically and flexibly.

2.2   Mobile Phone Activity Logging

Some earlier research works look for user's characteristic and behavior when a mobile device is either in use or standby. Especially for smartphones, data of sensors, processing, and communication could be analyzed, identified and utilized for more applications of activity recognition [1, 4]. Context gathering, learning, predicting, and monitoring analytically present solutions to the integration of context-aware mobile computing, cloud services and the user's physical surroundings. Moreover, other works address mobile applications of smartphones to analyze user's Accelerometer [8–10, 12]. However, data received by the smartphone depends on its position in the pocket, bag or hands. Smartphones are often rotated while locating in different places, directions and so on. Here we show a typical alpha rotation shown in Fig. 2 of the smartphone.

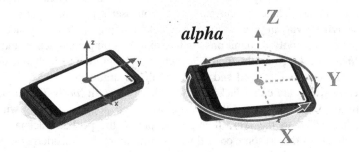

Fig. 2. An example of alpha rotation shows how smartphones might rotate with its coordinate frame.

2.3   Wearable Computer and Sensors

Research works on Google Glass[1] [2, 7] have shown the possibility of assistive use for patients. Besides, more other projects [11, 13, 14] are studying and discussing human motion through single '*body-worn*' Accelerometer sensor, electrode sensors, or '*armband*' and '*backpack*' wearable array sensors. The works in [15] present experiments in recognizing human activities such as blinking and reading via the latest designed smart glasses. In our studies, other projects also talk about analyzing users' behavior via Google Glass [5], and performing '*lifelogging*' processes [6] to upload taken images and texts. Another work in [16] uses '*textile integrated*' and '*wearable sensor array*' to achieve the classification of human motions.

---

[1] https://www.google.com/glass/start/.

3   System Evaluation

In order to learn how smartphones might sense differently compared to smart glasses during the task of activity recognition, we prepare two hardware devices with separated software application to evaluate our assumption. The evaluated sensors on both devices include Accelerometer, Gravity, Linear Acceleration, Gyroscope, and Rotation Vector.

3.1   System and Software

We start to look into how smart devices like smartphones and smart glasses to perform activity recognition in the experiments. Our Android software, '*Mobile4You*', is installed on the smartphone (Samsung S3 mini, Android 4.1) to collect logging data of sensors with the frequency of 20 Hz on each sensor, and each logging time is 20 s with 400 entries of recorded data. Another Android software is installed on the smart glasses (Google Glass, Explorer Edition XE 22), '*Glass4You*', which is similar to '*Mobile4You*' but with slight differences in the UI design and SDK implementations. The logging frequency is 5 Hz for each sensor, each logging time is 20 s, and total 100 entries of data are recorded on our smart glasses.

3.2   Experimented Sensor Values

Each sensor offers three values (x, y, and z-axis) and there are a total of 15 values of 5 sensors with 3 axes in each entry of data. For we target a near real-time response time, the first 5 s of data, called the first '*data block*', is taken into our consideration. Since the first and second entry of data are missing some values of sensors possibly due to hardware warm-up behavior, we collect the entries from the 3rd entry until the entry of during a period of 5 s on both devices.

Table 1. Data among 5 sensors and data for 5 s ('*data block*') are analysed, where smartphones (*SP*) and smart glasses (*SG*), C for coordinate axes of x, y, and z, MV as math values.

Number of Data / Sensor	Data per second (Hz)		'data block' as 5 seconds data		C	MV
	SP	SG	SP	SG		
A, G, LA, GS, R	20	5	100	25	*xyz*	*all*

Table 2. Definitions of each activity and subsets performed in the experiments while carrying smartphone and smart glasses.

	Smartphone		Smart-glasses
Biking	Random location	Fixed location	Face wearing
Jogging	Random location	Fixed location	Face wearing
Movie Watching	Random location	Fixed location	Face wearing
Video Gaming	Random location	Fixed location	Face wearing

In our design, each '*data block*' contains 5 s of entry and results in a series of mathematics expressions, which are *sum* (summation), *mean* (mean value), *var* (variance), *max* (maximum), and *min* (minimum) for each sensor with its axes shown in Table 1, where abbreviations show *A* (Accelerometer), *G* (Gravity), *LA* (Linear Acceleration), *GS* (Gyroscope), and *R* (Rotation Vector); and 'all' means the above 5 mathematics values.

3.3 Activities and Experiments

We experiment four types of activity, which are *Biking*, *Jogging*, *Movie Watching*, and *Video Gaming* while carrying both devices separately. When carrying the smartphone for the four activities, we measure data of two subsets of behavior, which are Fixed Location (the smartphone is put in the pocket), and Random Location (the smartphone is put in the hand, backpack, or on the table, etc.). Meanwhile, the user performs all four activities while wearing the smart glasses in the experiments without specific subsets in any activity, shown in Table 2.

Each activity or subsets require collecting 60 times (20 s for each time) of data to be the training datasets. In addition, the users collect another 20 times of data to be the testing dataset. Eventually, data collected by the smartphone manifests 8 subsets in four activities, and data of smart glasses containing only four activities.

In the experiments, a Support Vector Machine framework, *libsvm* (released version 3.20) [17], is applied to our system in both training and prediction process. Besides, according to our system design, *libsvm* has not only been deployed to our server for the training, testing and modeling purpose, but also integrated into our Android program for the testing and prediction purpose.

4 System Analysis

Our proposed system is designed to serve as both real time services in data processing, classification and activity recognition, and batch processing services running at the backend servers, which deal with data computation and computed results of *Feature Selection* and *F-Score* in the training process. Moreover, *Classification* and *Recognition Accuracy*, and *Time Consumption* in *Execution* and *Responsive Time* are also measured in our work.

4.1 Feature Extraction

Feature Extraction is an important stage in our experiments for activity recognition. In order to learn how selected features may impact on the results of accuracy, the studies of feature strategy are conducted to understand them. Our strategy is based on *Feature Dimension* according to our presented works, and *Feature Selection* and *F-Score* of the dimensions in the system.

4.1.1 Feature Dimension

The current approach focuses on the dimensions of generated mathematics values in a '*data block*', which has continuous data within 5 s from 5 sensors on smart glasses. Thus, a total number of 75 dimensions or vectors (5 sensors, 3 axes, 5 math values) are collected, shown as Eq. (1).

$$fs_t = \{v_0, v_1 \ldots \ldots \ldots \ldots \ldots, v_{n-2}, v_{n-1}\} \tag{1}$$

where $fs(t)$ means a Set of all feature dimensions or vectors containing math values of t seconds; n is the number of vectors.

4.1.2 Feature Selection and F-Score

Support Vector Machine (SVM) (Boser et al. 1992; Cortes and Vapnik 1995) methods are effective to classify data, but do not receive or select important features automatically to complete the classification tasks. In the experiments, the questions of what features are important and how many features should be selected to perform well in activity recognition have been raised. Therefore, the filters and thresholds of each sensor are considered to possibly identify and answer those questions.

Since some dimensions of data are possibly less effective or non-discriminative to classify the datasets, we exploit the technique of *F-Score* [18] to measure how important some features are, and they must be used to improve or maintain accuracy of recognition and eliminate unnecessary dimensions in the computation cost under certain thresholds, shown as Eq. (2) according to *F-Score*.

$$F(i) \equiv \frac{\left(x_i^{(+)} - x_i\right)^2 + \left(x_i^{(-)} - x_i\right)^2}{\frac{1}{n_+ - 1} \sum_{k=1}^{n_+} \left(x_{k,i}^{(+)} - x_i\right)^2 + \frac{1}{n_- - 1} \sum_{k=1}^{n_-} \left(x_{k,i}^{(-)} - x_i\right)^2} \tag{2}$$

The results of calculating *F-Score* show how effective some features are, and the ranking of features based on each *F-Score* provides us with more information of how features should be considered more, and filtered based on defined thresholds. Here we demonstrate the *F-Score* rankings of top 10 feature dimensions for activity recognition on smart glasses and smartphones, shown in Figs. 3(a, b), where S means which sensor, C means the coordinate axis, and MV means mathematics value.

In Fig. 3(a) on smart glasses, we observe the top 3 features score much higher than the rest ones, which are *var* of '*A y-axis*', *var* of '*LA y-axis*', and *var* of '*LA z-axis*'. On the other hand, the scores of the smartphone in Fig. 3(b) seem more average among those top 10 selected features, which might hint us the importance of the fixed '*on-body*' locations/positions is significant while users performing mobile activity recognition, instead of not fixed or randomly locating the device.

Furthermore, according to the smart glasses, we not only pay more attention to important features that should be watched, but other possible vector spaces that could be eliminated, and how those effective features should have been translated to identify

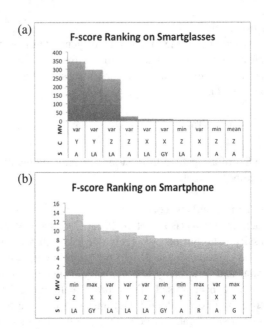

Fig. 3. (a) Top 10 features with *F-Score* ranking on smart glasses, where *GY* means *GS*. (b) Top 10 features with F-score ranking on smartphone.

head motions in the proposed activity experiments. Moreover, the question of how and why these features help in classifying proposed activities is raised.

4.2   Classification

In the experiment, the training model predicts all the testing four activities and builds the classifier. In order to look into how activities on sensors affect these features while wearing the smart glasses, we evaluate further information from experiments of two distinct categories, which could help us learn more informative results of head motions. Each category of '*Sports*' (*Biking* vs. *Jogging*) and '*Entertainment*' (*Movie Watching* vs. *Video Gaming*) discusses the specific features of head motions to separate the activities in each category. Here we take 10 s sensor data of each activity as our examples. From our analysis of sensor data in the ranking, we are able to identify the most effective features and head motions for classification quickly.

4.2.1   Biking Vs. Jogging

Our studies show that top scoring features are more effective in classifying activities. When we look into these features of these two activities. The activities show their specific characteristics in *var* from data distribution in *A* and *LA*, shown in Fig. 4. In *Biking* and *Jogging*, our data distribution suggests that the glass wearer's head motions may shake more frequently while *Jogging*, where appears more *var* in '*A*, y-axis' (Fig. 4(a)) movements. *LA*, of y and z-axis in Figs. 4(b, c) show in different velocities in the two activities. Meanwhile, smaller x-axis spins of '*GS* x-axis' in Fig. 4(d) appear while *Jogging* is performed, compared to bigger x-axis spins of *Biking*.

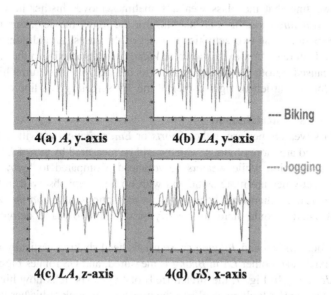

4(a) *A*, y-axis   **4(b) *LA*, y-axis**

4(c) *LA*, z-axis   **4(d) *GS*, x-axis**

Fig. 4. Sensor data of top features on smart glasses for *Biking* and *Jogging* (x-axis: 10 s, y-axis: value of entry data).

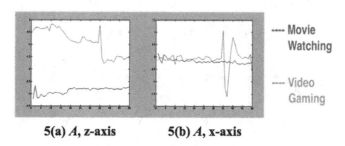

5(a) *A*, z-axis   **5(b) *A*, x-axis**

Fig. 5. Sensor data of top features on smart glasses for *Movie Watching* and *Video Gaming*. (Color figure online)

4.2.2 Movie Watching Vs. Video Gaming

When glass wearers perform *Movie Watching* and *Video Gaming*, they are more static than doing exercise. Often movements are '*head-up*' as looking up and '*head-down*' as looking down motions in our measurements. Our data shows that the important feature is '*A* z-axis', in Fig. 5(a), helping to classify these 2 activities quickly. For instance, the glass wearer often performs head-up in *Movie Watching* (blue line of Fig. 5(a)) compared to '*head-down*' in *Video Gaming* (green line of Fig. 5(a)).

We conclude that nodding behavior of head motions is identical to our '*head-up*' following with '*head-down*' immediately, which are more related to variations of '*A z-* axis'. The direction of the user's sight is closely related to this feature.

Though we find that the glass wearer sometimes moves his/her head randomly while *Movie Watching* (possibly our laughing for the funny movies), this feature can still help to separate these two activities in most of the cases. In addition, some head motions in the feature of '*A x-axis*' shown in *Video Gaming* activity in the experiments are possibly caused by our car racing game, which makes the user turns his/her head occasionally looking at left or right corner of the TV screen (green line of Fig. 5(b)).

4.2.3 Sports Vs. Entertainment

When the glass wearers perform either *Sports* or *Entertainment* activities, their characteristics in speed are more obvious, which could be measured by *var* of *LA* especially in the forward direction while wearers move ahead. Compared to *Sports* activities, *Entertainment* activities are more static and with no huge *var* observed in the feature dimensions of *LA*. Furthermore, behavior of head motions of '*head-up*' and '*head-down*' of '*A z-axis*' could help to classify proposed two static activities in the experiments.

In Fig. 6, both *Biking* and *Jogging* cause user's head shaking vertically in different *var* of '*A, y-axis*', a smoother *LA* in *Biking* is measured, and *GS* rotates bigger spins in *Biking* than *Jogging*. In Fig. 7, the stretch (red) of '*A, z-axis*' tells how high or down the user is facing and/or looking at. When the user turns to look at his/her left or right, the stretch of x-axis in *A* tells the angle of that turn.

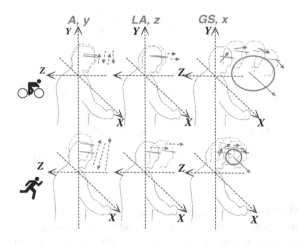

Fig. 6. *Sports* head motions on smart glasses.

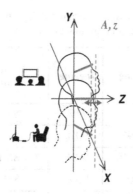

Fig. 7. *Entertainment* head motions on smart glasses.

4.3 Recognition Accuracy

Our goal targets high accuracy of activity recognition both on smart glasses (SG) and smartphones (SP). The experiments of activity recognition on smart glasses and the smartphone are conducted to observe the three actions. Thus, we locate the smartphone device with fixed position and random location while doing the proposed activities. On the other hand, activity recognition of smart glasses wearing is also performed.

In the experiments, we fix the locations and directions of the smartphone in the pocket, compared to random locations of that smartphone is put in the pocket, held in the hand, or located on the table. The results of activity recognition in three actions show that smart glasses wearing performs better than both fixed location as well as random locations of the smartphone, shown in Table 3. Therefore, more experiments on smart glasses are focused and studied.

In the experiments, we take different numbers of selected feature to study how accurate our activity recognition could be while wearing smart glasses. Currently, we experiment our activity recognition in two groups, A and B, which are based on the selection of top 5 scoring features and top 10 scoring features in the *F-Score* rankings.

Table 3. Activity recognition on the SP is compared to fixed locations (SP-fixed-loc), randomly located (SP-random), and SG as wearing.

Activity Test	Biking	Jogging	Movie Watching	Video Gaming
SP- random	58%	67%	44%	38%
SP- fixed-loc	80%	76%	50%	45%
SG- wearing	89%	90%	86%	83%

Table 4. W1/W2/W12 on smart glasses are evaluated for activity recognition with the numbers of selected features (A and B are chosen groups as G).

G Test	Activity	Biking	Jogging	Movie Watching	Video Gaming
A	W1	87%	93%	83%	80%
A	W12	89%	90%	81%	83%
A	W2	85%	90%	86%	85%
B	W1	90%	95%	83%	81%
B	W12	88%	92%	87%	85%
B	W2	88%	91%	85%	87%

Besides, in order to look into how accurate of activity recognition in different '*data block*', we take various portions of data to be our test cases, which are Window 1 (W1) as the first '*data block*', Window 2 (W2) is the second '*data block*', and Window 1–2 (W12) is the second half of W1 coming with the first half of W2, as results shown in Table 4.

In the comparisons of two groups, we observe that group B is slightly better than A in some cases. Besides, from the averages of recognition accuracy of W1/W12/W2 of four activities in two groups, we obtain the total average of these two groups around 87 %, as shown in Table 5.

Table 5. The averages of recognition accuracy in 4 activities on smart glasses with W1/W2/W12 are evaluated.

	A			B		
Window	W1	W12	W2	W1	W12	W2
AVG%	86.75	86.0	86.5	87.25	88.0	87.75
Total AVG	87 %					

4.4   Time Consumption

The total time consumption in *Execution Time* consists of two major parts, which are the time spent on *Data Pre-Processing* and *Classification*, and the time spent in the rest parts of computation such as *Warm-Up* time of sensor and waiting for the first '*data block*'. Our analysis shows upon *Classification* to complete the recognition task, which means we assume the time will be spent since the beginning of *Warm-Up*, till either with or without *Batch-Processing* time (send data to the backend server). In addition, the testing of *Responsive Time* by considering '*window size*' (the size of '*data block*') and *Overlapping* shows the possibility of being more reactive in our proposed system.

4.4.1 Execution Time

Data in our experiments shows some values of sensor omitted in the first 2 entries. For that reason, we skip 0.4-s warm-up and continue for 5 s. The process of *Data Pre-Processing* to generate math values takes around 0.2-s. Following with the *Classification* process on the Android program, it takes around 0.45-s in average to complete the task of activity recognition with the training model on it. Thus, it is expected to complete activity recognition for the smart glasses within around 6.05 s since the beginning of the task.

While the training model is either not available or the newer one is needed, *Batch-Processing* will be required to transmit a '*data block*' to the backend server for the process of *Classification*, which takes another 0.96-s to upload data in a WiFi (upload average speed of 5.56 Mbps) networking environment in order to be classified.

Therefore, the total execution time accumulates time of data processing and computation for *Classification*, as well as possible network communication time, which take either 6.05 s to be finished on the smart glasses, or additional *Batch-Processing* added to be finished in 7.01 s (Fig. 8).

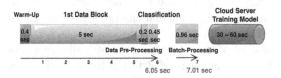

Fig. 8. *Classification* of activity recognition is completed by the smart-phone, or more *Batch-Processing* is required.

4.4.2 Responsive Time

The experiments in verifying '*window size*' and applying the *Overlapping* technique help to show the potentiality of being more reactive. The size of data is tested to see how activity recognition could perform. In order for considering all activities, our experiments show that accuracy in separating two activities, *Movie Watching* and *Video Gaming*, on smart glasses may reduce at this moment, when the size of data is smaller than 25 entries of 5 s, such that 15 or 20 collected entries drop average 7.05 % more failure in the experiments.

While performing experiments in our work, we verify the metrics of accuracy measurement for W1, W12 and W2. *Overlapping* technique could help the system react more quickly to achieve the result. Thus, the minimal *Responsive Time* on smart glasses for activity recognition is achieved in the proposed system, which could be less than 3 s (2.5 s) shown in Fig. 9.

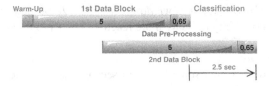

Fig. 9. *Responsive time* of activity recognition is achieved by more frequent data computation of *over-lapping*.

5 Discussion

Our contribution aims to build a user-centric and real-time system to perform recognitions of user's activity via sensing their head motions. By selecting top features from our ranking mechanisms, the system could quickly construct the behavioral patterns, learning model, and help to reduce the computation cost. We also demonstrate how special '*head-tracking*' characteristics of each user among the experimented activities help to achieve the results effectively.

The current work includes four example activities performed by testing users during their casual time of sports and entertainment, although there are many other possible more activities in our daily life. However, we believe that our work is the beginning step to study and understand how user's activity should be predicted and recognized in the continuous learning and analyzing environment, while eye-wearing wearable computers are conducted.

Due to the limitation of detected frequency of hardware sensors at present, our smartphone provides more amounts of data (20 Hz) than the smart glasses (5 Hz). However, we assumed more information of smartphone might give us better results while executing our feature selection and ranking process, but the outcomes seem to feedback the opposite answer. We anticipate the future design of smart glasses will come out with more accurate and refined sensors compared to the smartphone to help our new findings while efficient power consumption has been considered and resolved as well.

We also find that the most useful sensor data are among *A* (Accelerometer), *LA* (Linear Acceleration), and *GS* (Gyroscope) in our current proposed activities. However, there might be more possibilities and combinations of sensor data analysis beyond those three in our future experiments of any newly targeted activity. Moreover, we expect the eye-wearing wearable computers to understand and help users more, through a regular daily logging and life logging in our future experiments, as well as the future practical use by humans to bring us more research possibilities and living convenience.

6 Conclusion and Future Work

We study and analyze sensor data of both wearable computers and smartphones, and focus on how '*head-tracking*' might provide more useful information for user's activity recognition. By annotating and extracting features of user's '*head-mounted*' behavior in our proposed activities, the system shows high accuracy of activity recognition, user-centric and real-time classifications for human's head motions.

Our future work will bring us to design more user-friendly and scalable wearable applications, more recognitions on complex activity, diverse input data of various types for Machine Learning analysis, and combinational services for on-going observations in furthermore contexts of glass wearing experiences. Applications from many personalized analyses to interesting wearable services are examples for our upcoming works.

References

1. Lockhart, J.W., Pulickal, T., Weiss, G.M.: Applications of mobile activity recognition. In: 2012 Proceedings of the ACM Conference on Ubiquitous Computing. ACM (2012)
2. McNaney, R., et al.: Exploring the acceptability of google glass as an everyday assistive device for people with Parkinson's. In: Proceedings of the 32nd Annual ACM Conference on Human Factors in Computing Systems. ACM (2014)
3. Adomavicius, G., Tuzhilin, A.: Context-aware recommender systems. In: Ricci, F., Rokach, L., Shapira, B., Kantor, P.B. (eds.) Recommender Systems Handbook, pp. 217–253. Springer, Berlin (2011)
4. Briem, V., Hedman, L.R.: Behavioural effects of mobile telephone use during simulated driving. Ergonomics **38**(12), 2536–2562 (1995)
5. Ishimaru, S., et al.: Shiny: an activity logging platform for Google Glass. In: Proceedings of the 2014 ACM International Joint Conference on Pervasive and Ubiquitous Computing: Adjunct Publication. ACM (2014)
6. Gouveia, R., Karapanos, E.: Footprint tracker: supporting diary studies with lifelogging. In: Proceedings of the SIGCHI Conference on Human Factors in Computing Systems. ACM (2013)
7. Mazilu, S., et al.: GaitAssist: a wearable assistant for gait training and rehabilitation in Parkinson's disease. In: 2014 IEEE International Conference on Pervasive Computing and Communications Workshops (PERCOM Workshops). IEEE (2014)
8. Khan, A.M., et al.: Human activity recognition via an accelerometer-enabled-smartphones using kernel discriminant analysis. In: 2010 5th International Conference on Future Information Technology (FutureTech). IEEE (2010)
9. Anjum, A., Ilyas, M.U.: Activity recognition using smartphones sensors. In: 2013 IEEE Consumer Communications and Networking Conference (CCNC). IEEE (2013)
10. Shoaib, M., Scholten, H., Havinga, P.J.: Towards physical activity recognition using smartphones sensors. In: IEEE 10th International Conference on Ubiquitous Intelligence and Computing, 2013 and 10th International Conference on Autonomic and Trusted Computing (UIC/ATC). IEEE (2013)
11. Kern, N., Schiele, B., Schmidt, A.: Multi-sensor activity context detection for wearable computing. In: Aarts, E., Collier, R.W., van Loenen, E., de Ruyter, B. (eds.) EUSAI 2003. LNCS, vol. 2875, pp. 220–232. Springer, Heidelberg (2003)
12. Randell, C., Muller, H.: Context awareness by analysing accelerometer data. In: The Fourth International Symposium on Wearable Computers. IEEE (2000)
13. Parkka, J., et al.: Activity classification using realistic data from wearable sensors. IEEE Trans. Inf Technol. Biomed. **10**(1), 119–128 (2006)

14. Krause, A., Smailagic, A., Siewiorek, D.P.: Context-aware mobile computing: learning context-dependent personal preferences from a wearable sensor array. IEEE Trans. Mob. Comput. **5**(2), 113–127 (2006)
15. Ishimaru, S., et al.: Smarter eyewear: using commercial EOG glasses for activity recognition. In: Proceedings of the 2014 ACM International Joint Conference on Pervasive and Ubiquitous Computing: Adjunct Publication. ACM (2014)
16. Teichmann, D., et al.: Human motion classification based on a textile integrated and wearable sensor array. Physiol. Meas. **34**(9), 963 (2013)
17. LIBSVM: LIBSVM (2015). http://www.csie.ntu.edu.tw/~cjlin/libsvm/
18. Chen, Y.-W., Lin, C.-J.: Combining SVMs with various feature selection strategies. In: Guyon, I., Nikravesh, M., Gunn, S., Zadeh, L.A. (eds.) Feature Extraction, vol. 207, pp. 315–324. Springer, Berlin (2006)
19. Apple Watch: Apple Watch (2015). https://www.apple.com/tw/watch/
20. Epson Moverio BT-200: Epson 2016. http://www.epson.com/cgi-bin/Store/jsp/Landing/moverio-bt-200-smart-glasses.do
21. Sony SmartEyeglass Developer Edition: Sony (2016). http://developer.sonymobile.com/products/smarteyeglass/

Network Security

Minimizing Confident Information Coverage Breach in Rechargeable Wireless Sensor Networks with Uneven Recharging Rates

Zehui Xiong and Bang Wang[(⊠)]

The School of Electronic, Information and Communications,
Huazhong University of Science and Technology (HUST), Wuhan, China
wangbang@hust.edu.cn

Abstract. In this paper, we study the problem of minimizing the network coverage breach in a rechargeable wireless sensor network (RWSN). Due to the node density and charging capability constraint, it may happen that a RWSN cannot provide required area coverage some time, yet it may recover later on after obtaining enough recharged energy. To minimize the coverage breach, we propose a family of sensor scheduling algorithms, each of which uses an utility function to greedily choose an active node in each step. Furthermore, we consider a new confident information coverage model that is more efficient for environment monitoring applications. Since this new coverage model takes into consideration of the collaborations in between sensors, it may still exist coverage-redundant active sensors after the scheduling. We then propose another redundancy removal algorithm to further optimize the selected active nodes. Simulation results show that our algorithm with both coverage and energy capability considerations can outperform the traditional coverage-based scheduling algorithm in terms of much smaller breach rate.

1 Introduction

Wireless Sensor Networks (WSN) have many applications in precision agriculture [1], where sensors are deployed to monitor the soil temperature, humidity and salinity. Network coverage which can reflect the monitoring performance has been widely used to evaluate the quality of service of a WSN [15]. The sensors' sensing capability and quality can be abstracted by the *coverage model*, which, however, can be defined in different ways due to the wide range of sensor types and functionalities [15]. Although the simplistic disk coverage has been widely used, it may not be the most appropriate one for such monitoring applications. In this paper, we consider a novel *confident information coverage* (CIC) model [16], which is based on the theory of field reconstruction and can be used for many physical phenomenon monitoring applications. In Sect. 2, we will briefly introduce the CIC model.

Network lifetime is another important performance metric. In traditional non-rechargeable WSNs, network lifetime is often defined as the maximum time

© Springer International Publishing Switzerland 2016
X. Huang et al. (Eds.): GPC 2016, LNCS 9663, pp. 213–228, 2016.
DOI: 10.1007/978-3-319-39077-2_14

duration till the required network coverage cannot be assured by all available sensor nodes. As such non-rechargeable battery-powered have only limited operation time, therefore the whole network lifetime is not infinite. In order to extend network lifetime, *sensor activity scheduling* can be used to organize sensors into a series of set covers and then work alternatively, each satisfying the network coverage requirement.

Recently, *rechargeable sensor nodes* that can harvest energy from environment have been proposed to be used in WSNs to improve network lifetime [3–5,10,11,13,14,18–21]. A good survey on how energy harvesting sensor nodes can be used to improve WSN performance can be found in [14]. Most existing works have studied the problem of scheduling rechargeable sensor nodes for target coverage based on the simplistic disk model [4,5,11–13,18–20]. They assume an energy harvesting sensor network is with limited lifetime and they consider the continuous coverage similar as in the non-rechargeable WSNs. Their common objective is to schedule sensor activity efficiently to prolong the lifetime while ensuring the coverage requirement continuously. Furthermore, in most of these studies [3,4,11,12,17,20], a centralized controller is assumed to know the exact battery level information and locations of all nodes. However, most of these studies have not considered the different charging capabilities for sensors located at different geographic locations.

A WSN consisting of all rechargeable nodes can achieve infinite lifetime in theory. However, due to the node density and charging capability constraint, it may happen that a RWSN cannot provide required area coverage some time, yet it may recover later on after obtaining enough recharged energy. We call this temporarily loss of coverage requirement as *coverage breach*, which was previously termed for traditional non-chargeable WSNs for target coverage yet with feedback bandwidth constraint [2,17]. In [2], sensor activity scheduling based on coverage contribution has been proposed to minimize coverage breach; While in [17], both coverage contribution and residual energy have been considered. But both of them have not considered the charging capability in rechargeable WSNs, yet applying the simplistic disk model for target coverage.

In this paper, we study the minimum coverage breach problem in a rechargeable WSN based on the CIC model. To solve this problem, we propose a family of greedy heuristic active sensor selection algorithms for constructing set covers each satisfying the application coverage requirement. In the set coverage construction, the algorithms greedily select one active sensor node with the maximum utility at each step. We design several utility functions, which take into consideration of the coverage contribution, remaining energy and predicted charging energy. Since this new CIC model considers the collaborations in between sensors, it may still exist coverage-redundant active sensors after the scheduling. We then propose another redundancy removal algorithm to further optimize the selected active nodes. Simulation results show that our algorithm with both coverage and energy capability considerations can outperform the traditional coverage-based scheduling algorithm in terms of much smaller breach rate.

The rest of the paper is structured as follows. The system model is introduced in Sect. 2 and we precisely define our problem in Sect. 3, Sect. 4 presents a family of greedy heuristic solutions. Simulation results are provided in Sect. 5, and Sect. 6 concludes the paper.

2 Preliminaries

2.1 Confident Information Coverage

The CIC model [16] is based on the theory of field reconstruction. We assume that a specific physical phenomenon within the sensing field needs to be monitored. Let $z^t(x)$ denote the true value of the physical attribute at a reconstruction point x, and $\hat{z}^t(x)$ denote its estimated value. We use the time-average root mean square error (RMSE) to evaluate the reconstruction quality for each reconstruction location, that is,

$$\Phi(x) \equiv \sqrt{\frac{1}{T}\sum_{t=1}^{T}(z^t(x) - \hat{z}^t(x))^2}. \tag{1}$$

Given a reconstruction function and reconstruction requirement ε, a space point x is called being Φ-covered, if $\Phi(x) \le \varepsilon$. A sensor field is said being completely Φ-covered, if all the space points within the field are Φ-covered.

In many applications, the physical phenomenon can be modeled as a second-order stationary stochastic process. We can adopt the widely used *ordinary Kriging* [6,7] as a reconstruction function. Furthermore, we use only those sensor nodes located within the *correlation range* of a space point for its attribute reconstruction. This is due to that the spatial correlation of a physical phenomenon is often within a limited range. We note that after some further mathematical transformations, whether a point is Φ-covered can be determined by the geometric relations among the point and the sensors within its correlation range.

2.2 Energy Charging Model

Each rechargeable sensor node can harvest energy by its solar panel, but it can only be charged in the sleep state, since in many cases each node is equipped with only one rechargeable battery with a simple switch circuitry [9,20]. We adopt an approximate one-day energy charging model for each solar panel [8], which uses a quadratic curve to model the solar energy harvested in the daytime; While in the night, the harvested energy is zero:

$$E^c(k) = E^{max} \times (-\frac{1}{36}\kappa^2 + \frac{2}{3}\kappa - 3), \qquad \kappa = \mod (k, 24), k = 1, 2, \ldots \tag{2}$$

where E^{max} is the maximum charging rate and $\kappa = \mod(k, 24)$ is to obtain the remainder after k is divided by 24 h of a day.

Table 1. Symbols and notations

Symbol	Notation
$\mathcal{S}$	The set of all rechargeable nodes
$N(k)$	The number of the nodes (slots)
$i(k)$	The index of the nodes (slots)
S_i^{max}	The maximum energy storage of the node i
E_i^{init}	The initial energy of the node i
E_i^{max}	The maximum charging rage of the node i
$E_i^r(k)$	The remaining energy of the node i at the beginning of the slot k
$E_i^s(k)$	The consumed energy of the node i in the slot k
$E_i^c(k)$	The charged energy of the node i in the slot k
C_k	The set cover in the slot k
ε	The CIC RMSE threshold
$\Phi(C_k)$	The Φ-coverage ratio of the set cover C_k
Φ_{th}	The network Φ-coverage requirement

In practice, since the solar panel and recharge battery are not cheap, the solar panel size and battery storage capacity are generally not made very large. The charging rate is determined by the size of a solar panel. So the maximum battery capacity can be set to store the maximal chargeable energy in a whole day. On the other hand, it is possible that different nodes are equipped with different sizes of solar panel. Furthermore, solar power generation depends on the intensity of solar radiation, and obstruction of sunlight can impact on the charging rate. In a large sensor field, sensor nodes are widely distributed at different locations, and it is not uncommon that some sensor nodes may be within the shadow of foliage and crops for different times. Therefore, the charging rates are uneven across sensor nodes.

3   Problem Statement

We consider a randomly deployed WSN consisting of rechargeable sensor nodes, each equipped with a solar panel and a rechargeable battery. We assume that each sensor node can be in one of two states: *active* and *sleep*. In the active state, a sensor node samples the physical phenomenon and consumes an amount of the energy stored in its battery. Furthermore, a sensor node in the active state cannot charge its battery. In the sleep state, a sensor node consumes negligible energy, but it can charge its battery.

In traditional non-rechargeable WSNs, the battery of each sensor node is with limited capacity and is not rechargeable. Therefore, the operational time of a sensor node is not infinite, and so is a non-rechargeable WSN. Sensor activity scheduling is a common approach to extend the network operational time by alternatively activating only a subset of sensors at a time. The scheduled active sensors need to meet the network coverage requirement. The network lifetime is often defined as the maximum time duration till the network coverage cannot be guaranteed by all available sensors.

In rechargeable WSNs, a sensor node can be recharged after its battery depletion. In theory, the operational time of a rechargeable node can be infinite, and so is a rechargeable WSN. However, as a sensor node cannot charge all the time, like in the night and in the active state, the totally available sensors with enough battery energy may not be enough at sometimes, which can lead to *coverage breach*, i.e., the network coverage requirement cannot be achieved even with all sensors being active sometimes. In this paper, we study the coverage breach problem in such a rechargeable WSN.

Coverage breach can be avoided by deploying more nodes and/or equipping larger solar panel and rechargeable battery, but this approach is too expensive. In a rechargeable WSN, coverage breach is not permanent, but can be self-recovered after sensor nodes are recharged. We can adopt the sensor scheduling approach to alternatively activate sensors, such that the coverage requirement can be satisfied by active sensors, yet the network breach can be minimized.

In this paper, we divide the continuous time line into consecutive slots with equal length. In one slot, a sensor can be in either active or sleep state. In the beginning of each slot, a sensor node is called a *candidate* if its remaining energy can support the whole slot. In the beginning of each slot, we select active sensors from all candidates to form a *set cover* by which the network coverage requirement can be achieved. The worst case is that a coverage breach occurs, even if all the candidates are active. If this happens, we have two options: One is still to activate all candidates to only fulfill partial coverage requirement; The other is to deactivate all nodes such that they can have chances to recharge. In this paper, we choose the latter option, as our main objective is to minimize the average breach rate in a long term viewpoint, other than differentiating breaches.

Table 1 summarizes the symbols and notations. We next provide the problem formulation as follows. Consider a long term duration consisting of K slots, the breach rate is defined as

$$BR = \frac{1}{K} \sum_{k=1}^{K} (\Phi(C_k) < \Phi_{th}), \tag{3}$$

where $\mathbb{I}(\cdot)$ is an indicator function. $\mathbb{I}(\Phi(C_k) < \Phi_{th}) = 1$, if $\Phi(C_k) < \Phi_{th}$; Otherwise, it equals to 0. Note that a set cover can be an empty set, which means no rechargeable nodes been selected to be active.

The problem of minimizing coverage breach rate can be formulated as:

$$\underset{K}{\text{Minimize}} \quad BR = \frac{1}{K} \sum_{k=1}^{K} \mathbb{I}(\Phi(C_k) < \Phi_{th})$$

$$\text{Subject to} \quad 0 \le E_i^r(k) \le S_i^{max}, \quad \forall k = 1, 2, .., K, \forall i \in \mathcal{S};$$

$$E_i^r(k) > E_i^s(k), \quad \forall k = 1, 2, .., K, \forall i \in C_k;$$

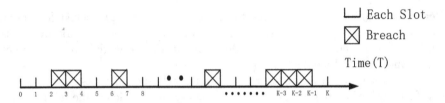

Fig. 1. Illustration of breach schemes.

Where

$$E_i^{init} = S_i^{max}, \forall i \in \mathcal{S};$$
$$E_i^r(k+1) = \min\{E_i^r(k) + E_i^c(k), S_i^{max}\},$$
$$\forall k = 1, 2, .., K, \forall i \notin C_k;$$
$$E_i^r(k+1) = \max\{E_i^r(k) - E_i^s(k), 0\},$$
$$\forall k = 1, 2, .., K, \forall i \in C_k;$$
$$\mathbb{I}(\Phi(C_k) < \Phi_{th}) \in \{0, 1\}, \forall k = 1, 2, .., K;$$

Remarks:

- The first constraint guarantees that the remaining energy does not exceed the maximum storing energy of each sensor s_i across the lifetime and it is non-negative.
- The second constraint guarantees that the remaining energy of each selected active sensor is not smaller than consumed energy in a time slot.

We further illustrate our problem in Fig. 1. We consider a long duration of K slots. There may exist coverage breach in some time slots. For example in Fig. 1, C_3 is a breach slot. In a breach slot, all the rechargeable sensor nodes will switch to the sleep state. Note from Fig. 1, the required Φ-coverage can still be guaranteed in the 5th slot, if some nodes have recharged enough energy in the 4th slot. Therefore, although a RWSN can in theory work infinitely, coverage breach may happen due to the lack of sensor density and charging capability. For this new characteristic of RWSNs, few work have been done before for minimizing coverage breach. Although an optimum solution to the minimum breach rate problem may be found through exhaustive search for all possible set covers in all slots, its computation complexity is very prohibitive. In the next section, we propose a family of greedy selection algorithms to approach this problem.

4   Heuristic Solutions for Breach Minimization

In the beginning of each slot, the proposed algorithm constructs a set cover to satisfy the network coverage requirement. The set cover is initiated as an empty set. The basic idea of these algorithms is the same: A set cover is constructed by greedily selecting the sensor with the largest utility to be included into the set

Table 2. Pseudo-codes for set cover construction

Algorithm 1. Energy-efficient Greedy Scheduling Algorithm

Input: S: all the rechargeable sensors; Φ_{th}: required Φ-coverage;
Define: S_C: set of selected sensors; $\Phi(S_C)$: current Φ-coverage;
$\mathcal{I}$: candidate sensor nodes set;

01: $S_C = \mathcal{I} = \emptyset$; $\Phi(S_C) = 0$;
02:   **For** each $s_i \in S$ in the kth slot
03:     **if** $E_i^r(k) > E_i^s(k)$
04:       $\mathcal{I} = \mathcal{I} \cup \{s_i\}$;
05:   **EndFor**
      /* Until the coverage requirement is satisfied
          or no candidate can be found */
06:   **While** $\Phi(S_C) < \Phi_{th}$ **or** $\mathcal{I} \neq \emptyset$
      /* Greedy select a sensor with the largest utility */
07:       $s_i = \arg \max_{i \in \mathcal{I}} U(s_i)$;
08:       $S_C = \{s_i\} \cup S_C$;
09:       Compute $\Phi(S_C)$;
10:   **EndWhile**
11:   **If** $\Phi(S_C) < \Phi_{th}$
12:       $S_C = \emptyset$;
13:   **else**
14:       $S_C = RR(S_C)$;
15:   **EndIf**
16: **return** S_C;

---

cover in each step, until the coverage requirement is satisfied or all the candidates are included into the set cover.

Table 2 provides the core pseudo-codes of the proposed algorithms. In the beginning of each iteration, we first obtain the candidate sensor sets $\mathcal{I}$ (line 4). In each iteration of the **While** loop, it constructs one set cover until the required Φ-coverage is guaranteed or the candidate set is empty (line 6). In each iteration for sensor selection, we choose the one with the largest utility (line 7). When it cannot find a set cover to provide required Φ-coverage, a coverage breach happens and all selected sensor nodes switch to sleep state (line 12); Otherwise, we implement the redundancy removal algorithm to optimize the constructed set cover (line 14). We next present our proposed utility functions and redundancy removal algorithms.

4.1   Utility Function

Coverage Contribution: The first utility function is purely based on the Φ-coverage contribution. For a sensor s_i, its Φ-coverage contribution is defined as the newly increased Φ-coverage ratio, if it is included into the set cover C_k:

$$\Delta\Phi(s_i) = \Phi(C_k \cup \{s_i\}) - \Phi(C_k) \tag{4}$$

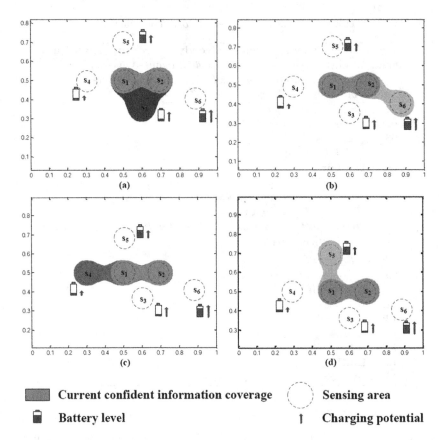

Fig. 2. Illustration of scheduling scheme. (Color figure online)

According to the CIC property, if a single sensor is used for Φ-coverage, its covered area is actually the disk coverage model, i.e., a disk centered at itself with a radius r. However, when two sensors within the correlation range are used for Φ-coverage, their covered area is in general more than the union of their respective coverage disks. For example, in Fig. 2, we use a disk to illustrate the coverage of a single sensor; yet the yellow region surrounding the sensors s_1 and s_2 is the Φ-covered area by the two sensors. Clearly, the concept of Φ-coverage expands the disk coverage, yet it can still maintain the same coverage quality in terms of the RMSE of Φ-covered area being larger than the same threshold.

Therefore, when computing the Φ-coverage of $\Phi(C_k \cup \{s_i\})$, not only the area within the sensing radius s_i should be considered, but also the area that could be covered by the collaboration of s_i and some sensors in C_k within the correlation range of s_i. For example, in Fig. 2(a)–(d), the blue, green, magenta and cyan area represents the coverage contribution $\Delta\Phi(s_3)$, $\Delta\Phi(s_4)$, $\Delta\Phi(s_5)$, and $\Delta\Phi(s_6)$, respectively. Among them, the sensor s_3 has the largest coverage contribution.

The first utility function is hence defined as:

$$U(s_i) = \Delta\Phi(s_i). \tag{5}$$

The above utility function is efficient in selecting the least number of sensors. However, it may happen that a sensor could be selected into multiple consecutive set covers, which leads to its loss of recharging opportunities and even renders its temporarily shutdown. Coverage breach may happen due to such *temporary death* of some sensor nodes, which might become even more prominent in a rechargeable WSN with uneven charging rate. Therefore, a utility function should also take energy into consideration.

Coverage Contribution and Remaining Energy: The storage capacity of the rechargeable battery is limited due to its high cost. Therefore, for a fully charged sensor node, if the scheduling algorithm puts it into the sleep sate, it is a waist of its recharging opportunity; Whereas other sensor nodes in the active state with less residual energy could miss the opportunity for harvesting energy. Therefore, we include the remaining energy into the utility function as follows:

$$U(s_i) = \frac{E_i^r(k)}{S_i^{max}} \times \Delta\Phi(s_i). \tag{6}$$

Here we compute the battery level of sensor i by its remaining energy divided by its maximum battery storage. Compared with Eq. (5), the above utility function takes the remaining energy into consideration, which may help to improve the energy balance across all sensors. For example in Fig. 2, among $s_3, ..., s_6$, the sensor s_6 has the largest utility. Its selection may help to reduce the risk that some other sensor losses of charging opportunity.

Coverage Contribution and Predicted Energy: Considering the fact of uneven charging rates, the prospective energy level may be different in the spatial domain, which is another critical factor we should consider. We assume that the amount of energy harvested by the sensor in a certain future time period is estimable [8]. Here we denote the prospective energy level as the predicted energy divided by the maximum battery storage. We thus consider to increase the likelihood for a sensor with high prospective energy level to charge its energy such that from the whole network perspective, more environment energy can be exploited. Hence we define the next utility function:

$$U(s_i) = \frac{S_i^{max}}{E_i^c(k)} \times \Delta\Phi(s_i). \tag{7}$$

With the above utility the sensor nodes which cannot harvest plenty of energy, for example s_4, should give the charging opportunity to those sensors with high perspective energy level, such s_3, s_5 or s_6, in order to increase the energy inflow to the whole network.

Table 3. Redundancy removal algorithm

Sub-algorithm: The Redundancy Removal Algorithm
Input: a set cover S_C;
Output: the optimized set cover S_C;
/* A eligibility test to eliminate redundant nodes */

01: $\mathcal{C} = \emptyset$;
02: **For** $\forall s_i \in S_C$
      /* Remove the sensors from the set cover one by one */
03: $S_C = S_C - \{s_i\}$;
04: Compute $\Phi(S_C)$;
      /* If the remaining sensors cannot Φ-cover the target field */
05:     **if** $\Phi(S_C) < \Phi_{th}$
06:         $S_C = S_C \cup \{s_i\}$;   /*restore it */
07:     **else**
08:         $\mathcal{C} = \mathcal{C} \cup \{s_i\}$;
09:         $S_C = S_C \cup \{s_i\}$;
10:     **endif**
11: **EndFor**
12: **if** $\mathcal{C} = \emptyset$ /* there are no redundant nodes */
13:     **return** S_C;
14: **else**
15:     $s_i = \arg\min\limits_{s_i \in \mathcal{C}} \frac{U(s_i)}{\Delta\Phi(s_i)}$;
      /* delete one with lowest utility function */
16:     $S_C = S_C - \{s_i\}$;
17:     $S_C = RR(S_C)$;
18: **endif**

Coverage Contribution, Remaining Energy and Predicted Energy:
Based on the above discussions, we know that there are three main factors
impacting on the selection of a sensor node, namely, coverage contribution,
remaining energy and predicted energy. Therefore, we propose another utility
function to combine all the three factors as follows:

$$U(s_i) = \frac{E_i^r(k)}{E_i^c(k)} \times \Delta\Phi(s_i). \tag{8}$$

Compared with Eqs. (6) and (7), the above utility function assigns a higher priority to a sensor node with higher remaining energy as well as lower recharging potential. As it makes some balance in between of using abundant remaining energy and charging more environment energy, it can increase the likelihood of more charging energy for the whole network for future usage while without dramatically depleting a single sensor. For example from Fig. 2, we should compare the battery level, perspective energy level and coverage contribution to compute the utility of candidate sensors $s_3, ..., s_6$, and then select s_5 for its highest utility.

4.2   Redundancy Removal

The greedy nature of the proposed algorithms implicitly imposes a constraint of nonreversible selection. That is, once a sensor node is selected, it will not be removed from the set cover. The only exception is that the set cover cannot fulfill the network Φ-coverage requirement, and all the sensor nodes in the set cover are dismissed and converted back into the sleep state.

This irreversibility of the greedy algorithms needs to be considered in our Φ-coverage model. Note that in the Φ-coverage model, the area covered by a set of sensors is also dependant on the geometric relations in between these sensors. Therefore, after a sensor has been newly included, it not only covers some previously uncovered area, but also changes the geometric relations among the sensors being selected. Therefore, this inclusion of a new sensor may change the Φ-coverage structure of the whole field. So we need to recheck the coverage redundancy after the set cover construction.

We next propose a *redundancy removal* (RR) algorithm. A redundant node is defined as such a node that its deletion from the set cover does not compromise the network coverage requirement. The basic idea of the proposed RR algorithm is to iteratively remove one redundant node with the smallest utility at a step, until the network coverage cannot be satisfied if further deletion is performed.

Table 3 presents the pseudo-codes of the proposed RR algorithm. In each iteration of the **For** loop, the algorithm checks the coverage redundancy of constructed set cover. If redundancy does not exist, return the set cover (line 13). Otherwise, we will remove the redundant sensor in terms of its utility step by step (line 15–17). Note that a redundant sensor has its coverage contribution equal to zero. Therefore, we redefine the utility for redundant sensor node as $\frac{U(s_i)}{\Delta\Phi(s_i)}$ (line 15). Ties are broken randomly. After deleting one redundant sensor nodes, we should recheck the redundancy (line 17).

5   Simulation Results

Our simulations are written in MATLAB 7.10.0 (2012a). We simulate a rechargeable WSN randomly deployed in a $1\,\mathrm{km} \times 1\,\mathrm{km}$ sensor field. For the CIC model, the correlation range is set to $0.4\,\mathrm{km}$, and the reconstruction RMSE requirement ε is set to 0.2. For each rechargeable node, we use Eq. (2) as its charging model and set one hour as a slot. We also normalize the energy charging and consumption with respect to a slot. The initial energy or the maximum energy storage of all sensor nodes is set to 1 slot and the energy consumed in each slot is set to 0.2 slot.

We call the algorithms using different utility functions as CC using Eq. (5), CC-RE using Eq. (6), CC-PE using Eq. (7), and CC-REPE using Eq. (8). We use a uniform distribution to model the uneven charging rates across sensors. The maximum charging rate E^{max} of each node is set to be uniformly distributed within $[0.1, \mathcal{K}]$. Therefore, we change the value of $\mathcal{K}$ to change the uneven charging degree. We simulate a long period of 500 slots and all results are average over 20 different network deployments.

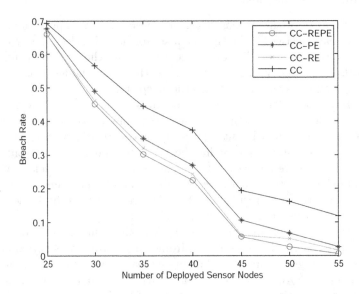

Fig. 3. Comparison of the breach rate against the number of sensor nodes. The maximum charging rate is uniformly distributed within $[0.1, 0.6]$ or $\mathcal{K} = 0.6$.

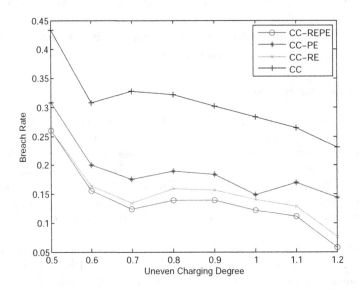

Fig. 4. Comparison of breach rate against uneven recharging degree. The number of deployed nodes is 40.

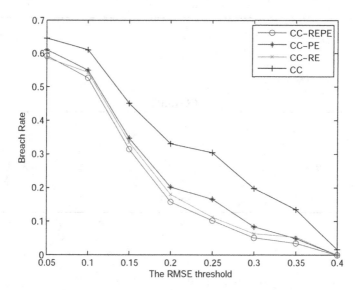

Fig. 5. Comparison of breach rate against different RMSE thresholds. The number of deployed nodes is 40; $\mathcal{K} = 0.6$.

Figures 3 and 4 compare the breach rate for the four algorithms against the number of deployed nodes and the uneven charging degree, respectively. It is not unexpected that the breach rate decreases with the increase of number of sensors, and with the increase of uneven charging degree on the whole. It can also be observed that the proposed algorithms with energy consideration outperform the CC algorithm without energy consideration. Furthermore, the CC-REPE algorithm achieves the smallest breach rate. This indicates that our greedy selection algorithms can maximally reduce the coverage breach when the utility function takes both the remaining energy and predicted energy charging into the scheduling consideration.

Figure 5 plots the breach rate against different network RMSE thresholds. It is observed that the breach rate decreases with the increase of the RMSE threshold. Again the CC-REPE algorithm achieves the smallest breach rate among the algorithms. In the CIC model, the network RMSE determines the reconstruction quality requirement. When the RMSE requirement is relaxed, the number of sensors which can collaborate to provide CIC coverage for a same field can be generally reduced. Hence more sensor nodes could have more time to harvest energy and the breach rate can be reduced.

We further use the Fig. 6 to illustrate the breach distribution of four proposed utility functions among the simulation of the 500 time slots. A *burst breach* is defined as a coverage breach spanning two or more consecutive breach slots. Here we define the number of breach slots in each burst breach as *burst value*, namely, the degree of burst breach. In the Fig. 6, the burst value can be reflected by the thickness and the shade of bar. Figure 7 compares the number of total breached

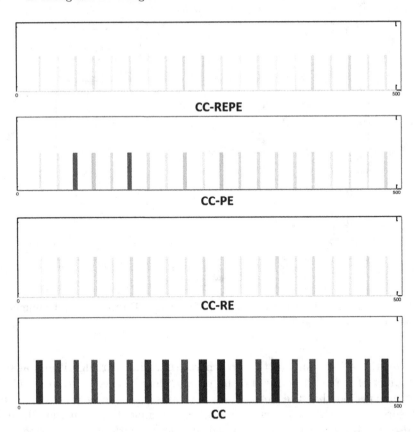

Fig. 6. Illustration of breach distribution in terms of four utility functions. The number of deployed nodes is 40; $\mathcal{K} = 0.6$.

slots and the number of different predefined burst breach for the four utility functions. It is clearly seen that the utility functions taking energy into account can improve the performance of network compared with the purely coverage-based CC algorithm. Moreover, CC-REPE outperforms the other two in terms of both of the number of breach slot and burst breach. This is because that the CC-REPE considers both of remaining energy and charging potential, which might help to balance the energy distribution not only in the temporal domain for individual sensors, but also in the spatial domain for the whole network.

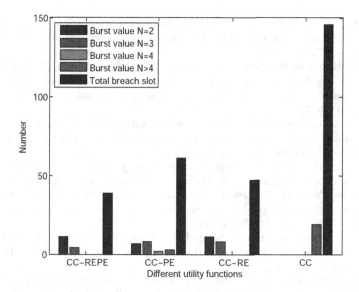

Fig. 7. Comparison of burst breach and breach time slots of different score functions. (Color figure online)

6 Conclusion

In this study, we have studied the problem of minimizing breach rate in rechargeable sensor networks and proposed a family of greedy selection algorithms to organize sensor nodes into a series of set covers which work alternatively based on the novel CIC model, each satisfying applications coverage requirement. Moreover we implement the redundancy removal algorithms (RR) to optimize the constructed set cover. Simulation results demonstrate that the utility function CC-REPE which consider the coverage benefit, remaining energy and predicted energy outperforms the others in terms of the smallest breach rate. Our future work will further consider the connectivity and design efficient distributed scheduling algorithms.

Acknowledgement. This paper is supported in part by the National Natural Science Foundation of China (No. 61371141), and the Fundamental Research Funds for the Central Universities (No. HUST2015QN081).

References

1. Camilli, A., Cugnasca, C.E., Saraiva, A.M., Hirakawa, A.R., Corrêa, P.L.P.: From wireless sensors to field mapping: anatomy of an application for precision agriculture. Comput. Electron. Agric. **58**(1), 25–36 (2007). (Elsevier)
2. Cheng, M.X., Ruan, L., Weili, W.: Coverage breach problems in bandwidth-constrained sensor networks. ACM Trans. Sens. Netw. **3**(2), 2198–2216 (2007)

3. Dewitt, J., Patt, S., Hongchi Shi: Maximizing continuous barrier coverage in energy harvesting sensor networks. In: IEEE International Conference on Communications (ICC), pp. 172–177 (2014)
4. Eto, M., Katsuma, R., Tamai, M., Yasumoto, K.: Efficient coverage of agricultural field with mobile sensors by predicting solar power generation. In: IEEE International Conference on Advanced Information Networking and Applications (AINA), pp. 62–69 (2015)
5. Fu, N., Suppakitpaisarn, V., Kimura, K., Kakimura, N.: Maximum lifetime coverage problems with battery recovery effects. In: IEEE Global Communications Conference (GLOBECOM), pp. 118–124 (2014)
6. Harrington, B., Huang, Y., Yang, J., Li, X.: Energy-efficient map interpolation for sensor fields using kriging. IEEE Trans. Mob. Comput. $8(5)$, 622–635 (2008)
7. Hernandez-Penaloza, G., Beferull-Lozano, B.: Field estimation in wireless sensor networks using distributed kriging. In: IEEE International Conference on Communications (ICC), pp. 724–729 (2012)
8. Huan, X., Wang, B., Mo, Y., Yang, L.T.: Rechargeable router placement based on efficiency and fairness in green wireless mesh networks. Comput. Netw. $78(4)$, 83–94 (2015). (Elsevier)
9. Kar, K., Krishnamurthy, A., Jaggi, N.: Dynamic node activation in networks of rechargeable sensors. In: INFOCOM 2005, Proceedings IEEE of the 24th Annual Joint Conference of the IEEE Computer and Communications Societies, vol. 3, pp. 1997–2007 (2005)
10. Lexie, D., Lin, S., Wu, J.: Adaptive battery charge scheduling with bursty workloads. In: IEEE Global Communications Conference (GlOBECOM), pp. 708–713 (2012)
11. Pryyma, V., Turgut, D., Bölöni, L.: Active time scheduling for rechargeable sensor networks. Comput. Netw. $54(4)$, 631–640 (2010). (Elsevier)
12. Ren, X., Liang, W., Wenzheng, X.: Quality-aware target coverage in energy harvesting sensor networks. IEEE Trans. Emerg. Top. Comput. $3(1)$, 8–21 (2015)
13. Severini, M., Squartini, S., Piazza, F.: Energy-aware lazy scheduling algorithm for energy-harvesting sensor nodes. Neural Comput. Appl. $23(7-8)$, 1899–1908 (2013). (Springer)
14. Sudevalayam, S., Kulkarni, P.: Energy harvesting sensor nodes: survey and implications. IEEE Commun. Surv. Tutorial $13(3)$, 443–461 (2011)
15. Wang, B.: Coverage problems in wireless sensor networks: a survey. ACM Comput. Surv. $43(4)$, 1–53 (2011)
16. Wang, B., Deng, X., Liu, W., Yang, L.T., Chao, H.-C.: Confident information coverage in sensor networks for field reconstruction. IEEE Wireless Commun. $20(6)$, 74–81 (2013)
17. Wang, C., Thai, M.T., Li, Y., Wang, F., Wu, W.: Minimum coverage breach and maximum network lifetime in wireless sensor networks. In: IEEE Global Communications Conference (GLOBECOM), pp. 1118–1123 (2007)
18. Yang, C., Chin, K.-W.: Novel algorithms for complete targets coverage in energy harvesting wireless sensor networks. IEEE Commun. Lett. $18(1)$, 118–121 (2014)
19. Yang, C., Chin, K.-W.: A novel distributed algorithm for complete targets coverage in energy harvesting wireless sensor networks. In: IEEE International Conference on Communications (ICC), pp. 361–366 (2014)
20. Yang, C., Chin, K.-W.: On complete target coverage in wireless sensor networks with random recharging rates. IEEE Wirel. Commun. Lett. $4(1)$, 50–53 (2015)
21. Yoo, H., Shim, M., Kim, D.: Dynamic duty-cycle scheduling schemes for energy-harvesting wireless sensor networks. IEEE Commun. Lett. $16(2)$, 202–204 (2012)

An Improved Dynamic ID Based Remote User Authentication Scheme for Multi-server Environment

Qimin Sun, Jongho Moon, Younsung Choi, and Dongho Won[✉]

College of Information and Communication Engineering, Sungkyunkwan University,
2066 Seobu-ro, Jangan-gu, Suwon-si, Gyeonggi-do 440-746, Korea
{qmsun,jhmoon,yschoi,dhwon}@security.re.kr

Abstract. Mutual authentication has been widely used to verify the legal user and server over a common communication channel. To ensure secure connection between user and server, a large number of remote mutual authentication schemes for multi-server have been proposed by researchers. However, there is a common feature that the identity of user is static in the login phase, which may leak some information of user. Therefore, a good deal of smart card based anonymous multi-server remote user authentication scheme have been proposed to overcome this problem. Recently, Banerjee et al. pointed out that Li et al.'s scheme is vulnerable to user impersonates attack and stolen smart card attack. Later, they proposed an improved protocol to fix this problem. However, we found that Banerjee et al.'s scheme is still vulnerable to user impersonation attack and off-line password guessing attack. Finally, we proposed an enhanced scheme to eliminate the security vulnerability.

Keywords: Authentication scheme · Smart card · Dynamic-id

1 Introduction

Recently, the popularity of internet and development of computer technologies for multi-server make the exchange of valuable resources and remote communication feasible. Therefore, to protect the communication between user and server via a insecure channel, remote user authentication has become the most important security mechanism. Among all of them, the password based authentication scheme is the most commonly used technique. Many password based authentication schemes with smart card to verify the login request of legitimate remote user have been proposed. In 1981, Lamport [1] proposed a password based authentication scheme with insecure communication though it provides no mechanisms for user anonymity. Hwang et al. [2] proposed a Non-interactive password authentication without password tables in 1990. However, the user who wants to log in not only required to severally register with every server, but also must store a good deal of different password in the memory. In order to solve

© Springer International Publishing Switzerland 2016
X. Huang et al. (Eds.): GPC 2016, LNCS 9663, pp. 229–242, 2016.
DOI: 10.1007/978-3-319-39077-2_15

this problem, Horng [3] constructed an enhanced version of remote user authentication scheme for multi-server. Their scheme is based on the notion of one-way functions, trapdoor one-way functions and Lagrange interpolating polynomials.

Since then, a mass of user authentication schemes have been proposed. Some of these scheme are applied to multi-server environment [4]. Some of these schemes use smart card to enhance authentication's security [6,7]. However, a common flaw among all of them is static identity of user, which may result in leakage of information of user. In 2007, Wang and Liao [8] proposed an improved remote user authentication scheme for multi-server using dynamic ID to provide user anonymity. Later, Hsiang and Shih [9] pointed out that their scheme is vulnerable to masquerade attack, insider attack. Besides, Liao and Wang's scheme cannot achieve mutual authentication. To solve these problems, Hsiang and Shih proposed an improvement on Liao and Wang's scheme. Unfortunately, Lee et al. [10] analyzed Hsiang and Shih's scheme, and claimed that Hsiang and Shih's scheme is still susceptible to masquerade attack. Furthermore, their scheme cannot provide mutual authentication. Lee et al. [10] proposed an enhanced scheme but it has been pointed out that it is still insecure by Li et al. [11]. Recently, Banerjee et al. [12] claimed that the weakness of Li et al.'s dynamic ID based remote user authentication scheme and showed Li et al.'s scheme cannot resist stolen smart card attack and user impersonation attack during authentication process. To overcome this identified problem, they proposed an enhanced smart card based authentication scheme and claimed that it improves all the identified weakness of Li et al.'s scheme. However, through carefully analysis, we found that Banerjee et al.'s scheme is vulnerable to off-line password guessing attack, outsider attack and user impersonation attack. Therefore, we proposed an improved dynamic ID based remote user authentication scheme for multi-server environments using smart cards to tackle these problems. This paper is organized as follows: in Sect. 2, we review Banerjee et al.'s user authentication scheme. The security flaws of Banerjee et al.'s scheme are shown in Sect. 3. The Sect. 4 is our improved scheme. In the Sect. 5, we discuss the security and performance of our improved scheme. Finally, our conclusion is given in Sect. 6.

2   Review of Banerjee et al.'s Scheme

This section includes a brief overview of Banerjee et al.'s remote user authentication scheme. The notations used throughout this paper are summarized in Table 1. In their scheme, registration center RC chooses the master secret key x and secret number y to compute $h(x\|y)$ and $h(y)$, then shares them with server S_j over a secure channel. Their scheme consist of four phases: registration phase, login phase, authentication phase, and password change phase. The details of four phases are described as follows.

2.1   Registration Phase

This phase is invoked whenever user U_i wants to access the server. In this phase, user U_i registers to server S_j to obtain a legitimate smart card when server S_j

Table 1. Notations

Notations	Description
U_i	ith user
S_j	jth server
RC	Trusted registration center
ID_i	Unique identification of U_i
PW_i	Password of U_i
SID_j	Unique identification of S_j
CID_i	Dynamic ID of U_i to preserve user anonymity
$h(\cdot)$	A one-way hash function
$\oplus$	Exclusive-OR operation
$\parallel$	Message concatenation operation

has already been registered. For this purpose, user U_i sends a registration request to server S_j, then server S_j sends the smart card to U_i.

1. User U_i chooses his/her ID_i and PW_i, then generates a random number b and computes RPW_i by using $RPW_i = h(b \oplus PW_i)$. After that, user U_i sends ID_i and $RPW_i = h(b \oplus PW_i)$ to the registration center RC for registration via a secure channel.
2. After receiving the registration request message, RC first verifies whether ID_i has already existed in the registration record database or not. If holds, user U_i needs to chooses another ID_i. Moreover, RC checks the registration record of U_i, if U_i is a new user, RC initiates the value $N = 0$ and stores this value in the registration record database and computes,

$$A_i = h(x\|IDU), where IDU = h(ID_i\|N) \tag{1}$$
$$B_i = h(ID_i\|h(y)\|RPW_i) \oplus A_i \tag{2}$$
$$V_i = h(A_i\|h(y)\|RPW_i) \tag{3}$$
$$D_i = h(A_i \oplus h(x\|y)) \tag{4}$$
$$E_i = A_i \oplus h(x\|y) \tag{5}$$

3. Later, registration center RC issues a smart card to U_i which contains information $\{B_i, V_i, D_i, E_i, h(\cdot), h(y)\}$ via a secure channel.
4. Finally, user U_i securely stores random number b in the smart card. Now the updated smart card contains $\{B_i, V_i, D_i, E_i, b, h(\cdot), h(y)\}$.

2.2   Login Phase

When U_i wants to access to S_j, U_i inserts his/her smart card in the card reader first, inputs ID_i and PW_i, then the smart card performs the following steps:

1. The smart card computes $RPW_i = h(b \oplus PW_i)$, $A_i = h(ID_i\|h(y)\|RPW_i) \oplus B_i$, $V_i^* = h(A_i\|h(y)\|RPW_i)$ and check whether the computed V_i^* is equal to V_i. If holds, the legitimacy of the user is ensured, otherwise, the smart card rejects the login request.

2. Afterwards, the smart card generates a nonce number N_i and computes,

$$P_{ij} = E_i \oplus h(SID_j\|h(y)\|N_i) \tag{6}$$
$$CID_i = RPW_i \oplus h(D_i\|SID_j\|N_i) \tag{7}$$
$$C_1 = h(A_i\|D_i\|CID_i\|N_i) \tag{8}$$
$$C_2 = h(SID_j\|h(y)) \oplus N_i \tag{9}$$

3. Then, U_i submits $\{P_{ij}, CID_i, C_1, C_2\}$ to server S_j over a public channel.

2.3   Authentication Phase

After receiving the login request messages from U_i, the server S_j performs the following tasks to authenticate each other and agrees on an shared session key with user U_i. The steps of the authentication phase are as follows:

1. The server S_j computes the following information by using login message $\{P_{ij}, CID_i, C_1, C_2\}$ received from U_i.

$$N_i = C_2 \oplus h(SID_j\|h(y)) \tag{10}$$
$$E_i = P_{ij} \oplus h(SID_j\|h(y)\|N_i) \tag{11}$$
$$A_i = E_i \oplus h(x\|y) \tag{12}$$
$$D_i = h(A_i\|h(x\|y)) \tag{13}$$
$$RPW_i = CID_i \oplus h(D_i\|SID_j\|N_i) \tag{14}$$

2. After that, the server must verify the user's authenticity. Therefore, the server S_j computes $h(A_i\|D_i\|CID_i\|N_i)$ and check whether it is equal to C_1. If not, server S_j rejects this access and terminates this login. Otherwise, server S_j accepts this login request and generates a random number N_j to compute the following:

$$C_3 = h(SID_j\|D_i\|RPW_i\|N_j) \tag{15}$$
$$C_4 = RPW_i \oplus N_i \oplus N_j \tag{16}$$

Then, server S_j sends the message $\{C_3, C_4\}$ to user U_i over public channel for mutual authentication.

3. Upon receiving the response message, the user U_i gets N_j by using $N_j = C_4 \oplus N_i \oplus RPW_i$. After that, the user U_i calculates $h(SID_j\|N_i\|RPW_i\|D_i)$ and checks if the computed $h(SID_j\|N_i\|RPW_i\|D_i)$ is the same as the received C_3. If this hold, user U_i successfully authenticates S_j and computes the mutual authentication message $C_5 = h(SID_j\|N_i\|RPW_i\|D_i)$ and transmits it to the server S_j via a public channel.

4. Finally, the server S_j must calculate $h(SID_j\|N_i\|RPW_i\|D_i)$ first, and checks whether it is equal to the received message $\{C_5\}$. If C_5 is correct, server S_j and user U_i successfully completes the mutual authentication. Then, U_i and S_j can compute $SK = h(RPW_i\|D_i\|SID_j\|N_i\|N_j)$ as their shared session key for the following secure communications.

2.4 Password Change Phase

This phase is invoked whenever user U_i wants to change his password PW_i to be a new one. There is no need for a secure channel for password change, because it can be finished without logining to the registration center RC.

1. After inserting the smart card into the card reader, the user U_i inputs his/her identity ID_i and password PW_i.
2. The smart card computes $RPW_i = h(b \oplus PW_i)$, $A_i = h(ID_i\|h(y)\|RPW_i) \oplus B_i$, $V_i^* = h(A_i\|h(y)\|RPW_i)$ and checks if the V_i^* is the same as V_i. If they are same, user U_i can choose a new password PW_i^*, and smart card computes,

$$RPW_i^* = h(b\|PW_i^*) \tag{17}$$
$$B_i^* = h(ID_i\|h(y)\|RPW_i^*) \tag{18}$$
$$V_i^* = h(A_i\|h(y)\|RPW_i^*) \tag{19}$$

3. Finally, the smart card replaces B_i and V_i with B_i^* and V_i^* to finish the password change phase.

3 Security Analysis of Banerjee et al.'s Scheme

This section describes the security weakness of Banerjee et al.'s smart card based anonymous multi-server remote user authentication scheme. Their scheme cannot resist off-line password guessing attack and fails to provide mutual authentication. Moreover, a serious problem exists in the registration phase of Banerjee et al.'s scheme. A adversary who registers to the system as a legitimate user can get a smart card from server, and he/she extracts the secret value $h(x\|y)$ by using the information from the smart card and exploits this flaw to illegally attack user and server. Further, If an adversary is able to obtain the smart-card of user U_i and eavesdrop the login message $\{P_{ij}, CID_i, C_1, C_2\}$. It's simple for him/her to extract user's password PW_i from stolen smart-card. Thus, the protocol proposed by Banerjee et al. is still insecure. The detail steps of those attacks will be shown as follows.

3.1 Off-Line Password Guessing Attack

The only possibility of password guessing is either from smart card or login request of user U_i. We only consider the possibility of password guessing from login phase. If a malicious user A steals the smart card, eavesdrops the login message $\{P_{ij}, CID_i, C_1, C_2\}$, he/she can perform the off-line password guessing attack with secret value C_2 from login message, $(b, D_i, h(y))$ from smart card and computes as following,

1. The attacker A extracts C_2 from login message $\{P_{ij}, CID_i, C_1, C_2\}$ and obtains the secret value $(b, D_i, h(y))$ from stolen smart card.
2. Adversary A guesses a password PW_i^* of victim party U_i and computes,

$$CID_i^* = RPW_i \oplus h(D_i \| SID_j \| N_i) \tag{20}$$
$$= h(b \oplus PW_i^*) \oplus h(D_i \| SID_j \| C_2 \oplus h(SID_j \| h(y))) \tag{21}$$

where SID_j is a known parameter by all user.
3. The adversary A verifies whether $CID_i^* = CID_i$ or not. If they are equal, A obtains the correct password PW_i, otherwise, A repeats the above steps until the correct password PW_i is found. Therefore, the adversary A can successfully recover the password PW_i of user. Banerjee et al.'s scheme cannot resist off-line password guessing attack.

3.2   Outsider Attack

Outsider attack perpetrated by adversaries that do not have access to direct access to any of the authorized nodes in the network. However, the adversary may have access to the physical medium, particularly if user is dealing with wireless network. In Banerjee et al.'s scheme, there is a big design defect in the registration phase that if an adversary who is a legal user can register and get a smart card with information $\{B_i, V_i, D_i, E_i, b, h(\cdot), h(y)\}$. After that, he/she can compute the secret value $h(x\|y)$ by using $h(x\|y) = E_i \oplus B_i \oplus h(ID_i \| h(y) \| RPW_i)$. So that, it's easy for him/her to do other attack such as user impersonation attack to impersonate user U_i or extract the secret information of user U_i.

3.3   User Impersonation Attack

In this type of attack, the attacker impersonates as the legitimate user and forges the login message using the information obtained from the communication between user U_i and server S_j even if without the password PW_i and identity ID_i of user U_i. An adversary A registers to the system as a legitimate user and extracts the secret value $h(x\|y)$ and $h(y)$ through above attack.

1. First, the adversary A needs to eavesdrop the login message $\{P_{ij}, CID_i, C_1, C_2\}$ and extract (C_2, CID_i), then computes,

$$N_i = C_2 \oplus h(SID_j \| h(y)) \tag{22}$$
$$E_i = P_{ij} \oplus h(SID_j \| h(y) \| N_i) \tag{23}$$
$$A_i = E_i \oplus h(x\|y) \tag{24}$$
$$D_i = h(A_i \| h(x\|y)) \tag{25}$$
$$RPW_i = CID_i \oplus h(D_i \| SID_j \| N_i) \tag{26}$$

2. After that, this adversary A can choose a random nonce value N_i^* and calculates by using $(N_i^*, E_i, D_i, A_i, RPW_i)$ as following:

$$P_{ij}^* = E_i \oplus h(SID_j \| h(y) \| N_i^*) \tag{27}$$
$$CID_i^* = RPW_i^* \oplus h(D_i \| SID_j \| N_i^*) \tag{28}$$
$$C_1^* = h(A_i \| D_i \| CID_i \| N_i^*) \tag{29}$$
$$C_2^* = h(SID_j \| h(y)) \oplus N_i^* \tag{30}$$

3. This adversary can send the valid login request message $\{P_{ij}^*, CID_i^*, C_1^*, C_2^*\}$ to the server S_j as user U_i and this login request message is verified by the server S_j. After that, the server S_j computes $C_3 = h(SID_j \| D_i \| RPW_i \| N_j)$, $C_4 = RPW_i \oplus N_i \oplus N_j$, then sends the response message $\{C_3, C_4\}$ to the adversary A who is masquerading as the user U_i. The adversary can be successfully authenticated by server S_j because he/she knows all values that required to make login request message. Finally, after mutual authentication, the adversary masquerading as the user U_i communicates with server S_j by using common session key as $SK = h(RPW_i \| D_i \| SID_j \| N_i \| N_j)$.

3.4   Violation of the Session Key Security

In the part of weakness analysis of Banerjee et al.'s paper, they proposed that the secret information $h(x \| y)$ has been protected by registration center, thus it is impossible to compute a valid session key for adversary. However, the adversary can compute out the session key even if without secret information $h(x \| y)$. If he/she eavesdrops the message $\{P_{ij}, CID_i, C_1, C_2\}$ sent by user U_i and $\{C_3, C_4\}$ sent by server S_j, he/she can compute:

$$N_i = C_2 \oplus h(SID_j \| h(y)) \tag{31}$$
$$E_i = P_{ij} \oplus h(SID_j \| h(y) \| N_i) \tag{32}$$
$$D_i = h(E_i) \tag{33}$$
$$N_j = C_4 \oplus RPW_i \oplus N_i \tag{34}$$
$$RPW_i = CID_i \oplus h(D_i \| SID_j \| N_i) \tag{35}$$

After that, the adversary can successfully compute the session key as $SK = h(RPW_i \| D_i \| SID_j \| N_i \| N_j)$ because he/she knows the secret value (D_i, N_i, RPW_i, N_j). Therefore, the session key establishment of this protocol is incorrect.

4   The Proposed Scheme

In this scheme, we proposed an improved smart card based anonymous multi-server remote user authentication to resist all known attack. The scheme is illustrated in Fig. 1. Our scheme also consists of four phase: registration phase, login phase, authentication phase and password change phase. In the proposed scheme, the major changes is in the registration phase, login phase and authentication phase that are described in the following sub-section. Registration center

RC chooses the master key x and secret number y to compute $h(x\|y)$ and $h(y)$, then sends them to all registered user. Therefore, only registration center RC knows the master key x and secret number y. The notations used in our proposed scheme are summarized as Table 1 and the detailed steps of four phase are described as following.

4.1   Registration Phase

In this phase, everyone who was registered at the server can obtain a smart card. Before the remote user logins to the system, the user needs to perform the following steps:

1. Firstly, the user U_i inputs his/her identity ID_i, password PW_i, randomly generates a nonce b, and computes $RPW_i = h(b \oplus PW_i)$. Later, the user U_i submits ID_i and RPW_i to registration center RC through a secure channel.
2. After receiving the request, registration center RC checks the registration record of user U_i. If ID_i is already existed in the database of registration center, RC requests U_i to choose another ID_i, otherwise computes,

$$A_i = h(x\|ID_i) \tag{36}$$
$$B_i = h(A_i) \tag{37}$$
$$C_i = h(RPW_i\|ID_i\|h(y)) \oplus B_i \tag{38}$$
$$D_i = h(A_i \oplus h(x\|y)) \tag{39}$$
$$E_i = A_i \oplus h(x\|y) \tag{40}$$

where x and y is the secret value of the server S_j
3. Registration center RC stores $\{B_i, C_i, D_i, E_i, h(\cdot), h(y)\}$ in smart card and sends it to user U_i over a secure channel.
4. User U_i keys b into his/her smart card to finish this phase.

4.2   Login Phase

In the login phase, whenever the user U_i wants to log on the server S_j or access to some resources. User U_i inserts his/her smart card into a terminal, and keys ID_i and password PW_i. The smart card will perform the following operations:

1. The smart card calculates RPW_i as $RPW_i = h(b \oplus PW_i)$, and verifies whether $h(PW_i\|D_i\|h(y)) \oplus C_i$ is equal to the B_i stored in smart card or not. If not, the smart card drops the session. If holds, the smart card generates a random number N_i and computer as follows,

$$P_{ij} = E_i \oplus h(SID_j\|h(y)\|N_i) \tag{41}$$
$$CID_i = B_i \oplus h(D_i\|SID_j\|N_i) \tag{42}$$
$$M_1 = h(B_i\|D_i\|CID_i\|N_i) \tag{43}$$
$$M_2 = h(SID_j\|h(y)) \oplus N_i \tag{44}$$

2. Finally, the smart card sends the login request message $\{P_{ij}, CID_i, M_1, M_2\}$ to the service provider server S_j to log on the server S_j.

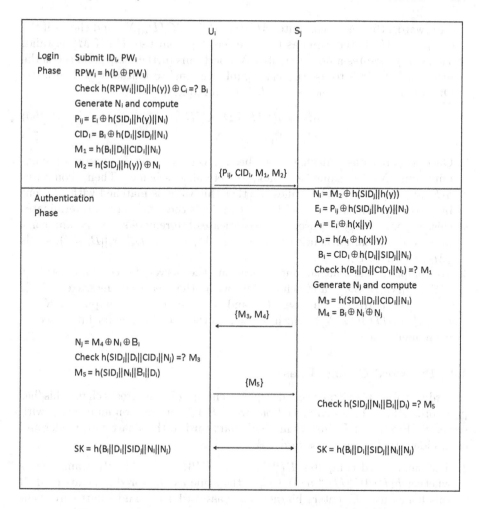

Fig. 1. Login and authentication phase of our proposed scheme

4.3 Authentication Phase

After a successful login, the smart card prepares for the authentication process. Upon receiving the login request message $\{P_{ij}, CID_i, M_1, M_2\}$, the server S_j verifies the authenticity of U_i by performing the following steps:

1. In order to authenticate user U_i, server S_j computes,

$$N_i = M_2 \oplus h(SID_j \| h(y)) \tag{45}$$
$$E_i = P_{ij} \oplus h(SID_j \| h(y) \| N_i) \tag{46}$$
$$A_i = E_i \oplus h(x \| y) \tag{47}$$
$$D_i = h(A_i \oplus h(x \| y)) \tag{48}$$
$$B_i = CID_i \oplus h(D_i \| SID_j \| N_i) \tag{49}$$

2. Afterwards, the server computes $M_1^* = h(B_i \| D_i \| CID_i \| N_i)$ and checks if the computed M_1^* is the same as the received M_1 from user U_i. If M_1^* is valid, server S_j generates a nonce number N_j, performs further steps and sends the message $\{M_3, M_4\}$ to user U_i via a public channel to mutually authenticate. Otherwise, server S_j rejects user U_i's login request.

$$M_3 = h(SID_j \| D_i \| CID_i \| N_j) \tag{50}$$

$$M_4 = B_i \oplus N_i \oplus N_j \tag{51}$$

3. Once the response message has been received, user U_i needs to compute out N_j as same as Banerjee et al.'s scheme. Then, computes $h(SID_j \| N_i \| CID_i \| D_i)$, verifies whether this value is matched with M_3 sent by server S_j. If it does not hold, user U_i rejects these message and terminates this session. Otherwise, user U_i authenticates the remote server S_j and computes the mutual authentication message $M_5 = h(SID_j \| N_i \| B_i \| D_i)$, sends $\{M_5\}$ to server S_j.

4. To complete the mutual authentication, the server S_j computes $M_5^* = h(SID_j \| N_i \| B_i \| D_i)$ and checks it with the received message $\{M_5\}$. If M_5^* is correct, the user U_i and the server S_j compute $SK = h(B_i \| D_i \| SID_j \| N_i \| N_j)$, which is taken as their session key for future secure communication.

4.4 Password Change Phase

According to the above mentioned requirement, user U_i can freely change his/her password PW_i to be an enhanced password PW_i^* without communicating with server S_j. First, user U_i inserts his/her smart card to the smart card reader and enters identity ID_i and password PW_i.

1. The smart card computes RPW_i, where $RPW_i = h(b \oplus PW_i)$ and checks whether $h(RPW_i \| ID_i \| h(y)) \oplus C_i$ is the same as B_i stored in smart card. If this holds, user U_i enters his/her new password PW_i^* and smart card computes (RPW_i^*, C_i^*) as follows,

$$RPW_i^* = h(b \| PW_i^*) \tag{52}$$

$$C_i^* = h(RPW_i^* \| ID_i \| h(y)) \oplus B_i. \tag{53}$$

2. Afterwards, the smart card replaces the old C_i with the new C_i^*. At the end of this step, the password will be successfully updated.

5 Security Analysis of the Proposed Scheme

In this section, we will analyze the security of the proposed scheme and demonstrate that the proposed scheme can resist most of known attack. At the end of this section, we will compare Banerjee et al.'s scheme [12], Li et al.'s scheme [11], Lee et al.'s scheme [11] and our proposed scheme. We assume the adversary can execute various attacks to steal secret information of user and server or impersonate user. The adversary will perform as following:

5.1 Insider Attack

Insider attack is a malicious attack perpetrated on a network or computer system by a person with authorized system access. During registration phase, the user U_i submits his/her password PW_i and identity ID_i to registration center RC over a secure channel. Therefore, it's difficult for adversary to eavesdrop the registration message. Furthermore, because the adversary don't know the master secret key x, y, thus even if the adversary can eavesdrop the registration message through some special attack, he/she would still not be able to gain password PW_i of user U_i. Thus, our scheme can against insider attack.

5.2 Off-Line Password Guessing Attack

In this type of attack, the adversary can eavesdrop the record messages and tries to guess identity ID_i and password PW_i from recorded message transmitted between user U_i and server S_j. In our proposed scheme, an attacker first tries to extract some informations that are related to password PW_i, and then tries to guess password PW_i of user U_i. However, the adversary cannot obtain the secret C_i from recorded message, even if this value was extracted, he/she has to guess the identity ID_i and password PW_i correctly at the same time. It is not possible to guess two parameters at the same time in real polynomial time. Thus, our scheme can against off-line password guessing attack.

5.3 Replay Attack

Replay attack is a form of network in which a valid data transmission is maliciously or fraudulently repeated or delayed. This is carried out either by the originator or by an adversary who intercepts the data and retransmits it, possibly as part of a masquerade attack by IP packet substitution. An adversary first eavesdrops the record message between user U_i and server S_j and tries to imitate user U_i to log on server S_j by replaying the eavesdropped message. However, because the random nonce is reserved in every session phase, if an adversary eavesdrops and replays any login request message, the replayed message will be detected and the server S_j will reject this request. Therefore, the adversary cannot obtain any information about user U_i or impersonate user. Thus, our scheme can against replay attack.

5.4 User Impersonation Attack

User impersonation attack means that an adversary successfully assumes the identity of one of the legitimate parties in a system or in a communication protocol to obtain some secret information of user U_i. If the adversary tries to masquerade as the legal user to log into the remote server S_j, he/she must enable to forge a login request $\{P_{ij}, CID_i, M_1, M_2\}$ to fool server S_j. Suppose an adversary eavesdrops login message $\{P_{ij}, CID_i, M_1, M_2\}$ and extracts C_2, P_{ij}. Then, he/she can compute N_i by using $N_i = C_2 \oplus h(SID_j \| h(y))$, E_i by using

$E_i = P_{ij} \oplus h(SID_j \| h(y) \| N_i)$. However, the adversary cannot compute A_i without the knowledge of $h(x\|y)$, thus he/she cannot compute B_i from intercepted communication parameters $(P_{ij}, CID_i, M_1, M_2, E_i, N_i)$ and cannot impersonate user U_i to fool server S_j to log on the server. Therefore, our scheme can against user impersonation attack.

5.5 User Anonymity

User anonymity is used for public access to remote server over an insecure channel. Anonymous access is the most common server access control method. It allows anyone to visit the public areas while hiding privacy information of user. In our scheme, user U_i's ID_i is not stored in memory of smart card, thus it's impossibility for adversary to extract user's identity from smart card. Even if the adversary can eavesdrop login message $\{P_{ij}, CID_i, M_1, M_2\}$ and extracts the encrypted secret value CID_i, he/she still cannot obtain the identity of user U_i. Thus, our scheme provides user anonymity.

5.6 Stolen Smart Card Attack

In this type of attack, an adversary steals a smart card and performs any operation to obtain private information from smart card. If an adversary extracts the secret value $\{B_i, C_i, D_i, E_i, b, h(\cdot), h(y)\}$ from stolen smart card, then it is impossible to compute secret value $h(x\|y)$ of server S_j for adversary. Even if the adversary can extract P_{ij}, CID_i, M_1, M_2 from eavesdropped login message of user U_i, he/she still cannot compute password PW_i of user U_i without knowing ID_i of user U_i. Therefore, no one can either extract secret value $h(x\|y)$ or guess the correct ID_i and PW_i in the same polynomial time. Thus, our scheme can against stolen smart card attack.

5.7 Perfect Forward Secrecy

Perfect forward secrecy is a very important part of ensuring the security of information of user and server. In our proposed scheme, the session key contains two secret values B_i and N_i that protected by $A_i = h(x\|ID_i)$, the ID_i will be changed with each user's identity. If some session key or long term private key of the server or user's password is exposed to the adversary, it will have no effect on established other session key. Thus, our scheme has perfect forward secrecy.

5.8 Performance and Security Comparison

In this phase, we will evaluate and compare the performance and security of the improved scheme with a few of previously proposed schemes. We mostly focus on the computations of registration, login and authentication phase, because the three phase are the most important part for a user authentication scheme. We define the notation T_h is time complexity of hash function, T_x is time complexity of operation XOR and T_c is time complexity of operation concatenation.

Table 2. Performance of the improved scheme and previously proposed schemes

Scheme	Total
Li et al.'s scheme	$25T_h+14T_x+44T_c$
Lee et al.'s scheme	$26T_h+7T_x+44T_c$
Banerjee et al.'s scheme	$26T_h+17T_x+48T_c$
Our proposed scheme	$26T_h+11T_x+41T_c$

Table 3. Security comparisons between the improved scheme and previously proposed schemes

Security component	Ours	Lee et al.	Li et al.	Banerjee et al.
Resist stolen smart card attack	Yes	No	Yes	No
Resist replay attack	Yes	Yes	Yes	Yes
Resist user impersonates attack	Yes	No	No	No
Resist insider attack	Yes	Yes	Yes	Yes
Resist off-line password guessing attack	Yes	No	No	No
Resist violation the session key security	Yes	Yes	Yes	No
Resist outsider attack	Yes	Yes	Yes	No
Securely chosen password	Yes	No	Yes	Yes
User anonymity	Yes	Yes	Yes	Yes
Mutual authentication	Yes	Yes	Yes	Yes
Perfect forward secrecy	Yes	No	No	No

Table 2 shows the performance of the improved scheme and previously proposed schemes. Because our proposed scheme has the minimum computation cost of operation concatenation and the second minimum computation cost of operation XOR. Besides, Table 3 lists the security comparison of our proposed scheme and other related schemes [10–12]. We can see that our proposed scheme not only provides user anonymity and perfect forward secrecy, but also can provide better security and resists most of known attack. Therefore, our scheme is more secure and efficient than previously proposed schemes.

6   Conclusion

In this paper, we analyzed the security of Banerjee et al.'s smart card based anonymous multi-server remote user authentication scheme and showed that Banerjee et al.'s scheme cannot resist off-line password guessing attack, outsider attack, user impersonation attack and violation the session key security. Later, we proposed an enhanced scheme that keeps better properties and provides better reparability of the attacks and automatically repairs the protocol with same security parameters. Thus, our proposed scheme is suitable for remote user authentication in multi-server since it provides security, reliability, and efficiency.

Acknowledgment. This work was supported by Institute for Information and communications Technology Promotion (IITP) grant funded by the Korea government (MSIP) (No.R0126-15-1111, The Development of Risk-based Authentication Access Control Platform and Compliance Technique for Cloud Security).

References

1. Lamport, L.: Password authentication with insecure communication. Commun. ACM **24**(11), 770–772 (1981)
2. Hwang, T., Chen, Y., Laih, C.S.: Non-interactive password authentication without password tables. In: IEEE Region 10 Conference on Computer and Communication System, vol. 1, pp. 429–431, September 1990
3. Horng, G.: Password authentication without using password table. Comput. Secur. **24**(8), 619–628 (1995)
4. Lin, I.C., Hwang, M.S., Li, L.H.: Improving the security of a flexible biometrics remote user authentication scheme. Future Gener. Comput. Syst. **19**, 1322 (2002)
5. Lee, H., Won, D.: Prevention of exponential equivalence in simple password exponential key exchange (SPEKE). Symmetry **7**(3), 1587–1594 (2015). doi:10.3390/sym7031587
6. Juang, W.S.: A new remote user authentication scheme for multi-server architecture. IEEE Trans. Consum. Electron. **50**, 22–23 (2001)
7. Li, C.T., Hwang, M.S.: An efficient biometrics-based remote user authentication scheme using smart cards. J. Netw. Comput. Appl. **33**, 1–5 (2010)
8. Liao, Y.P., Wang, S.S.: A secure dynamic ID based remote user authentication scheme for multi-server environment. Comput. Stand. Interfaces, October 2007. doi:10.1016/j.csi
9. Hsiang, H.C., Shih, W.K.: Improvement of the secure dynamic ID based remote user authentication scheme for multi-server environment. Comput. Stand. Interfaces **31**(6), 1118–1123 (2009)
10. Lee, C.C., Lin, T.H., Chang, R.X.: A secure dynamic ID based remote user authentication scheme for multi-server environment using smart cards. Expert Syst. Appl. **38**(11), 13863–13870 (2011)
11. Li, X., Ma, J., Wang, W., Xiong, Y., Zhang, J.: A novel smart card and dynamic ID based remote user authentication scheme for multi-server environments. Math. Comput. Model. **58**(1–2), 85–95 (2013)
12. Banerjee, S., Dutta, M.P., Bhunia, C.T.: An improved smart card based anonymous multi-server remote user authentication scheme. Int. J. smart home **9**(5), 11–22 (2015)
13. Choi, Y.S., Nam, J.H., Lee, D.H., Jung, J.Y.K.J.W., Won, D.: Security enhanced anonymous multi-server authenticated key agreement scheme using smart cards and biometrics. Sci. World J. **2014**, 15 (2014). Article ID 281305
14. Choi, Y., Lee, D., Kim, J., Jung, J., Nam, J., Won, D.: Security enhanced user authentication protocol for wireless sensor networks using elliptic curves cryptography. Sensors **14**(6), 10081–10106 (2014)
15. Kim, J., Lee, D., Jeon, W., Lee, Y., Won, D.: Security analysis and improvements of two-factor mutual authentication with key agreement in wireless sensor networks. Sensors **14**(4), 6443–6462 (2014)
16. Nam, J., Choo, K.K.R., Han, S., Kim, M., Paik, J., Won, D.: efficient and anonymous two-factor user authentication in wireless sensor networks: achieving user anonymity with lightweight sensor computation. PLoS ONE **10**(4), 1–21 (2015)

Mining Frequent Attack Sequence in Web Logs

Hui Sun, Jianhua Sun[✉], and Hao Chen

College of Computer Science and Electronic Engineering,
Hunan University, Changsha, China
{huisun,jhsun,haochen}@hnu.edu.cn

Abstract. As a crucial part of web servers, web logs record information about client requests. Logs contain not only the traversal sequences of malicious users but the operations of normal users. Taking advantage of web logs is important for learning the operation of websites. Furthermore, web logs are helpful when conducting postmortem security analysis. However, common methods of analyzing web logs typically focus on discovering preferred browsing paths or improving the structure of website, and thus can not be used directly in security analysis. In this paper, we propose an approach to mining frequent attack sequence based on PrefixSpan. We perform experiments on real data, and the evaluations show that our method is effective in identifying both the behavior of scanners and attack sequences in web logs.

Keywords: Log analysis · Web security · Web attacks · Sequential pattern mining

1 Introduction

The web is an important part of the Internet, and it becomes the largest publishing system in the world with its pragmatic natural attributes. With increased information sharing through network, attackers are attracted by the range and diversity of information, which causes the continued increase of attack frequency. They either endeavor to compromise the corporate network or the end-users access to the website by subjecting them to *drive-by-downloading* [13]. Among all these kinds of attacks, the attack for web servers is the most serious one with a variety of different ways, such as distributed denial of service and weak password guessing. Imaging that if a malicious user has intruded into a server that runs a database and network operating system, it would be relatively easy to obtain private information in the database or shutdown the network for a while. Under this circumstance, it is necessary to analyze the accident by finding attack footprints from log files, because the web logs contains the original information about client requests and run-time errors.

An entry will be added into access log when user request to the server, and the entry records client request information such as the time of request, client IP address, HTTP method, and so on. As one type of request users, attacker intrusions to server also be recorded. Thus, in web server's daily operation and

© Springer International Publishing Switzerland 2016
X. Huang et al. (Eds.): GPC 2016, LNCS 9663, pp. 243–260, 2016.
DOI: 10.1007/978-3-319-39077-2_16

security emergency response, web logs are always used to evaluate the risks of website. On the other hand, webmasters need to carry out investigation and evidence collection to find attackers by analyzing access log of the last few days, and then reconstruct the attack flow. A common method is using commands like "*grep*" (a tool using regular expressions to search text). In this way, certain keywords are searched in logs, then the records that contain specific keywords will be analyzed manually. However, this manual analysis is time-consuming and the analyzer is also expected to have a thorough knowledge on web security. Of course, there still exist many automatic analysis tools for web logs. For example, Piwik [3], Kibana [2], AWStats [1] and Splunk [4] are free open source software to analyze web logs. With these tools, we can perform searching, visualization, analyzing, and many other operations on web logs efficiently. The bad news is that these tools can just achieve some simple statistical data collection of deep analysis. Therefore, with data mining technology some researchers analyze user access patterns, which are called *Web Usage Mining*.

The data source of web usage mining mainly comes from access logs in web servers. Commonly, it is used to discover usage patterns and understand the need for web-based applications [5]. And web usage mining is widely used by companies [8,11,16] to improve service quality, to provide personalized services, and to find potential users. Actually, log mining in security plays a decisive role for webmasters and companies. It can be easier to know what the attacker is interested in, and whether 0-day is exploited in large-scale. However, web usage mining has been rarely applied to the field of web security. This paper focuses on the method of sequential pattern mining, which aims to learn the frequent attacking sequence from records logged by web servers.

In this paper, we make the following contributions:

- With sequential pattern mining, we can obtain frequent attacking sequences. In this paper, a method for mining frequent attacking sequences is proposed, which can not only reflect the attacker's intension, but also explore the common sequences of different security scanners.
- We distinguish scanners from malicious man-made attacks. The typical way of attacking a website is to first detect vulnerabilities of the website with scanners. Because the different behavior between the scanners and the manual requests, it is necessary to distinguish the man-made attack from the automatic tools before mining to make sure the accuracy of mined sequences.
- We explore the regular patterns of scanners. Scanners are typically black-box tools. It is beneficial to understand the internal working principle by mining attacking patterns of vulnerability scanners.
- We visualize the attack sequence with flowchart. Frequent sequence mining can help administrators to understand the attacker's behavior, which also can be utilized to display attacks sequence. The flowcharts are much intuitive for human investigation and can help webmasters to identify vulnerabilities to take further actions to protect the website.

2   Background and Motivation

This section presents an overview about the method of web usage mining and motivates the design of mining sequential attacking patterns. In addition, some representative web vulnerabilities that are often exploited in web applications are introduced in this part, which can help understand the typical payloads for each vulnerability.

2.1   Web Usage Mining

Generally, the data source of web usage mining comes from client click stream (always web server logs). The process is composed by three phases: the preprocessing, the pattern discovery, and the pattern analysis [12,14]. The preprocessing stage aims to clean up the raw data and transform the logs to what is more accurate and suitable for data mining. Transformed data are processed in the pattern discovery stage with specific data mining algorithms in order to find common rules. And in the final stage, useless patterns are filtered out.

Data Collection and Preprocessing. The raw documents are collected in this stage. The data for web usage mining usually come from three parts: server level, client level and proxy level. Among them, the server level is the most convenient for collection, including web log file, web page content and the website structure, etc. However, the collected data can not be used for modeling directly. It must be preprocessed to make sure the modeling in later steps more reliable. Ideally, the data should be in the format that just contains the page views of each user session. In general, the data preprocessing task involves data cleaning and filtering, user and session identification, and path completion [10,15,17].

- Clean up data. Filtering out error requests which are considered useless for understanding user actual behaviour. And then cleaning up the automatic requests (e.g., the requests for graphics files) which are not specifically requested by user. Another example for ineffectual requests in accessing records is web bots. Behaviour of web bots differs from human and not interested for web usage mining.
- User identification. The task of this part is to define each user, which help to implement access frequent sequence mining. The free-form structure of the Internet means that most users accessing on most websites are anonymous. The existence of local caches, corporate firewalls and proxies make it more difficult to identify each user. For instance, users who use the same proxy may access the site at the same time. Even more, the same user may request the web server on different machines or browsers. In order to improve the accuracy of user identification, lots algorithms have been proposed [6,18], while these algorithms have an adverse effect on realisation. Usually, web usage mining distinguishes each user by their IP address and operating system.
- Session identification. For each visitor, log files record which pages are requested, the order of the requests, and the duration of each page view.

Session identification divides each user's requests into many parts, which can reflect user continuous request to website [20]. A key factor for the quality of web usage mining is the real scale of session identification.

- Perform path completion. Not all pages requested by agent are recorded in log file. Just like when "back" button is pressed to return the page viewed before. The browser will go back to the page that has been cached locally rather than send a request to the web server again, and then the web logs will miss the record. This part tends to complete the paths which were requested by users but not recorded in the web logs [9].

Pattern Discovery Stage. The purpose of this stage is to establish the common patterns for users. The techniques in the pattern discovery stage include *statistical analysis, clustering and classification algorithms, frequent itemsets and association rules*, and *sequential patterns*. Among the above algorithms, statistical analysis, which is used to discover frequent access pages or average view time of a page, aims to improve the performance of the web system. At the same time, frequent itemsets and association rules also benefit to find out the frequent access pages or improve the struct design for the website. Clustering and classification algorithms divide the objects into multiple classes, and it is usually believed to be beneficial to market segmentation or information retrieval. Common sequential patterns expose users' visit patterns that reflect the access trends.

Pattern Analysis Stage. Not all patterns uncovered in the pattern discovery stage will be considered useful for analyzers. This stage filters out the rules and patterns that are common sense patterns. Hence, in this stage, we need to transform the patterns to comprehensible forms according to the actual application and keep the interesting, useful, and actionable patterns.

2.2 Web Application Security

According to numerous studies, the preferred method for attacking business's online assets is to exploit the vulnerabilities of their web applications. Vulnerability in web application is a security weakness that allows an attacker to bypass security checks or break system assurance. In the following, we discuss some common web vulnerabilities.

SQL Injection. In SQL injection, malicious codes are inserted into strings that are later passed to an instance of SQL Server for parsing and execution, which aims to get the higher authorized access in the database (e.g. administrator right to the database). For example, when users' input is not checked strictly, the request containing malicious codes will be submitted to the server, then the malicious statements are parsed into SQL statements to execute. SQL injection may lead to security risks such as the leakage of sensitive information, the modification and deletion of user data.

Cross-Site Scripting (XSS). XSS enables attackers to inject client-side script into web pages that will be viewed by other users. Most experts distinguish XSS flaws into non-persistent and persistent. The further division of these two groups is reflected XSS, persistent XSS, and DOM-based cross-site. In reflected XSS, the bait is an innocent-looking uniform resource identifier (URL), pointing to a trusted site but containing a XSS vector. The injected script will be executed by the victim's browser when the URL is clicked. While in persistent XSS, the data provided by attackers are saved by the server, and permanently displayed on "normal" pages returned to other users in the course of regular browsing. The DOM-based cross-site neither need the parse of web server nor the response to the malicious code. It is triggered by the DOM parser of the client browser. A cross-site scripting vulnerability may be used to steal the session cookie and bypass access controls (such as the same-origin policy).

Directory Traversal. It exploits insufficient security validation of users' input file names that contain "/", so that malicious users can achieve directory jump to traverse to parent directory on the server. The goal of this attack is to grant an application the access to files that are not allowed by the default privilege. In general, the path "/etc/passwd" that contains the password is a common file in Unix to demonstrate directory traversal. In order to detect this vulnerability, users always restructure the URL that contains sub-strings like "../" or its escape character "x5c./".

File Inclusion. The occurrence of this vulnerability is due to that the developers insert reusable code into a file openly and include it when these functions are called. Because there is no strict filtering on the entry function when calling the public file, the client can submit malicious functions to make the server execute, and achieve evil purposes.

Command Execute. A special URL constructed by attackers, and the URL contains commands expected to be executed by the server. It exploits that the server doesn't check strictly for those functions to be executed, and achieve the goals of getting server information, executing command or some Java code of server system, and uploading file to the server.

2.3 Motivation

It is widely reported that more than half of the security breaches target web applications, which indicates the importance of strengthening the security level of web applications. Clearly, organizations need a way to replace fragmented and manual penetration testing. There is a great demand for automated tools, so they can protect their global application infrastructures.

Based on the background of web application security and web usage data mining, we propose to mine sequential patterns for the web logs from the perspective of managing website more securely. Concretely, we intend to obtain common behaviors of attackers or black-box scanners. Given that, we need to find the potentially malicious records from the logs by matching common attacking payloads, and then locate the vulnerabilities or reveal the connection between different vulnerable pages.

3   Design and Implementation

In this section, we present the design and implementation of our system, and the main components and data flow is shown in Fig. 1. Similar to web usage mining, firstly, we collect the raw data that are mainly extracted from access logs. In addition, we collect payloads for each vulnerability. Secondly, different from common web usage mining, we remove normal requests from the logs and retain the records that may contain abnormal behavior. Thirdly, we distinguish users and their sessions in logs. When we identify each user, we divide the users into two categories: black-box scanners and malicious users. Then, we transform the target data into sequence database. After that, we use the algorithm Pre-fixSpan to mine frequent attack sequence patterns from the sequence database. At last, visualizing attack sequence be realized by the *dot* language, before that we maximized the sequences generated in the mining stage.

3.1   Data Collection

As depicted in Fig. 1, this is the first task before we process the web data. In this section, for vulnerabilities we illustrate what payloads are, and then we present some real payloads for certain vulnerability.

Payload Collection. Our intention is to discover abnormal behaviors from recorded requests. Hence, before preprocessing, a reference should be indicated to tell the system what kind of log entries contain possible attacks. Essentially, besides the original web data, we also need to collect payloads for real exploits.

Definition 1. *The payload of each vulnerability is the most substantive characteristic string or statements contained in the request URL, with which we can determine that the request attempts to exploit the vulnerability.*

Some common web vulnerabilities have been demonstrated. For example, we can confirm that XSS exploit is attempted when the string "<"' <img src=javascript:" appears in the URL. Usually, the payloads of the SQL injection

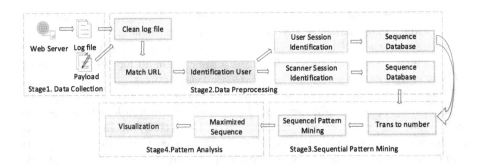

Fig. 1. The main process of frequent attack sequence mining.

DirectoryTraver:\..\..\..\..\..\..\   XSSAttack:>'><script>
DirectoryTraver:/\..\..\..\..\   XSSAttack:>"><script>
DirectoryTraver:/????/????/????/????/????   XSSAttack:</textArea><script>
DirectoryTraver:/..%5c..%5c..%5c..%5c..%5c..   XSSAttack:%3cimg%20src%3
DirectoryTraver:/..%5c../   XSSAttack:>"'><img src="javascript:alert
DirectoryTraver:/\x5c\x5c../   XSSAttack:" style="background:url(javascript:
DirectoryTraver:..\../../..\   XSSAttack:--><script>alert

Fig. 2. Part of payloads of XSS attack and Directory traversal.

attack contains basic database operations such as strings that contain *"select"*, *"union"* in the URL. We gather many other payloads and corresponding attack vectors, and store them in a single file. Figure 2 shows some web application attack payloads that we collect.

3.2 Data Preprocessing

The results of preprocessing will be used for data mining algorithm directly. Therefore, the consequences, whether good or not, such as the accuracy of user identification and session identification, will straightly affect the mining outcome. This section mainly introduce the procedure of data clean-up, user and session identification method. It is worth mentioning, in the stage of user identification, we will divide users into malicious user and scanners in order to improve the accuracy of analysis.

Cleaning Up Log File. It is well known that if the type of web servers is different, then their log formats are also different. The most widely used free web server in Unix and Linux platform is *W3C*, *Nginx* and *Apache Server*, and *IIS* is the native web server in Windows platform. Factors like security, logs and statistics, virtual host, proxy server, and integrated applications, should be considered when choosing a web server. Each request from a client as well as the response from the server is recorded in the log file automatically. So an entry in the log file can reflect a particular action performed by the user. Meanwhile, the format of log file is often customizable, and each field is separated by spaces. A sample web log of *Nginx* is shown in Fig. 3.

- Remote host field: This field is located in the first parts commonly, and it records Internet IP address of the remote host.
- Author user field: It provides the authenticated user information. If this field is not a hyphen, it means that a client has gained access to directories which are password protected.

```
124.133.7.42 - - [04/Aug/2015:13:29:44 +0800] "GET /search?c=%3A%E4%B8%AD%E5%9B%BD&t=1
HTTP/1.1" 200 12189 "http://www.baidu.com/" "Mozilla/5.0 (Windows NT 10.0; WOW64)
AppleWebKit/537.36 (KHTML, like Gecko) Chrome/43.0.2357.130 Safari/537.36" "-"
```

Fig. 3. A log record.

- Date/time field: This shows time zones and access time.
- Http request field: The Http request field consists of information that client's browser has requested to the web server. Essentially, this field may be partitioned into three areas: the request method, the uniform resource identifier, and the protocol.
- Status code: Obviously, not all client requests has succeeded, the status code field provides a three-digit response from the web server, indicating whether the request was successful or not, or if there was an error, we could know the error type. For example, 200 is OK, 304 is not-modified, etc.
- Transfer Volume (Bytes) field: This field expresses the size of the file sent by the web server to the client. Only when the GET request status code is 200, the number has a positive value.
- Referrer field: Listing the URL of the previously visited site that are linked to the current page.
- User agent field: This field is used to store client's browser and system information.

The log formats can be tailored to suit individual requirements. Certain fields might be chosen using the configuration file. We need to be aware of the structure of the log, and parse the string to IP, request time, method, URL, state and client field. The most common URLs are based on Http or Https protocol, and it is the breakthrough point of web security. Varieties of security threats are exploited by means of modifying the URL before sending requests to the server. It may cause a security problem if any level from the client to the server does not conduct filtering. According to this, we can find clues about attack by checking the record of the URL field.

After analyzing the structure of the log file, we can get the strings of attack payloads to match the URL, and then determine whether the user exhibit an attack behavior. Unlike common web usage mining whose data cleaning removes the exception requests and static requests, we remove normal requests, and retain the exceptional ones. More concretely, in this phase, if any payloads are contained in the URL, no matter which type of attack it belongs to, we store the record to a file suffixed with ".attack" and the string is reordered as access time, IP, browser and system of client, URL and status code. At the same time, we also maintain the type of each attack records. Figure 4 illustrates the segment of attack records that are generated after cleaning log files. Before user and session identification, the URL we got, is the raw request information of attacker, which might contain the string that is constructed by the attacker. And it is useless for analyzing the attack path, so we need to clean up the URL. We focus on the actual path that the attacker requests. In this step, we also transform the raw URL to the page it belongs to.

User Identification. Given that our goal is to get the user's common access sequence, we need to distinguish each user, and find the common attack behavior of them. The main task of user identification is to find out each attack who visits the website according to IP, system, browser and other information remained in the log after preprocessing. There are many effective algorithms proposed to

Attack Time	IP	Client Information	Vulnerability	URL	Response	Bytes
26/Jun/2015 :15:20:50	61.185. 194.159	mozilla/5.0 (windows nt 6.1; wow64) gecko/20110613 firefox/6.0a2	DirectoryTraver	/util/ barcode.php?ty pe=../../../../../ ../../../ ../../../etc/ passwd%00	200	941391
26/Jun/2015 :15:20:51	61.185. 194.159	mozilla/5.0 (windows nt 6.1; wow64) gecko/20110613 firefox/6.0a2	XSSAttack	/servlet/ %0arefresh:0;u rl=javascript:pr ompt(1)%0a1	200	941413
26/Jun/2015 :15:20:51	113.247.2 22.22	mozilla/5.0 (windows nt 6.1; wow64; rv:6.0a2) gecko/ 20110613 firefox/ 6.0a2	DirectoryTraver	/sdk/../../../../ ../../../../../../ ../../etc/ passwd	400	941568
26/Jun/2015 :15:20:52	113.247.2 22.22	mozilla/5.0 (windows nt 6.1; wow64; rv:6.0a2) gecko/ 20110613 firefox/ 6.0a2	Port DirectoryTraver	/?page=../../../ ../../../../../ etc/ passwd%00.jpg	200	941581
26/Jun/2015 :15:21:01	113.247.2 22.22	mozilla/5.0 (windows nt 6.1; wow64; rv:6.0a2) gecko/ 20110613 firefox/ 6.0a2	XSSAttack	/?search =<script>alert(1)</script>	200	941572
26/Jun/2015 :15:21:01	113.247.2 22.22	mozilla/5.0 (windows nt 6.1; wow64; rv:6.0a2) gecko/ 20110613 firefox/ 6.0a2	XSSAttack	/?search =%3cscript%3e alert(1) %3c%2fscript% 3e	200	941582

Fig. 4. The attack record of matching.

achieve user identification. The first general algorithm identifies different users by using the field of the IP and user agent. Others are based on cookies or extended property of the log. This method can distinguish users who are in the same proxy server effectively, and it provides higher accuracy. However, it requires both the server and the client to support cookie. In our implementation, we adopt the first method.

In daily operations of the website, besides suffering man-made attacks, the server is also scanned frequently by black-box testing tools. The man-made attack is different from automated tools. The records for scanners are not removed in the clean-up stage. The accuracy of the model mined from the data will be reduced if the two types of users mentioned above are mixed. Therefore, how to differentiate human attacks from scanners is also considered in order to improve the accuracy of analysis. The following are some methods that can be combined to make this distinction.

– Fingerprint of scanner. Different scanners usually have their own characteristics. A specific field such as the name of the scanner might be added into the request header.

- Trigger rules. Recording the times of users intercepted by the Web Application Firewall in a certain period. If the number is larger than the threshold allowed, you can assert the user is a scanner.
- Setting hidden links. The hidden links are invisible, and couldn't be clicked. While crawlers in scanners always catch all links including the hidden ones to detect vulnerabilities, so the hidden links are in the list of their requests. Especially, scanners based on Webkit will test the hidden links automatically to crawl more page to test. We can set a hidden link to induce scanners to request the link, which can help distinguish scanners from users.
- Cookie implantation. When the measured time under the condition of security rules triggered is lager than the threshold, a cookie is sent to the user. The client should carry the cookie when it requests the server next time, while most scanners can not achieve this operation. If the user requests next time without the cookie, we believe this user is a scanner. The advantage of cookie implantation is that it is more direct to find the scanner according to the next request.
- Response error ratio. This method is implemented by calculating the proportion of server response error in a certain duration, hence, it can detect sensitive directory scanning. Scanners based on dictionary file send request to each URL listed in the dictionary file, and then determine whether the path exists by getting the response returned by the server. By counting the number of return status of 404 for each user, we can ensure the user is a scanner when the number reaches a certain threshold.

Because the log data that we collect is in fixed format, considering the practical operability, we use the fingerprint approach to identifying scanners. In addition, we use the response error ratio method. We also consider if the number of attacks exceeds a certain frequency in a period. Combining these methods mentioned above with counting the number of response in the referrer field that are not 200, we can determine whether the user is a tool.

3.3   Attack Sequential Pattern Discovery

After preprocessing, two sequence databases are generated. One is the database of ordinary attackers, and the other is for scanners. We can conduct data mining algorithms on the two sequence databases separately to get the frequent sequence. In order to reduce the computational overhead, we convert each attack string to a corresponding number. Then, the pattern mining operation is performed based on these digital numbers.

Sequential pattern mining aims to find valuable patterns in a sequence database, which is based on a given mining support. More concretely, with mining we can find out all the frequent sequences for a given sequence database and minimum support threshold, and then remove the sequences that are duplications or contained by others. The *Sequence* is an ordered list of *itemsets* (A collection of one or more items, it can be expressed as $s = (x_1, x_2, x_3, \ldots, x_m)$, where x_k

represents an item), like $S = (s_1, s_2, s_3, \ldots, s_n)$, where s_k represents an item-set. The length of sequence, $|s|$, is the number of itemsets in the sequence. And the *Support* of a sequence W is defined as the fraction of sequences that contain W. *Frequent sequence* is a *subsequence* (A subsequence is that a sequence $< a_1, a_2, \ldots, a_n >$ is contained in another sequence $< b_1, b_2, \ldots, b_m > (m \geqslant n)$ if there exist integers $i_1 < i_2 < \ldots < i_n$, such that $a_1 \subseteq b_{i_1}, a_2 \subseteq b_{i_2}, \ldots, a_n \subseteq b_{i_n}$) whose support is $\geq minsup$.

Various sequential pattern mining algorithms have been proposed. Algorithms like AprioriAll [22], AprioriSome [21], GSP [22] are based on Apriori property to find the patterns in layers. The FreeSpan [7] and PrefixSpan are based on pattern-growth. The PrefixSpan is always preferable due to its performance and efficiency in large sequence databases, which is because that it generates less projection databases and less subsequence connections.

PrefixSpan. PrefixSpan is a kind of sequential pattern mining algorithm based on database projection, whose performance is better than GSP and AprioriAll. With the ability of handling large sequence databases, it is more widely used than other algorithms.

The *Prefix* in PrefixSpan means that: suppose that all the items are listed in alphabetical order. Given a sequence $\alpha =< e_1, e_2, \ldots, e_n >$ (where each e_i corresponds to a frequent element in S), and a sequence $\beta =< e'_1, e'_2, \ldots, e'_m >$ $(m \leqslant n)$ is called a prefix of α if and only if three conditions are satisfied: (1) $e'_i = e_i (i \leqslant m - 1)$, (2) $e'_m \subseteq e_m$, and (3) all the frequent items belong to $(e_m - e'_m)$ are alphabetically after those in e_m. Conversely, *Suffix* is that given a sequence $\alpha =< e_1, e_2, \ldots, e_n >$ (where each e_i corresponds to a frequent element in S), let $\beta =< e'_1, e'_2, \ldots, e'_{m-1}, e'_m > (m \leqslant n)$ be the prefix of α. Sequence $\gamma =< e''_m, e_{m+1}, \ldots, e_n >$ is called the suffix of α with regards to prefix β, denoted as $\gamma = \alpha/\beta$, where $e''_m = (e_m - e'_m)^2$.

PrefixSpan uses the divide-and-conquer strategy to generate more projected databases (let α be a sequential pattern in a sequence database S. The α-projected database, denoted as $S |_\alpha$, is the collection of suffixes of sequences in S with regards to prefix α), and the sizes of these databases are smaller than the raw sequence databases. The basic idea is to find out the frequent items whose frequency is greater than support, to generate their projection databases. For each projection database, the algorithm constructs the prefix pattern connected with the suffix mode to get frequent pattern.

Because Prefixspan does not need to generate candidate sequence patterns, it reduces the search space greatly. And it belongs to the growth pattern method, so compared with the original sequence database it reduces the size of projection database. The main cost of the algorithm is the construction of projection database. If the average length of sequences is large, it needs to build a projection database for each sequence pattern, then the time consumption increases correspondingly.

However, the average length of sequences in the database for scanners is too long for PrefixSpan. Certainly it will be, in scanning tools, tens of thousands of payloads waits to request each page of the website. In the course of our

---

Algorithm 1. Framework of our changed PrefixSpan.

Input:
  The set of Sequence Database, S;
  The minimum support threshold, $min\_support$;
Output:
  The set of sequential patterns, S';
 1: Scanning the Database S to extract the set of *Items* whose frequency is bigger
   than $min\_support$,
   $Items < -scan(sequenceDatabase)$
 2: for each $item \in Items$ do
 3: $\alpha < -item$;
 4: for all $sequences \in sequenceDatabase$
 5:   $SuffixSequence = Suffix(\alpha).removeitem(\alpha)$
 6:   $S \mid_\alpha= AppendSuffixSequence(SuffixSequence)$;
 7: end for
 8: for all $itemsequence \in \alpha$ do;
 9:   // extend the item in independence sequence like $a.iadd() = \{a, b\}$
10:   $\alpha' < -item.iadd()$;
11:   $l < -\alpha'.length$;
12:   $prefixspan(\alpha', l, S \mid_{\alpha'})$;
13:   // extension the item in a sequence like $a.sadd() = \{(a, b)\}$
14:   $\alpha'' < -item.sadd()$;
15:   $l < -\alpha''.length$;
16:   $prefixspan(\alpha'', l, S \mid_{\alpha''})$;
17: end for
18: end for

---

experiment, we find that the lengths of sequences in scanning tools' database can reach hundreds. In the generated frequent sequence, we find that there are lots of repeated items, which means that the pages in the website is request back in attack path, like $< a(bg)aad >$, and we don't care about that. What we just want to know is whether the sequence contains more new paths, we just need the path like $< a(bg)d >$ rather $< a(bg)aad >$. So after generating the projection database, we remove all the items belonging to prefix sequence.

The algorithm is shown in Algorithm 1. Firstly, the sequence database is scanned to obtain all the frequent items N (the frequent sequence whose length is 1). Secondly, we divide the complete collection of frequent sequences into n subsets with different prefix. For each item whose frequency is bigger than $min\_support$, the corresponding projection database is obtained. Thirdly, all items that belong to prefix sequences are removed. Lastly, the main loop is executed until no frequent sequence is found.

We present an example to clarify our algorithm. Suppose that the sequence database is $[< a(ac)ad(cf) >, < (ad)c(bc)a >, < (ef)(ab)(df)ab >, < eg(af)cac >]$ and the $min\_support$ is 70 %. In the first step, we find the frequent items whose frequency is bigger than 70 %, and the results are a, c, d, f. Then, for each item, for example a, we get its suffix sequences from the origin database. For the first sequence, the suffix for a is $< \_(ac)ad(cf) >$, and then we remove the item a from suffix sequence, leaving $< \_(\_c)\_d(cf) >$. Analogously, the new sequence database we get for a is $[< \_(\_c)\_d(cf) >, < (\_d)c(bc)\_ >, < (\_b)(df)\_b >, < (\_f)c\_c >]$. Next, we extend a to $< a, c >$ and $< (ac) >$, which aims to find new frequent sequence. If their frequency is bigger than $min\_support$, like $< a, c >$, they are added to the final results as parts of frequent sequences.

3.4 Pattern Analysis

It is difficult to evaluate the vulnerability directly just with the mined result. First, lots of sequential patterns are generated after sequential pattern mining, and we need to analyze each pattern. Second, the format of sequences is represented with normal digital numbers, and these numbers are unreadable for the analyzers. For example, $< 6\ 8\ (12\ 8)\ 16 >$ is an example pattern, but it is meaningless characters if not transformed to a readable form. In order to ensure the accuracy and readability of the patterns, the following two steps are performed.

Step 1: maximizing frequent sequences. In the generated frequent sequences, a large number of sequences are redundant, because many sequences are contained in other sequences. At this point, we need to delete the redundant sequences. For example, for a frequent-sequence set $< a(bc) >, < a(fd)(bc) >, < a >$, we can find that the first and the third sequence are contained in the second one, so we need to remove the first and the third sequence, keeping the sequence $< a(fd)(bc) >$.

Step 2: transforming the sequential pattern into graphical representation. In order to make the patterns more intuitive to understand what the vulnerabilities are and where is vulnerable, we translate the resulting patterns into the *dot* language. Before that we parse numbers in frequent sequences to strings. In the step of sequential pattern discovery, we transform path strings to numbers that are stored in a file. In this part, we transform each number back to the corresponding string.

For example, Fig. 5 shows parts of frequent sequences. The sequences like $< 0 >$, $< 0\ 2 >$, and $< 0\ (2\ 6)\ 8 >$, are contained in sequence $< 0\ (2\ 6)\ 8\ (11\ 16) >$, so in the first step, we delete these sequences. One of the final patterns in Fig. 5 is $< 0\ (2\ 6)\ 8\ (11\ 16)\ 182 >$. We translate the number

```
0 #
0 #2 #
0 #2 6 #
0 #2 6 #8 #
0 #2 6 #8 #11 #
0 #2 6 #8 #11 16 #
0 #2 6 #8 #11 16 #182 #
0 #2 6 #8 #11 16 #183 #
0 #2 6 #8 #11 16 #168 #
```

Fig. 5. Mined sequences.

```
fileinclude:/::0
xssattack:/::2
portsqlinject:/::6
clientsqlinject:/::8
clientfuzztesting:/::11
fromurlfileinclude:/::16
directorytraversal:/user::168
xssattack:/images::182
xssattack:/tpl::183
```

Fig. 6. Corresponding strings.

to strings according to Fig. 6, and the pattern is transformed to $<$*fileinclude:/ (xssattack:/ portsqlinjection:/) clientsqlinjection:/ (clientfuzztesting:/ fromurlfileinclude:/) xssattack:/*$>$. Lastly, the sequence can be illustrated in *dot* language.

4   Experimentation and Analysis

In this section, we evaluate our implementation of frequent attack sequence mining. To prove the effectiveness of our system, we use the access logs from the real world. The experimental data are the raw access logs that are collected on a company's web server (Nginx) from September 2014 to October 2015. The testing machine is a 64-bit system with 4 GB RAM and a 3.2 GHz Intel i5 processor installed.

We first pre-process log files with different sizes separately. Figure 7 depicts the times consumed when processing different log files in our experiment. We can see that the time of finding attack record increases linearly, and this is because that the time spent on matching payload and reading log file is in proportion to the size of raw log files. While the sudden increase of time is because that attack file size increases, when writing the attack record to file it consumes a lot of time. On the other hand, from the red starts of Fig. 7, we can see that the size of attack files based on the number of attack record is randomly distributed. Intuitively, we may think that the probability of containing attack records for large logs is higher than small logs, but the appearance of attacks in the dataset is actually random. It implies that large-scale attacks may be less unpredictable.

With different sizes of attacker files that are generated by matching attack payloads, users and sessions are identified, and the results are shown in Fig. 8. For all benchmarks, the time increases with the increase of attack file sizes. For this part, we first use the method of fingerprint method, the response error ratio, and counting the number of attacks (which are introduced in Sect. 3.2). By these methods mentioned above, we separate man-made attack from scanner tools, and then, for each user, we identify sessions.

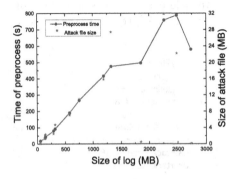

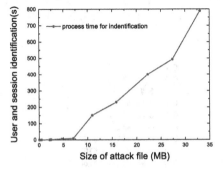

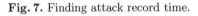

Fig. 7. Finding attack record time.

Fig. 8. User and Session identification time.

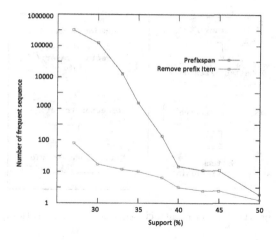

Fig. 9. Frequent sequences number of PrefixSpan and our algorithm.

After preprocessing log files, we have 52338 records of attack in total including 52090 records for scanners and 248 records for attackers. In order to evaluate the effectiveness of our improved Prefixspan algorithm, we compare it with the original Prefixspan. As shown in Fig. 9, with the decline of the support, the number of frequent sequences generated by PrefixSpan grow exponentially, while our algorithm generates much less frequent sequences than those that have the same support in Prefixspan. The main reason is that a large number of duplicate items has been removed after the projection database is generated. Correspondingly, the space of projection database is smaller.

In order to find sequential attack patterns from the man-made sequence database, we set the support with 3.5%, 5%, 7%, 9%, 10%, 12%, 14%, 16% to find more possible frequent attack sequences. Before generating the flowchart of attack, we transfer the sequence numbers to strings according to number-string file whose format is similar to Fig. 6. Then we transfer the patterns to the *dot* language. Table 1 shows the number of records generated with each support, and Fig. 10 illustrates the attack sequence generated by human when the support is 3.5%.

Then, we experiment on the sequence database for scanners. As illustrated in Table 2, we set the supports to be bigger than that of the man-made, which is because that there are many common sequences between scanners. We do not need to understand the sequence of each scanner. What we really need to find

Table 1. Number of frequent sequence record by man-made

Support(%)	3.5	5	7	9	10	12	14	16	18
Number	27	14	8	6	5	5	4	3	3

Table 2. Number of frequent sequence record in scanning tools

Support(%)	22	25	27	30	33	35	38	40	43
Number	2936	132	89	35	17	11	8	5	4

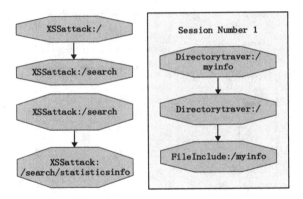

Fig. 10. The users' attack sequence of visualization.

is the common scanning sequence, and that is different from attackers' frequent sequences which are all important to understand the behaviors of attackers. So we set the supports with 22%, 25%, 27%, 30%, 33%, 35%, 38%, 40%, 43%. Table 2 shows the number of records generated with each support, and we perform the same steps as for man-made attack. Figure 11 displays parts of the attack records of scanners when the support is 22%.

By analyzing the results, we can conclude that for this website, the man-made attack sequence is biased to a specific page and a certain attack type,

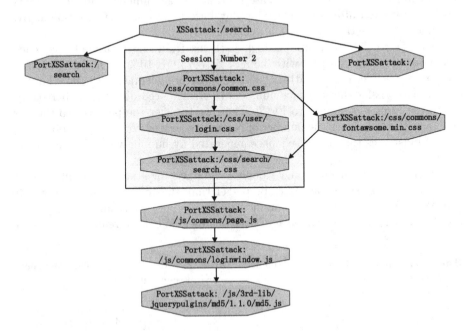

Fig. 11. The scanner attack sequence of visualization.

while scanners exhibit a wide varieties of attacks and more pages are involved. From the user attack sequence as shown in Fig. 10, we can see that the "/" page suffered from XSS attacks frequently, and the XSS attack against the page "/search" are also attempted. Or the attackers tried to use the XSS from page "/search" to "/search/statisticsinfo". Based on this, we can infer that there are contents that come from users' input, or the users are allowed to change the three pages that contain HTML tags. And XSS vulnerability may exist in these pages. In addition to the root directory, the attacker uses directory traversal to try to find the content in higher level directories to execute system command, and also perform "directorytraver" or "fileinclue" attack on page "/myinfo". Based on these information, the webmaster can check whether the pages of "/" and "/myinfo" can be bypassed by unprivileged users.

Figure 11 shows that the XSS attack sequence from scanners, it shows that for a certain type of general attack, the basic attacking paths share a lot similarity. Actually, many different types of attacks are found in the attack sequence, Fig. 11 only shows the XSS attack. With the patterns of attack sequences, we can distinguish scanners.

5   Conclusions and Future Work

This paper presents the design, implementation, and evaluation of sequential attack pattern mining in web logs. With efficient mechanisms, our system achieves the goals of discovering attack sequences of users and scanners to investigate the attack behaviors. We can pinpoint vulnerable pages and understand the internal-path of scanners. In the future, we plan to investigate new ways to identify the type of attacks to improve the accuracy, for example, using automatic classification algorithms. On the other hand, we are also interested in identifying black-box scanners by using the patterns generated by our system.

Acknowledgment. This research was supported in part by the National Science Foundation of China under grants 61173166, 61272190, and 61572179, the Program for New Century Excellent Talents in University, and the Fundamental Research Funds for the Central Universities of China.

References

1. Awstats. http://www.awstats.org/
2. Kibana. https://www.elastic.co/products/kibana
3. Piwik. http://piwik.org/
4. Splunk. http://www.splunk.com/
5. Cooley, R., Mobasher, B., Srivastava, J.: Data preparation for mining world wide web browsing patterns. Knowl. Inf. Syst. **1**, 5–32 (1982)
6. Dziczkowski, G., Wegrzyn-Wolska, K., Bougueroua, L.: An opinion mining approach for web user identification and clients' behaviour analysis. In: 2013 Fifth International Conference on Computational Aspects of Social Networks (CASoN), pp. 79–84. IEEE (2013)

7. Han, J., Pei, J., Mortazavi-Asl, B., et al.: FreeSpan: frequent pattern-projected sequential pattern mining. In: Sixth ACM SIGKDD International Conference on Knowledge Discovery & Data Mining, pp. 355–359. ACM (2000)

8. He, J.: Mining users potential interested in personalized information recommendation service. J. Mod. Inf. (2013)

9. Li, Y., Feng, B.Q., Mao, Q.: Research on path completion technique in web usage mining. In: International Symposium on Computer Science and Computational Technology, pp. 554–559. IEEE (2008)

10. Kewen, L.: Analysis of preprocessing methods for web usage data. In: 2012 International Conference on Measurement, Information and Control (MIC), pp. 383–386. IEEE (2012)

11. Mele, I.: Web usage mining for enhancing search-result delivery and helping users to find interesting web content. In: Proceedings of the Sixth ACM International Conference on Web Search and Data Mining, pp. 765–770. ACM (2013)

12. Nasraoui, O.: Web data mining: exploring hyperlinks, contents, and usage data. ACM SIGKDD Explor. Newsl. **10**, 23–25 (2009)

13. Provos, N., Mcnamee, D., Mavrommatis, P., et al.: The ghost in the browser analysis of web-based malware. In: Usenix Hotbots (2007)

14. Srivastava, J., Cooley, R., Deshpande, M., et al.: Web usage mining: discovery and applications of usage patterns from web data. ACM SIGKDD Explor. Newsl. **1**(2), 12–23 (2000)

15. Suresh, R.M., Padmajavalli, R.: An overview of data preprocessing in data and web usage mining. In: 2006 1st International Conference on Digital Information Management (2006)

16. Ting, I.H., Kimble, C., Kudenko, D.: Applying web usage mining techniques to discover potential browsing problems of users. In: IEEE International Conference on Advanced Learning Technologies, pp. 929–930. IEEE Computer Society (2007)

17. Varnagar, C.R., Madhak, N.N., Kodinariya, T.M., et al.: Web usage mining: a review on process, methods and techniques. In: International Conference on Information Communication and Embedded Systems (ICICES) 2013, pp. 40–46. IEEE (2013)

18. Wang, T., He, P.L.: User identification in web mining and iris recognition technology. Comput. Eng. **34**(6), 182–184 (2008)

19. Pei, J., Han, J., Mortazavi-Asl, B., et al.: Mining sequential patterns by pattern-growth: the PrefixSpan approach. IEEE Trans. Knowl. Data Eng. **16**(11), 1424–1440 (2004)

20. Qin, C., Liao, C.: Session identification based on linked referrers and web log indexing. Comput. Syst. Sci. Eng. **25**(8), 273–286 (2013)

21. Agrawal, R., Srikant, R.: Mining sequential patterns. In: Proceedings of ICDE, pp. 3–14. IEEE Computer Society (1995)

22. Srikant, R., Agrawal, R.: Mining sequential patterns: generalizations and performance improvements. In: Apers, P., Bouzeghoub, M., Gardarin, G. (eds.) EDBT 1996. LNCS, vol. 1057, pp. 1–17. Springer, Heidelberg (1996)

Practical Server-Aided k-out-of-n Oblivious Transfer Protocol

Xiaochao Wei, Chuan Zhao, Han Jiang, Qiuliang Xu$^{(\boxtimes)}$, and Hao Wang

School of Computer Science and Technology, Shandong University, Jinan, China
{weixiaochao2008,wanghao0605}@163.com, zhaochuan.sdu@gmail.com,
{jianghan,xql}@sdu.edu.cn

Abstract. Oblivious transfer (OT) is an important cryptographic primitive. In this paper, we propose a practical server-aided k-out-of-n oblivious transfer (OT_n^k) protocol based on the Decisional Diffie-Hellman (DDH) assumption. Our construction is the first one that is applicable in cloud computing environment. Unlike the original OT which only contains the receiver R and sender S, the server-aided OT setting also contains cloud servers who provide a vast amount of computational resources, therefore the sender and receiver can outsource the computational work to the cloud servers. In the proposed protocol, the receiver R sends only two group elements to the sender S, and S sends $2n$ group elements back to R. The computation cost of R and S is the most efficient comparing with other known schemes. In our protocol, the receiver R computes $2k + 3$ modular exponentiations and the sender computes $2.5n$ modular exponentiations. The communication rounds of the protocol is three, including one extra round from the receiver R to the cloud servers. The choices of the receiver R is protected against the sender S and cloud servers, meanwhile, the input values of S which are not chosen are still secret to R.

Keywords: k-out-of-n oblivious transfer · Server-aided · Decisional Diffie-Hellman assumption · Cloud computing

1 Introduction

1.1 Background

Oblivious transfer (OT) is an important basic cryptographic primitive, which can be used in many cryptographic protocols [1–7]. An oblivious transfer protocol involves two participants, the sender S and the receiver R, where the sender S has some input values and the receiver R aims at obtaining part of these values via interacting with S. Meanwhile, the protocol must meet the following requirements: (1) The sender S does not know what R chooses; (2) The receiver

This work is supported by the National Natural Science Foundation of China under grant No. 61173139 and No. 61572294.

X. Huang et al. (Eds.): GPC 2016, LNCS 9663, pp. 261–277, 2016.
DOI: 10.1007/978-3-319-39077-2_17

can only obtain the values of its choice and get no information about the other values. Since Rabin firstly proposed the notion of OT, it has been studied widely and in many aspects. In this paper we are mainly concerned with the k-out-of-n oblivious transfer protocol (OT_n^k), in which the receiver R wants to obtain k values from the sender's n input values, where $k < n$. For the reason that the OT protocol is the bottleneck when constructing other cryptographic protocols, how to construct efficient and practical OT protocol is the main research topic for cryptography researchers.

Recently, as the rapid development of cloud computing, more and more computational costs are outsourced to the cloud, which has a vast amount of computational resources. With the help of cloud, the users avoid numerous complex computations, and such that some schemes become very efficient and even practical. In the cryptographic field, many schemes and protocols, such as attribute-based encryption (ABE) [8], identity-based encryption (IBE) [9], secure multiparty computation (SMPC) [10,11] and other cryptographic schemes [12,13], are constructed in the cloud computing setting with better efficiency. However, protecting the users's privacy against untrusted cloud server providers (CSP) is a thorny and urgent problem. Therefore, when outsourcing cryptographic schemes or protocols to the cloud, we must view the cloud servers as honest-but-curious, which means that they want to obtain users's private information for the reason of competition, benefit and politics. To the best of our knowledge, there have no works yet on constructing k-out-of-n oblivious transfer protocols in cloud computing environment, and so that we provide the first server-aided (or cloud-assisted) k-out-of-n oblivious transfer protocol in this paper.

1.2   Related Work

Rabin [14] introduced the notion of OT and proposed a scheme based on quadratic residue modulo a composite. Even et al. [15] presented an extension form of OT called 1-out-of-2 OT (OT_1^2) and gave a protocol based on any enhanced trapdoor permutation. Brassard et al. [16] firstly proposed 1-out-of-n OT (OT_n^1), which is also known as "all-or-nothing disclosure of secrets" (ANDOS). Since then, lots of OT_n^1 protocols [17–23] were proposed based on different security assumption. It is worth mentioning that, Peikert et al. [24] presented a new abstraction called dual-mode cryptosystem which can be used to construct OT_2^1 protocols. The proposed protocols are universally composable with the help of common reference strings (CRS). Furthermore, it can be extended to 1-out-of-2^k lossy encryption scheme, which would yield a 1-out-of-2^k OT protocol. The concrete constructions of the dual-mode cryptosystem are mainly based on the Decisional Diffie-Hellman (DDH) problem, the Quadratic Residuosity (QR) problem and the learning with errors(LWE) problem. Among them, the DDH construction can transfer strings, but the QR and LWE construction can only transfer single-bit.

Considering k-out-of-n OT, Mu et al. [25] proposed three OT_n^k protocols based on RSA encryption, Nyberg-Rueppel signature and ElGamal encryption, and the non-interactive OT_n^k protocol is most efficient with $O(n)$ encryptions respectively. Chu and Tzeng [26] presented efficient two-round OT_n^k protocols based on DDH assumption. The main idea behind the protocol is that, the receiver R constructs a k-degree polynomial $f(x)$ satisfying that $f(i) = 0$ for each $i \in \{\sigma_1, \cdots, \sigma_k\}$, where $\{\sigma_1, \cdots, \sigma_k\}$ is the set of the receiver's choice. Then R chooses another random k-degree polynomial $g(x)$ to mask $f(x)$ and sends the masked choices $A_0, A_1, \cdots, A_{k-1}$ to the sender S. After receiving these values, S computes $B_i = g^{f(i)} h^{g(i)}$ and treats B_i as the public key of the ElGamal cryptosystem and then encrypts its input values to transfer to R. At last, the receiver decrypts the corresponding values it chooses. The protocol is secure against semi-honest sender and receiver, and the participants computes $(k+2)n+3k+2$ exponentiations and sends $2n+k+1$ group elements overall. Camenish et al. [27] proposed an adaptive OT_n^k protocol with full simulation based on the q-Power Decisional Diffie-Hellman (q-PDBH) assumption, which is not standard. Green and Hohenbergerand [28] also presented a fully simulatable adaptive OT_n^k protocol, which is based on the Decisional Bilinear Diffie-Hellman (DBDH) assumption. Except for numerous modular exponentiations, these protocols also need complex bilinear operations. Zeng et al. [29] presented two practical frameworks for k-out-of-n OT with security against covert and malicious adversaries. The frameworks are constructed using a variant of smooth projective hash and also the technique of cut-and-choose is used to achieve the security of full simulation. However, the technique of cut-and-choose has an inherent disadvantage that protocols using this technique have error probability when simulating the corrupted party. Therefore, the above frameworks of OT_n^k are with statistic security. The frameworks can ce implemented from the DDH assumption, the decisional n-th residuosity assumption, the decisional quadratic residuosity assumption and so on. The DDH-based instantiation is most efficient with six interactive rounds and the participants should compute $40(n+k)$ public key encryptions overall. Basing on the above work, Zeng et al. [30] proposed a framework of OT_n^k protocol with the security against covert adversaries. If the deterrence factor is set to be $1/2$, the DDH-based instantiation costs $8.5n - k$ exponentiations, and the communication round of the proposed protocol is four. Recently, Guo et al. [31] proposed a cryptographic notion called subset membership encryption (SME), which can be used to construct two round OT_n^k protocol against semi-honest adversaries. The proposed protocol are based the n-BDHE, (f,n)-DHE and n-BSDH assumptions. Furthermore, the sender invokes n encryption algorithms and the receiver invokes k decryption algorithms, where the two algorithms both cost numerous modular exponentiations and complex bilinear operations. We emphasize that compared with our scheme the above protocols are all constructed in traditional setting where there not exist cloud servers, such that our protocol is more practical in cloud computing environment.

1.3   Our Contribution

In this paper, we aim to construct efficient and practical OT_n^k protocol in the cloud computing environment for the first time, which is based on the decision

Diffie-Hellman (DDH) assumption. Our proposed protocol is secure against semi-honest sender and receiver, which means that the privacy of the sender and receiver is protected when completing the full protocol. Compared with other original OT_n^k protocol, to our best knowledge, our protocol is the most efficient. For the communication cost, the receiver only sends two group elements to the sender and the sender sends $2n$ group elements to the receiver which is independent of k. Regarding modular exponentiations computed by the parties, the receiver and sender compute $2k + 3$ and $2.5n$ separately, therefore the computational complexity of our protocol is just $O(n + k)$, not $O(nk)$ in some other schemes.

Our proposed protocol has the following advantages.

1. Our work firstly considers how to construct OT_n^k protocol in the server-aided (cloud-assisted) setting. In the traditional k-out-of-n oblivious transfer setting, there exist only two parties, the sender and receiver, and they interact with each other in real protocol. Therefore, they must compute complex computational task by themselves. Differently, in our server-aided setting, there also exist two cloud servers, which help the participants to compute numerous modular exponentiations. As a result, the computational complexity of the participants is improved. We emphasize that the two servers are honest-and-curious and independent, which means that they will not collude with each other, as well as the sender or the receiver. The above assumption is reasonable in real life. For example, many famous public cloud providers Amazon EC2, Windows Azure or Google Computer Engine, will not collude with each other in view of benefit, privacy and reputation. Therefore, our server-aided oblivious transfer model is reasonable and practical in the era of cloud computing.

2. Our proposed OT_n^k protocol is the most efficient comparing with other protocols. The idea behind our protocol mainly benefits from the DDH-based instantiation of the dual-mode cryptosystem presented in [24], which means that the receiver constructs two tuples satisfying that only one is a Diffie-Hellman tuple. We extend this $(1,2)$-dual-mode into a general (k, n)-dual-mode, where the receiver constructs n tuples satisfying that only k of them are Diffie-Hellman tuples, using the technique of oblivious polynomial evaluation. In detail, the receiver constructs a k-degree polynomial whose roots are its choices and sends the k coefficients of $f(x)$ in masked state. Then the sender and two servers evaluate the polynomial obliviously and generate n tuples satisfying that only k of them are Diffie-Hellman tuples. At last, the sender transfers its own input values using the above n tuples and the receiver can only obtain the desired k values it chooses. Furthermore, our protocol protects the receiver's choice against the sender and cloud servers, and the sender's input values which are not chosen by the receiver are still secret to the receiver.

1.4   Organization

This paper is organized as follows. In Sect. 2 we give the problem statement of the server-aided OT_n^k protocol. In Sect. 3 we introduce the preliminaries and definition of security used in our protocols. In Sect. 4 we give a specific construct of our server-aided OT_n^k protocol and prove its correctness and security. Furthermore, we analyse the efficiency of the proposed protocol and compare our result with other known schemes. In Sect. 5 we conclude the paper and give the future work.

2 Problem Statement

2.1 Design Goals

In the traditional k-out-of-n oblivious transfer setting, there exist two parties, which are denoted by sender and receiver. The sender has n input values and the receiver wants to obtain k ($k \leq n$) from them according to its choice. Meanwhile, the sender does not know the choice of the receiver, and the receiver can only obtain the desired values it chooses. In the previous known protocols, the sender and receiver interact with each other by sending messages and the receiver obtains the desired output values finally. Therefore, both the sender and the receiver must execute numerous computational tasks, and the efficiency of the protocols is not optimistic. With the emergence and development of cloud computing, many cryptographic schemes have been outsourced to the cloud serves with the improvement of efficiency. Our motivation is to construct practical OT_n^k protocol with the help of cloud servers. In the server-aided OT_n^k protocol, most of the computational tasks are outsourced to the cloud servers and therefore the efficiency of the sender and receiver is improved. However, in view of the untrusted cloud servers, the privacy of the user should also be protected. Therefore, the server-aided OT_n^k protocol must also satisfy that the privacy of the sender and receiver is secret to the cloud servers.

2.2 The System Model

In our server-aided k-out-of-n oblivious transfer setting, there are three kinds of participants: the sender S, the receiver R and the cloud server. The sender and receiver are identical to the corresponding participant in the original k-out-of-n oblivious transfer protocol, where the sender has n input values and the receiver wants to obtain k values randomly from them. Differently, in the server-aided setting, there exist two servers that (1) don't have any input and output in the OT_n^k protocol; (2) are independent to each other, which means that they won't collude; (3) has a vast amount of computational resources. Concretely, the sender and receiver outsource their computational tasks to the cloud servers without revealing any information about their inputs and outputs to the cloud servers.

The system model of our server-aided k-out-of-n oblivious transfer setting is described in Fig. 1, which contains three phases inside. Concretely, the receiver sends messages corresponding to its own input to the sender and the two cloud servers in Phase 1. We emphasise that the receiver's input is secret if and only if the two cloud servers do not share the messages received from the receiver with each other. Then in Phase 2 the two cloud servers send messages they compute separately to the sender. Finally in Phase 3, the sender combines the messages it receives from the receiver and cloud servers, and the reconstructs the final messages which are used to transfer the sender's input values to the receiver. Then the receiver decrypts and obtains the desired output values.

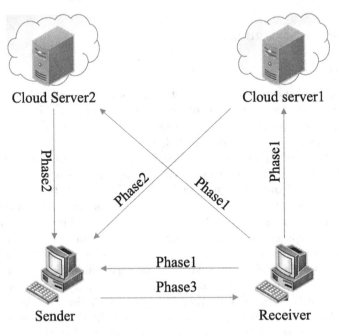

Fig. 1. The system model of server-aided OT

2.3   The Security Model

In this paper, we are concerned with the server-aided k-out-of-n oblivious transfer protocol, where the participants have access to two cloud servers. In order to define the security of server-aided protocol, we refer to the definition of security for the secure multi-party computation (MPC) in the server-aided setting [10,11]. In our scheme, the two cloud servers are honest-but-curious and independent. Considering the property of honest-but-curious, it means that the cloud servers will run the protocol according to the specification honestly, however they are willing to get other extra information about the input of the sender or receiver from the received message transcript. For the independent property, as discussed in [10,11], it means that corrupted parties do not necessarily collude with each other. Concretely, the two cloud servers will not collude with either the sender or the receiver, and in other words, they will only provide the ability of computation and transfer the messages to the sender or receiver according to the protocol specification. What's more, the two servers themselves will not communicate with each other. The above requirements are reasonable in many real life scenarios, where the two servers come from different cloud providers.

We now define the security of the sender S and receiver R separately. In our server-aided OT_n^k protocol, the messages sent by R to the servers and S contain the information of R's input, therefore when we define the security of the receiver R, we must consider its privacy against the servers and sender separately. This is different with the definition of R's security in original k-out-of-n oblivious transfer protocol, where we only consider the sender. Considering the security of the sender, in the protocol S only sends messages to the receiver, so that we will only define the security of S against the receiver R. Assuming that the sender S has n input values $x_1, \cdots, x_n$ and R's k choice are $\sigma_1, \cdots, \sigma_k$. If the cloud servers are honest-but-curious and independent, a server-aided OT_n^k protocol with security against semi-honest sender and receiver should meet the following requirements:

1. **Receiver's security against cloud servers:** We use the indistinguishability to define R's security against cloud servers. For any two different sets of R's choices, $C = \{\sigma_1, \cdots, \sigma_k\}$ and $C' = \{\sigma_1', \cdots, \sigma_k'\}$, the corresponding transcripts of messages sent by R to the servers are indistinguishable.
2. **Receiver's security against sender:** R's security against sender is the same as the definition above. That is, for any two different sets of R's choices, $C = \{\sigma_1, \cdots, \sigma_k\}$ and $C' = \{\sigma_1', \cdots, \sigma_k'\}$, the corresponding transcripts of messages sent by R to the sender are indistinguishable.
3. **Sender's security against receiver:** For any choice set $C = \{\sigma_1, \cdots, \sigma_k\}$ of the receiver R, the encryptions of S's unselected input values should be indistinguishable from the random ones.

3 Preliminaries

3.1 The Security Assumption

Decision Diffie-Hellman (DDH). Let $\mathbb{G}$ be a group of order q with generators g, where q is a prime. Given (g, g^a, g^b, g^c) where $a, b, c \in_R Z_q$, decide whether $ab \equiv c (mod q)$ or not is difficult. In another words, the DDH assumption is that the following two distribution ensembles are computationally indistinguishable:

- $X_1 = (g, g^a, g^b, g^{ab})$ where $a, b \in_R Z_q$.
- $X_2 = (g, g^a, g^b, g^c)$ where $a, b, c \in_R Z_q$ and $c \neq ab$.

3.2 A Special Function - *RAND* Function

Given a group $\mathbb{G}$ of order q with generators g, we show how a quadruple (w, x, y, z) is called a Diffie-Hellman tuple, where $w, x, y, z \in \mathbb{G}$. If there exists a value $a \in Z_q$ such that $y = w^a$ and $z = x^a$, we say that the tuple (w, x, y, z) is a Diffie-Hellman tuple in the group $\mathbb{G}$. On the contrary, if there not exist such a value, then the tuple (w, x, y, z) is called a non-Diffie-Hellman tuple in the group $\mathbb{G}$.

The $RAND$ function is defined over a quadruple in the group $\mathbb{G}$. Concretely, the function $RAND(w, x, y, z) = (u, v)$ satisfies that $u = (w)^s \cdot (y)^t$ and $v = (x)^s \cdot (z)^t$, where $s, t \leftarrow \mathbb{Z}_q$ are random. The $RAND$ function has the following property:

- If (w, x, y, z) is a Diffie-Hellman tuple satisfying that $x = w^a$ and $z = y^a$, then for $(u, v) \leftarrow RAND(w, x, y, z)$ it holds that $u^a = v$.
- If (w, x, y, z) is a non-Diffie-Hellman tuple, then the distributions $(w, x, y, z, RAND(w, x, y, z))$ and $(w, x, y, z, g^\alpha, g^\beta)$, where $\alpha, \beta \leftarrow \mathbb{Z}_q$ are random, are equivalent.

3.3   Computationally Indistinguishability

Two distribution ensembles $X = \{X(a, n)\}_{a \in \{0,1\}^*; n \in N}$, $Y = \{Y(a, n)\}_{a \in \{0,1\}^*; n \in N}$ are said to be computationally indistinguishable, denoted by $X \overset{c}{\equiv} Y$, if for every probabilistic polynomial-time(PPT for short) algorithm D there exists a negligible function $\varepsilon(n)$ such that for every $a \in \{0, 1\}^*$ and every $n \in N$,

$$|\Pr[D(X(a, n)) = 1] - \Pr[D(Y(a, n)) = 1]| \leq \varepsilon(n).$$

4   Server-Aided k-out-of-n Oblivious Transfer Protocol

4.1   Server-Aided OT_n^k Protocol

In this section, we present a server-aided OT_n^k protocol against semi-honest sender and receiver in the cloud computing environment, where the cloud servers are honest-but-curious and independent.

Server-Aided k-out-of-n Oblivious Transfer $\pi_{OT_n^k}$

- **Functionality:** $\mathcal{F}_{OT_n^k}$
    - **Inputs:** The sender S has n values $(x_1, \cdots, x_n)$ and the receiver R has k values $(\sigma_1, \cdots, \sigma_k) \in \{1, \cdots, n\}$. In addition, two servers $Server_1$ and $Server_2$ have no input.
    - **Auxiliary input:** Both parties have a security parameter 1^n and a group $\mathbb{G}$ of prime order q with a generators g_0.
- **Protocol:**
    1. The receiver R chooses n random values $y_1, \cdots, y_n, \leftarrow \mathbb{Z}_q$ and sends them to the server S_1 and S_2.
    2. The receiver chooses a polynomial $f(x) = (x - \sigma_1)(x - \sigma_2) \cdots (x - \sigma_k) + \beta = a_0 + a_1 x + \cdots + x^k \bmod q$, where $\beta \leftarrow \mathbb{Z}_q$ and computes $(g_0)^{a_i}$ for each $i = 0, 1, \cdots, k - 1$. Then R sends $(g_0)^{a_0}, (g_0)^{a_1}, \cdots, (g_0)^{a_t}$ to the server $Server_1$ and $(g_0)^{a_{t+1}}, \cdots, (g_0)^{a_{k-1}}$ to the server $Server_2$, where $t < k - 1$ (i.e. we set $t = \lfloor \frac{k-1}{2} \rfloor$).

3. The server $Server_1$ computes $g_1 = (g_0)^{y_1}, \cdots, g_n = (g_0)^{y_n}$. Then, for $i = 1, \cdots, n$, $j = 0, 1, \cdots, t$, the server $Server_1$ computes $((g_0)^{a_j})^{y_i} = (g_i)^{a_j}$. At last, $Server_1$ computes the following matrix,

$$
\begin{bmatrix}
(g_1)^{a_0 \cdot 1^0} & (g_1)^{a_1 \cdot 1^1} & \cdots & (g_1)^{a_t \cdot 1^t} \\
(g_2)^{a_0 \cdot 2^0} & (g_2)^{a_1 \cdot 2^1} & \cdots & (g_2)^{a_t \cdot 2^t} \\
\vdots & \vdots & \vdots & \vdots \\
(g_n)^{a_0 \cdot n^0} & (g_n)^{a_1 \cdot n^1} & \cdots & (g_n)^{a_t \cdot n^t}
\end{bmatrix}
$$

and then computes

$$
\begin{bmatrix}
h_1^1 = (g_1)^{a_0 \cdot 1^0 + a_1 \cdot 1^1 + \cdots + a_t \cdot 1^t} \\
h_2^1 = (g_2)^{a_0 \cdot 2^0 + a_1 \cdot 2^1 + \cdots + a_t \cdot 2^t} \\
\vdots \quad \vdots \quad \vdots \quad \vdots \\
h_n^1 = (g_n)^{a_0 \cdot n^0 + a_1 \cdot n^1 + \cdots + a_t \cdot n^t}
\end{bmatrix}
$$

and sends $(g_1, \cdots, g_n)$ and $(h_1^1, \cdots h_n^1)$ to the sender S. In addition, the server $Server_1$ sends the number of the values $(g_0)^{a_0}, (g_0)^{a_1}, \cdots, (g_0)^{a_t}$ (in fact, it is the number of the coefficients sent by R to $Server_1$), denoted as c_1, to S.

4. The server $Server_2$ computes $g_1 = (g_0)^{y_1}, \cdots, g_n = (g_0)^{y_n}$. Then, for $i = 1, \cdots, n$, $j = t+1, \cdots, k-1$, the server $Server_2$ computes $((g_0)^{a_j})^{y_i} = (g_i)^{a_j}$. At last, $Server_2$ computes the following matrix,

$$
\begin{bmatrix}
(g_1)^{a_{t+1} \cdot 1^{t+1}} & \cdots & (g_1)^{a_{k-1} \cdot 1^{k-1}} & (g_1)^{1^k} \\
(g_2)^{a_{t+1} \cdot 2^{t+1}} & \cdots & (g_2)^{a_{k-1} \cdot 2^{k-1}} & (g_2)^{2^k} \\
\vdots & \vdots & \vdots & \vdots \\
(g_n)^{a_{t+1} \cdot n^{t+1}} & \cdots & (g_n)^{a_{k-1} \cdot n^{k-1}} & (g_n)^{n^k}
\end{bmatrix}
$$

and then computes

$$
\begin{bmatrix}
h_1^2 = (g_1)^{a_{t+1} \cdot 1^{t+1} + \cdots + a_{k-1} \cdot 1^{k-1} + 1^k} \\
h_2^2 = (g_2)^{a_{t+1} \cdot 2^{t+1} + \cdots + a_{k-1} \cdot 2^{k-1} + 2^k} \\
\vdots \quad \vdots \quad \vdots \quad \vdots \\
h_n^2 = (g_n)^{a_{t+1} \cdot n^{t+1} + \cdots + a_{k-1} \cdot n^{k-1} + n^k}
\end{bmatrix}
$$

and sends $(g_1, \cdots, g_n)$ and $(h_1^2, \cdots h_n^2)$ to the sender S. In addition, the server $Server_2$ sends the number of the values $(g_0)^{a_{t+1}}, \cdots, (g_0)^{a_{k-1}}$ (in fact, it is the number of the coefficients sent by R to $Server_2$), denoted as c_2, to S.

5. S checks whether $c_1 + c_2 = k$ and the values $(g_1, \cdots, g_n)$ sent by $Server_1$ and $Server_2$ are identical, if not, S aborts. Then, for $i = 1, \cdots, n$, S computes

$$
h_i = h_i^1 \cdot h_i^2 = (g_i)^{a_0 + a_1 \cdot i + \cdots + a_t \cdot i^t + a_{t+1} \cdot i^{t+1} + \cdots + a_{k-1} \cdot i^{k-1} + i^k} = g_i^{f(i)}.
$$

6. R chooses a random σ_i from $(\sigma_1, \cdots, \sigma_k)$ and computes $g_{\sigma_i} = (g_0)^{y_i}$. Then R computes $g = (g_{\sigma_i})^r$, $h = (g)^\beta$, and then sends (g, h) to S.

7. The sender S operates in the following way:
   - Define the function $RAND(w, x, y, z) = (u, v)$, where $u = (w)^s \cdot (y)^t$ and $v = (x)^s \cdot (z)^t$, and the values $s, t \leftarrow \mathbb{Z}_q$ are random.
   - For every $i \in \{1, \cdots, n\}$, S computes $(u_i, v_i) = RAND(g_i, g, h_i, h)$ and sends the receiver the values (u_i, w_i) where $w_i = v_i \cdot x_i$.

8. The receiver outputs as follows:
   - For σ_i, R computes $x_{\sigma_i} = w_{\sigma_i}/(u_{\sigma_i})^r$.
   - For every $\sigma_j \neq \sigma_i \in (\sigma_1, \cdots, \sigma_k)$, R computes $x_{\sigma_j} = w_{\sigma_j}/(u_{\sigma_j})^{r \cdot y_{\sigma_i} \cdot z}$, where $z = (y_{\sigma_j})^{-1} \bmod q$.

4.2   The Correctness of the Server-Aided OT_n^k Protocol

Assuming that all the participants run the protocol honestly, we analyse the correctness of the server-aided OT_n^k protocol. Concretely, we show that the receiver R can obtain the values it chooses. Intuitively speaking, as shown in the above protocol, the polynomial $f(x) - \beta = (x - \sigma_1)(x - \sigma_2) \cdots (x - \sigma_k)$ constructed by R has k roots $(\sigma_1, \cdots, \sigma_k)$, which means that $f(\sigma_1) = \cdots = f(\sigma_k) = \beta$. Therefore, for each $\sigma_i \in (\sigma_1, \cdots, \sigma_k)$, $(g_{\sigma_i})^{f(\sigma_i)} = (g_{\sigma_i})^\beta$. Note that the values (g, h) are computed by the receiver R satisfying that $h = g^\beta$, and such that the tuple $(g_{\sigma_1}, g, (g_{\sigma_i})^{f(\sigma_1)}, h) \cdots (g_{\sigma_k}, g, (g_{\sigma_k})^{f(\sigma_k)}, h)$ are all Diffie-Hellman tuples. According to the property of the $RAND$ function, the values transferred using these DH tuples can be decrypted by R. We show how to compute the desired values as follows:

1. For $i = \sigma_i \in \{\sigma_1, \cdots, \sigma_k\}$ (R chose in step 6), the tuple $(g_i, g, h_i, h) = (g_i, (g_i)^r, h_i, (h_i)^r)$ is a DH tuple, so we have that

$$\frac{w_i}{(u_i)^r} = \frac{(g)^s \cdot (h)^t \cdot x_i}{((g_i)^s \cdot (h_i)^t)^r} = \frac{(g)^s \cdot (h)^t \cdot x_i}{((g_{\sigma_i})^r)^s \cdot ((h_{\sigma_i})^r)^t} = \frac{(g)^s \cdot (h)^t \cdot x_i}{(g)^s \cdot (h)^t} = x_i \quad (1)$$

2. For each $i \neq \sigma_i \in \{\sigma_1, \cdots, \sigma_k\}$ (R chose in step 6), the tuple $(g_i, g, h_i, h) = (g_i, (g_{\sigma_i})^r, h_i, (h_{\sigma_i})^r) = (g_i, (g_{\sigma_i})^r, (g_i)^\beta, ((g_{\sigma_i})^r)^\beta)$ is also a DH tuple, so we have that

$$\frac{w_i}{(u_i)^{r \cdot y_{\sigma_i} \cdot (y_i)^{-1}}} = \frac{(g)^s \cdot (h)^t \cdot x_i}{((g_i)^s \cdot (h_i)^t)^{r \cdot y_{\sigma_i} \cdot (y_i)^{-1}}} = \frac{(g)^s \cdot (h)^t \cdot x_i}{((g_{\sigma_i})^r)^s \cdot ((h_{\sigma_i})^r)^t} = x_i \quad (2)$$

3. For each $i \notin \{\sigma_1, \cdots, \sigma_k\}$, $f(i) \neq \beta$, the tuple $(g_i, g, h_i, h) = (g_i, (g_{\sigma_i})^r, (g_i)^{f(i)}, ((g_{\sigma_i})^r)^\beta))$ is not a DH tuple, so we have that

$$\frac{w_i}{(u_i)^{r \cdot y_{\sigma_i} \cdot (y_i)^{-1}}} = \frac{(g)^s \cdot (h)^t \cdot x_i}{((g_i)^s \cdot (h_i)^t)^{r \cdot y_{\sigma_i} \cdot (y_i)^{-1}}} = \frac{((g_{\sigma_i})^r)^s \cdot ((g_{\sigma_i}^\beta)^r)^t \cdot x_i}{((g_{\sigma_i})^r)^s \cdot ((g_{\sigma_i}^{f(i)})^r)^t} \neq x_i$$

$$(3)$$

In conclusion, the receiver R can obtain the values it chooses correctly.

4.3   The Security of the Server-Aided OT_n^k Protocol

We firstly show that the privacy of the receiver is protected against the two independent and honest-but-curious servers. As shown in the protocol, the information associated with R's input only contains the k coefficients of the polynomial $f(x)$. The receiver constructs the polynomial $f(x)$ using its own inputs $(\sigma_1, \cdots, \sigma_k)$, and then divides $f(x)$ into two polynomials $f_1(x)$ and $f_2(x)$, satisfying that $f(x) = f_1(x) + f_2(x)$. Assuming that, if R sends all the values $(g_0)^{a_0}, (g_0)^{a_1}, \cdots, (g_0)^{a_{k-1}}$ to only one server (i.e. $Server_1$), then the server can computes $(g_0)^{f(1)}, (g_0)^{f(2)}, \cdots, (g_0)^{f(n)}$. It's clear that there are k values among them equal to $(g_0)^\beta$, and therefore the server can deduce the inputs of the receiver R. However, in the above protocol, the $Server_1$ and $Server_2$ obtain the coefficients of $f_1(x)$ and $f_2(x)$ separately, such that they can computes $((g_0)^{f_1(1)}, \cdots, (g_0)^{f_1(n)})$ and $((g_0)^{f_2(1)}, \cdots, (g_0)^{f_2(n)})$. However, $f_1(x)$ and $f_2(x)$ don't have the property of the polynomial $f(x)$, which means there exists k values $(\sigma_1, \cdots, \sigma_k)$ such that $f(\sigma_1) = \cdots = f(\sigma_k) = \beta$. Therefore, if one server only obtains the values $((g_0)^{f_1(1)}, \cdots, (g_0)^{f_1(n)})$ or $((g_0)^{f_2(1)}, \cdots, (g_0)^{f_2(n)})$, it can't get extra information about the inputs of the receiver. Furthermore, the two servers are independent to each other, therefore they can't get R's input values using their own information.

Considering the privacy of the receiver against the sender. In the protocol, the view of S only contains the n tuples (g_i, g, h_i, h), where $i = 1, \cdots, n$. It's clear that, for each $\sigma_i \in (\sigma_1, \cdots, \sigma_k)$, the tuple $(g_{\sigma_i}, g, h_{\sigma_i}, h)$ is a Diffie-Hellman tuple, and for each $i \notin (\sigma_1, \cdots, \sigma_k)$, the tuple (g_i, g, h_i, h) is a non-Diffie-Hellman tuple. Because the DDH problem is difficult in group $\mathbb{G}$, the sender S can't distinguish which tuple is a Diffie-Hellman tuple, and therefore S can't get the inputs of R from its own view.

Now, we analyse the sender's privacy against the malicious receiver, who wants to get extra information about the sender's input values it doesn't choose. Let's consider the malicious behaviors of R, it may construct the polynomial $f(x)$ incorrectly, which satisfies that $f(1) = \cdots = f(n)$. It's inevitable that the degree of such a polynomial is more than k (in fact, it is n). However, upon receiving the coefficients of $f_1(x)$ and $f_2(x)$ from R, the $Server_1$ and $Server_2$ transfer the number of the coefficients of $f_1(x)$ and $f_2(x)$ to the sender S, and furthermore S checks whether the sum of the two numbers equals to k. Using this technique, the degree of the polynomial $f(x)$ is just k, therefore number of Diffie-Hellman tuples among all the n tuples $(g_1, g, h_1, h), \cdots, (g_n, g, h_n, h)$ is also k. Upon receiving the input values of the sender which are "encrypted" by the n tuples, the receiver can only obtain the desired k values it chooses, and gets no extra information about the other values.

We now give the formal proof of the protocol:

Theorem 1. *If the servers $Server_1$ and $Server_2$ are honest-but-curious and independent, then protocol $\pi_{OT_n^k}$ meet the receiver's security requirement against the servers.*

Proof. In our protocol, the servers $Server_1$ and $Server_2$ receive partial coefficients (in encrypted form) of the polynomial $f(x)$ constructed by the receiver. We will show that $Server_1$ and $Server_2$ can not deduce the roots of $f(x)$ from their own received messages. Assuming that $f(x) = (x - \sigma_1)(x - \sigma_2) \cdots (x - \sigma_k) + \beta = a_0 + a_1 x + \cdots + x^k$, where $\sigma_1, \cdots, \sigma_k$ are the choices of the receiver and $\beta \in \mathbb{Z}_q$. As shown in the protocol, the receiver divides $f(x)$ into two polynomials $f_1(x)$ and $f_2(x)$, where $f_1(x) = a_0 + a_1 x + \cdots + a_t x^t$ and $f_2(x) = a_{t+1} x^{t+1} + \cdots + x^k$, and then transfers $(g_0)^{a_0}, \cdots, (g_0)^{a_t}$ to $Server_1$ and $(g_0)^{a_{t+1}}, \cdots, (g_0)^{a_{k-1}}$ to $Server_2$. Using these values, $Server_1$ can compute $(g_0)^{f_1(1)}, \cdots, (g_0)^{f_1(n)}$ and $Server_2$ can computes $(g_0)^{f_2(1)}, \cdots, (g_0)^{f_2(n)}$. Note that the polynomial $f(x)$ satisfies that $f(\sigma_1) = \cdots = f(\sigma_k) = \beta$, such that among the n values $(g_0)^{f(1)}, \cdots, (g_0)^{f(n)}$, there are k values equal $(g_0)^\beta$. However, the values $(g_0)^{f_1(1)}, \cdots, (g_0)^{f_1(n)}$ and $(g_0)^{f_2(1)}, \cdots, (g_0)^{f_2(n)}$ may not have this property. Assuming that there exist two values $i, j \in (1, \cdots, n)$ satisfying that $(g_0)^{f_1(i)} = (g_0)^{f_1(j)}$, because $Server_1$ doesn't know $f_2(x)$ and then it can't make sure whether $(g_0)^{f_2(i)} = (g_0)^{f_2(j)}$ and $(g_0)^{f_1(i)} \cdot (g_0)^{f_2(i)} = (g_0)^{f_1(j)} \cdot (g_0)^{f_2(j)} = (g_0)^\beta$ or not. Therefore, whether $i, j \in (\sigma_1, \cdots, \sigma_k)$ or not is random for $Server_1$. In other words, $Server_1$ has no advantage guessing the receiver's choice, even if it uses the information sent by the receiver. It's identical for the $Server_2$, we omit it. In conclusion, the receiver's privacy is protected against $Server_1$ and $Server_2$.

Theorem 2. *If the Decision Diffie-Hellman assumption holds in group $\mathbb{G}$, and the servers $Server_1$ and $Server_2$ are honest-but-curious and independent, then protocol $\pi_{OT_n^k}$ meet the receiver's security requirement against the sender.*

Proof. Note that, after receiving messages from the receiver and the two servers, the sender S constructs n tuples. As shown in the above protocol, there are exactly k of the n tuples are Diffie-Hellman tuples, whose discrete logarithms are identical. Furthermore, these k Diffie-Hellman tuples are related to the receiver's input choice. Assuming that the sender can get some extra information about R's choice, it means that S knows which tuple is a Diffie-Hellman tuple and which one is a non-Diffie-Hellman tuple. Therefore, we can construct a polynomial-time machine $\mathcal{D}$, which invokes S as a sub-routine, to solve the DDH problem, which is hard in the group $\mathbb{G}$.

We choose two sets of choice C and C', where $C = \{\sigma_1, \cdots, \sigma_k\}$ and $C' = \{\sigma_1', \sigma_2', \cdots, \sigma_k'\}$. We define the view of the sender in the protocol are the transcripts of the messages sent by the receiver and servers to the sender, denoted as $View_S^C$, where C is the receiver's choice set. We have that $View_S^C = ((g_1, h_1), \cdots, (g_n, h_n), (g, h))$, which contains n tuples where only k tuples are Diffie-Hellman tuples (i.e. if the choice set is C, the tuples $(g_{\sigma_1}, g, h_{\sigma_1}, h), \cdots, (g_{\sigma_k}, g, h_{\sigma_k}, h)$ are Diffie-Hellman tuples, and if the choice set is C', the tuples $(g_{\sigma_1'}, g, h_{\sigma_1'}, h), \cdots, (g_{\sigma_k'}, g, h_{\sigma_k'}, h)$ are Diffie-Hellman tuples). Without loss of generality, let $\sigma_i \in C$ and $\sigma_i \notin C'$, it's clear that the tuple $Tuple_C = (g_{\sigma_i}, g, h_{\sigma_i}, h)$ is a Diffie-Hellman tuple when the choice set is C, and the tuple $Tuple_{C'} = (g_{\sigma_i}, g, h_{\sigma_i}, h)$ is a non-Diffie-Hellman tuple when the choice set is C'. Since the indistinguishability is preserved under multiple samples, if we want to distinguish the distribution of $View_S^C$ and $View_S^{C'}$, we just need to distinguish $Tuple_C$ and $Tuple_{C'}$. Assuming that a polynomial-time distinguisher $\mathcal{D}$ can distinguish $View_S^C$ and $View_S^{C'}$ with a non-negligible probability ϵ, we construct another distinguisher $\mathcal{D}'$, which can invoke $\mathcal{D}$ to solve the DDH problem with the probability of at least $\epsilon - 2/q$. However, this is impossible, and so that $View_S^C$ and $View_S^{C'}$ are Computationally indistinguishable.

Theorem 3. *If the Decision Diffie-Hellman assumption holds in group $\mathbb{G}$, and the servers $Server_1$ and $Server_2$ are honest-but-curious and independent, then protocol $\pi_{OT_n^k}$ meet the sender's security requirement against the receiver.*

Proof. In the last step of the above protocol, the sender uses the n tuples to encrypt its own input values separately and then transfers the encrypted values to the receiver. Among the n tuples, there are k tuples corresponding to the receiver's choice are Diffie-Hellman tuples, and the other $n - k$ tuples are all non-Diffie-Hellman tuples. According to the property of the $RAND$ function, if a tuple is a non-Diffie-Hellman tuple, then the result of the $RAND$ function of this tuple is random in group $\mathbb{G}$. Assuming that the receiver's choice is $(\sigma_1, \cdots, \sigma_k)$, for each $\sigma \notin (\sigma_1, \cdots, \sigma_k)$, the corresponding tuple $(g_\sigma, g, h_\sigma, h)$ is a non-Diffie-Hellman tuple. Without loss of generality, let $a, b \leftarrow \mathbb{Z}_q$ such that $h_\sigma = (g_\sigma)^a$ and $h = g^b$, where $a \neq b$. In order to prove that $RAND(g_\sigma, g, h_\sigma, h)$ is random in $\mathbb{G}$, we only should show that $Pr[RAND(g_\sigma, g, h_\sigma, h) = (g_0^\alpha, g_0^\beta)] = \frac{1}{q^2}$, where $\alpha, \beta \leftarrow \mathbb{Z}_q$ are random. Note that, $RAND(g_\sigma, g, h_\sigma, h) = ((g_\sigma)^s \cdot (h_\sigma)^t, (g)^s \cdot (h)^t)$, where $s, t \leftarrow \mathbb{Z}_q$ are random. Therefore, the above probability is taken over the random values s, t. Let $g = (g_\sigma)^\gamma$, where $\gamma \leftarrow \mathbb{Z}_q$, then the tuple $(g_\sigma, g, h_\sigma, h) = (g_\sigma, (g_\sigma)^\gamma, (g_\sigma)^a, (g_\sigma)^{b \cdot \gamma})$. And so $RAND(g_\sigma, g, h_\sigma, h) = ((g_\sigma)^s \cdot (g_\sigma)^{a \cdot t}, (g_\sigma)^{s \cdot \gamma} \cdot (g_\sigma)^{b \cdot \gamma \cdot t}) = ((g_\sigma)^{s+at}, (g_\sigma)^{s \cdot \gamma + b \cdot \gamma \cdot t})$. Therefore, we just require that $s + at = \alpha$ and $s \cdot \gamma + b \cdot \gamma \cdot t = \beta$. Let s, t be the variables of the above equations, these equations have a single pair of solution if and only if the following matrix

$$\begin{pmatrix} 1 & a \\ \gamma & \gamma \cdot b \end{pmatrix}$$

is invertible. Because $a \neq b$, then the determinant of the matrix is $\gamma \cdot b - \gamma \cdot a = \gamma \cdot (b - a) \neq 0$, such that the above matrix is invertible. Therefore, there exists a single pair values s, t satisfying that $s + at = \alpha$ and $s \cdot \gamma + b \cdot \gamma \cdot t = \beta$. Because s, t are chosen separately from $\mathbb{Z}_q$ randomly with the probability $\frac{1}{q}$, so that the above probability is just $\frac{1}{q^2}$, which implies that the encryptions of S's unselected input values is indistinguishable from the random elements in $\mathbb{G}$.

This completes the proof of the security of the server-aided OT_n^k protocol.

4.4 The Efficiency of the Server-Aided OT_n^k Protocol

The number of the rounds of communication in the protocol is exactly 3. The first round, the receiver sends R messages to the sender S, $Server_1$ and $Server_2$ in parallel. Then the $Server_1$ and $Server_2$ send the values computed by themselves to the sender S in the second round. In the final round, the sender S transfers its input values which are "encrypted" by tuples to receiver R, and then R decrypts the values it chooses and obtains the desired outputs.

Regarding exponentiations computed by the participants, we have the following:

1. The receiver R computes $2k + 3$ exponentiations overall, which contain k for computing $((g_0)^{a_0}, (g_0)^{a_1}, \cdots, (g_0)^{a_k})$, 3 for the values (g_{σ_i}, g, h) and k for decrypting $(x_{\sigma_1}, \cdots, x_{\sigma_k})$.

2. The sender S computes $4n$ exponentiations which are of the form $x^a \cdot y^b$ in the $RAND$ function. Note that invoking the $RAND$ function one time costs 4 exponentiations. Each of these double exponentiations costs only 1.25 the cost of the standard exponentiations, therefore the sender computes $2.5n$ exponentiations overall.

3. The $Server_1$ and $Server_2$ compute $2nk + 2n - k$ exponentiations overall, which contains $2n$ for $g_1 = (g_0)^{y_1}, \cdots, g_n = (g_0)^{y_n}$ ($Server_1$ and $Server_2$ both compute these values), nk for

$$
\begin{bmatrix}
((g_0)^{a_0})^{y_1} & ((g_0)^{a_0})^{y_2} & \cdots & ((g_0)^{a_0})^{y_n} \\
((g_0)^{a_1})^{y_1} & ((g_0)^{a_1})^{y_2} & \cdots & ((g_0)^{a_1})^{y_n} \\
\vdots & \vdots & \vdots & \vdots \\
((g_0)^{a_{k-1}})^{y_1} & ((g_0)^{a_{k-1}})^{y_2} & \cdots & ((g_0)^{a_{k-1}})^{y_n}
\end{bmatrix}
$$

and $(n-1)k$ for

$$
\begin{bmatrix}
(g_2)^{a_1 \cdot 2^1} & \cdots & (g_2)^{a_{k-1} \cdot 2^{k-1}} & (g_2)^{2^k} \\
(g_3)^{a_1 \cdot 3^1} & \cdots & (g_3)^{a_{k-1} \cdot 3^{k-1}} & (g_3)^{3^k} \\
\vdots & \vdots & \vdots & \vdots \\
(g_n)^{a_1 \cdot n^1} & \cdots & (g_n)^{a_{k-1} \cdot n^{k-1}} & (g_n)^{n^k}.
\end{bmatrix}
$$

Finally, we count the number of group elements sent by each participant in the protocol:

1. The receiver R sends k group elements $((g_0)^{a_0}, (g_0)^{a_1}, \cdots, (g_0)^{a_{k-1}})$ to the $Server_1$ and $Server_2$ overall.
2. The receiver R sends only 2 group elements (g, h) to sender S.
3. The sender S sends $2n$ group elements $(u_1, w_1), \cdots, (u_n, w_n)$ to the receiver R.
4. The $Server_1$ sends $2n$ group elements $(g_1, \cdots, g_n)$ and $(h_1^1, \cdots h_n^1)$ to the sender S. The $Server_2$ sends $2n$ group elements $(g_1, \cdots, g_n)$ and $(h_1^2, \cdots h_n^2)$ to the sender S. Overall, the $Server_1$ and $Server_2$ send $4n$ group elements.

In Table 1, we compare our protocol with the known OT_n^k protocol.

Table 1. The comparison with known OT_n^k protocols

Protocol	Assumption	Round	Exponentiation	Bilinear map	Cloud server
[26]	DDH	2	$(k+2)n + 3k + 2$		No
[28]	DBDH	$\geqslant 12$	$\geqslant 4n + 17.5k + 23.25, \geqslant n$	$\geqslant 3n + 5k$	No
[29]	DDH	6	$40(n+k)$		No
[30]	DDH	4	$8.5n - k$		No
Our work	DDH	3	$2.5n + 2k + 3$		Yes

Note: The protocol of [28] is based on pairing, let $\hat{e} : G \times G \longrightarrow \widehat{G}$ be a bilinear map, such that we need two values to describe the exponentiation cost in the group G and $\widehat{G}$. Furthermore, we only compare the exponentiations cost of the sender and receiver, excluding the cost of cloud servers.

5 Conclusion

In this paper, we presented a server-aided (or cloud-assisted) OT_n^k protocol in the cloud computing environment for the first time. The proposed protocol is based on the standard DDH assumption and doesn't need any set-up phase. The number of the communication rounds is only three, which contain one round for the receiver sends messages to the sender and cloud servers, one round for the cloud servers send messages to the sender and on round for the sender sends messages back to the receiver. The sender and sender send $2n+2$ group elements to each other, which is independent to k, and also, they compute $2.5n + 2k + 3$ exponentiations overall. To our best knowledge, our protocol is the most efficient one comparing with other known OT_n^k protocol. Furthermore, the privacy of the sender and receiver is protected in the protocol. In the future, we will consider to construct server-aided OT_n^k protocols in malicious adversaries model, where the collusion between corrupted adversaries is allowed, which is more complex and difficult.

References

1. Yao, A.C.: How to generate and exchange secrets (extended abstract). In: 27th FOCS, pp. 162–167 (1986)
2. Goldreich, O., Micali, S., Wigderson, A.: How to play any mental game C A completeness theorem for protocols with honest majority. In: 19th STOC, pp. 218–229 (1987)
3. Goldreich, O.: Foundations of Cryptography: Volume 2 C Basic Applications. Cambridge University Press, Cambridge (2004)
4. Lindell, Y., Pinkas, B.: An efficient protocol for secure two-party computation in the presence of malicious adversaries. In: Naor, M. (ed.) EUROCRYPT 2007. LNCS, vol. 4515, pp. 52–78. Springer, Heidelberg (2007)
5. Hazay, C., Lindell, Y.: Protocols, Efficient Secure Two-Party: Techniques and Constructions. Springer, Heidelberg (2010)

6. Lindell, Y., Pinkas, B.: Secure two-party computation via cut-and-choose oblivious transfer. In: Ishai, Y. (ed.) TCC 2011. LNCS, vol. 6597, pp. 329–346. Springer, Heidelberg (2011)

7. Lindell, Y.: Fast cut-and-choose based protocols for malicious and covert adversaries. In: Canetti, R., Garay, J.A. (eds.) CRYPTO 2013, Part II. LNCS, vol. 8043, pp. 1–17. Springer, Heidelberg (2013)

8. Li, J., Huang, X., Li, J., Chen, X., Xiang, Y.: Securely outsourcing attribute-based encryption with checkability. IEEE Trans. Parallel Distrib. Syst. **25**(8), 2201–2210 (2014)

9. Li, J., Li, J., Chen, X., Jia, C., Lou, W.: Identity-based encryption with outsourced revocation in cloud computing. IEEE Trans. Comput. **64**(2), 425–437 (2015)

10. Kamara, S., Mohassel, P., Raykova, M.: Outsourcing multi-party computation. Cryptology ePrint Archive, 2011/272 (2011)

11. Kamara, S., Mohassel, P., Riva, B.: Salus: a system for server-aided secure function evaluation. In Proceedings of the ACM Conference on Computer and Communications Security, pp. 797–808 (2012)

12. Chen, X., Li, J., Ma, J., Tang, Q., Lou, W.: New algorithms for secure outsourcing of modular exponentiations. IEEE Trans. Parallel Distrib. Syst. **25**(9), 2386–2396 (2014)

13. Chen, X., Li, J., Susilo, W.: Efficient fair conditional payments for outsourcing computations. IEEE Trans. Inf. Forensics Secur. **7**(6), 1687–1694 (2012)

14. Rabin, M.O.: How to exchange secrets by oblivious transfer. Technical report, Harvard University (1981)

15. Even, S., Goldreich, O., Lempel, A.: A randomized protocol for signing contracts. Commun. ACM **28**(6), 637–647 (1985)

16. Brassard, G., Crépeau, C., Robert, J.M.: All-or-nothing disclosure of secrets. In: Odlyzko, A.M. (ed.) CRYPTO 1986. LNCS, vol. 263, pp. 234–238. Springer, Heidelberg (1987)

17. Brassard, G., Crepeau, C., Robert, J.M.: Information theoretic reductions among disclosure problems. In: Proceedings of 28th Annual Symposium on Foundations of Computer Science (FOCS 1987), pp. 427–437. IEEE (1987)

18. Brassard, G., Crepeau, C., Santha, M.: Oblivious transfers and intersecting codes. IEEE Trans. Inf. Theory **42**(6), 1769–1780 (1996)

19. Naor, M., Pinkas, B.: Oblivious transfer with adaptive queries. In: Wiener, M. (ed.) CRYPTO 1999. LNCS, vol. 1666, pp. 573–590. Springer, Heidelberg (1999)

20. Stern, J.P.: A new and efficient all-or-nothing disclosure of secrets protocol. In: Ohta, K., Pei, D. (eds.) ASIACRYPT 1998. LNCS, vol. 1514, pp. 357–371. Springer, Heidelberg (1998)

21. Naor, M., Pinkas, B.: Efficient oblivious transfer protocols. In: Proceedings of 12th Annual Symposium on Discrete Algorithms (SODA), pp. 448–457 (2001)

22. Aiello, W., Ishai, Y., Reingold, O.: Priced oblivious transfer: how to sell digital goods. In: Pfitzmann, B. (ed.) EUROCRYPT 2001. LNCS, vol. 2045, p. 119. Springer, Heidelberg (2001)

23. Tzeng, W.-G.: Efficient 1-out-n oblivious transfer schemes. In: Naccache, D., Paillier, P. (eds.) PKC 2002. LNCS, vol. 2274, p. 159. Springer, Heidelberg (2002)

24. Peikert, C., Vaikuntanathan, V., Waters, B.: A framework for efficient and composable oblivious transfer. In: Wagner, D. (ed.) CRYPTO 2008. LNCS, vol. 5157, pp. 554–571. Springer, Heidelberg (2008)

25. Mu, Y., Zhang, J., Varadharajan, V.: m out of n oblivious transfer. In: Batten, L.M., Seberry, J. (eds.) ACISP 2002. LNCS, vol. 2384, pp. 395–405. Springer, Heidelberg (2002)

26. Chu, C.-K., Tzeng, W.-G.: Efficient k-out-of-n oblivious transfer schemes with adaptive and non-adaptive queries. In: Vaudenay, S. (ed.) PKC 2005. LNCS, vol. 3386, pp. 172–183. Springer, Heidelberg (2005)

27. Camenisch, J.L., Neven, G., Shelat, A.: Simulatable adaptive oblivious transfer. In: Naor, M. (ed.) EUROCRYPT 2007. LNCS, vol. 4515, pp. 573–590. Springer, Heidelberg (2007)

28. Green, M., Hohenberger, S.: Blind identity-based encryption and simulatable oblivious transfer. Cryptology ePrint Archive, 2007/235 (2007)

29. Zeng, B., Tang, X., Xu, P., Jing, J.: Practical frameworks for t-out-of- oblivious transfer with security against covert and malicious adversaries. Cryptology ePrint Archive, 2011/001 (2011)

30. Zeng, B.,Tartary, C., Xu, P., Jing, J., Tang, X.: A practical framework for t-out-of-n oblivious transfer with security against covert adversaries. IEEE Trans. Inf. Forensics Secur. **7**(2) (2012)

31. Guo, F., Mu, Y., Susilo, W.: Subset membership encryption and its applications to oblivious transfer. IEEE Trans. Inf. Forensics Secur. **9**(7), 1098–1107 (2014)

Improved Power Analysis Attack Based on the Preprocessed Power Traces

Xueyang Han, Qiuliang Xu[✉], Fengbo Lin, and Minghao Zhao

School of Computer Science and Technology, Shandong University, Jinan, China
xueyanghan@hotmail.com, {xql,linfb}@sdu.edu.cn, zhaominghao@hrbeu.edu.cn

Abstract. In recent years, side-channel attacks have become a most powerful attack performed on cryptographic devices. And many side-channel attack methods have sprung up, such as time attacks, electromagnetic radiation attacks, power analysis attacks including simple power attack, differential power attack, correlation power attack, etc. And the correlation power attack has become the most common side-channel attack. In this paper, we introduce a method to improve the correlation power attack (CPA). Our method is mainly to preprocess the recorded power consumption of a cryptographic device. During the procedure, we introduce a four-dimension vector to express the basic unit which we deal with. And also we give the steps of performing our improved CPA (named as ICPA). Then the experiment shows that the ICPA method enhances the efficiency. Meanwhile, we briefly show that preprocessing power traces increases the signal-to-noise ratio (SNR) comparing with non-preprocessed power traces.

Keywords: Side-channel attack · Correlation power attack · ICPA · Power model · SNR

1 Introduction

In side-channel attacks, power analysis attack are the most widely used methods. Because of its easiness of implementation, high success rate and high effectiveness, since put forward, it attracts many researchers to study. Power analysis attacks mainly measure the power consumption when physical cryptographic devices encrypt or decrypt input data, then use statistical methods to crack the cryptographic algorithm and to get the secret key. According to the analysis principle of side-channel information, it can be divided into simple power analysis (SPA), differential power analysis (DPA) and correlation power analysis (CPA). In power analysis attacks, the leaked information is recorded as power traces. In order to perform CPA, it is necessary to collect enough power traces.

The success rate of such attacks largely depends on the measured data and the power model. In classical CPA, attackers first choose a proper intermediate result of executed algorithm, then measure the power consumption (that is

This work is supported by the National Natural Science Foundation of China under grant No. 61173139 and No. 61572294.

© Springer International Publishing Switzerland 2016
X. Huang et al. (Eds.): GPC 2016, LNCS 9663, pp. 278–289, 2016.
DOI: 10.1007/978-3-319-39077-2_18

recorded as power traces), thirdly calculate the hypothetical intermediate values and mapping them to power consumption values, finally perform correlation analysis on the hypothetical power consumption and measured power traces. As a result, the higher the correlation coefficient is, the better the hypothetical consumption and the measured power trace match. So the hypothetical key is more likely to be the real one.

But in the classical CPA steps, CPA directly deals with the recorded power traces. Inevitably, there are lots of noises in them which have an non-ignorable effect on the results. In this paper, we improve the correlation power attack by preprocessing recorded power traces. The main difference of our method is that the ICPA method is based on a new group of power traces (we call it 'the difference power traces') calculated by the recorded power traces, not on the original recorded power traces. In this way, we eliminate the const component and some electronic noise for every power trace. In order to acquire the difference power traces, we give two scenarios. In first scenario, we pick one power trace from recorded power traces as a base power trace. In second scenario, we collect another group of power traces of the cryptographic device fed with constant input, and calculate the base power trace by these traces. Based on the base power trace, new power traces can be obtained by calculating the difference of power traces and the base power trace. It's well known lots of power traces should be collected to perform CPA, which takes much time. As for the ICPA, we record fewer power traces and take less sampling time than CPA but get approximate or even higher correlation coefficient. In second scenario, the time of recording power traces of constant input is much less than the saved time of sampling time.

The article structure consists of the following components. First, we briefly introduce the Hamming weight model [1] and the signal-to-noise ratio concepts. Then we introduce a vector expression method to express the unit of power traces and to demonstrate how to preprocess the recorded power traces. Meanwhile we introduce the difference Hamming weight and briefly show that it simulates the difference power consumption well. After that we reveal the total steps of the ICPA and show it graphically. We use a simple experiment to exhibit the results of the ICPA. In the end, we give an outline of some future works.

2   Related Work

The side-channel attack refers to passing by the complicated analysis of the encryption algorithm and using the physically leaked information such as execution time, power consumption, electromagnetic radiation etc. of cryptographic algorithms' hardware implementation, combined with statistical theory to crack password system or exploit secret information of cryptographic devices. Nowadays, it tends to be more diverse.

Since proposed, side-channel attacks have received people's attention. In 1995, Paul Kocher first puts forward the concept of time attack [2]. Time attack gets the secret key of some encryption algorithms (such as DES, AES, RSA) by accurately measuring the time consumed by a physical device. This is the first article on side channel attacks. In 1998, power analysis attack [2] is first proposed by Kocher. In the side-channel attack, power analysis attacks are the most effective and easiest ways to implement, and therefore favored by many cryptographic scholars. The basic working principle of power analysis attacks is to analyse the correlation between the instantaneous power consumption of a device and the device's operations and data it performs. In 1999, Kocher et al. first proposed SPA method in [2] and successfully attacked the DES algorithm implemented by hardware. SPA is a direct analysis technology to the power consumption collected during the execution of the cryptographic algorithm. At the same time, DPA is proposed by Kocher et al. in the literature [2]. Different from SPA attack, DPA attack does not need to get hold of the implementation details of cryptographic algorithm, and has certain immunity to noise. Currently DPA has developed a variety of forms, Mono-Bit DPA, Multi-Bit DPA, First-Order DPA, Higher-Order DPA and so on. Its standard form [3] shows that DPA is based on divide-conquer strategy, that is to say different parts of the key (usually referred to "sub-key") resume separately. Later, Messerges [4] apply this method to public key cryptosystem. Then Walter, Klima and others analyse RSA algorithm further. In 1999, Chari put forward the concept of correlation power analysis [5], they realized the AES algorithm on ST16 smart card, and successfully carried out the attack with CPA. Brier et al. [6] give a full insight on the data leakage and use the correlation power analysis (CPA) to identify the parameters of the leakage model. Then they show that efficient attacks can be performed against unprotected implementations of many algorithms such as DES or AES. In 2006, Le [7] and others summarize and expand the concept of the multi-bit DPA, proposed Partitioning Power Analysis (PPA). The energy is divided into multiple sets not only two and the difference is not the difference between two sets, but the algebra weighted sum of multi-means of power traces.

In early study, DPA mainly focused on attacking some specific algorithms (such as DES, RSA and ECC, etc.) and equipments (such as smart cards, DSP processors, etc.) and defenses are made according to the characteristics of DPA. In [8], Chari et al. put forward some general DPA countermeasures and formal methods to assess the effectiveness of these defensive countermeasures. Dakshi put forward the evaluating method [9] for electromagnetic leakage. Its core idea is to analyse the leaked electromagnetic quantitatively by the signal detection theory, combined with information theory. The literature [10] demonstrates a safety performance assessment method of power consumption leakage. This method analyses the security of the differential power attack mainly by the Hamming weight model.

3   Preliminaries

Before focusing on our target attacking method, we specify the definition of basic notations and concepts.

3.1 Hamming Weight Model

Classically, most power consumption analysis are based upon the Hamming weight model or the Hamming distance model which are commonly considered to be good models for power consumption. If we have a data word D, $D = d_0 d_1 \cdots d_j \cdots d_{m-1}$, with the bit values $d_j = 0$ or 1. Its Hamming weight is defined as

$$H(D) = \sum_{j=0}^{m-1} d_j \tag{1}$$

Namely, it is the number of bits set in D. If D is composed of m independent and uniformly distributed bits, its mean is $E(H(D)) = m/2$ and variance is $Var(H(D)) = \sigma^2_{H(D)} = m/4$. As for the Hamming distance, it always accompany with an initial state R. And the Hamming distance of D is depicted as $H(D \otimes R)$, so the Hamming weight is indeed a special case of the Hamming distance when R equals zero.

In power analysis attacks, there are many power models that can simulate power consumption, such as bit model, Hamming weight model and Hamming distance model, etc. Until now, it is widely believed that the consumed power depends on the energy required to flip the bits from one state to the next. So the Hamming weight model and distance model is a proper way to model the power consumption. The number of flipping bits from X to Y can be depicted as $H(X \otimes Y)$. In power analysis, the component X can be the chosen intermediate result, which is a function of a input data and a hypothetical key. The component Y is a reference state which is a constant machine word. So in general we substitute V's Hamming weight $H(V)$ for $X \otimes Y$'s Hamming distance $H(X \otimes Y)$. Therefore the power model for the data dependency can be written as:

$$W = \alpha H(V) + \beta \tag{2}$$

where α is a scalar gain between the Hamming weight $H(V)$ and the power consumed W, and β stands for the remaining power consumption except the data dependency part.

3.2 Signal-to-Noise Ratio (SNR)

Power analysis attacks exploit a fact that the measured power consumption of cryptographic devices depends on the processed data and the performed operations. Besides, there are two additional non-ignorable factors in practice, the noise component and a constant component. Therefore, for each point of a power trace, it is possible to model the point as the sum of the above four factors.

$$P_{total} = P_{op} + P_{data} + P_{el.noise} + P_{const} \tag{3}$$

The components P_{op}, P_{data}, $P_{el.noise}$, P_{const} stand for the operation-dependent component, data-dependent component, the noise component and a const component, respectively. In a digital environment, an SNR is the ratio between the signal and the noise component of a measurement. When it comes to power consumption, the signal can be described as $P_{op} + P_{data}$ and the noise as $P_{el.noise}$ if we considered the input data bits is uniformly distributed. So the SNR can be calculated by the formula:

$$SNR = \frac{Var(P_{op} + P_{data})}{Var(P_{el.noise} + P_{const})}. \tag{4}$$

4   Getting Preprocessed Power Traces

In this section, we introduce another method to express the recorded power traces. Every point of a power trace is depicted as a vector. The preprocessed power traces is calculated based on this expression.

4.1   Vector Expression of a Power Trace Point

In the first step of power analysis attack, a large number of power traces should be recorded when the devices encrypt or decrypt different data blocks. Each point of a power trace can be modeled as formula (3). Because four components are independent with each other, they can be expressed as a four-dimension vector (we call it power trace vector):

$$\overrightarrow{P_{total}} = (P_{op}, P_{data}, P_{el.noise}, P_{const}) \tag{5}$$

Now, we give some definitions and properties here:

(1) Additivity

$$\overrightarrow{P_{total_1}} + \overrightarrow{P_{total_2}} = (P_{op_1}, P_{data_1}, P_{el.noise_1}, P_{const_1})$$
$$+ (P_{op_2}, P_{data_2}, P_{el.noise_2}, P_{const_2})$$
$$= (P_{op_1} + P_{op_2}, P_{data_1} + P_{data_2}, P_{el.noise_1} + P_{el.noise_2}, P_{const_1} + P_{const_2}) \tag{6}$$

(2) Scalar-multiplication

$$\lambda \overrightarrow{P_{total}} = \lambda(P_{op}, P_{data}, P_{el.noise}, P_{const})$$
$$= (\lambda P_{op}, \lambda P_{data}, \lambda P_{el.noise}, \lambda P_{const_1}) \tag{7}$$

where λ is a scalar number.

(3) The length of power trace vector

$$\|\overrightarrow{P_{total}}\| = \sqrt{P_{op}^2 + P_{data}^2 + P_{el.noise}^2 + P_{const}^2} \tag{8}$$

Note, for the same point of a power trace, the length of power consumption vector doesn't equal to P_{total}. But they have a similarity: both of them increase with the increase of each component. The vector $\overrightarrow{P_{total}}$ direction stands for the direction of the voltage or electronic current, which is similar to the sign of P_{total}.

4.2   Preprocessing Recorded Power Traces

In general, we choose second scenario to get the base power trace. In this scenario, we collect two groups of power traces G^A and G^B. G^A is fed with const input while G^B with the random input. The base power trace is based on the group G^A. For each point of the base power trace, it's represented as:

$$\overrightarrow{P_{total}^{base}} = (P_{op}^{base}, P_{data}^{base}, P_{el.noise}^{base}, P_{const}^{base}) \tag{9}$$

where P_{total}^{base} can be the mean of group G^A, that is

$$\overrightarrow{P_{total}^{base}} = \frac{1}{N} \sum_{i=1}^{N} \overrightarrow{P_{total_i}} \tag{10}$$

in which N is the number of power traces collected in group G^A. The vector $\overrightarrow{P_{total}^{base}}$ can be calculated according to the properties (additivity and scalar-multiplication), given in the formulas (6) and (7). The method to calculate each point vector of new power traces is as follows:

$$\overrightarrow{T_j} = \overrightarrow{P_{total_j}} - \overrightarrow{P_{total}^{base}} = (P_{op_j} - P_{op}^{base}, P_{data_j} - P_{data}^{base}, P_{el.noise_1} - P_{el.noise}^{base}, P_{const_j} - P_{const}^{base}) \tag{11}$$

Because of fixed operations executed in device, The P_{op} component is identical in every $\overrightarrow{P_{total}}$. And it is the same to P_{const} component if we keep all traces collected in the same external environment. Obviously, there are two components in $\overrightarrow{T_j}$ that equal to 0. Therefore, the formula (11) can be simplified as follows:

$$\overrightarrow{T_j} = (0, P_{data_j} - P_{data}^{base}, P_{el.noise_1} - P_{el.noise}^{base}, 0) \tag{12}$$

In the new power traces (we also call it difference power traces), the signal corresponds to $data_j - P_{data}^{base}$ and the noise corresponds to $P_{el.noise_1} - P_{el.noise}^{base}$. According to the SNR definition (4) and the formula (12), the signal-to-noise ratio SNR of the difference power traces is apparently bigger than SNR in (4), noticing that $Var(P_{op})$ equals 0 because of the same performed operations when it is applied to specific power consumption attacks.

4.3   Corresponding Difference Hamming Weight Model

It is commonly known that Hamming weight model can simulate the power consumption well. According to the difference power traces, we use a difference Hamming weight model as follows and show that it is a good simulation for difference power consumption.

$$W^* = W^r - W^c = \alpha(H(r) - H(c)) + (\beta_r - \beta_c) \tag{13}$$

Correlation analysis refers to analysing the relative degree of two or more relevant variables. Traditionally, it is usual to use the correlation factor ρ_{XY} to evaluate the linear fitting rate of variables X and Y. As for the difference of Hamming weight and the difference power consumption, we introduce $\rho_{W^* H^*}$ to describe the relationships.

$$
\rho_{W^* H^*} = \frac{cov(W^*, H^*)}{\sigma_{W^*} \sigma_{H^*}} = \frac{\alpha \sigma_{H^*}}{\sigma_{W^*}} = \frac{\alpha \sigma_{H^*}}{\sqrt{\alpha^2 \sigma_{H^*}^2 + \beta^{*2}}}
$$

$$
= \frac{\alpha \sqrt{m}}{\sqrt{m \alpha^2 + 4 \sigma_{\beta^*}^2}} = \frac{1}{\sqrt{1 + \frac{4\sigma_{\beta^*}^2}{\alpha^2 m}}} \tag{14}
$$

with $H^* = H(r) - H(c)$ and $\beta^* = \beta_r - \beta_c$. Here, the input of Hamming weight $H(r)$ is a random number and the input of $H(c)$ is constant. The two groups of input comes from the input of G^B and G^A, respectively. β_r and β_c are the corresponding noise, respectively. The equation has the property: $|\rho_{W^* H^*}| \leq 1$. When the variance of noise tends to 0, we get a perfect Hamming weight model $|\rho_{W^* H^*}| = 1$.

5   The Improved Correlation Power Attack

In classic CPA attacks, there exists a general attack strategy which contains several basic steps. Compared to this, the ICPA has some different operations in each step. Based on our method introduced above, our method is mainly composed of the four following steps.

Step 1: Select an Attacking Point. In the first step, we should select an intermediate result in the encryption algorithm as the attacked point. Be aware that the intermediate result should be a result of a function $f(r_i, k_j)$ where r_i and k_j are known to us. In fact, r_i may be the input data, and k_j is a part of the hypothetical key.

Step 2: Measuring the Power Consumption and Calculate the Difference Power Traces. There are two parts in this step. Firstly, we recorded the power consumption by some special equipments when the cryptographic device performs encryption operations. Here we use two input modes. The first input mode is applied in G^A and the other input mode is applied in G^B. In the first input mode, we write every input as $r_1, r_2 \cdots r_i \cdots r_d$. Note that r_i is generated by a random generator, so each input r_i is most likely to be different from each other. However in the second input mode, all inputs $c_1, c_2 \cdots c_i \cdots c_d$ is the same, that is to say, $c_1 = c_2 = \cdots = c_i = \cdots = c_d$. Respectively, the recorded trace of each input is denoted by T_i^r or T_i^c, where $1 \leq i \leq d$. Note that d is the number of our input data or recorded traces.

Secondly, we calculate the difference power traces. Every difference power trace can be calculated by the operation $T_i^* = T_i^r - T^{base}$. This operation is based on the difference of power trace vector at the same time point. The base trace T^{base} is the mean of T_i^c. Figure 1 shows the process of getting the difference power traces. In the figure, the subscript s stands for the length of a power trace.

Step 3: Calculating the Hypothetical Difference Power Consumption.
The aim of this step is to obtain the hypothetical difference power consumption.
Firstly we calculate the hypothetical intermediate value $f(r_i, k_j)$ with $1 \leq i \leq d$
and $1 \leq j \leq K$. The k_j is a hypothetical key and K is the number of possible
choices which usually equals to 256. So the key space of hypothetical key can
be denoted as $(k_1, k_2, \cdots, k_K)$. Then under the technique of the difference
Hamming weight model proposed before, we use the hypothetical intermediate
values to simulate the difference power consumption $H_{i,j}^*$. Figure 2 shows the
overall process of how to get the difference Hamming weight.

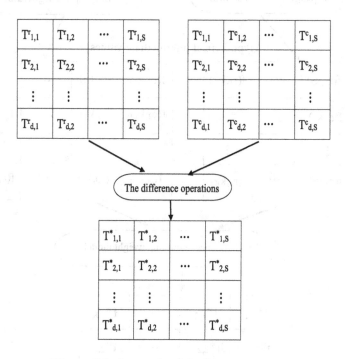

Fig. 1. Calculating the difference power traces

**Step 4: Correlating the Hypothetical Difference Power Consumption
with the Difference Power Traces.** In this step, we calculate the correlation coefficient to response the relationships between the hypothetical difference
power consumption and the difference power traces. As we all know the correlation coefficient $\rho_{(X,Y)}$ is a commonly used way to measure a linear relationship
between two variables. And we have proved that the difference Hamming weight
model is a good simulation for the difference power consumption in the last
section. Plenty of power trace samples is necessary to estimate the correlation
coefficient.

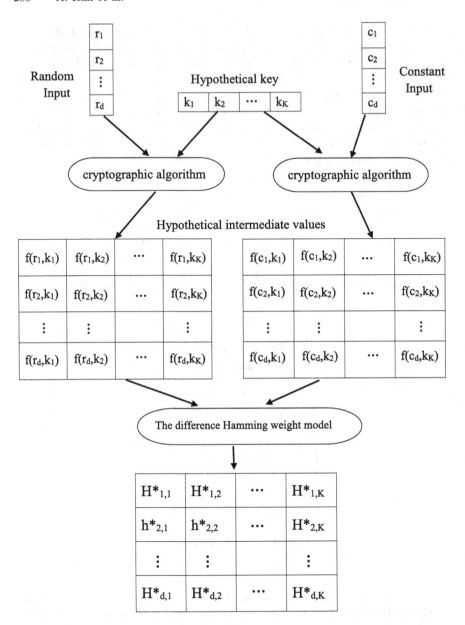

Fig. 2. The process of calculating the hypothetical power consumption

$$\rho_{(T^*, H_j^*)} = \frac{N \sum_{i=1}^{N} \|\overrightarrow{T_i^*(t)}\| H_j^* - \sum_{i=1}^{N} \|\overrightarrow{T_i^*(t)}\| \sum_{i=1}^{N} H_j^*}{\sqrt{N \sum_{i=1}^{N} \|\overrightarrow{T_i^*(t)}\|^2 - (\sum_{i=1}^{N} \|\overrightarrow{T_i^*(t)}\|)^2} \sqrt{N \sum_{i=1}^{N} H_j^{*2} - (\sum_{i=1}^{N} H_j^*)^2}} \tag{15}$$

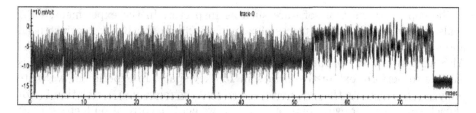

Fig. 3. Record power trace

In this formula, the $\overrightarrow{T_i^*(t)}$ stands for the value in $\overrightarrow{T_i^*}$ at time t. The largest correlation coefficient $\rho_{(T^*, H_j^*)}$ shows that the hypothetical key k_j is most likely to be the real key used in the cryptographic device.

6   Results of the ICPA

In this section, we compare the performance between CPA and the ICPA. The experimental is performed on an IC chip which integrates AES algorithm without countermeasures. The environment is composed of a power tracer, an

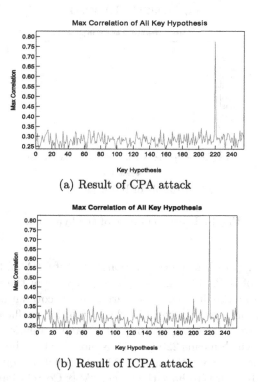

(a) Result of CPA attack

(b) Result of ICPA attack

Fig. 4. The first byte of key hypothesis

oscilloscope and a set of software such as Inspector. In the experiment, CPA deals with recorded power traces shown in Fig. 3. In the ICPA, we just need about 80 % recorded power traces to calculate the difference power traces. The AES algorithm uses the round key byte by byte in the AddRoundKey step, it is feasible to perform exhaustive attack in 256 key space. In experiment we write programs to calculate the new power traces and the maximum correlation factor of each key byte. For every byte of AES key, we get 256 correlation factors. Each hypothetical key byte corresponds to one correlation factor. Then we create line chart. Each group contains two figures below.

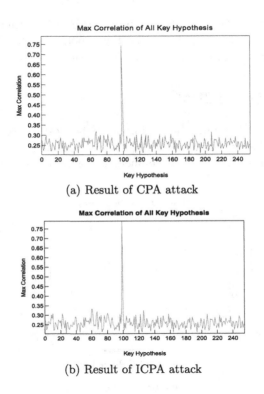

(a) Result of CPA attack

(b) Result of ICPA attack

Fig. 5. The second byte of key hypothesis

The figure (a) represents the correlation factor of CPA and the figure (b) is about the results of ICPA attack. Here are line charts of the first two bytes of AES round key. From the line chart, we learn that the correlation factor of wrong hypothetical keys converge to zero while the correlation coefficient of the correct key guess is close to 1. In Fig. 4, the biggest "Max Correlation" appears on the x-coordinate 220, which means $220(0xDC)$ is most likely to be the real key byte. Both figure (a) and (b) have the biggest "Max Correlation" on the x-coordinate 220, but apparently figure (b) have the bigger "Max Correlation" here. Hence we increase the "Max Correlation" of the correct key by about 6.4 %. As for Fig. 5, the value is increased by about 6.6 %. Because we use fewer power traces and acquire equivalent or even better results, the ICPA method is more efficient.

7   Conclusion and Future Work

In this paper, we introduce a method to improve the power analysis attack. The main idea is to reduce some noise in recorded power traces. In order to preprocess power traces, we introduce a data structure to express the basic unit of power traces. Every power unit is modeled as a vector. The difference power traces are based on the vector expression and the base power trace. Then we demonstrate full steps of the ICPA. The experiment above shows that ICPA uses fewer power traces and get better results.

In the next future, we'll work further on the following aspects. Firstly, more experiments should be carried out on the cryptographic devices with countermeasures or other cryptographic algorithm. Secondly, we'll research on other side-channel analysis and compound attack based on this method.

References

1. Akkar, M.-L., Bévan, R., Dischamp, P., Moyart, D.: Power analysis, what is now possible. In: Okamoto, T. (ed.) ASIACRYPT 2000. LNCS, vol. 1976, pp. 489–502. Springer, Heidelberg (2000)
2. Kocher, P., Jaffe, J., Jun, B.: Differential power analysis. In: Wiener, M. (ed.) CRYPTO 1999. LNCS, vol. 1666, pp. 388–397. Springer, Heidelberg (1999)
3. Mangard, S., Oswald, E., Standaert, F.-X.: One for all–all for one: unifying standard differential power analysis attacks. IET Inf. Secur. 5(2), 100–110 (2011)
4. Messerges, T.S.: Using second-order power analysis to attack DPA resistant software. In: Paar, C., Koç, Ç.K. (eds.) CHES 2000. LNCS, vol. 1965, pp. 238–251. Springer, Heidelberg (2000)
5. Chari, S., Jutla, C., Rao, J., Rohatgi, P.: A cautionary note regarding evaluation of AES candidates on smart-cards. In: Proceedings of the 2nd Advanced Encryption Standard Candidate Conference, Rome, Italy, 22–23 March 1999
6. Brier, E., Clavier, C., Olivier, F.: Correlation power analysis with a leakage model. In: Joye, M., Quisquater, J.-J. (eds.) CHES 2004. LNCS, vol. 3156, pp. 16–29. Springer, Heidelberg (2004)
7. Le, T.-H., Clédière, J., Canovas, C., Robisson, B., Servière, C., Lacoume, J.-L.: A proposition for correlation power analysis enhancement. In: Goubin, L., Matsui, M. (eds.) CHES 2006. LNCS, vol. 4249, pp. 174–186. Springer, Heidelberg (2006)
8. Chari, S., Jutla, C.S., Rao, J.R., Rohatgi, P.: Towards sound approaches to counteract power-analysis attacks. In: Wiener, M. (ed.) CRYPTO 1999. LNCS, vol. 1666, pp. 398–412. Springer, Heidelberg (1999)
9. Agrawal, D., Archabeault, B., Rao, J.R.: The EM side-channel: attacks and assessment methodologies. In: Kaliski Jr., B.S., Koç, Ç.K., Paar, C. (eds.) CHES 2002. LNCS, vol. 2523, pp. 29–45. Springer, Heidelberg (2003)
10. Mangard, S.: Hardware countermeasures against DPA – a statistical analysis of their effectiveness. In: Okamoto, T. (ed.) CT-RSA 2004. LNCS, vol. 2964, pp. 222–235. Springer, Heidelberg (2004)

Preserving User Location Privacy
for Location-Based Service

Xiaojuan Chen[1,2] and Yi Mu[2(✉)]

[1] Department of Information Management, Rongchang Campus,
Southwest University, Chongqing, China
[2] School of Computing and Information Technology, University of Wollongong,
Wollongong, NSW 2522, Australia
{xiaojuan,ymu}@uow.edu.au

Abstract. Location privacy has been a great concern to users who need the location based service on networked devices such as mobile phones and personal computers. Location based service usually relies on a location server, which is commonly regarded as semi-trusted or honest-but-curious. To protect user privacy their location information must be protected against the location server. We propose a protocol which captures user location privacy, while the user can still receive the requested service from a service provider, and does not reveal the user's exact location to the location server. Our approach offers the applicability to real-world applications.

Keywords: Location privacy · Security · Applied cryptography

1 Introduction

With the advances of computer and communication technologies, electronic commerce has become part of people's daily life. The introduction of the Global Positioning System (GPS) to networked devices, location based services have become increasingly popular. Location based services provide services for users based on their locations. For example, with such services, a user can query which bank, restaurant, hospital, etc. is the closest to his current location. These services can bring greatly convenience and benefits to our lives. However, in these cases, once the user obtains a service, his location is also disclosed to the service provider. User's personal information, especially location data, could be illegally betrayed and abused by some dishonest service providers because of commerce benefits. Some service providers could analyse customer's interest such as hobby, locus, health condition and so on, according to their queries and contents visited or shopping habit and history. It is a serious threat to the user's privacy. Therefore, despite of the many boots provided by the service provider, most users do not want to reveal their location to the service provider due to concerns on personal privacy. It may cause some users to suffer losses of social reputation,

X. Huang et al. (Eds.): GPC 2016, LNCS 9663, pp. 290–300, 2016.
DOI: 10.1007/978-3-319-39077-2_19

finance, etc. Therefore, location privacy is a major concern. To resolve this problem, several technologies about preserving location privacy have been published, such as [7, 13, 14, 16, 23–25].

In general, location Privacy is regarded as a particular and important type of data privacy. However, location is indispensable information for the users who want to get a location based service. For instance, when a large machinery or household appliances are broken or out of order, maintenance department needs to know the user's location in order to provide the service. However, the user might be unwilling to disclose his location or address to the service provider except someone who is on-site service personnel. This case presents a problem which can not be settled by common service software.

Considering the location privacy for users, we devise a scheme that can preserve user's location privacy, meanwhile, user can obtain a service from the service provider. We suppose some service providers provide a service only to users who are in a specific geographical area. Users who want to get a service firstly register to the service provider with their locations. When the service provider received a service request, the provider firstly checks whether or not the location belongs to his service region and is registered. If yes, he will provide the service to the user. In this process, the service provider can not know the exact location of this user.

We seek to find a solution that can resolve this problem and satisfy this requirement with cryptographic primitives. About this topic, there are some research works, especially published in this paper [7], which adopts a homomorphic encryption scheme when a user contacts with the service provider. Firstly, the user encrypts his request which contains user's geographical location and then sends this ciphertext to the service provider. The server searches on the location database and encrypts this result which is matched the search content, then returns the encrypted records to the user. The user decrypts it and gets a service he requested, while his location privacy is protected against the service provider.

However, this method is not applicable to our scenario, since our service provider provides the service only to the client whose location has registered at the server. Therefore, the service provider has known all the user's locations. When a user sends a request, the service provider knows that this user is a registered user but does not know user's exact location, as he is only one of registered users. In order to resolve this problem, we propose a protocol to meet this requirement and achieve location privacy.

The rest of the paper is organized as follows. In Sect. 2, we briefly review related to our work. In Sect. 3, we give the detail of our system and present the research problem we address. In Sect. 4, we provide all preliminaries and definitions for our scheme. In Sect. 5, we propose a protocol for user location privacy. In Sect. 6, we analyse the security of our scheme. In Sect. 7, we present a protocol for an application scenario. In Sect. 8, we give a conclusion.

2   Related Work

There are various approaches in the literature about preserving location privacy in the location based service. Generally, these approaches can be summarised as follows:

- Obfuscation or cloaking
- Private information retrieval
- Encryption

A classical obfuscation approach aims to protect personal location information [6], which obfuscates the user location, that lets the location be a coarse instead of a actual location. Based on the spatial cloaking algorithms, we can hide or blur the user's actual location information [3,14,15,25]. The spatial cloaking algorithm proposed by Chow and Mokbel [5] can distinguish between location privacy and query privacy. It is an important and widely used in preserving location privacy that k-anonymity can hide the user's location among $k - 1$ neighbours [8,9,18]. Some methods with this idea is to send a box of locations but not only the actual one. Also, some papers rely on a third party who is responsible for constructing a cloaking region, which includes another $k - 1$ users locations and the user's true location. These papers [16,24] using k-anonymity technology can blur the user's location into a region with a minimum size threshold.

Private information retrieval [4] was proposed by Chor, Benny and Kushilevitz, etc. It can be applied for protecting the location information while the location data are stored on a database. To the database server, location information is not revealed when the user access k replicated copies of location data and retrieve privately information stored on a database. With the Private information retrieval scheme, Craig Gentry and Zulfikar Ramzan proposed a novel approach [11] which is used to retrieve data from a database while the user's content of queries or the identity is not disclosed. Applying private information retrieval, this technique [13] does not need a third part trust server, because the privacy is achieved via cryptographic technology. It achieves stronger privacy in contrast to the former approaches.

With the development of mobile communication technology and the widespread using of GPS, location-based services (LBS) become very popular. Preserving location privacy is an imperative requirement [12]. This paper makes an overview the two types of privacy: query privacy and trajectory anonymization from the dual perspective. They proposed a classification of anonymization techniques for the private queries. For the trajectory anonymization, they summarized two different paradigms from the privacy-preserving trajectory publications.

Encryption techniques have been frequently used for protection location privacy, for example [1,7,23]. Fully homomorphic encryption was proposed firstly by Gentry [10]. A homomorphic encryption scheme allows that any party can operate or calculate on ciphertext without knowing the related plaintexts [22]. These schemes can construct privacy-preserving protocols.

Applied Paillier encryption [20], Michael Herrmann presented a scheme that can collect privacy-preserving aggregate statistics on the locations users share with each other [17]. The service provider can perform some verification work.

A problem about social networking was considered by Narayanan et al. [19]. They introduced the proximity testing with privacy which is an indispensable and thriving type of location-based service. Under this testing, a pair of friends can be notified in a certain distance while their locations do not revealed to anyone. In another paper [21], with homomorphic encryption, Sedenka proposed a secure computation of distance and a proximity testing over a sphere. The protocols allow two parties to compute their mutual distance while their locations are not disclosed to each other.

An interesting scheme was presented by Bilogrevic et al. [2]. They proposed a scheme, which allows a group of users to find an optimal meeting location but their preference locations are not revealed to the service provider or to the other users. Applied the homomorphic encryption, the server is responsible for computing the distance between the user's preference locations but does not know the actual locations. It can be applied to the mobile devices and applications.

3 System Description

Our system consists of three main entities: (i) a set of registered users $U = \{u_1, u_2, ..., u_n\}$, (ii) a third-party trusted server, and (iii) a service provider. Users want to obtain a location based service from the service provider while their locations are not revealed to the service provider. The service provider provides some services such as push-based and delivering coupons or other service information only to customers who have registered. The third-party trusted server blinds the user's exact location.

We assumed that the users hold a networked computing device which can communicate with the trusted server directly through a fixed or wireless infrastructure such as the Internet. Furthermore, this communication channel is assumed a secure channel. The same is true between trusted server and service provider. The network equipments are able to complete public-key cryptographic operations, for instance digital signature, encryption and decryption. Furthermore, we supposed that each user $u_i \in U$ has a fixed location $L_i = (x_i, y_i)$. Here, our scheme considers a two-dimensional position coordinate system which is generally adequate and can be easily extended to three-dimensional coordinates system. These coordinates are corresponded to real geographic coordinates, by the user's network device or through an optional third party location service, for example Google My Location.

In the system, we identify a user only by his location. The service provider has constructed a list of locations of the all the registered users as $L = \{L_i\}_{i=1}^{N}$, and sent the L to the third-party trusted server.

The service provider is usually assumed semi-trusted or honest-but-curious. That is, it is honest to correctly implement the protocol but might attempt to find the location information with the information they have received from users. To protect user privacy, we introduce a trusted proxy or trusted server, who can help to randomize the user location, so that the service provider can only know whether or not a user's location is registered but cannot find his real location. We assume that all valid users have registered their locations at the service provider. During a run of the protocol, the service provider can only be convinced that the corresponding user is one of the registered users, but does not know which location is his.

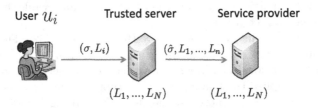

Fig. 1. The system model.

As an example shown in Fig. 1, we provide our basic system model. The registered user u_i who wants to get a service from the service provider signs his location with his private signing key to form a signature σ and sends it along with his location L_i to the trusted server via a secure channel. The trusted server has stored all the locations of the registered users. It can process the location data and is trusted by all the users. The trusted server verifies whether or not the location belongs to the L. If yes, it will blind the user's exact location to form a new signature $\hat{\sigma}$ with a list of selected locations $(L_1, ..., L_n)$, $n \leq N$, from L (L_i is also included) and then send $\hat{\sigma}$ and $(L_1, ..., L_n)$ to the service provider. Note that the order of elements in $(L_1, ..., L_n)$ has selected at random. The service provider can check if $\hat{\sigma}$ is a valid signature on $(L_1, ..., L_n)$ but is unable to find which location is for the requester. In other words, after verification, the service provider can only know the user is a registered user.

4   Preliminaries and Definitions

In this section, all preliminaries and definitions our protocol needs are as follows:

4.1   Definitions

Our protocol is a main signature scheme. Our scheme consists of four algorithms: Keygen, Sign, Randomise, and Verify, for key generation, signing, and randomizing the original signature from a user, and verifying a signature, respectively.

- Keygen: Taking as input the security parameter λ, it outputs a pair of public and private keys: PK, SK.

- Sign: Taking as input a private key SK and a message m, it returns a signature σ.
- Randomise: Taking as input a signature σ and a random number, it returns a randomized signature $\hat{\sigma}$.
- Verify: Taking as input a public key PK and a signed message (M, σ) or $(M, \hat{\sigma})$, it returns True, otherwise $\bot$.

4.2 Security Model

In our system, we have assumed that the trusted server is fully trusted, therefore, we can omit it. So, in this security model, we consider two kinds of adversaries, namely, service provider, and outside attackers. The service provider is assumed to be honest-but-curious and should not know the exact location of the user. Outside attackers want to obtain the locations of users. We assume that all the communication channels among the three parties are secure in order to prevent the outsider from obtaining the location information of users. We define the privacy properties against these adversaries as follows:

Definition 1. *(Type I Adversary: Location privacy against the honest-but-curious service provider.) After the execution of the protocol, the Type I Adversary can only know whether the user was registered but cannot find the exact location of the user.*

The adversary receives the full location information of all users; however, it should not able to find the exact location of the user, who has registered and requested a service.

Definition 2. *(Type II Adversary: Location privacy against outside attackers) After the execution of the protocol, the outside attackers can not find the exact location of this user who requests a service, even if it could eavesdrop the information in the communication among all parties.*

Type II Adversary can only eavesdrop the communication flows from the secure channels. These attacks can be prevented by using secure channels. If our protocol is secure against Type I adversary, then it should be secure against Type II adversary.

4.3 Bilinear Pairing

We simply describe the necessary facts about bilinear maps and bilinear maps groups. Let G and G_T be two multiplicative cyclic groups of prime order p with generator g. Let $e : G \times G \to G_T$ be a bilinear map. We employ the following properties:

- Bilinearity: $e(g^a, h^b) = e(g, h)^{ab}$, for all $a, b \in Z_p$, and $g, h \in G$.
- Non-degeneracy: $e(g, h) \neq 1_{G_T}$, where $g, h \in G$. That is, there exists no the map of all pairs in $G \times G$ to the identity in G_T.
- Computability: For all $g, h \in G$, there exists an algorithm to efficiently compute the map $e(g, h)$.

5   Protocol

Suppose that user u_i wants to obtain a service while the location privacy should be protected against the service provider. Let user u_i be located at L_i, $i \in [1, 2, ...N]$. We take the location coordinate $(x_i, y_i) = L_i$ as the message, which is to be signed by the user. Let S be the third-party trusted server, who helps protecting the user's location information. The service provider can provide a location based service for registered users without knowing the exact location of users. We suppose the service provider has a list of location coordinates which include the locations of all the registered users. We denote this list as $L = \{L_1, L_2, ..., L_N\}$. L is also known to the trusted server.

Let G, G_T be both multiplicative cyclic groups of prime order p with generator g. There exists a bilinear map: $e : G \times G \rightarrow G_T$. We adopt a collision-resistant hash function, $H : \{0, 1\}^* \rightarrow G$ for signing a message.

- **Setup.** The public/private keys are generated as following. The algorithm chooses a $g, g_2 \in G$. The user randomly chooses $\alpha \in Z_p$ and then computes $Y = g^\alpha$, where α is the private key and must be kept secret. The public key is the tuple (g, g_2, Y).

- **Sign.** The user u_i chooses randomly $r_i \in_R Z_p$, and then computes g^{r_i}. The user's signature on L_i is constructed as:

$$\sigma = (\sigma_0, \sigma_i) = (g_2^\alpha H(L_i)^{r_i}, g^{r_i}).$$

u_i sends the (σ, L_i) to the trusted server.

- **Randomise.** The trusted server checks if $L_i \in L$. If it outputs false, abort. Otherwise, check if $\sigma = (\sigma_0, \sigma_i)$ is a valid signature of message m_i by checking:

$$e(\sigma_0, g) \stackrel{?}{=} e(g_2, Y)e(H(L_i), g^{r_i}).$$

If the result is false, abort; otherwise accept.

Then the trusted server chooses randomly $L_1, ..., L_{n-1}$, $(n < N)$ from the list L. Adding L_i to it, the trusted server reorders the set by shuffling randomly to form $L_1, ..., L_n$. He then selects at random $r_1, ..., r_n \in Z_p$ and computes $g^{r_1}, ..., g^{r_n}$ and

$$\hat{\sigma} = (\sigma_0', \sigma_1, ..., \sigma_n)$$
$$= (\sigma_0 \cdot H(L_1)^{r_1} \cdots H(L_n)^{r_n}, g^{r_1}, ..., g^{r_n}).$$

The trusted server sends $\hat{\sigma}$ and $(L_1, ..., L_n)$ to the service provider.

- **Verify.** The service provider verifies:

$$e(\sigma_0', g) \stackrel{?}{=} e(g_2, Y)e(H(L_1), \sigma_1) \cdots e(H(L_n), \sigma_n)$$

If the equation holds, accept the request; otherwise abort.

The correctness of signature verification can be easily verified:

$$e(\sigma_0, g) = e(g_2^\alpha H(L_i)^{r_i}, g)$$
$$= e(g_2^\alpha, g)e(H(L_i)^{r_i}, g)$$
$$= e(g_2, g^\alpha)e(H(L_i), g^{r_i})$$
$$= e(g_2, Y)e(H(L_i), g^{r_i})$$

and

$$e(\sigma_0{}', g)$$
$$= e(\sigma_0(H(L_1)^{r_1} \cdots H(L_n)^{r_n}, g)$$
$$= e(\sigma_0, g)e(H(L_1), g^{r_1}) \cdots e(H(L_n), g^{r_n})$$
$$= e(g_2, Y)e(H(L_1), \sigma_1)e(H(L_2), \sigma_2) \cdots e(H(L_n), \sigma_n)$$

6 Security Analysis

The security of our protocols depends on the security of the signature scheme. We assume that the underlying signature scheme is secure.

Security Against Type I Adversary. For service provider, we have assumed it is honest-but-curious. The service provider only holds a list of locations for registered users. During a protocol run, it will receive a randmized signature. As we have assumed that the signature scheme is secure, then it is impossible to find the location information of the user, and can only know whether the user is a registered user. Therefore, the protocols are secure against the service provider.

Security Against Type II Adversary. Outside adversaries can be blocked by standard network security techniques. In fact, if our protocol is secure against Type I adversaries, then it is secure against Type II adversary.

In summary, our protocol is secure in the presence of all the adversaries. In this model, while participants follow prescribed protocol, user's location privacy could be preserved.

7 An Application Scenario

We provide an example for implementing our scheme (see Fig. 2). Suppose there is a service provider who provides repair services for electronic equipments of households such as TV sets, refrigerators, washing machines, etc. However, the identities of householders should be protected against the service provider. Perhaps an on-site service are provided for some important people. In order to achieve it, we separate the service provider into two servers: registration server and service provider, where the registration server provides the registration service to its clients and the service provider provides the service. The trusted server is also responsible for informing the repairman to deliver the requested service to the client.

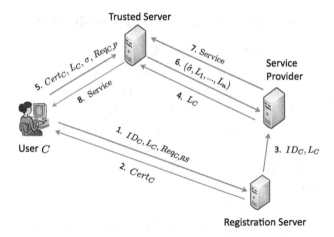

Fig. 2. The application scenario.

We construct the protocol as two phases: Registration and Service. We denote by C a client, RS the registration server, P the trusted server (or proxy), and SP the service provider. Our protocols are given below.

Registration

1. $C \rightarrow RS$: $ID_C, L_C, Req_{C,RS}$
2. $RS \rightarrow C$: $Cert_C$
3. $RS \rightarrow SP$: ID_C, L_C
4. $RS \rightarrow P$: L_C

   where ID_C denotes the identity of the client, L_C is his location, $Req_{C,RS}$ the request for registration services, and $Cert_C$ the certificate for the client to use the services. $Cert_C$, signed by the registration server, contains the identification of the client.

Service

5. $C \rightarrow P$: $Cert_C$, L_C, σ, $Req_{C,P}$
   P checks if $Cert_C$ is valid. If not, abort; otherwise, verifies the signature σ. $Req_{C,P}$ denotes the location-based service request.
6. $P \rightarrow SP$: $\hat{\sigma}$, Request SP verifies the randomised signature $\hat{\sigma}$ to decide if the request should be approved.
7. $SP \rightarrow P$: yes/no, if yes, deliver the service via P; otherwise, exit. P decides if the requested service should be delivered according to the result of signature verification.
8. $P \rightarrow C$: Service

8   Conclusion

Location privacy is an important private information to users. In this paper, we proposed a novel protocol for preserving location privacy based on a signature scheme from bilinear pairing. We described the details of our system and show how to protect user location privacy, while the service can still be delivered to the user. With the digital signature scheme from bilinear pairing, location privacy can be achieved. We applied our protocol to a practical scenario. After implementing of our protocol, user can obtain the requested service and his location privacy can be achieved.

Acknowledgment. This work was supported by "Fundamental Research Funds for the Central Universities" of China (No.XDJK2016C108) and the youth fund of Southwest University (No. 20700907).

References

1. Ashouri-Talouki, M., Baraani-Dastjerdi, A., Selçuk, A.A.: GLP: a cryptographic approach for group location privacy. Comput. Commun. **35**(12), 1527–1533 (2012)
2. Bilogrevic, I., Jadliwala, M., Joneja, V., Kalkan, K., Hubaux, J., Aad, I.: Privacy-preserving optimal meeting location determination on mobile devices. IEEE Trans. Inf. Forensics Secur. **9**(7), 1141–1156 (2014)
3. Cheng, R., Zhang, Y., Bertino, E., Prabhakar, S.: Preserving user location privacy in mobile data management infrastructures. In: Danezis, G., Golle, P. (eds.) PET 2006. LNCS, vol. 4258, pp. 393–412. Springer, Heidelberg (2006)
4. Chor, B., Kushilevitz, E., Goldreich, O., Sudan, M.: Private information retrieval. J. ACM **45**(6), 965–981 (1998)
5. Chow, C.-Y., Mokbel, M.F.: Enabling private continuous queries for revealed user locations. In: Papadias, D., Zhang, D., Kollios, G. (eds.) SSTD 2007. LNCS, vol. 4605, pp. 258–275. Springer, Heidelberg (2007)
6. Damiani, M.L., Bertino, E., Silvestri, C.: Protecting location privacy through semantics-aware obfuscation techniques. In: Trust Management II–Proceedings of IFIPTM : Joint iTrust and PST Conferences on Privacy, Trust Management and Security, June 18–20, 2008, Trondheim, Norway, pp. 231–245 (2008)
7. Gahi, Y., Guennoun, M., Guennoun, Z., El-Khatib, K.: Privacy preserving scheme for location-based services. J. Inf. Secur. **3**(2), 105–112 (2012)
8. Gedik, B., Liu, L.: Location privacy in mobile systems: a personalized anonymization model. In: 25th International Conference on Distributed Computing Systems (ICDCS 2005), 6–10, June 2005 Columbus, OH, USA, pp. 620–629 (2005)
9. Gedik, B., Liu, L.: Protecting location privacy with personalized k-anonymity: architecture and algorithms. IEEE Trans. Mob. Comput. **7**(1), 1–18 (2008)
10. Gentry, C.: Fully homomorphic encryption using ideal lattices. In: Proceedings of the 41st Annual ACM Symposium on Theory of Computing, STOC, Bethesda, MD, USA, May 31–June 2, 2009, pp. 169–178 (2009)
11. Gentry, C., Ramzan, Z.: Single-database private information retrieval with constant communication rate. In: Caires, L., Italiano, G.F., Monteiro, L., Palamidessi, C., Yung, M. (eds.) ICALP 2005. LNCS, vol. 3580, pp. 803–815. Springer, Heidelberg (2005)
12. Ghinita, G.: Private queries and trajectory anonymization: a dual perspective on location privacy. Trans. Data Priv. **2**(1), 3–19 (2009)

13. Ghinita, G., Kalnis, P., Khoshgozaran, A., Shahabi, C., Tan, K.-L.: Private queries in location based services: anonymizers are not necessary. In: Proceedings of the ACM SIGMOD International Conference on Management of Data, SIGMOD 2008 (2008)
14. Gruteser, M., Grunwald, D.: Anonymous usage of location-based services through spatial and temporal cloaking. In: Proceedings of the First International Conference on Mobile Systems, Applications, and Services, MobiSys, San Francisco, CA, USA, 5–8 May 2003
15. Gruteser, M., Liu, X.: Protecting privacy in continuous location-tracking applications. IEEE Secur. Priv. 2(2), 28–34 (2004)
16. Hashem, T., Kulik, L.: "don't trust anyone": Privacy protection for location-based services. Pervasive Mob. Comput. 7(1), 44–59 (2011)
17. Herrmann, M., Rial, A., Díaz, C., Preneel, B.: Practical privacy-preserving location-sharing based services with aggregate statistics. In: 7th ACM Conference on Security and Privacy in Wireless and Mobile Networks, WiSec 2014, Oxford, United Kingdom, 23–25 July, pp. 87–98 (2014)
18. Mokbel, M.F., Chow, C., Aref, W.G.: The new Casper: query processing for location services without compromising privacy. In: Proceedings of the 32nd International Conference on Very Large Data Bases, Seoul, Korea, 12–15 September, pp. 763–774 (2006)
19. Narayanan, A., Thiagarajan, N., Lakhani, M., Hamburg, M., Boneh, D.: Location privacy via private proximity testing. In: Proceedings of the Network and Distributed System Security Symposium, NDSS 2011, San Diego, California, USA, 6–9 February 2011
20. Paillier, P.: Public-key cryptosystems based on composite degree residuosity classes. In: Stern, J. (ed.) EUROCRYPT 1999. LNCS, vol. 1592, pp. 223–238. Springer, Heidelberg (1999)
21. Sedenka, J., Gasti, P.: Privacy-preserving distance computation and proximity testing on earth, done right. In: 9th ACM Symposium on Information, Computer and Communications Security, ASIA CCS 2014, Kyoto, Japan, 03–06 June, pp. 99–110 (2014)
22. Stehlé, D., Steinfeld, R.: Faster fully homomorphic encryption. In: Abe, M. (ed.) ASIACRYPT 2010. LNCS, vol. 6477, pp. 377–394. Springer, Heidelberg (2010)
23. Sun, Y., Porta, T.F.L., Kermani, P.: A flexible privacy-enhanced location-based services system framework and practice. IEEE Trans. Mob. Comput. 8(3), 304–321 (2009)
24. Sweeney, L.: k-anonymity: a model for protecting privacy. Int. J. Uncertain. Fuzziness Knowl.-Based Syst. 10(5), 557–570 (2002)
25. Teerakanok, S., Vorakulpipat, C., Kamolphiwong, S.: Anonymity preserving framework for location-based information services. In: International ACM Conference on Management of Emergent Digital EcoSystems MEDES 2010, Bangkok, Thailand, 26–29 October, pp. 107–113 (2010)

Towards Secure Private Image Matching

Zaid Ameen Abduljabbar[1,2], Hai Jin[1(✉)], Ayad Ibrahim[2], Zaid Alaa Hussien[1,3],
Mohammed Abdulridha Hussain[1,2], Salah H. Abbdal[1], and Deqing Zou[1]

[1] Cluster and Grid Computing Lab, Services Computing Technology
and System Lab, School of Computer Science and Technology,
Huazhong University of Science and Technology, Wuhan 430074, China
zaidalsulami@yahoo.com, hjin@hust.edu.cn
[2] University of Basrah, Basrah, Iraq
[3] Southern Technical University, Basrah, Iraq

Abstract. Currently, image matching is being used in many daily
life applications such as *content-based image retrieval* (CBIR), computer vision, and near duplicate images. Hence, a number of matching methods have been developed. However, most proposed methods
do not address the challenges involved when confidential images are
used in image matching between two security agencies. Thus, interest to
develop a secure method, particularly one that can be used in privacy-
preserving image matching, is growing. This paper addresses the challenge of privacy-preserving image matching between two parties where
images are confidential. The descriptor set of the queried party needs to
be generated and encrypted properly with the use of a secret key at the
queried party side before being transferred to the other party. We present
the development and validation of a secure scheme to measure the cosine
similarity between two descriptor sets. The method can work without
using any image encryption, sharing, and trusted third party. We conduct several empirical analyses on real image collections to demonstrate
the performance of our work.

Keywords: Secure private image matching · Feature protection · Secure
multiparty computing · Surf descriptors · Homomorphic encryption

1 Introduction

Digital images have become a significant part of our lives because of the development of the Internet and the growing demand from various multimedia fields.
This demand raises the need for efficient and robust *private image matching*
(PIM) methods in many real-world applications, including social media [1,2]
business community [3], and e-health [4]. In the context of private image retrieval,
similar images are usually brought together such that similar images can be
retrieved efficiently once a query image is sent. In general, PIM method is a
set of operations through which two parties determine their common matching values without disclosing extra information. Hence, PIM only requires the
magnitude of similarity rather contents similarity.

© Springer International Publishing Switzerland 2016
X. Huang et al. (Eds.): GPC 2016, LNCS 9663, pp. 301–315, 2016.
DOI: 10.1007/978-3-319-39077-2_20

According to [5], *private matching* (PM) can be classified into three scenarios. In the first scenario, the parties involved, namely *Alice* and *Bob*, both must learn the final results of PM as a result of the so-called symmetric PM. The second scenario involves a non-symmetric PM where only one party learns if a commonality of values exist. The third scenario seeks to determine the number of common elements rather than whether values match exactly. All these requirements have been met and addressed using different PM protocols.

We employ the second scenario in a secure manner to meet the requirements of actual security applications. Simply stated, in some cases, protecting the privacy of images during the matching process is necessary. Consider the following example to determine the importance of a security issue. Suppose a security agency is searching for data related to a potential terrorist suspect. The agency may wish to check whether images related to the suspect can be found in local police databases. However, for security purposes, neither the agency nor the local police want to reveal their images unless a need to share exists. One way to identify such a need is to detect similarities between the agency's query (in the form of images) and the local police's image collections. Once the need for sharing information is verified, the agency and local police can exchange only shared information. During the process of identifying similar images, the best choice for both parties is not to disclose the query image and the database, and has the former learn only of the existence of any commonality of image matching values (second scenario). Such a process is referred to as *secure private image matching* (SPIM).

Most *image matching* (IM) approaches define an image representation and a distance metric that reduce the amount of data stored per image and the time cost of database search. Feature vectors (descriptors) of each image in the database are extracted and stored. During the matching, the descriptors of the query image are compared against their counterparts in the database to determine the most relevant image. However, keeping descriptors in their clear text may reveal information on some objects in the image. Thus, such descriptors should be encrypted in such a way that their distances are preserved without decryption.

In this paper, we address the question of how to search for similar images between two parties in a privacy-preserving manner without losing image confidentiality. Given image I, *Alice* would like to determine whether there are images in *Bob's* collection D that are similar to I (e.g., duplicate, near duplicate, somewhat close, etc.) without disclosing either I or D. We focus primarily on security, where protecting the descriptors of images is necessary. Specifically, our scheme uses cosine similarity [6], a well-known metric to score matching images, and employs homomorphic encryption [7] to protect the confidentiality of descriptors. The method allows only the inquiring side to see the matching value. Hence, only *Alice* is interested in determining whether she has any image in common with *Bob*, without worrying about the leakage of unnecessary information.

Most feature vectors are either global vectors, such as global color histogram or local vectors such as *scale-invariant feature transform* (SIFT) descriptors

[8,9] and *speeded up robust features* (SURF) descriptors [10,11]. The first model generates an extreme compressed feature vector for each image. Such model can effectively identify global similarities, e.g., how many colors two images share. The second model searches the image to identify the interest key points invariant to scale and orientation. A feature descriptor is generated for each key point. In this paper, we will focus on local features model, which has the advantage of identifying local similarities, e.g., scenes and objects.

The contributions of this paper are as follows. First, a trivial solution to achieve secure and private image matching is to utilize a *trusted third party* (TTP). *Alice* sends I to the TTP and *Bob* sends D to the TTP, and then TTP can investigate and inform *Alice* whether images similar to I can be found in *Bob's* collection. However, in real life situations, finding a completely trustworthy third party is a difficult task. Our work does not require such a third party. Second, the applications of SPIM often suffer from significant overhead for the image encryption operation. Our scheme can work without image encryption and still maintain the privacy of the parties involved.

The rest of this paper is organized as follows. Related works are reviewed and discussed in Sect. 2. Section 3 introduces the security requirements and problem definition. Section 4 provides the proposed scheme. Experimental results are provided in Sect. 5, and conclusions and future works are drawn in Sect. 6.

2 Related Works

Ever since Freedman et al. [12] brought up the first solution using private matching mechanism to prevent the leakage of unnecessary information between two parties, a number of authors have subsequently proposed different private matching mechanisms. These mechanisms typically conform to the different requirements of such parties in PM or are the results of fine-tuning to achieve low overhead in term of computational cost. However, most of these schemes suffer from drawbacks. Keeping this in view, we will present related works pertaining to PM and its drawbacks. Works within the context of private image matching will also be highlighted.

The important factors in the field of PM are the protocol of *private set union* (PSU) [4,13,14] and *private set intersection* (PSI) [12,15–17], respectively. Cristofaro et al. [18] reveal that these two approaches do not provide adequate privacy on the server end and thus, a server could compromise privacy. In [18], a scenario is proposed where users are allowed to learn only the magnitude of the shared values instead of the exact values. Such scenario uses the *Private Set Union Cardinality* (PSI-CA) and a third-party server. Similarly, Lu et al. [19] proposed a system to search encrypted multimedia databases stored on a server maintained by a third-party service provider. Under both [18,19], the server should not know its stored data and using third-party services where communication has a way through it, it does probably not keep maintaining the privacy aspect of the matching values. Our work obviates the use of any third party for security purposes.

Shashank et al. [20] applied *private information retrieval* (PIR) techniques to protect the privacy of the query image when searching over a public database. However, such method assumes that the database is public when such database is supposed to be private. The proposed methods in [18–20] are also not suitable for evaluating similarity. Both approaches can achieve an exact match, thereby limiting the ability to develop efficient solutions.

In [21], Agrawal et al. proposed a method for private matching using double encryption under the assumption that $x \in X, E(E'(x)) = E'(E(x))$, where E is the encryption function. To determine the common elements between two parties, the authors proposed using the crypto-hash function. Initially, such function should be decided between the parties involved. Thus, this approach encourages a curious party to utilize a brute force attempt using the same hash function to determine uncommon elements over a finite domain of elements. In our work, we avoid the use of any hash function to prevent a curious user from obtaining additional information.

3   Security Definition and Problem Statement

3.1   Security Definition

Our security definition follows the *secure multiparty computing* (SMC) definition of Goldreich et al. [22] and private matching (second scenario) [5]. We assume that the parties involved are semi-honest. A semi-honest party follows the steps of the protocol using the party's correct input, but attempts to utilize what it sees during the execution of the protocol to compromise security. This model guarantees that parties who follow the protocol correctly cannot gain any knowledge on the other party's input data except for the output to only queried party. No additional information is disclosed and information that can be inferred from its own input is avoided.

Table 1. Common symbols used

Symbol	Meaning
N	Size of descriptors
M	Number of images in *Bob's* collection
K	Number of descriptors of *Alice's* image
P	Number of descriptor of each one of *Bob's* images

3.2   Problem Statement

The common notations listed in Table 1 are used throughout this paper. Our proposed scheme includes two parties, namely, *Alice* and *Bob*, each of whom has a collection of images. We assume that the images of both parties are private. Given an image I of *Alice*, we are interested in determining whether *Bob's* collection contains an image similar to I without disclosing *Bob's* database to *Alice* and vice-versa. We evaluate the similarity of two images under the local feature vector model, in which each image is represented as a set of vectors. Let $D = Img_1, ..., Img_m$ denote the set of m images in *Bob's* collection. Without disclosing I to *Bob* and D to *Alice*, our objective is to find a set of images in D similar to I without disclosing the matching results to *Bob*. We term such protocol as SPIM. Formally, SPIM is defined as

$$SPIM(I, D) = \alpha_1, \alpha_2, ..., \alpha_m \tag{1}$$

SPIM returns the m similarity scores $\alpha_1, \alpha_2, ..., \alpha_m$ to *Alice* instead of returning the actual images. At another time, *Alice* can retrieve the similar image from *Bob*. To evaluate the similarity between two images, each party initially extracts the feature vectors for each image in its own collection. Several metrics are used to evaluate the similarity between the sets of the two feature vectors such as Euclidean distance and cosine similarity [6]. The cosine similarity between vectors v_1 and v_2 of size n can be defined as follow:

$$CSIM(v_1, v_2) = \frac{\sum\limits_{i=1}^{n} v_1[i].v_2[i]}{\|v_1\|.\|v_2\|} \tag{2}$$

where $\|v\|$ is the Euclidian length of vector v, and is defined as the following:

$$\|v\| = \sqrt{\sum\limits_{i=1}^{n} v[i]^2} \tag{3}$$

Given normalized vectors $\vec{V}_1$ and $\vec{V}_2$, cosine similarity can be written as:

$$CSIM(\vec{V}_1, \vec{V}_2) = \sum\limits_{i=1}^{n} \vec{V}_1[i].\vec{V}_2[i] \tag{4}$$

Here

$$\vec{V}[i] = \frac{v[i]}{\|v\|} \tag{5}$$

Given two images, Im_1 and Im_2, of the two feature vector sets $F_1 = \{v_1, v_2, ..., v_k\}$ and $F_2 = \{s_1, s_2, ..., s_p\}$, respectively. Algorithm 1 illustrates how the distance between two feature vector sets can be measured through the cosine similarity while preserving privacy.

Table 2 shows a trivial example for *Alice* image which is represented by a set of three vectors of size 5. The first three columns are the feature vectors, while

Algorithm 1. Insecure Image Distance Calculation

Input: two feature vectors $F_1 = \{v_1, v_2, \ldots, v_k\}$ and $F_2 = \{s_1, s_2, \ldots, s_p\}$ of two images.
    All vectors v_i and s_i are of the same size n.
Output: $Dist$: distance between F_1 and F_2.
$Dist = 0$;
For $i = 1$ to k **do**
  Compute $\vec{v}_i$ as in Equation (5)
  For $j = 1$ to p **do**
  Compute $\vec{s}_i$ as in Equation (5)
  $D_j = 1 - CSIM(\vec{v}_i, \vec{s}_j)$
  End for//j
  $Dist = Dist + min(D_j), \forall j = 1, \ldots, p$
End for//k
$Dist = Dist/k$

Table 2. *Alice's* image

Alice image					
F1			$\vec{F}_2$		
v_1	v_2	v_3	$\vec{v}_1$	$\vec{v}_2$	$\vec{v}_3$
1	3	3	0.1348	0.5145	0.75
5	2	1	0.6742	0.343	0.25
2	4	2	0.2697	0.686	0.5
3	1	1	0.4045	0.1715	0.25
4	2	1	0.5394	0.343	0.25

the last three columns are their corresponding normalized versions. Similarly, Table 3 illustrates the collection of *Bob*, which consists of two images. Also this table is interpreted in the same way as Table 2.

To compute the distance between *Alice's* image and the first image in *Bob's* collection, we have to compute distance between the feature vector sets F_1 and F_2. The distance between F_1 and F_2 can be calculated as follows:

$$Dist_1 = (min((1 - CSIM(\vec{v}_1, \vec{s}_1)), (1 - CSIM(\vec{v}_1, \vec{s}_2)), (1 - CSIM(\vec{v}_1, \vec{s}_3))) + \ldots + min((1 - CSIM(\vec{v}_3, \vec{s}_1), (1 - CSIM(\vec{v}_3, \vec{s}_2), (1 - CSIM(\vec{v}_3, \vec{s}_3))))/3 = (min(0.225, 0.225, 0.1766) + min(0.1067, 0.1375, 0.1991) + min(0.1981, 0.2367, 0.1918))/3 = (0.1766 + 0.1067 + 0.1918)/3 = 0.1584$$

Similarly, the distance between F_1 and F_3 is $Dist_2 = 0.1375$. Thus, we can conclude that the second image in *Bob's* collection is more similar to *Alice's* image than the first one, because it has a shorter distance.

As shown in the above example, the main step in evaluating similarity between two images is the dot product between their corresponding normalized vectors. Therefore, once we know how to calculate the dot product in a

Table 3. *Bob's* collection

Bob collection of two images											
F_2			F_3			$\vec{F}_2$			$\vec{F}_3$		
s_2	s_2	s_3	x_1	x_2	x_3	$\vec{s}_1$	$\vec{s}_2$	$\vec{s}_3$	$\vec{x}_1$	$\vec{x}_2$	$\vec{x}_3$
2	1	3	2	3	3	0.3592	0.1796	0.5388	0.417	0.7746	0.6882
1	2	2	1	2	2	0.1796	0.3592	0.3592	0.2085	0.5164	0.4588
3	4	1	0	1	1	0.5388	0.7184	0.1796	0	0.2582	0.2294
1	3	1	3	0	1	0.1796	0.5388	0.1796	0.6255	0	0.2294
4	1	4	3	1	2	0.7184	0.1796	0.7184	0.6255	0.2582	0.4588

privacy-preserving manner, we can calculate the distance between any two images without sharing their contents.

In the following subsection, we will demonstrate a homomorphic encryption-based protocol [23] for computing the dot product operation in a privacy-preserving mode. We then show how to utilize such a protocol as a tool in designing our proposed SPIM.

3.3 Secure Dot Product Based on Homomorphic Encryption

Homomorphic encryption is a probabilistic public key encryption [7,23]. Let $HE_{pk}(x)$ and $HD_{pr}(y)$ be the encryption and decryption functions in this system with public key pk and private key pr. Without private key pr, no adversary can guess the plaintext x in polynomial time. Furthermore, $HE_{pk}(x)$ has a semantic security [24] property, which means no adversary can compute any function of the plaintext from the ciphertext set. Interestingly, the full homomorphic encryption has two amazing properties, namely: additive and multiplicative. Additive property allows adding two encrypted numbers, i.e., $HE_{pk}(x1) \times HE_{pk}(x2) = HE_{pk}(x1 + x2)$. Given a constant c and a ciphertext $HE_{pk}(x)$, the multiplicative property works as follows: $HE_{pk}(x)^c = HE_{pk}(c \times x)$. In this paper, we adopt Paillier's system [25] for the practical implementation because of its efficiency.

Let u and v be secure vectors of *Alice* and *Bob*, respectively. *Both* vectors are of the same size n. Below we show how homomorphic encryption can be used to compute the secure dot product between u and v. At the beginning, *Alice* encrypts her private vector component-wise, i.e., $z_i \leftarrow HE_{pk}(u_i)$, and sends the encrypted vector z to *Bob*. Upon receiving z, *Bob* computes the encrypted component-wise product between z and v based on the multiplicative property, (i.e., $y_i = z_i^{vi}, for all i = 1, ..., n$). He then sums up these products based on the additive homomorphic property to compute the encrypted dot product *EDot* such as: $EDot = y_1 + y_2 + ... + y_n$. After receiving *EDot* from *Bob*, *Alice* uses her private key pr to decrypt it and to obtain the plaintext value of $u \times v$, i.e., $HD_{pr}(EDot) = u \times v$. Note that *Alice's* private vector u is not revealed to *Bob* because only encrypted values of u are sent to *Bob*. Therefore, without prior knowledge of *Alice's* private key, neither u vector nor matching plaintext can be recovered by semi-trusted *Bob* or any adversary. Thus, this method meets the requirement of second scenario as explained in Sect. 1 with respect to privacy-preserving.

4   Our Proposed Scheme

Before providing our proposed scheme, we briefly explain the method used to extract the feature vectors for the image collection.

4.1   Feature Extraction

In this paper, we utilize the SURF algorithm [10,11], which is a novel scale and rotation-invariant detector and descriptor. SURF approximates or even outperforms previously proposed SIFT algorithm [8,9], which is patented, with respect to repeatability, distinctiveness, and robustness, yet can be computed and compared much faster. Generally speaking, SURF extracts the feature vectors of the provided image as follows. First, SURF selects several interest points at distinctive locations in the image, such as corners, blobs, and T-junctions. Such points are selected in such a way that enables the detector to find the same physical interest points under different viewing conditions. Next, the neighborhood of every interest point is represented by a feature vector. This descriptor has to be distinctive and time robust to noise, detection displacements, and geometric and photometric deformations. The descriptor vectors are matched between different images. Matching is based on a distance between the vectors, e.g., the Euclidean distance, or cosine similarity.

Formally, given the image *Im*, we use the SURF algorithm to generate its feature vectors $F = \{v_1, v_2, ..., v_k\}$, where k is the number of interest points in the provided image. Note that different images may differ in the number of descriptors k. Figure 1 illustrates the interest points of Lena image and their counterparts in the same image after rotation.

4.2   Secure Private Image Matching (SPIM)

The implementation of SPIM utilizes the homomorphic encryption to evaluate similarity. The main steps are highlighted in Algorithm 2. Our proposed protocol distributes scores calculation between the two participant parties and is composed of two phases, initialization and matching phases. In the first phase, each party computes the feature vector set for each image in its own collection and then normalizes each vector to enable assessment of the cosine similarity.

We demonstrate the proposed scheme using SURF descriptors in this paper, although this scheme is applicable to other feature vectors. To match her private image, *Alice* goes into two rounds. In the first round, she encrypts her feature vector set and sends them to *Bob*. Once *Bob* receives *Alice's* encrypted vectors, he employs the *secure_dot_product* subroutine (as explained in Algorithm 3) to

Fig. 1. SURF interest point of two images

return the dot product matrix of the input vector set and the feature vector set of each image in his collection. The details of the above listed subroutine are explained in Subsect. 3.3. Without loss of generality and to make the presentation clearer, we assume that all *Bob's* images have the same number p of descriptors. At the second round, *Alice* uses her private key to decrypt the dot product terms and obtain the actual values, which will be employed in assessing the similarity scores as explained in Algorithm 1. Hence, without the knowledge of *Alice's* private key no adversary is able to get the right matching scores, even the *Bob*.

4.3 Time and Communication Complexity Analysis

In this section, we measure the complexity of our proposed scheme in terms of computing time and communication cost. For computing time complexity, at the first round of *Alice's* side, the encryption represents the most expensive operation, which is bounded by $O(k)$, where k is the number of descriptors in the input image. At *Bob's* side, the secure dot product subroutine runs m times, and each time it takes the complexity of $O(k.p)$. Thus the overall computing time complexity of this step is $O(m.k.p)$. Decryption represents the most expensive operation in the second round of *Alice's* side, which bounded by $O(m.k.p)$ operations. With respect to the communication cost, we can summarize it as follows: in the first round, *Alice* sends $k.n$ values to *Bob* and *Bobs* sends back $m.p.k$ values to *Alice*. Suppose that each value has b-bit long, then the total communication cost is bounded as: $O(b(k.n + m.p.k))$ bits.

5 Experimental Results

In this section, we report the experimental results of the proposed scheme on a real image database containing 1000 color images from the Corel dataset [26]. The images are grouped by content into 10 categories. Each category contains 100 images. These categories include *African, Beach, Architecture, Buses,*

Algorithm 2. Secure Private Image Matching

Input: I: *Alice's* image.

$\quad\quad D = \{Img_1, ..., Img_m\}$: *Bob's* collection.

Output: $\alpha_1, \alpha_2, ..., \alpha_m$: the similarity scores.

Initialization:

Alice:

-Generate the homomorphic encryption public key pair (pr, pk).

-Send pk to *Bob*.

-Use SURF algorithm to extract the feature vector set $F = \{v_1, v_2, ..., v_k\}$ for the image I, all vectors v_i are of the same size n.

-Compute $\overrightarrow{v}_i$ as in Eq. (5), for $i = 1, ..., k$, and replace it with v_i in F.

Bob:

For each image $Im_j \in D, \forall_j = 1, ..., m$

- Use SURF algorithm to extract the feature vector set $F_j = \{s_1, s_2, ..., s_p\}$.

- Compute $\overrightarrow{s}_i$ as in Eq. (5), for $i = 1, ..., p$, and replace it with s_i in F_j.

Matching:

Alice:(*first round*)

For $i = 1$ to k **do**

Encrypt the elements of vector $\overrightarrow{v}_i$ as:

$\quad z_{ij} \leftarrow HEnc_{pk}(\overrightarrow{v}_{ij})$ for all $j =, 1, ..., n$

Endfor //i

- Send z to *Bob*

Bob:

For $m = 1$ to M **do**

- Get the feature vector set F_m of image m.

- Compute the secure dot product set between the *Alice's* vector set and the vector set of image m as:

$\quad\quad Dot\{m\} = Secure\_dot\_product(Z, F_m);$

Endfor//m

- Send $Dot\{m\}$ to *Alice*.

Alice:(*second round*)

- Receive Dot from *Bob*, where each element in Dot is a matrix of $[k, p]$ dimensions.

- **For** $m = 1$ to M **do**

Set X to be matrix m of Dot.

$Sum = 0$;

For $i = 1$ to k **do**

For $j = 1$ to p **do**

$\quad sub_j = 1 - HDec_{pr}(X_{ij})$ // this is because: distance=1-similarity

Endfor//j

$min = minimum(sub)$

$Sum = Sum + min$;

Endfor//i

Compute the distance with image m as:

$\alpha_m = sum/k$

Endfor//m

Algorithm 3. Secure_dot_product(Z, F)

Input: two feature vector sets Z and F of sizes k and p, respectively.
Output: $Dot[k, p]$: the encrypted sup-product terms between Z and F vectors.
For $i = 1$ to k **do**
  For $j = 1$ to p **do**
    $Dot_{ij} = HDec_{pk}(0);$ // initial value
    For $t = 1$ to **do**
      $Dot_{ij} = (Z_{it}^{v_{jt}}) \times Dot_{ij}$
    Endfor$//t$
  EndFor$//p$
Endfor$//k$

Dinosaurs, Elephants, Flowers, Horses, Mountain, and *Food.* Image sizes are either 256×384 or 384×256. Our experiments are conducted on a 2.2 GHz Intel i7-4702MQ processor, with a Windows 7 operating system of 64-bits, and 8 GB RAM. We use MATLAB R2008a to implement our experiments. We use Java class to implement Paillier cryptosystem. For the SURF descriptors, the size of each descriptor is 64 elements, i.e., $n = 64$. The normalized vectors are scaled by a user specific factor to convert the normalization (between 0 and 1) into an integer numbers because the encryption function is applied only on integer values. The SURF vectors are already normalized to vector units and thus not require normalization.

5.1 Effectiveness

In this experiment, we test the ability of our proposed scheme to retrieve the most similar images to the provided query. Figure 2 shows samples of our results. The first column represents the provided image queries. The other columns show the returned images arranged according to their similarity to their corresponding query. The columns show that our scheme can usually retrieve images in the same category as that of the query image.

5.2 Efficiency

In this experiment, we investigate the performance of our proposed scheme in term of matching time. Our scheme requires n exponentiations and n homomorphic additions to compute the distance between each two vectors. Such expensive operations cause our scheme to become slower than the non-secure scheme. Figure 3 illustrates the average time cost of our scheme against the non-secure scheme. In both cases, results are drawn as the number of image queries increased. Every query image is matched against 1000 images. The average time cost of our scheme to match a single query is about 3.4 s, while the other scheme requires 0.48 s. The additional time cost of our work can be considered as a reasonable cost for achieving a secure matching. Our ongoing research focuses on reducing the feature vector set of each image to improve the efficiency.

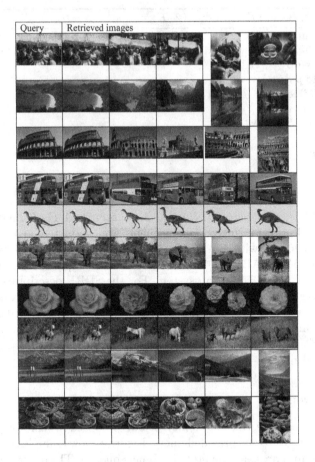

Fig. 2. Selected result of retrieved images

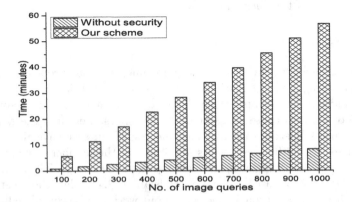

Fig. 3. Matching time

5.3   Protection Against an Adversary

As our scheme uses a private key to encrypt the feature vectors of *Alice*, hence, no adversary, including *Bob*, can obtain the correct matching scores if they have no knowledge of the key. In this experiment, we attempt to determine how difficult it would be for *Bob* to attempt to learn the matching scores using a set of invalid private keys. The first row in Fig. 4 shows the retrieved image under the valid private key. The remaining rows show the retrieved images under invalid keys. The first column represents the provided image queries.

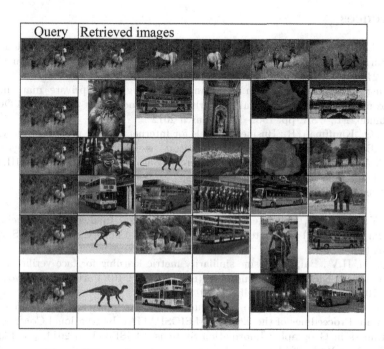

Fig. 4. Effect of private key on security image matching

6   Conclusion

Conducting image matching while preserving confidentiality is a challenging task. This paper presents a secure scheme that evaluate similarity between image collections of two parties without compromising their privacy. We utilize the homomorphic properties to design a secure protocol to achieve cosine similarity between two feature vector sets. Specifically, we use SURF descriptor to extract feature vectors. Interestingly, our proposed framework for secure private image matching is not limited to a specific feature vectors and instead can work under different features. The practical value of our work is demonstrated through several experimental results. Following this line of research, our future work will attempt to improve the performance of the matching time to scale for massive databases. We intend to apply clustering techniques to select representative descriptors for each image because clustering selects fewer descriptors. Thus, distance calculation could be largely reduced and consequently decreasing matching costs.

Acknowledgment. This work is supported by National 973 Fundamental Basic Research Program of China under grant No. 2014CB340600.

References

1. Li, M., Cao, N., Yu, S., Lou, W.: FindU: privacy-preserving personal profile matching in mobile social networks. In: Proceedings of 2011 INFOCOM, Shanghai, China, pp. 2435–2443. IEEE Press, April 2011
2. Zhang, R., Zhang, Y., Sun, J., Yan, G.: Fine-grained private matching for proximity-based mobile social networking. In: Proceedings of 2012 INFOCOM, Orlando, FL, USA, pp. 1969–1977, March 2012
3. Dai, Q., Kauffman, R.: Business models for Internet-based e-procurement systems and B2B electronic markets: an exploratory assessment. In: Proceedings of the 34th Annual Hawaii International Conference on System Sciences, Maui, HI, USA, pp. 1–10, January 2001
4. Frikken, K.: Privacy-preserving set union. In: Katz, J., Yung, M. (eds.) ACNS 2007. LNCS, vol. 4521, pp. 237–252. Springer, Heidelberg (2007)
5. Li, Y., Tygar, J., Hellerstein, J.: Private matching. In: Lee, D.T., Shieh, S.P., Tygar, J.D. (eds.) Computer Security in the 21st Century, pp. 25–50. Springer, USA (2005)
6. Nguyen, H.V., Bai, L.: Cosine similarity metric learning for face verification. In: Kimmel, R., Klette, R., Sugimoto, A. (eds.) ACCV 2010, Part II. LNCS, vol. 6493, pp. 709–720. Springer, Heidelberg (2011)
7. Choi, S., Ghinita, G., Bertino, E.: Secure mutual proximity zone enclosure evaluation. In: Proceedings of the 22nd ACM SIGSPATIAL International Conference on Advances in Geographic Information Systems, SIGSPATIAL 2014, pp. 133–142. ACM, New York (2014)
8. Lowe, D.: Distinctive image features from scale-invariant keypoints. Int. J. Comput. Vis. **60**(2), 91–110 (2004)
9. Chao, J., Huitl, R., Steinbach, E., Schroeder, D.: A novel rate control framework for SIFT/SURF feature preservation in H.264/AVC video compression. IEEE Trans. Circ. Syst. Video Technol. **25**(6), 958–972 (2015)
10. Bay, H., Ess, A., Tuytelaars, T., Gool, L.V.: Speeded-up robust features (SURF). Comput. Vis. Image Underst. **110**(3), 346–359 (2008)
11. Truong, D.-D., Ngoc, C.-S.N., Nguyen, V.-T., Tran, M.-T., Duong, A.-D.: Local descriptors without orientation normalization to enhance landmark regconition. In: Huynh, V.N., Denoeux, T., Tran, D.H., Le, A.C., Pham, B.S. (eds.) KSE 2013, Part I. AISC, vol. 244, pp. 401–413. Springer, Heidelberg (2014)
12. Freedman, M.J., Nissim, K., Pinkas, B.: Efficient private matching and set intersection. In: Cachin, C., Camenisch, J.L. (eds.) EUROCRYPT 2004. LNCS, vol. 3027, pp. 1–19. Springer, Heidelberg (2004)
13. Hazay, C., Nissim, K.: Efficient set operations in the presence of malicious adversari. J. Cryptology **25**(3), 383–433 (2012)

14. Hong, J., Kim, J.W., Kim, J., Park, K., Cheon, J.H.: Constant-round privacy preserving multiset union. Cryptology ePrint Archive, Report 2011/138 (2011). http://eprint.iacr.org/

15. Kissner, L., Song, D.: Privacy-preserving set operations. In: Shoup, V. (ed.) CRYPTO 2005. LNCS, vol. 3621, pp. 241–257. Springer, Heidelberg (2005)

16. Jarecki, S., Liu, X.: Efficient oblivious pseudorandom function with applications to adaptive ot and secure computation of set intersection. In: Reingold, O. (ed.) TCC 2009. LNCS, vol. 5444, pp. 577–594. Springer, Heidelberg (2009)

17. Hazay, C., Lindell, Y.: Efficient protocols for set intersection and pattern matching with security against malicious and covert adversaries. In: Canetti, R. (ed.) TCC 2008. LNCS, vol. 4948, pp. 155–175. Springer, Heidelberg (2008)

18. De Cristofaro, E., Gasti, P., Tsudik, G.: Fast and private computation of cardinality of set intersection and union. In: Pieprzyk, J., Sadeghi, A.-R., Manulis, M. (eds.) CANS 2012. LNCS, vol. 7712, pp. 218–231. Springer, Heidelberg (2012)

19. Lu, W., Swaminathan, A., Varna, A.L., Wu, M.: Enabling search over encrypted multimedia databases. In: Proceedings of Media Forensics and Security, SPIE, San Jose, CA, USA, vol. 7254, pp. 18–29 (2009)

20. Shashank, J., Kowshik, P., Srinathan, K., Jawahar, C.: Private content based image retrieval. In: Proceedings of IEEE Conference on Computer Vision and Pattern Recognition, Anchorage, AK, USA, pp. 1–8. IEEE Press, June 2008

21. Agrawal, R., Evfimievski, A., Srikant, R.: Information sharing across private databases. In: Proceedings of the 2003 ACM SIGMOD International Conference on Management of Data, SIGMOD 2003, pp. 86–97. ACM, New York (2003)

22. Goldreich, O., Micali, S., Wigderson, A.: How to play any mental game. In: Proceedings of the Nineteenth Annual ACM Symposium on Theory of Computing, STOC 1987, pp. 218–229. ACM, New York (1987)

23. Goethals, B., Laur, S., Lipmaa, H., Mielikäinen, T.: On private scalar product computation for privacy-preserving data mining. In: Park, C., Chee, S. (eds.) ICISC 2004. LNCS, vol. 3506, pp. 104–120. Springer, Heidelberg (2005)

24. Goldwasser, S., Micali, S., Rackoff, C.: The knowledge complexity of interactive proof-systems. In: Proceedings of the Seventeenth Annual ACM Symposium on Theory of Computing, STOC 1985, pp. 291–304. ACM, New York (1985)

25. Paillier, P.: Public-key cryptosystems based on composite degree residuosity classes. In: Stern, J. (ed.) EUROCRYPT 1999. LNCS, vol. 1592, pp. 223–238. Springer, Heidelberg (1999)

26. Corel test set. http://wang.ist.psu.edu/_jwang/test1.tar

Author Index

Printed in the United States
By Bookmasters